American Nonpublic Schools

Otto F. Kraushaar

American Nor

public Schools

Patterns of Diversity

The Johns Hopkins University Press

Baltimore and London

The Johns Hopkins University Press, Baltimore, Maryland 21218
The Johns Hopkins University Press Ltd., London

Library of Congress Catalog Card Number 75-186475
ISBN 0-8018-1384-0

Contents

List of Tables and Figures

Tables

Figures

Preface

This book is about the nonpublic or private (we use these terms interchangeably) schools of America—their history, goals, significance, problems, and prospects. It was undertaken in the belief that these schools, which at their crest educated approximately 6.5 million children in about 19 thousand elementary and secondary schools, constitute an important resource in America's dual system of public and private schooling, a resource which is currently in serious jeopardy. Important public policy decisions which will affect the welfare of these schools for decades to come are on the agenda of the states and the federal government—and before the people; decisions in which much is at stake for both public and private schools, decisions involving conflicting issues of peculiar complexity and consequence. I hope this book, which is addressed to laymen and professionals alike, may help clarify the main issues. While I do not expect the reader to agree with all the positions taken in this book, I trust it will help to bring greater clarity in his own thinking about the basic issues.

The three parts of the book represent different approaches to and the treatment of different aspects of this far-ranging topic. Part 1 is chiefly introductory and historical, and is based on library research and considerable reading in the proliferating contemporary literature about the problems of schools. Our aim here was to sketch the historical circumstances under which various types of nonpublic schools—church-related and independent—arose, and how the schools responded and developed.

Part 2 is an attempt to characterize and differentiate the nonpublic schools from within by canvassing the background, outlook, attitudes, and expectations of the following constituencies: parents, students, teachers, school heads, trustees. The descriptions and conclusions advanced in part 2 are based primarily on data gathered by means of a nationwide questionnaire survey and impressions gathered during school visits. The goals and procedures employed are described briefly in appendix 1. With the usual overoptimism of project researchers, we gathered data quite beyond our capacity to analyze and present them, and what is reported in part 2 and elsewhere represents only a small selection, focused usually on activities that were observed also during school visits. We believe the data to be reliable and representative; where we have presented data that seemed to us of marginal reliability we have inserted a caveat in the text. The reader who may be inclined to question the data should be reminded that there are no others at all covering the whole range of nonpublic schools.

After pondering and trying out various ways of using the findings to exhibit the rich diversity of private school types, we settled on collapsing the data into the major categories of Catholic, Protestant, Jewish and independent schools.[1] This enabled us to draw general comparisons and contrasts in many aspects of school goals and practices, but we tried also to inform the reader of the important deviations within the generalizations.

If part 2 is largely descriptive and only occasionally normative, part 3 is an effort to grapple with the major issues of public policy regarding nonpublic schools and to assess the changing role of private schooling as it affects the prospects of nonpublic schools of all types.

The point of this book is not to argue the superiority of private over public schools, but rather to defend the dual system of private *and* public schools. The torrent of criticism to which urban public schools are subjected encourages intellectuals and critics in an ideological swing towards private schools; it is, however, more of a swing away from moribund bureaucratic schools and toward a more desirable alternative than it is a positive movement on behalf of private schools. It seems obvious that the public schools will continue to carry the major burden of schooling the young. But it seems equally obvious that for the public schools to acquire a virtual monopoly in educating the young would be a major social disaster. As public institutions become ever more impersonal and grow out of scale with people, the need for alternatives, choices, and options increases.

It was part of my original intention to include a chapter or two dealing comparatively with private schooling in the countries of western Europe and the British Commonwealth, where examples abound. Such a comparative study is needed and would, I believe, be an eye opener to many Americans who see the question of nonpublic schools chiefly as a black-white First Amendment issue. But the scope of our project, even without such an addition, was already overly ambitious to the point of presumption.

---

[1] Two points should be emphasized here, lest the reader miss our scattered references to them in the text. (1) Episcopal and Friends schools, though Protestant in their affiliation, are usually, except where otherwise noted, included in the independent school group with which they closely identify, rather than with the other Protestant schools. (2) The Jewish schools do not appear in many comparisons simply because the returns from these schools were meager and we have doubts as to their representativeness. Data concerning Jewish schools were used when they pointed strongly and consistently in one direction, especially when the data findings were supported by school visits and other evidence.

My debts are many and large. This book would not have been possible without the unflagging interest, assistance and counsel of Mr. Cary Potter, president
of the National Association of Independent Schools (NAIS) in Boston. Picking
up the threads of negotiations, begun in 1949, which strove to secure funding
for a study of independent schools, he laid the groundwork for the grant which
was provided by the Danforth Foundation of St. Louis, whose officers, together
with Mr. Potter, invited me to direct the study. Originally entitled "A Study of
the American Independent School," the project soon outgrew its boundaries and
became in fact, though not in name, a study of American private schools as a
whole. With Mr. Potter's help, the growth of the project and the plan to conduct
an enlarged questionnaire was underwritten by a grant from the Independence
Foundation of Philadelphia, which also covered the cost of the Gallup poll,
"How the Public Views Nonpublic Schools," commissioned by the study and
published in July, 1969. Mr. Potter was instrumental also in securing a subsidiary
grant from the E. E. Ford Foundation for the purpose of engaging assistance for
the study of the history of nonpublic schools and problems relating to their
control and accreditation. Also at Mr. Potter's urging, Professor Livingston Hall,
of the Harvard Law School, and Mrs. Elizabeth Hall, a member of this study's
Advisory Commission, asked the study to harbor and administer a probe of
student unrest in independent schools, a problem of special interest to the
Educational Practices Committee of the NAIS. That linkage had the happy
consequence of bringing to our staff Alan R. Blackmer, for the express purpose of
utilizing the study's resources to investigate the unrest question, and led to the
publication, in February, 1970, of *An Inquiry Into Student Unrest in Independent Secondary Schools*, with Mr. Blackmer as author. Thanks to the keen interest of the Halls, this offshoot of the larger study was funded by a cluster of
small foundation grants, which are acknowledged in the "Foreword" of Mr.
Blackmer's book. I shall always be grateful to Cary Potter for his friendship and
his enlivening and sustaining influence on the study and its various outgrowths.

My debt is great to members of the study's Advisory Commission, particularly its chairman, Dr. Richard Sullivan of the Carnegie Corporation in New
York, formerly president of Reed College, and more recently president of the
American Association of Colleges. I enjoyed the invaluable privilege of receiving
the advice, criticism and encouragement of individual members of the Advisory
Commission, as well as their collective insights during the periodic formal meet-
ings; but I was granted complete freedom in reaching final conclusions and in
writing the book. The members of the commission were the Reverend John B.
Coburn, formerly dean of the Episcopal Theological Seminary, Cambridge,
Massachusetts, a teacher in a Harlem Street Academy, and now rector at the St.
James Church in New York City; Professor James Coleman of the Department of
Social Relations, Johns Hopkins University; the Honorable Edith Green, con-

gresswoman from Oregon and chairman of the U.S. House of Representatives Special Subcommittee on Education; Fred Hechinger, education editor of the *New York Times*; Mrs. Elizabeth Hall, president, Simon's Rock College, Great Barrington, Massachusetts; Floyd S. Michael, professor of school administration, Northwestern University, formerly superintendent of Evanston Township High School; Dr. Rixford Snyder, director of admissions, emeritus, of Stanford University; William L. Pressly, president of the Westminster Schools, Atlanta, Georgia; James A. Linen III, president of *Time*, Inc.; and Dr. Sullivan. I am grateful to them individually and collectively for guidance, encouragement and friendship. John Coburn's comments on early drafts of the racial chapter were particularly helpful, as were Richard Sullivan's on the first three chapters. The expert counsel of Dr. James Coleman was invaluable at crucial stages in the building of the questionnaires and the analysis of the results. To Fred Hechinger I am indebted for invigorating discussions of the role of private schools in a public-school–dominated society.

I owe a special debt to Dean Theodore Sizer of the Harvard Graduate School of Education (HGSE), who not only made available office facilities and library and computer services, but followed the development of the study with friendly interest and advice. Much of the burden of finding suitable working quarters for the study staff during the period of flux occasioned by the construction of the new HGSE library fell on the shoulders of Dr. Richard R. Rowe and W. Ronald Wormser, associate deans of HGSE, who resolved these logistical problems with thoughtful concern. Dr. Richard Jay Light, assistant professor of education at HGSE, consulted with us regarding the sampling plan of our questionnaire survey, and Dr. Allan B. Ellis, lecturer and research associate in education at Harvard, and associated with the New England School Development Council, advised us on various aspects of the study, including computer services. Dr. William G. Spady, now associated with The Ontario (Canada) Institute for Studies in Education, served as a consultant in the preparation of the questionnaires. Ralph O. West, director of evaluation for the Commission on Independent Secondary Schools, under the New England Association of Colleges and Secondary Schools, gave us the benefit of his extensive deliberations about the problems of school accreditation, state control and teacher certification. Our chapter 12 is much the better for his advice. I cannot conclude these acknowledgments to Harvard and Boston colleagues without expressing my debt to Dr. Robert Ulich, James Bryant Conant Professor of Education, emeritus, at Harvard, whose friendly lunch-table conversations and rich knowledge of comparative education I found stimulating and rewarding.

The staff of the study was augmented for six weeks during the early spring of 1961 by eight educators who were invited to help conduct the 60 school visits: Carl Andrews, Jr., at the time headmaster of the Collegiate School in New York;

Preface

Nathaniel S. French, professor of education, University of Massachusetts at Amherst; Edward F. Krueger, assistant executive secretary of Christian education, Northern Illinois District, Lutheran Church—Missouri Synod; David Mallery, program director, Friends Council on Education, and director of studies, National Association of Independent Schools; Francis Parkman, consultant, NAIS, and formerly headmaster of St. Mark's School; the Reverend Anthony Polini, O. Praem., principal of the Bishop Neumann High School in Philadelphia; and David C. Twitchell, director of the Lowell Field Study, HGSE, and formerly headmaster of the Thacher School in California and of the Pomfret School in Connecticut. The experience of associating with this interdenominational group during the visits and in pre- and post-visit sessions proved to be very enlightening. I owe a double debt to Francis Parkman who, in addition to the school visits, drew up an early draft of chapter 9 on school finance.

The unstinting cooperation of the chief officers of the national school associations greatly facilitated our work. Letters of endorsement accompanying the questionnaires addressed to church schools under their general surveillance were written by Monsignor James C. Donohue, at the time director of the Division of Elementary and Secondary Education, United States Catholic Conference (USCC); Dr. William A. Kramer, at the time secretary of Schools, Lutheran Church–Missouri Synod, to whom I am indebted for many favors, including comments on an early draft of chapter 2; the Reverend John Paul Carter, secretary, National Association of Episcopal Schools; Dr. John F. Blanchard, Jr., executive director, National Association of Christian Schools; Dr. John A. Vander Ark, director, National Union of Christian Schools; Dr. T. S. Geraty, associate secretary, Department of Education, General Conference of Seventh-Day Adventists; Dr. Joseph Kaminetsky, Torah Umesorah–National Society for Hebrew Day Schools. Cary Potter contributed a similar letter for NAIS schools. The nature of our study and a plea for cooperation had been presented in early 1968 at a conference in Washington, D.C., attended by Dr. Walter W. Howe, associate secretary, Department of Education, General Conference of Seventh-Day Adventists; Dr. Louis Nulman, director of research, Torah Umesorah; the Reverend C. Albert Koob, O. Praem., president, National Catholic Education Association, to whom I am greatly indebted also for other favors, including his comments on the original draft of chapter 2; the Reverend Paul V. Siegfried, executive secretary–treasurer, Jesuit Educational Association; Dr. Edward R. D'Alessio, at the time coordinator of governmental programs, USCC. We like to think that the initial conference and the cooperation of the represented groups in this study helped pave the way for the growing spirit of collaboration among nonpublic schools.

How much we owe to Dr. Donald A. Erikson, professor of education at the University of Chicago, and an experienced, penetrating student of nonpublic school affairs, is made manifest by the references in our text to his books and articles. But our debt to him is even larger. He read and commented on early drafts of the chapters that now comprise part 1 and a position paper which became the basis for chapter 12. Chapter 9 on the racial question benefited by the comments of Dr. Norman Dorsen, professor of law and director of Arthur Hays Civil Liberties Program, New York University School of Law.

How is one to thank the hundreds of school heads, teachers, students, parents and trustees who took the time to fill out questionnaires or to participate in the interviews, which often became lively talk fests? I hope this book, to which they are anonymous contributors, may be at least a token reward for their generous patience and the willingness to open their hearts and minds about their school.

To the staff of the NAIS—John Chandler, Jr., Edward Yeomans, Frank R. Miller, Richard P. Thomsen, John P. Downing, William L. Dandridge, and Adele Q. Ervin—we pay tribute for assistance of many kinds in connection with almost every aspect of this undertaking.

My largest debt of all is owed to our study staff. A. D. Ayrault, now headmaster of the Lakeside School, Seattle, Washington, was assistant director of the study for the first two years and thereafter continued to assist us in commenting on early drafts of the first six chapters. The conception of the study's goals and the construction of the questionnaire survey owe much to his intellectual curiosity and resourcefulness. Dr. David R. Drew, now with the Office of Research, American Council on Education, served for a year as staff sociologist, and carried out in a spirited way the difficult task of expediting the preparation and administration of the survey, and programming the results. Mrs. Cherry Collins, a graduate student at HGSE, prepared lucid summaries of selected scholarly literature on the early history of schools. It was our good fortune to have Mrs. Victoria Blair-Smith as secretary and research assistant until marriage and motherhood called her to other tasks; but she continued her interest in the project, and has been personally helpful in many ways. Mrs. Susan Allen, computer program aid, and Mrs. Linda Roulston, secretary, though they served on the staff for only brief periods, are remembered for their skillful work.

The primary reason why the staff, which grew and diminished as the workload fluctuated, worked so well together is Mrs. Ann Couch. Project secretary in name, she was much more than that in fact. While participating in the study as research assistant, with a special knack for digging out statistical facts and doing intelligible takeoffs from computer printouts, she managed also to cope with the telephone, arrange appointments and travel plans, handle the correspondence, scan the newspapers and journals for significant news about schools, deal thoughtfully with any personality conflicts that arose, prepare the tables for this book, and type most of the manuscript through seemingly endless revisions. It was a prodigious feat.

Preface

Dr. Alan R. Blackmer, on joining the staff in the fall of 1968, bore the title of study associate, but he was truly the right-hand man. His career as dean at Phillips Academy, Andover, and teacher of English there, and his wide-ranging consultantships and keen insight into the process of education in independent schools placed him in a position to be helpful in manifold ways. I am immensely grateful not only for his intelligent, devoted collaboration but for good fellowship. After he completed his investigation of student unrest, noted above, we worked together, interpreting the results of the survey and discussing daily many aspects and problems of private schooling. In addition to combing the computer printouts for important findings, he did the original draft of chapter 12 and helped revise successive drafts of each chapter as I completed them. In the process he corrected my grammar, syntax and punctuation, and frequently saved me from egregious overstatements and rhetorical superfluities.

Finally, I must record my deep gratitude for the generous financial assistance and remarkable patience of the foundations that funded this undertaking: to the Danforth Foundation of St. Louis which provided the original and sustaining grants, and in particular to Merrimon Cuninggim, president, and Gene L. Schwilck, vice president, of the foundation; to the Independence Foundation of Philadelphia, particularly to Robert A. Maes, president, for support enabling us to extend the scope of the study; and to the E. E. Ford Foundation of New York City for a subsidiary grant enabling us to probe several problems more deeply and thoroughly. Needless to say, the conclusions and judgments reached by this study, as well as its imperfections, are my own responsibility.

The accelerating tempo of startling developments in the educational world during the many months while this book was in preparation necessitated rewriting certain passages again and again in the hope of staying ahead of the rapid obsolescence of facts, theories, and methods. But there comes a time when one has to write "finis," knowing full well that "the never-ending flight of future days," in Milton's words, will once again cast all in doubt.

Cambridge, Massachusetts   O.F.K.
Baltimore, Maryland
September 1971

I

Private Schools in Historical Perspective

I

1

An Overview of Private Schooling

*"What would be the attitudes
of a society
capable of such
continuous renewal?
First of all,
it would be
characterized by pluralism—
by variety,
alternatives, choices,
and multiple foci
of power and initiative."*

John W. Gardner[1]

Private Schools as Alternatives

The continuing conflict in recent years between the Old Order Amish schools and local school officials in Ohio, Kansas, Wisconsin, Iowa and Michigan dramatizes two radically different approaches to the education of young people. The educational philosophy of the deeply religious Plain People, who trace their history back to the Anabaptist movement of the Protestant Reformation, rests on the desire to perpetuate the ideals of a small, rural, self-sufficient, religious society, within the context of a closely knit family and church community. The public school in the form of the little red country schoolhouse of song and legend suited the Amish well enough. Though even its modest facilities included modern improvements that were proscribed in Amish homes, the country school

[1]"What Kind of Society Do We Want?" *Boston Evening Globe*, September 23, 1969, p. 56.

3

treated the Amish child as a member of the community rather than as an oddball, and managed to impart satisfactorily the basic skills in reading, writing and arithmetic through the eighth grade. That and a little contact with "English" children were all the Amish asked of the school. The rest of the Amish adolescent's critical teen period would be spent under parental tutelage on the farm, in the marketplace or in the kitchen, learning by doing, achieving adulthood by relating directly to his Amish peers and developing his religious commitment and his personality within the bounds of the Amish community.

But as the era of the farm and small town gave way to urbanization, the country school was replaced by the consolidated, comprehensive school in which the Amish child felt quite out of place. With mass education came the trend toward the stereotyping of pupils, the professionalization of teaching, bureaucratic control, compulsory education laws, the prescription of minimum standards, and the complex apparatus of accreditation, certification and credentialism. As the schools became more standardized in order the better to serve a technological society, they functioned for the Amish as a culturally alienating and disorienting influence. The whole trend of the public schools posed to the Plain People a dire threat to their beliefs, their culture and their very existence as a group. So they did what beleaguered or dissenting minorities have done all through American history—and are still doing—they built their own schools. An Amish private school was founded as early as 1925 in Delaware. But it was not until 1937 that the establishment of Amish schools began in earnest. There are now over 200 in operation, and their number is growing.[2]

They are a "problem" to public school officials legally responsible for enforcing attendance and other school laws which the Amish refuse to obey. In one of these skirmishes, a local Iowa official reportedly said: "We are going to assimilate these people, whether they want to be assimilated or not."[3] But the unyielding Amish think otherwise. During the most recent embroilment at New Glarus, Wisconsin, over the refusal of Amish children to attend the public high school after completing the eighth grade in their own parochial school, a bearded Amish father said, "We don't want our children involved in worldly things. Eight grades in our school is all we need."[4]

[2]See John A. Hostetler, *Amish Society*, rev. ed. (Baltimore: Johns Hopkins Press, 1968), chap. 9.

[3]*Ibid.*, p. 205. For a dramatic account of the Iowa showdown see Donald A. Erickson, ed. *Public Controls for Nonpublic Schools* (Chicago: University of Chicago Press, 1969), pp. 15-57.

[4]*New York Times*, February 16, 1971, p. 35. The Wisconsin Supreme Court overturned an earlier ruling in favor of the public schools, saying, "There is not such a compelling state interest in two years of high school education as will justify the burden it places upon the appellants' free exercise of their religion." The Wisconsin authorities have appealed the decision to the Supreme Court of the U.S. This marks the first time that a state compulsory

The Amish case rests, in the last analysis, on the freedom to practice and transmit a particular religious culture and a way of life without undue interference or harassment by the state. They are, by all accounts, hard-working, thrifty, productive farmers, with a strong preference for a simple life in unpolluted, rustic surroundings. Crime, unemployment, juvenile delinquency and abject poverty are virtually unknown among them. They are conscientious objectors not only to military service but to war, to mass society, to modern technology and to the deification of the state. In a strange way many of the convictions of the Amish are echoed today in the young people's communes. Yet because of their self-chosen isolation the Amish do not fulfill the conventional ideal of the good citizen in modern nationalized society. Unequivocally, it is God, not the state, to whom they give their highest obedience and loyalty.

The inconclusive forays against the Amish by local school officials raise fundamental issues regarding the limits of the state's power to define and compel adherence to its own educational philosophy, and the limits of the parental right to choose for the child an education designed to perpetuate a special form of group life, even though that choice may restrict the child's future options. There is no simple or final resolution of this dilemma, which involves such a tangled web of religious, educational, ethnic, political, economic, constitutional, and just plain human considerations. Today the sympathy of the public is evidently largely with the Amish, who are seen as harmless people being hounded by insensitive officialdom seeking to force compliance at a cost to the Amish of all that they hold to be most precious. Who can say that failure to conform to mainstream's values is harmful to children? The suspicion that conformity *is* harmful appears to be the reason for the rejection of "the system" by some young people today. And yet, just as few thoughtful persons would deny the right to the free exercise of religion, neither would they deny that minimum educational standards of some sort are necessary as safeguards against child abuse, fraud, and social anarchy. We shall be concerned with these issues in various contexts throughout this book.

The Amish experience illustrates clearly the long-standing concern in the United States over the religious and moral education of the young—until recent times the predominant rationale for the creation of private schools. Even today about eighty-five per cent of all nonpublic schools are church affiliated, and of that group over three-fourths are Roman Catholic. The private school is thus

---

education law has been successfully challenged on grounds of religious liberty. It is interesting to note that the Amish, who shy away from litigation, were defended by a group of influential Protestants, Catholics and Jews calling themselves the National Committee for Amish Freedom. Stephen Arons, fellow of the Center for the Study of Public Policy, Cambridge, Mass., presents an illuminating analysis of the Wisconsin decision in "Compulsory Education—the Plain People Resist," *Saturday Review*, January 15, 1972, pp. 52–57.

mainly a religious and more specifically a Catholic phenomenon. It was only after Catholics became convinced that the public schools were basically an establishment of Protestant religion that they began, late in the nineteenth century, building parochial, diocesan and order schools in earnest. Many of the multi-denominational Protestants, moreover, also found the watered-down Protestant humanism of public schools wanting. The proliferation of competing sects prompted certain denominations—notably the Lutheran, Episcopal, Friends, Christian Reformed, Seventh-Day Adventist, and various of the numerous "Christian" sects—to establish schools in order to raise their young in the true faith and its familiar special culture. The same desire motivated Orthodox Jewish leaders in founding Hebrew day schools. Even the nondenominational independent schools generally owe their origin to founders who evinced a strong desire to transmit nonsectarian but nonetheless distinctly Protestant, middle class moral and religious ideals, but with strong emphasis also on superior academic attainments. More recently the founding of Black Muslim schools in Detroit, Chicago, New York, Los Angeles, Washington, and Atlanta reflects the desire of black parents to provide for their children a secular education under a religious discipline. We shall deal with these developments later at greater length.

The public schools, whose purpose is to serve the whole population, aim to provide for every child, regardless of his religious background or group loyalties, access to a secular education which must perforce be religiously "neutral." These schools have been chary, under the Supreme Court's interpretation of the First Amendment, even to suggest that there might be an organic relationship between religion and education. The problem posed for those who take such relationship for granted is clear. "As long as the 'non-sectarianism' of the public schools meant a non-denominational Protestantism," says Will Herberg, theologian and sociologist of religion, "most American Protestants approved of excluding religion from the public school; now that 'non-sectarianism' has come to mean non-religion, however, the idea does not seem so persuasive." The result is that countless "Protestant voices have joined the many Catholic voices and the still few though multiplying Jewish voices" in proclaiming the centrality of religious education.[5] Thus, for parents who seek a religious education for their children, the answer is the choice of an appropriate church school. And since this is a legitimate choice, some parents and church school leaders conclude the state should assist them financially in maintaining these denominational alternatives.

The religious community still serves many Americans as the primary context of self-identification and social belonging, and the choice of a specific religious schooling entails well-defined ethnic, cultural, and, to some extent, socioeconomic and vocational values. It is up to the parent to decide whether such an

---

[5] John Cogley, ed., *Religion in America* (New York: Meridian Books, 1958), p. 138.

education places the child in a psychologically stronger position to make his way in the societal mainstream with its riptides of competing values,[6] or whether the public school way with its approach to social values through commonality, secularism, and heterogeneity is the better path.

Private schools exist, of course, to serve other than religious ends. The numerically small but educationally important group of independent schools is sought after chiefly for their academic superiority, though the high degree of student selectivity practiced by these schools, associated usually with high prestige and social status as well as family tradition, often exerts a significant influence on parental choice. Most but not all of these schools are nondenominational. Episcopal, Quaker and a few Catholic "private" (order) schools for which academic excellence is a major concern tend to identify with the independents. But even in many of the purely nonsectarian schools, religion plays a prominent part as a basis for moral education. Not infrequently such schools owe their origin to a church body.

The chief rationale of the independent school is to offer a "better" education than that available in the public school. Most parents desire for their children the best education within their reach. But "better" and "best" in this connection mean different things to different people. The best may mean academically or intellectually best, but not necessarily. What makes a given education "better" or "best" depends not only upon the available options but upon the value perspective of the parent who chooses. A recent survey entitled "How the Public Views Nonpublic Schools" found that "the reason cited most often by those who believe the quality of education is best in the private school is that the student receives more personal attention. . . . There is a strong tendency to judge quality by the way students are dealt with as individuals."[7] Most independent schools are relatively small and familial and have a favorable student-teacher ratio. These characteristics, as well as the ability of these schools to offer good intellectual training and rather rich opportunities in sports and extracurricular activities, figure strongly in the parental choice of such a school. It is a matter of priorities. The parent who chooses a church school as "best" usually assigns the top priority to education in a religious environment but looks also for a good education in secular subjects; he may in fact believe they are inseparable. The

[6] Andrew M. Greeley and Peter H. Rossi in *The Education of Catholic Americans* (Chicago: Aldine Publishing Co., 1966) offer some cautiously presented evidence in support of this view as it pertains to Catholic schooling. See especially pp. 191–98. In "Contradictory Studies of Parochial Schooling: An Essay Review," *School Review* 76 (Winter 1967): 425–36, Donald A. Erickson finds grounds for a similar view of the outcome of Lutheran schooling.

[7] "How the Public Views Nonpublic Schools," a public opinion survey by Gallup International, sponsored and published by "A Study of the American Independent School" (Cambridge, Mass., July 1969), p. 3.

parent who chooses an independent school as "best," while he gives special weight to the school's academic attainments and associated characteristics, expects a good outcome also in character education; many would contend that the two are inseparable elements of a good education.

Besides functioning as religious and academic alternatives to the public schools, private schools also fill special needs that public schools in many localities are not equipped to meet. Boarding schools are a case in point. Nonpublic schools also fill many other needs, among them schools for mentally defective, emotionally disturbed, or physically impaired children, tutoring schools, choir schools, schools based on a special pedagogical concept such as the Rudolf Steiner method or other free, experimental, or community school concepts, and schools designed to meet the special needs of minority groups, such as the black community schools that are sprouting in most urban centers. Throughout much of American history private schools were the mainstay of the nation's schools; and after the spread of the public schools private venturing has supplemented, extended and enriched the opportunities which the state makes available to children through its public schools.

What Is Private about Private Schools

It is often remarked about nonpublic schools that while they are privately managed they are essentially public in function. The current arguments in support of state aid for private schools use this fact as the major premise. Putting aside for now the question of their public function, we propose in this section to examine more closely what is private about private schools.

Right off one can say that compared to public schools they are usually fairly small; they are privately managed and financed, and stand in a special relation to their students because the students or parents choose the school and the school the student. The one is not required to attend, and the other is not required to admit. All this is clear enough for general purposes, but a closer look reveals that it is not quite that simple. In fact, every generalization about the control, funding, selectivity, size, and so on, of nonpublic schools is obliged to take into account variables which do not fit the customary stereotypes of independent or church-related schools.

In school governance, for example, "private control" assumes many forms and is exercised in many different ways. The distinctively private way, following the model of the private college, is governance by an autonomous, self-perpetuating board of trustees who delegate much of their power and authority to the school head. This type of governance is typical of the independent schools. Many church-affiliated schools are presently in the throes of adopting it. Catholic parish schools were traditionally managed by a local pastor, priest or nun with some help from the parish council or board, but with precious little accountability to or interference from higher administrative echelons. But the trend is simultaneously toward governance by parish boards of education with genuine policy-making powers, and toward greater administrative integration of discrete units under diocesan boards of education. To the extent that Catholic diocesan and parish schools are subject to the general control of the dioceses, the schools are linked into systems; but whether they are run as a tight or a relaxed ship depends chiefly upon the local bishop, who is vested with virtually auto-cratic powers—though there is a growing tendency to exercise those powers with restraint. Catholic private academies, on the other hand, are separately con-trolled by one or another of the many religious orders.

The governance of Protestant schools is so diverse, it is difficult to generalize except to say that school governance tends to follow the pattern of church governance. Lutheran and Seventh-Day Adventist schools, the two largest Prot-estant "systems," are under fairly firm hierarchical guidance, although some individual schools retain a high degree of local autonomy. As for the member schools of the National Union of Christian Schools (NUCS) and the National Association of Christian Schools (NACS)—the former composed of parentally controlled, essentially Calvinist oriented schools, and the latter made up of schools under a variety of controlling bodies having certain evangelical principles in common—governance by parents' associations of congregationally elected boards or committees is the rule, and the schools guard their autonomy jeal-ously. The national offices function chiefly as service agencies with little power to direct or control. Episcopal schools are a special case. Although in theory the power resides in the bishops and the church hierarchy, in practice central control is relaxed and often ignored, so that the schools have a large measure of autonomy under their local boards of trustees.

Another commonly recognized characteristic of privatism is the derivation of financial support from client fees, endowment or other investment income, and philanthropy—in other words, from nonpublic funds. Again this is subject to exceptions. In the world of higher education, private universities have come to rely heavily upon public subsidies, while public institutions are beating the drums for private as well as public support. In consequence, the difference between public and private institutions of higher education have been noticeably blurred, but without subjecting private colleges, it should be noted, to a danger-ous degree of public control. The line, however, between public and private elementary and secondary schools remains more sharply marked, not merely because the latter thus far receive only marginal support from public funds in most states, but because they are privately governed alternatives in fulfilling compulsory education laws. No one is compelled by law to go to college, but schooling up to the legally defined leaving age is compulsory. This fact puts the case for the public support of the private school in a somewhat different light from that of the private college.

Still another characteristic of privatism in education is the practice of selective admissions based variously on mental aptitude, religious affiliation, ethnic kinship, social status and family background, or—failing all else—the ability to pay. Again, this is not uniquely a private school characteristic. Some public schools—the Bronx High School of Science and the Boston Latin School come to mind—practice selective admissions either openly on the basis of aptitude or special talent, or as a tacitly acknowledged academic pecking order among schools in a given municipality. On the client's side, in choosing a school, the desire to be "with one's own kind," however "kind" may be defined, is a powerful motive. It is prominent among the reasons why some parents choose a private over a public school, and no less prominent in accounting for the migration of families from city to suburb, because the public schools there are generally better. Because this desire bulks so large in the bad conscience of our time, private schools are struggling to recruit "a better ethnic mix," while public schools are earnestly bussing students to achieve at least a measure of racial integration. The desire to be "with one's own kind" also prompts members of the black community to demand schools of their own; whether they be public or private doesn't really matter much to them, just so they are *theirs* and are designed to meet their specific needs.

Mutuality of choice functions only within limits in many nonpublic schools. Church bodies have been known in the past to impose heavy sanctions, virtually compelling parents to enroll children in the denomination's schools, so that for all practical purposes the option of attending the local public school was psychologically all but closed. Financial restrictions also limit the choice of many who might prefer a private over a public school. And on the school's side, whether in church-related or independent schools, the selection of students is naturally restricted by the institution's proclaimed goals and constituency, or by less apparent but subtly applied screening policies. Nevertheless, within the limits of various restrictions on choice, the nonpublic school "chooses" its students in a way that most public schools cannot because they are under the obligation to take virtually all children from the given district.[8] We suspect that this mutuality

[8] Richard O. Carlson of the University of Oregon distinguishes and characterizes several types of "client-organization relationships" based on the presence or absence of selectivity. The public school is a "domesticated" organization in that it is protected by the society it serves. It is guaranteed a steady flow of clients without competition, and there is therefore no struggle for survival in this type of organization. "Existence is guaranteed,... [and] funds are not closely tied to quality of performance." Private schools, by contrast, are "wild" in that they are engaged in a struggle for survival, and are unprotected at vulnerable points. They must therefore learn to adapt to the changing environment. See Daniel E. Griffiths, ed., *Behavioral Science and Educational Administration*, Yearbook of the National Society for the Study of Education, no. 63, part 22 (Chicago: University of Chicago Press, 1964), pp. 264–73.

of voluntary choice by student and school, to the degree that it is present, is one of the very significant educational differences between private and public schools.

The difference stems from the fact that the public school finds itself with a building full of youngsters who are delivered to its doorstep unsolicited, including some who would prefer to be elsewhere, while the private school opens with a complement of students who were formally accepted by the school and who chose it. It should not be surprising to find that the difference in morale and in attitude toward learning and teaching in these two situations is often very great. Though the psychological benefits of voluntariness are not precisely measurable, it is plain from the basic assumptions that underlie current proposals for educational reform that lack of choice or voluntariness can be a major impediment not only to the learning process but to the school's incentive to improve itself. Voluntary choice provides a constructive basis for the growth of mutual responsibility and trust between the student and the school, with both parties having a stake in making the relationship work. The knowledge that either party is free to terminate the relationship leaves both free to concentrate on the business in hand instead of merely going through the motions or playing games of evasion. Moreover, the exercise of choice maintains an educational free market which provides some public measure at least of the performance of competing schools as well as an incentive to improvement. Some public school critics suggest that more real competition among public schools, as well as among private and public schools, might provide significant new incentives to reform.[9]

The typical private school is not only unitary and relatively autonomous; it is with but a few exceptions a relatively small school that enrolls only a manageable group of students—usually a smaller number than the minimum effective size set for public comprehensive high schools by Dr. James B. Conant in *The American High School Today*.[10] Catholic elementary and secondary schools are

[9] See James S. Coleman's "Incentives in American Education," *Educate* (September 1969), pp. 18-24. Also Christopher Jencks, "Is the Public School Obsolete?" *The Public Interest* no. 2 (Winter 1966): 18-27. Feasibility studies under grants from the Office of Economic Opportunity are being conducted in preparation for experimental demonstration projects using educational vouchers to pay the cost of education in public and private schools.

[10] New York: McGraw-Hill, 1959. In his view a high school graduating fewer than 100 annually is too small to be capable of providing a comprehensive curriculum, that is, one providing academic courses for the college bound as well as vocational courses for terminal students. For private schools that specialize in one type of curriculum a minimum enrollment is less critical. In 1965-66 three-quarters of all nonpublic secondary schools enrolled less than 400 students. *Statistics of Nonpublic Elementary and Secondary Schools, 1965-66*, OE 20111 (Washington, D.C.: Office of Education, Department of Health, Education and Welfare, 1968), p. 19. Among the exceptions is the Punahou School, Honolulu, Hawaii, with an enrollment (in grades 1-12) of 3,480—the largest nonsectarian private school in the United States. On the other hand, there are schools so tiny that one is

somewhat larger on the average than other nonpublic schools. Most nonpublic schools are small by choice; some remain small because they lack reputation and clients, or the money or incentive to grow. But whether a school is small by choice or by the force of circumstances it is characteristic of private schools to regard smallness and direct human relations, unburdened by bureaucratic complexities, as essential. The aim is to provide a familial, personalized education under a headmaster or principal who accepts a broad delegation of power. Many public schools, on the other hand, under the necessity of dealing with large numbers efficiently and economically, delegate the decision-making powers to a hierarchy of professional administrators, who because of the scale of operations are often remote from the students and the day-to-day educational process.

There are subtle resemblances, however, between certain public and private schools, resemblances in style and atmosphere. It is often remarked that smaller high schools in affluent suburbs or exurbs in some ways resemble elite private day schools. Similarly, certain Catholic diocesan high schools, apart from the religious symbols which are usually much in evidence, resemble gray area urban public high schools. This is true also of some urban Lutheran schools. The suburban and elite schools have in common the accent on college preparation and a student body drawn largely from a relatively homogeneous middle and upper middle class background. Resemblances between urban denominational high schools and the public high schools derive from the fact that both serve a more heterogeneous socioeconomic clientele with both blue- and white-collar family backgrounds and with a variety of occupational destinations in prospect for the graduates.

Recent Enrollment Patterns

Considering the fact that nonpublic schools in the United States enrolled annually during the 1960s about six and a half million elementary and secondary school pupils, the American public appears to be surprisingly uninformed about them, how they operate, what types there are, and how they differ. The Gallup survey, "How the Public Views Nonpublic Schools," found that "by almost every test the public reveals little knowledge about nonpublic schools, especially about private non-church schools," even those in their own communities. The respondents professed little knowledge of how these schools are supported, how much it costs to attend or what assistance might be available in the form of scholarships. But despite this lack of information or immediate interest in private schools, 73 per cent of those interviewed across the nation thought it would

prompted to ask, What is a school? There is an approved school in North Carolina enrolling just four pupils, all in the fourth grade; and another, also approved, consisting of a father teaching his four children in his own home.

be a good idea to include private and parochial as well as public schools in plans for new cities built from the ground up on open land. Among respondents living in communities where private schools exist, 84 per cent favored the inclusion of private schools in new cities. It is evident that these schools, though little known, are widely accepted as a natural expression of a pluralistic society, even by many who choose to send their children to public schools. The overwhelming majority believe "there should be a right to choose."[11]

It is not surprising, then, that church-affiliated and independent schools are still prominent on the American educational scene a century and a half after the birth of the modern public school. But unlike the private colleges which now educate about 25 per cent of all college students, nonpublic schools at present educate only about 13 per cent of all students enrolled in elementary and secondary institutions. Until near the end of the nineteenth century private secondary schools played a much more prominent role. The major shift from private to public secondary schooling is a phenomenon of the past eighty years. But in the period beginning soon after the Second World War and extending into the sixties, the rate of growth of the nonpublic schools overall exceeded that of the public schools. Little notice has been taken of the fact that so much of the growth of nonpublic schools occurred as recently as the fifties and sixties.

The fluctuations of private school enrollment are instructive (see table 1). In 1879 the private academies, then in a steep decline, and the preparatory departments of private colleges which temporarily took over much of the burden of college preparation, between them enrolled a whopping 73 per cent of secondary school students. During the next decade, the number plummeted to 32 per cent, reflecting the rapid growth of public high schools. By 1920, immediately after the First World War and after three decades of phenomenal expansion of the public school system, the combined enrollment in elementary and secondary private schools dropped sharply to 7 per cent. It was the highwater mark of the melting-pot philosophy with its side effects of xenophobia, the passage of discriminatory immigration laws and suspicion of everything foreign in the name of Americanism.

A slow climb in nonpublic school enrollment began during the twenties, aided in part by the short-lived economic prosperity of that period and spurred in 1925 by the Supreme Court's landmark decision in the case of *Pierce* v. *Society of Sisters*.[12] This decision, the Magna Charta of nonpublic schools in the United

---

[11]See pp. 4–5, of the Gallup survey cited above, n. 7. A companion survey entitled "The Public's Attitude Toward the Public Schools," sponsored by CFK, Ltd., using the same national sample as the private school survey, revealed that 49 per cent of those interviewed say they knew "very little" about the public schools, even those in their own community. Schooling is a topic about which many people evidently have firm opinions but little knowledge.

[12]268 U.S. 510 (1925).

13

Table 1

ELEMENTARY AND SECONDARY SCHOOL ENROLLMENT
IN THE UNITED STATES, 1879 TO 1965[a]

In thousands

	Elementary (K–8)			Secondary (9–12)			
Year	Public	Private	Per Cent Private of Total Elementary	Public	Private	Per Cent Private of Total Secondary	Combined Per Cent Private of Total
1879	–	–	–	27	74	73.3	–
1889–90	–	–	–	203	95	31.9	–
1899–1900	14,984	1,241	7.6	519	111	17.6	7.6
1909–10	16,899	1,558	8.4	915	117	11.3	8.6
1919–20	19,379	1,486	7.1	2,200	214	8.9	7.3
1929–30	21,279	2,310	9.8	4,399	341	7.2	9.4
1939–40	18,832	2,153	10.3	6,601	458	6.5	9.3
1949–50	19,387	2,708	12.3	5,725	672	10.5	11.9
1959–60	27,602	4,640	14.4	8,485	1,035	10.9	13.6
1965	30,577	4,976	14.0	11,597	1,329	10.3	13.0
1970	32,430	4,170	11.4	13,330	1,360	9.3	11.0

[a]Data for 1879 and 1889–90, available for secondary schools only, are from *Report of the U.S. Commissioner of Education: 1900-1901*, p. xcv. Data for 1899–1900 to 1965 are from *Digest of Educational Statistics, 1969* (Washington, D.C.: National Center for Educational Statistics, Office of Education, U.S. Department of Health, Education and Welfare, 1969), table 3, p. 3. Data for 1970 are based on estimates, as reported in *Digest of Educational Statistics*, 1970, table 1, p. 2.

States, established the private school's constitutional right to exist and the parent's right to choose a private school. Under the hammer blows of the Great Depression in the thirties, private secondary school enrollment dwindled to 6 per cent, but elementary enrollment rose to 10 per cent. The trend was upward again during the forties, continuing through the Second World War and after. Then it accelerated rapidly during the fifties until the elementary and secondary enrollment combined crested at 13.6 out of a hundred in 1959-60. By 1969-70, the latest year for which national statistics are available, nonpublic elementary schools declined to 11.4 per cent, while the combined total of elementary and secondary students dropped to 11 per cent.

Though the percentages seem small, the total number of students attending nonpublic schools at the peak in 1965—roughly 6.5 million out of the 48.5 million enrolled in all types of elementary and secondary schools—is far from negligible. Quite apart from the human benefits conferred, in financial terms alone (assuming an average cost during the 1960s of $500 per student in public schools, and an average annual enrollment in nonpublic schools of 6.2 million) the operation of nonpublic schools saved the states an expenditure of roughly $31 billion on education.

The importance of nonpublic schools takes on added dimensions in certain metropolitan areas having large concentrations of nonpublic school students. For example, in ten of the nation's 212 Standard Metropolitan Statistical Areas, in 1960, more than one elementary pupil out of three was enrolled in nonpublic schools, including such populous centers as Philadelphia, Milwaukee, Cincinnati, and Jersey City. And Chicago, Pittsburgh, St. Louis, Cleveland, and New York show more than one out of four pupils in a nonpublic school.[13]

It is well to view and present private school enrollment trends in the perspective of the school age population as a whole. The decade of the sixties saw a dramatic increase in public school enrollment, but the prediction for the near future is for a relatively stable school population. As for the private schools, in the late 1960s there was talk in educational circles about a "private school explosion," which was regarded by some as a middle class movement away from the common schools.[14] No such explosion is apparent in the statistics for 1965–66.[15] The recent decline in Catholic school enrollments has in fact reversed the growth trend of nonpublic schools as a whole. The differential trends among various segments of the nonpublic school world are worth reviewing, for they provide important clues as to what is happening.

Since Catholic schools alone account for about 77 per cent of the total of nonpublic schools, what happens in that domain greatly affects the total. The widely publicized financial straits of Catholic parochial schools in many dioceses, whatever the contributing causes may be, are a major factor in the decline of the number of Catholic elementary schools as well as in their total enrollment. In 1969–70 Catholic schools enrolled 16.8 per cent fewer students than in their peak year of 1964–65, when over 5,600,000 children attended them.[16] On the other hand, schools of the younger evangelical Protestant sects

[13] Donald A. Erickson and Andrew M. Greeley, "Non-Public Schools and Metropolitanism," in *Metropolitanism—Its Challenge to Education*, ed. Robert J. Havighurst; Yearbook of the National Society for the Study of Education, no. 67 (Chicago: University of Chicago Press, 1968), pp. 287–88. The figures are based on the U.S. census for 1960.

[14] See, for example, Richard E. Morgan, *The Politics of Religious Conflict: Church and State in America* (New York: Pegasus, 1968), p. 39, and n. 35, pp. 141–42.

[15] The U.S. Office of Education conducts a census of private schools only at four or five year intervals. The next survey is to cover statistics for 1970–71. If past experience is a guide, one should expect a lag of two or three years before the statistics are available in printed form. The National Catholic Educational Association, in cooperation with the U.S. Office of Education and helped by grants from the Carnegie Corporation of New York, has set up a national data bank for Catholic school statistics. The first report presented data covering Catholic schools from 1967–68 through 1969–70. In 1970 the Association contracted with the U.S. Office of Education to gather data for the National Center for Educational Statistics concurrently with the 1970–71 NCEA project.

[16] *A Statistical Report on Catholic Elementary and Secondary Schools for the Years 1967–68 to 1969–70* (Washington, D.C.: National Catholic Educational Association, 1970). The number of Catholic schools declined by 11.2 per cent during the same period, and the

appear to be growing rapidly in both numbers and enrollment.[17] But since this growth starts from a very small base, the numbers involved do not begin to counterbalance even the relatively fractional losses suffered by the vast Catholic school system. The same must be said of the steady growth of Episcopal elementary schools and the rapid proliferation of Jewish all-day schools. Moreover, the fact that the schools of some of the older Protestant denominations, the Missouri Synod Lutheran and the Christian Reformed in particular, as well as the Seventh-Day Adventists, register slight declines in the immediate past serves to refute the explosion rumor.

The proliferation of predominantly black private schools of many kinds is another recent phenomenon: storefront or street academies, Black Muslim schools, freedom schools, community schools, mini-schools, block schools—some under Protestant or Catholic auspices—and elite prep and military schools for middle class blacks. They aim to fill social and educational needs to which local public schools are not responding effectively. But here again, important as these ventures are both for themselves and as experimental models, the numbers of schools and students involved are small.

With opposing racial motivations, in some areas of the South white citizens' councils are attempting to evade enforced integration by establishing private segregated academies. There is no way of determining precisely how numerous they are, since most southern states do not publish statistics about private schools.[18]

Reliable statistics are available, however, to assess the enrollment growth pattern over the past five years of the approximately 630 reporting member schools of the National Association of Independent Schools (NAIS), which, although its membership of approximately 780 is predominantly nondenominational, includes some Episcopal, Friends and a few Catholic schools. In general, the coeducational day schools of the NAIS group show the steadiest growth,

---

professional staff changed from approximately two-thirds religious to over one-half religious. Meanwhile, the pupil-teacher ratios improved from 38:1 in 1964–65 to 29:1 in 1969–70 among the elementary schools, and from 20:1 to 18:1 in the secondary schools.

[17]For example, the "Independent Christian School Census" conducted annually by the NACS shows an average increase of enrollment in member and nonmember Christian schools (not clearly defined denominationally) of about 19 per cent from 1966–67 to 1968–69. *NACS School Directory, 1968–69* (Wheaton, Ill.: National Association of Christian Schools, 1969), p. 4. The officers of NACS foresee a comparable growth in the years immediately ahead.

[18]"The Southern Regional Council estimated in October, 1969, that 300,000 students were attending segregated private schools (including older ones) . . . apparently ten times as many as before the 1964 Civil Rights Act. The Council is now revising its figures upward, to 400,000 or more." See Reese Cleghorn, "The Old South Tries Again," *Saturday Review*, May 16, 1970, p. 76.

especially at the elementary level, separate sex day schools are doing less well, boarding schools show a recent decline, while military schools are finding it necessary to stress their academic accomplishments in order to survive. Overall, the schools of the NAIS group show in recent years a slow but steady growth, but at a rate slower than that of the public schools.[19] It suggests that costly elite schooling is in relatively lower demand than five years ago.

Another sector of private education experiencing a ferment of growth is the group of new, "free" or community schools which are sprouting up in major population centers from coast to coast. Allen Graubard of the Department of Humanities, M.I.T., upon completing a study of these schools early in 1972 under a research contract with the Department of Health, Education and Welfare, estimated that there were between 450 and 500 in existence. They function as uniquely humanistic educational laboratories, unhampered by bureaucratic restrictions but plagued by money problems, so that the mortality rate is high. Yet they keep on coming.[20]

Combining these sources of information, statistical and otherwise, leads to the following general conclusion: a ground swell of private school growth began soon after the Great Depression of the 1930s, the trend accelerated significantly after the Second World War, and crested in the midsixties. Since then, the decline in Catholic school enrollment has evidently more than offset increases in small but growing groups of Protestant and Jewish schools, black schools, segregationist academies, and experimental free, community elementary schools.

Each passing year records the demise of private schools, even long-established ones. It would be strange indeed if, in a time of vertiginous change, some forms of private schooling, that served well another era, were not found wanting and obsolete. Yet while the future of many private schools or groups of schools is far from secure, the idea of private venture schools as alternatives to public schools shows no sign of losing its appeal. On the contrary, the critics and frustrated reformers of public education turn naturally to private-venture schooling to try out new ideas and to seek a fresh start. To assess and to respond to the changing needs of American society has been from the beginning a major function of private schools. The function remains while the form changes. The problem of the established schools is how to exercise the function in forms that are relevant and adaptable in a time when the only constant is change.

---

[19] "Annual Statistics, NAIS Member Schools," *Report of the National Association of Independent Schools*, no. 35 (Boston, Mass., December 1970).

[20] See "Study of Free Schools—New Schools Directory Project," a paper delivered in January 1972 before the Educational Staff Seminar, Institute for Educational Leadership, George Washington University. See also Bonnie B. Stretch, "The Rise of the Free School," *Saturday Review*, June 20, 1970, p. 73.

2

The Panorama of Denominational Schools

*"The important thing
to recognize is that,
above the sphere of politics
and the natural man's gamble
for power, there rises
a realm of the spirit,
of religion,
which unites individuals
belonging to different nations
by forces and motives
of an entirely different order.
In this way there arises
a unity and interconnection among men
that operates in continual opposition
to the demands
of mere political expediency,
which, for all its veneer
of intellectual refinements,
remains at bottom so crude."*

Ernst Troeltsch[1]

Religious Pluralism and the Schools

"On my arrival in the United States," Alexis de Tocqueville noted in the 1830s, "the religious aspect of the country was the first thing that struck my attention; and the longer I stayed there, the more I perceived the great political consequences resulting from this new state of things."[2] The truth of Tocqueville's observation is well illustrated by the schools. From earliest colonial times until well into the nineteenth century Americans commonly assumed that religion is the fundament of a complete education. There were, of course, notable exceptions. Benjamin Franklin and Thomas Jefferson, for example, were less respectful of sectarian religion than most of their contemporaries. Perhaps this is one of

[1] *Christian Thought in Its History and Application*, ed. Baron F. von Hügel (New York: Meridian Books, Living Age Edition, 1957), p. 173.

[2] Alexis de Tocqueville, *Democracy in America*, ed. Phillips Bradley (New York: Alfred A. Knopf, 1945), 1:308.

19

the reasons why neither Jefferson's nor Franklin's plan for the reform of schools was carried out. In the main, until well into the nineteenth century schooling was regarded as a function of the church, and denominational groups accepted this responsibility regardless of whether or not state aid was available to them. However, public support for various types of denominational schools, as well as religious instruction in the public common schools where they existed, were the rule rather than the exception.

As progressive urbanization and large-scale immigration wrought increasing heterogeneity in the population, the threat of burgeoning factionalism and the tensions inherent in competitive religious pluralism became manifest. The rapid growth of industry and the spread of science and rationalist philosophy in the nineteenth century brought a wave of skepticism and secularism which eventually led an influential segment of the public to question the propriety of religious instruction in the public schools as well as the policy of state support for denominational schools. But the religious roots were deep and the process of secularization took time. Long after the First Amendment became effective, religion continued to hold a prominent place in public and private education. Public aid to church schools generally increased until about 1820, and persisted, though on a diminishing scale, even after the Civil War. Even the official disestablishment of New England Congregationalism in the second and third decades of the century appeared to have little immediate effect. The churches and church schools had by that time learned to live in and cope with a secularized political environment. In fact, denominationalism made a virtue out of the mandated separation of church and state by stimulating the burgeoning church groups to vigorous competition in education, as well as in proselytizing.[3]

By the middle of the nineteenth century, however, the principal issue in education was the state's share of the responsibility in the founding and support of schools. Early in the national period, the states proceeded generally on the principle of subsidiarity, that is, they founded public schools only when voluntary effort was clearly incapable of coping with the need. But even before the end of the first half of the nineteenth century unprecedented demands were levied on education. The massive influx of immigrants, the accelerating pace of industrialization, and the explosive force of the westward movement combined to rupture the continuity with the more staid past. The private academy movement, funded either privately or in partnership with government, strove valiantly to expand in order to fill the rapidly growing need for secondary schooling. But as events were to show, voluntary effort by the churches and by private philanthropy combined was inadequate, and so in the second half of the century

[3] See Bernard Bailyn, *Education in the Forming of American Society* (Chapel Hill: University of North Carolina Press, 1970), pp. 102-14.

state-sponsored and -supported schools progressively assumed a growing share of the burden. And as this occurred, there emerged the hardy dilemma regarding the place and nature of religious instruction in the public schools.

The public schools that sprang up in response to the pressure of new demands reflected from the beginning the doctrinal views and values of the old-church Protestant majority. In Horace Mann's grand design the public schools were to be all things to all kinds of children. The common school was not only to provide a good education in secular subjects, it was to shape in the minds of the young a religiously rooted common value system forming the moral bedrock of American republicanism. Mann, himself a practicing Unitarian, believed that the schools could instruct the young in religion without being sectarian. But as experience was to show, it was too thin a line to be held for long. Mann could not have foreseen in the 1840s the progressive exclusion of religion from the public schools that took place during the next one hundred and twenty years. But with the advantage of hindsight we can see that the Supreme Court's 1963 decision in *Abington School District* v. *Schempp*, prohibiting prayers and Bible reading as a formal exercise in public school classrooms, was in the making for over a century, and that *Schempp* marked only the most recent and drastic step in the gradual elimination of religion from the public school.

Given this development, it was inevitable that the public schools could not satisfy families that believed deeply in the importance of bringing up their children in the tenets and special culture of a particular faith. By the mid-nineteenth century many Catholics saw the public school as essentially a hostile establishment of Protestant religion, and as such a threat to Catholic faith and culture. At the same time, the newly emerging evangelical Protestant sects, brimming with renewed vigor and holy vitality, charged that the watered-down religion purveyed by the public school was "godless." And so the unsolvable issue of religion in the public schools became an added incentive for Protestants, Catholics, and, later, for Jews to build their own schools in which the true faith could be transmitted.

But the pathway of the church schools was strewn with obstacles. To many Americans, freshly conscious of their Americanism, the public school seemed, in the closing decades of the nineteenth century, the only institution capable of inculcating democratic virtue and American ideals. Fired by the heady patriotism of manifest destiny, the rise of the Common Man, and the optimistic belief in the inexorable progress of democratic institutions, the American citizen regarded the public school as one of the chief bulwarks of the republic, and private venturing in education, hitherto accepted as both natural and desirable, came to be viewed with suspicion and even hostility. Legislative measures designed to outlaw or curb private and denominational schools appeared in many states during the 1870s and 1880s and later. It was not until 1925, in the famous

Oregon case, *Pierce* v. *Society of Sisters*, that the United States Supreme Court confirmed once and for all the right of parents to send their children to parochial or other private schools of their choice, but it also reaffirmed the right of the state to supervise nonpublic schools.

Given this long tutelage in "the school question," as it came to be called, the persistence and growth of religiously affiliated schools in the United States, especially since the end of the Second World War, need not be a puzzling phenomenon. Unlike so many private colleges that have dropped their denominational ties under the secularizing influence of postindustrial society and "the academic revolution,"[4] the schools of various religious denominations, as we noted above, grew rapidly even as recently as the fifth and sixth decades of this century—in fact more rapidly than did the public schools. To be sure, the denominational affiliates include some schools wherein religion is now, for the students at least, little more than a hallowed tradition or a ceremonial backdrop for a demanding academic program, however much headmasters and chaplains may struggle to restore religion to an integral place in the school program. But this is only what one would expect, given the trend of the time. The striking fact is the persistence of many schools with a strong religious orientation. Catholic, Protestant, and Jewish schools continue to conceive their religious mission as central, and as transcending even their growing commitment to academic learning. This phenomenon is one aspect of the confusing trend towards "religiousness in a secularist framework" on the one side and the contrasting "secularism of religious people" on the other, which Will Herberg identified as "the problem posed by the contemporary religious situation in America."[5]

A deeper understanding of this phenomenon and of how the denominational schools are intertwined with the growth of America and its public schools necessitates an excursion into the origin and history of major church school groups. It is a subject about which too little is known. Academic historians have paid these schools little attention, and public school historians, such as Ellwood Patterson Cubberley, either give them short shrift or treat them as mere false starts or regrettable aberrations along the way to the glorious rise and triumphant procession of the public school system.[6] It must be said of most denominational educators too, the Catholics and Lutherans excepted, that they have not taken

---

[4] In the sense in which this phrase is used by Christopher Jencks and David Riesman to describe the professionalization of education. See *The Academic Revolution* (New York: Doubleday and Co., 1968).

[5] *Protestant, Catholic, Jew*, rev. ed. (Garden City, N.Y.: Doubleday and Co., Anchor Books, 1960), p. 3.

[6] See Lawrence Cremin, *The Wonderful World of Ellwood Patterson Cubberley: An Essay on the Historiography of American Education* (New York: Columbia University Teachers College, Bureau of Publications, 1965). The author points out the peculiarly evangelistic spirit which imbued the writing of public school histories between 1910 and 1950.

the time from their daily problems to appraise the educational accomplishments of their denomination in the perspective of history. The literature in the history of most Protestant schools ranges from scant to nonexistent. The following accounts of denominational schools are no more than an introduction to a field that, cultivated more thoroughly, could greatly enhance our understanding of the pluralistic society of contemporary America.

The Rise and Development of Catholic Schools

The response of the Roman Catholic leadership to the Protestant-oriented public schools was to build up in the course of little more than a century the world's largest private school system, a formidable structure, though not really a "system" in the strict sense. It consisted, in 1968, of parochial, diocesan and religious order schools, numbering over 12,000 elementary and secondary schools enrolling about five million students annually. It was a prodigious feat, accomplished in the face of severe internal stresses brought on by the ethnic heterogeneity of the Catholic immigrants who poured into America and by the external pressures of strong anti-Catholic bias persisting in the United States until recent decades.[7]

Because of its international organization, American Catholicism, unlike Protestantism, was for a long time regarded not as a native religious movement but as a conglomerate of foreign constituents migrating to these shores from all the countries of western Europe. True, some of the Protestant churches of colonial times, especially those of English and Dutch origins, were just as much outposts of European churches. But the Protestant state churches of the colonial era were transformed by the Revolutionary War into voluntary churches within the American pluralistic society. For the Roman Catholics the process of Americanization took much longer, chiefly because the foreign contingent of its membership was explosively enlarged by successive waves of immigrants from many countries of western Europe. Earliest on the scene were the "old family" Catholics—the English in Maryland, the French in Louisiana, the Spanish in the southwest—people of assured social position possessing a rich cultural heritage. In contrast, the later immigrants were frequently impoverished, uneducated peasants, many of them victims of persecution and famine, who brought with them little more than their undeveloped capacities and the fervent hope for a fresh start. Compared with the other immigrant Catholic nationality groups, the Irish enjoyed superiority not only in numbers but in the possession of the English tongue; and so they soon dominated the growing church. The church's

[7]See John Tracy Ellis, *American Catholicism*, 2nd rev. ed. (Chicago: University of Chicago Press, 1969), pp. 192–96; and Robert D. Cross, "Origins of the Catholic Parochial Schools in America," *The American Benedictine Review* (June 16, 1965): 194–209.

task was to graft onto this Irish trunk the diverse branches of its foreign language constituencies: the Germans, Poles, Slavs, Italians, French-Canadians, Spanish-Americans, Ukrainians, and Lithuanians. While the Irish played an indispensable role in Americanizing the Catholics of other nationalities, some of the better-educated national groups, the German Catholics in particular, resisted most vigorously being assimilated to the Irish-dominated Church in America. That struggle came to a head in a petition addressed in 1890 to the Holy See by Peter Paul Cahensly, urging the establishment in America of dioceses along ethnic and cultural instead of geographical lines—a plan which, had it succeeded, would have balkanized the national church, Protestant fashion, into a federation of quasi-independent ethnic churches. Most American bishops joined their Irish constituents in opposing this scheme, which was rejected by the Holy See.[8] Nevertheless, the parochial schools and other Catholic welfare institutions generally continued to reflect, right up to the present day, the varied needs of the ethnic subcultures embraced by the church, but within the framework of firm church policy which in its own way furthered a slow but steady assimilation to Catholic Americanism.[9]

The assimilation of Catholic Americans was hampered also by tensions of another sort which provoked a conflict among the church leaders over what the Americanization of Catholics involved. The dramatic situation in New York attracted national attention. John Hughes, the embattled archbishop of New York and a forceful spokesman for a separatist Catholic America, voiced the fear that hasty assimilation of Catholics, whatever their ethnic backgrounds, would lead to a loss of faith. That fear was prompted by, and in turn affected, the anti-Catholic hysteria and violence of the nativist Know-Nothing party, which maintained that Catholicism was a satanic conspiracy bearing dark schemes to subvert republican government and all true religion.[10] When in the 1840s Bishop

---

[8] An interesting contemporary exception is the accommodation that the Ukrainian parishes of Chicago, Illinois, have managed to obtain. Instead of being subject to Cardinal Cody of the Chicago archdiocese, they have their own bishop, who is directly responsible to a Ukrainian cardinal in Rome. See Donald A. Erickson's comments in *Crisis in Illinois Nonpublic Schools; Final Research Report to the Elementary and Secondary Nonpublic Schools Study Commission*, State of Illinois (Springfield, December 29, 1970), pp. 4–10. John Tracy Ellis notes, in *American Catholicism*, that the Ukrainian Greek Catholic diocese was first established in 1913, and in 1924 the Holy See erected the Greek Rite diocese of Pittsburgh (p. 130).

[9] See Will Herberg's illuminating condensation, "Catholicism in America," in *Protestant, Catholic, Jew*, chap. 7, pp. 136–71. Herberg sees each of the major religions as a distinct melting pot within the all-embracing national one.

[10] Lloyd P. Jorgenson's "The Birth of a Tradition" contains a fresh account of the Protestant-Catholic conflict over religion in the Protestant-oriented public schools and the inflammatory anti-Catholic propaganda which erupted into violence during the 1840s. *Phi Delta Kappan*, June 1963, pp. 407–14.

Hughes became embittered by the failure to secure state aid for Catholic free charity schools in New York City, his position vis-à-vis the Protestant-Catholic conflict hardened, and in the ensuing controversy more and more Catholics saw themselves as a besieged religious culture within a society whose dominant Protestant values were hostile to and corrupting of the Catholic way.[11] Schooling in the Catholic culture took on a new urgency. "The time has almost come," the archbishop declared in 1850, "when it will be necessary to build the schoolhouse first and the church afterward."[12]

An older strain of thought, going back to Bishop John Carroll of Maryland, took a less dramatic turn, emphasizing that in the pluralistic society of the United States Catholics enjoyed an environment in which the church could grow as nowhere else in the world.[13] As long as Catholics were a suspected and persecuted minority, they fell back on the pluralism of the American religious community as a guarantee of their own right to survive separately in a Protestant-dominated society. But once Catholic schools and colleges became numerous, they too functioned as an Americanizing influence, gradually transforming the immigrant "shanty" Irish into "lace curtain" Irish, and more recently into the wall-to-wall suburban Irish, until they identified fully "with the emerging conception of American society as an over-all community of religious communities."[14] And with the gradual subsidence of anti-Catholic rancor, American Catholics developed in time a sense of national patriotism so strong as to identify, in the minds of some, Irish Catholicism with the essence of true Americanism.

Catholic schools in America are deeply marked by the special history of Catholicism in this country. Though they trace their ancestry back over three centuries to the Jesuit founding of schools in Maryland, because penal codes in the early colonies made virtual pariahs out of the Catholic and his children, the growth of the church and its school in colonial times was shadowy and slow.[15]

---

[11] "Between 1795 and 1825 the State of New York, which did not as yet have a public school system, gave financial aid, through the nominally non-sectarian 'Public School Society,' to every educational institution in the city, practically all of which were operated by the churches." Neil G. McCluskey, S. J., *Catholic Education Faces Its Future* (Garden City, N.Y.: Doubleday and Co., 1969), p. 60. See also Nathan Glazer and Daniel Patrick Moynihan, *Beyond the Melting Pot* (Cambridge Mass.: M.I.T. Press, 1964), pp. 234–38.

[12] Quoted in Robert D. Cross, *The Emergence of Liberal Catholicism in America* (Cambridge, Mass.: Harvard University Press, 1958), p. 137.

[13] See Andrew M. Greeley, *The Catholic Experience: An Interpretation of the History of American Catholicism* (Garden City, N.Y.: Doubleday and Co., 1967), pp. 19–20.

[14] Herberg, *Protestant, Catholic, Jew*, p. 151.

[15] By 1820 the estimated Catholic population in the United States was only about 195,000. From that point on, due largely to the swelling tide of immigrants, Catholic population more than doubled in virtually every decade up to 1900. "Estimates of today's

25

As the national period opened, not a single Catholic school was in existence. And no wonder, since the didactic *New England Primer*, on which millions of pupils were weaned, contained admonitions such as, "Child, behold the Man of Sin, the Pope, worthy of thy utmost hatred. . . ."[16] But by 1840 Catholic schools numbered "at least 200 with about half of these west of the Alleghenies."[17] Then as the public school movement spread, with its King James Bible, Protestant prayers and hymns, Catholic leaders were thrown increasingly on the defensive. Efforts to negotiate compromises in the form of combining public and parochial schooling for the benefit of Catholics and Protestant denominations succeeded in some localities, but seldom for long.

The First Plenary Council of Baltimore in 1852, surveying the outbreaks of anti-Romanism, bloody riots and church burnings spread over the preceding decades, exhorted Catholic parishes to found and support their own schools. But it remained for the decrees of the Third Plenary Council of Baltimore in 1884 to reject the public school on confessional grounds as a danger to faith and morals, to *order* the erection of a parish school "near every church . . . within two years" under stiff sanctions, and to bid Catholic parents send their children to Catholic schools.[18] Immediately back of the council's radical decrees lay the papal "Instruction" of 1875, which was influenced by the relentless crusade waged against the public schools by James A. MacMaster, the fiery Catholic lay editor of the *Freeman's Journal*. The issue now was not so much the Protestant orientation of the public schools, since that had abated somewhat, though it remained as a residual complaint. "A new enemy had energed," writes Father Neil G. McCluskey. The concern of Catholic bishops, shared with many Protestants, was for the all-out battle which was shaping up between truth and error, between religious and secular learning. It was Darwinism in particular that triggered the conflict between religion and science in the closing decades of the nineteenth century.[19]

What happened in the third Baltimore council proves again that the Catholic church was not the monolith which Protestant mythology had long held it to be. The Vatican could instruct and the bishops could propose, but it was the Catholic pocketbook, the fluctuating state of the national economy, and the exigencies of internal migration that eventually disposed. At the time of the council's

---

Catholic population vary between forty-five and fifty million, or 23–25 per cent of the total population." McCluskey, *Catholic Education*, p. 51. The statistics on earlier years are from John L. Thomas, *The American Catholic Family* (Englewood Cliffs, N.J.: Prentice-Hall, 1956), p. 108.

[16] McCluskey, *Catholic Education*, p. 53.

[17] Ellis, *American Catholicism*, p. 56.

[18] McCluskey, *Catholic Education*, pp. 82–83.

[19] *Ibid.*, p. 83.

decree, about 37 per cent of Catholic parishes had schools. That figure rose in the interim, but by 1900 it was down slightly.[20] Nor did the decree of the third Baltimore council silence liberal prelates who, like Archbishop John Ireland of St. Paul, continued to appeal for compromises and cooperation with the public schools. Parochial schools, he insisted, should not be seen as the norm but as the last resort. But this view did not prevail with the majority of the Catholic leadership. "Probably the major reason for the failure of Ireland's detente," observes Robert D. Cross, "was the unwillingness of most public school authorities to make special arrangements for minority groups."[21]

Since then, the debate over the place of Catholic schools has continued unabated among clergy and laymen, with the school expansionists having the better of it for the first six decades of the present century. Catholic schools grew rapidly during the period beginning immediately after the Second World War, then leveled off in the early sixties, and after the peak year of 1965 began an accelerating decline. With a sharp decrease in available teachers from the religious orders and the employment of lay teachers whose salaries must be at least comparable with public school salary scales, school costs have soared. Many Catholic educators are loath to cover the increased cost by escalating fees, lest they end by serving not only a diminishing but a middle class clientele selected on the basis of ability to pay.

The rich variety of Catholic schools is not widely understood or appreciated because non-Catholics tend to think of them all in terms of a prevailing but outdated parochial elementary school stereotype. There are basically three main types: parochial schools, diocesan schools, and "private" schools and academies operated and staffed by various of the many religious orders. The diocesan and order schools not only differ in essential respects from the parochials, the parochials themselves are very diversified, reflecting as they do local, ethnic, regional, class, and other differences. Many are conventional schools on the fringe of a city or in a suburb, serving mainly the children of lower middle, middle and upper class neighborhoods. Others, such as the Catholic Urban Community School in Cleveland, and St. Ann's, located in a "Model Cities" area of Baltimore, are in the slums of big cities. St. Ann's enrolls about 220 black children, half of them non-Catholic, in an ungraded "informal" classroom program. Schools of this type often utilize buildings of former congregations whose members have fled to the suburbs.[22] On the other hand, Camden Catholic High

---

[20] By 1968, however, it had risen to 57 per cent. Thus Macaulay's remark that "the Irish are distinguished by qualities which make them interesting rather than prosperous" was true of the nineteenth- but not of the twentieth-century Irish.

[21] "Origins of the Catholic Parochial Schools in America," p. 208.

[22] See "Three Perky Black Parochials," by Edgar L. Jones, in *Baltimore Evening Sun*, February 6, 1971.

School, in New Jersey, a comprehensive, innovative diocesan school, enrolls a cross-section of students resembling that of a fairly typical public high school serving an urban gray area with adjacent segments of suburbia.

Among the schools conducted by various Catholic religious orders, which also provide most of the staff for parish and diocesan schools, are the "private academies," with aims and traditions as diverse as the orders that sustain them or the pupils who attend. Some exhibit the elitist traits of the NAIS schools. Archmere Academy near Wilmington, Delaware, a boarding school conducted by the Norbertine Order, and Fordham Preparatory School, a Jesuit institution in New York City, are good examples. By contrast, LaSalle Military Academy, on Long Island, directed by the Christian Brothers, offers "a thoroughly Christian boarding high school in an atmosphere of military discipline and courtesy." The range of ethnic interests among the Catholic religious orders is illustrated by the St. Labre Indian Mission School at Ashland, Montana, not far from the scene of Custer's last stand. This K–12 boarding school is the nucleus of a mission conducted by the Capuchin Fathers, which includes besides the school a manufacturing plant in arts and crafts employing Indians from the adjacent Cheyenne reservation. The school also functions as a social and recreational center for adults from the immediate area. Another illustration of the range of the church's ethnic interests is the group of Ukrainian Catholic parish and diocesan schools in Chicago, unique institutions which are responsible through their own bishop directly to the Vatican.

Although financial stringency is the widely publicized reason for the present-day decline of Catholic schools, there are others not so well aired. Catholics have not only become Americanized in the twentieth century; they have risen rapidly into the middle and upper classes of American society with predictable changes in their attitudes toward Catholicism itself and the place of separate Catholic schools. One result of the upward mobility of Catholics is the gradual attenuation of the distinctive ethnic and religious elements of the schools. And this in turn makes them a less attractive apostolate for many of the nuns, brothers and priests who formerly subsidized them with money or contributed services. Mary Perkins Ryan's slender book, *Are Parochial Schools the Answer?*[23] while acknowledging that Catholic schools did yeoman's service in easing the process of acculturation for millions of Catholic immigrants and thus made Americanization a less traumatic experience, also alleges that the schools are a product of the "siege mentality" of the nineteenth-century church, a state of mind unsuited to the climate of our time. Whatever the merits or demerits of her book, it succeeded in provoking a general reassessment of the goals of Catholic schooling and a critical review of the church's established priorities in the light of present social, educational, and spiritual needs. Other voices have called for a reassess-

---

[23] New York: Holt, Rinehart and Winston, 1964.

ment of Catholic priorities. For example, Monsignor James C. Donohue urged the church to concentrate its educational effort and resources, first, on the educational needs of the urban ghetto; second, on religious education of adults and youth by various means; and third, on the operation of elementary and secondary schools.[24] This proposal would effect a reversal of the church's current priorities, under which the lion's share of the effort and available resources goes to the schools.

Catholic prelates, educators and laymen are in the midst of a searching reappraisal. Leading Catholic educators freely predict a continuing decline in school enrollment with the expectation that by 1975 it will be about half of the six million that the schools enrolled at their crest. Now that state aid to non-public schools is being debated in most states—a number already provide marginal aid in a variety of forms—the nature and future of Catholic schools is not only a matter of lively interest educationally but of immediate practical concern. If Catholic schools were to be phased out in large numbers, the loss to educational diversity alone would be incalculable, and the added cost to the American taxpayer would assume critical proportions.

The other arm of the universal Catholic Church, Byzantium, or the Greek Orthodox Church, is less well known in the United States partly because its membership is numerically much smaller, and partly because most of the various Orthodox groups are under old-country ecclesiastical jurisdiction, while they have developed in this country a strongly separatist but sophisticated community organization. Prior to 1945, Orthodox day schools were very few. Perhaps it was the fear of being submerged in the societal mainstream that spurred the rapid growth of day schools in the period after the Second World War. Unfortunately, little information about these schools is available nationally. But if one may generalize from those that have been studied at close range in Chicago, the schools are typically parochial in ownership and control and maintain a tradition of congregational autonomy and close rapport with the Orthodox community. They resemble the Jewish day schools in dividing the day into a block of secular academic studies patterned on the public school curriculum, followed by an extensive program of Greek language, cultural, and religious studies.[25]

Schools of the Protestant Denominations

The historical development of Protestant schools mirrors the long history of sectarian fission as well as the ethnic diversity that Protestantism cloaks. These schools were strongly conditioned, moreover, by the fact that up to the end of

[24]"New Priorities in Catholic Education" in *America*, April 13, 1968, pp. 476–79. Monsignor Donohue was at that time Director of Elementary and Secondary Education for the United States Catholic Conference.

[25]*Crisis in Illinois Nonpublic Schools*, pp. 4-55 to 4-60.

the nineteenth century American Protestants could regard the public school as their own creation. In the colonial period only the most separatist of sects, or those which were determined to carry on instruction in a foreign tongue and keep alive the memory of the ancestral home were disposed to found parochial schools. This pattern continued in the early national period as long as the common school was under the control of local districts and thus readily reflected the dominant Protestant beliefs and mores. But once the movement for centralization of public school control was well advanced and the constitutional mandate for separation of church and state became a public issue, doctrinal religion began to disappear from the common school. Opposition to this trend by those who wanted the public schools to remain not only Christian but Protestant was often heated but nonetheless unavailing.[26] Religious neutralism or outright secularism seemed the only just course for the common school, once the issue of the rights of conscience and freedom of belief had been raised.

The response to this trend by the Calvinists, Lutherans, Episcopalians, Quakers, and the Dutch Reformed was to found their own parochial elementary schools. Congregationalists, Methodists, and Baptists, on the other hand, were more disposed to accept the secular education offered by the state, but urged their constituents to supplement that schooling with religious instruction in the church and home. Though the Protestant parochial school movement was relatively strong in the first half of the nineteenth century, the heyday was not destined to arrive until much later—not until after the chauvinism of the early 1920s had subsided. Partly as a result of the growing secularization of the public schools, and partly as a conscious effort of the third generation to reidentify with ethnic and religious cultures which had been an embarrassment to the second generation, the founding of denominational schools was resumed with vigor. But now the educational zeal of old-line Protestant denominations, with a tenuous history of schools stretching back to colonial times, was matched by new sects which had come into being or had been renewed in the fires of the nineteenth-century evangelical revival movement. Methodists and Baptists of various special persuasions, Seventh-Day Adventists, Assembly of God churches, the Christian Reformed group, and many other small, proliferating, independent sects are responsible for much of the very recent growth of Protestant denominational schools.

The Protestant denominations which are deeply committed to maintaining full-time schools are characterized usually by a clear sense of sectarian identity, which the school is expected to strengthen. The size of the denomination has little to do with it. There are well over two hundred Protestant denominations in

[26] See William K. Dunn, *What Happened to Religious Education?* (Baltimore: Johns Hopkins Press, 1958), pp. 150–88.

the United States, most of them claiming fewer than fifty thousand adherents. Only eighteen count at least a half million members. The Seventh-Day Adventists—a denomination of relatively recent origin with a strong identity but with a constituency of only about 400,000 in the United States—is more deeply committed to education, in proportion to its membership, than any other Protestant body. On the other hand, the Missouri Synod Lutherans represent a large branch of an old-line church that deliberately remained insulated to some extent from the mainstream of American life for almost a century. With the help of its large school system, it has maintained a clear self-definition right to the present.

Among the old-church Protestants, the Lutherans are the most deeply committed to parochial schooling. The largest group is affiliated with The Lutheran Church—Missouri Synod, an international body with headquarters in St. Louis, Missouri. At various times in the past, twenty different Lutheran Synods maintained parochial schools. But besides the conservative Missouri Synod only the even more conservative and much smaller Wisconsin Evangelical Lutheran Synod still maintains a substantial number of schools. However, in the American Lutheran Church, constituent bodies of which in times past supported parochial education, the schools are again growing, slowly but appreciably, and most noticeably in California, where transplanted middle-westerners have sparked a revived interest in Lutheran education.

The educational undertaking of Lutheranism as a whole traces its contribution through three centuries of American history.[27] It began with the original Lutheran settlements of Swedes, Dutch and Germans in colonial Delaware, Maryland, Pennsylvania, New Jersey, New York, Virginia, the Carolinas and Georgia. In many of these enclaves, the setting up of a school was the first order of business.[28] Lutheranism in America grew rapidly in the nineteenth century as a result of the streams of German and Scandinavian immigrants—religious dissenters who came to America in search of religious freedom as well as economic opportunity. Desirous of perpetuating the mother tongue and their cherished European culture, they congregated in pioneering enclaves scattered over the plains, villages, forest clearings and along the rivers of the central and north central states, where they founded congregations, schools, colleges, seminaries, foreign language newspapers, publishing houses, chapters of the *Deutsche*

---

[27]See Walter H. Beck, *Lutheran Elementary Schools in the United States*, 2nd ed. (St. Louis: Concordia Publishing House, 1965), chap. 16. For current statistics about Lutheran schools, see the annual *School Statistics* report of the Board of Parish Education, Lutheran Church—Missouri Synod.

[28]The Lutherans in Pennsylvania, although a minority group, created the largest denominational school system in the country (240 schools by 1820) before the advent of public education. See Beck, *Lutheran Elementary Schools*, pp. 47 and 73.

Verein, the *Männerchor*, the *Turnverein* and other social and cultural agencies. Not uncommonly in a new settlement a log cabin Lutheran parochial school, serving non-Lutheran as well as Lutheran children, was the first educational institution, teaching the school subjects in the mother tongue with some instruction in English also. St. Lorenz Lutheran School in the farming community of Frankenmuth, Michigan, is an illustration. Established in 1846 as a pioneer school for children of Indians, Bavarian missionaries, and farmers newly settled in the area, it enrolls even today over half of the elementary school pupils in the town. Throughout the nineteenth century the Lutheran Church in America remained splintered into a multitude of synods differentiated either by ethnic origins or on credal grounds or both. It was not until the period between the two world wars and later that long-discussed proposals for mergers came to fruition, resulting in seven national Lutheran bodies. They conduct, all told, 1,444 elementary and 51 secondary schools in the United States.[29]

The history of Lutheran schools, replete with ups and down, reflects the changing social and political problems encountered by the Lutherans in the process of gradual Americanization. After a period of vigorous growth in colonial times, the schools increased steadily from the mid-nineteenth century until after the Civil War, and again from the turn of the century to the First World War.[30] Much of this growth took place under the stress of severe challenges. In the late eighties, for example, the burgeoning public school system, abetted by a tide of militant Americanism, provoked repeated efforts in various states to eliminate all nonpublic schools by state enactments. Antiprivate-school forces in Wisconsin and Illinois managed to pass such laws. A swift defense by Catholics, Lutherans and other religious groups brought about their repeal in short order. Yet the battle was far from over. During the ensuing decades similar legislative proposals for the abolition of parochial and foreign language schools continued to be mounted in about a dozen states, with those in Michigan, Nebraska and Oregon proving to be the most threatening. These persistent efforts to compel all children to attend public schools were laid to rest finally by the U.S. Supreme Court's landmark decision in *Pierce* v. *Society of Sisters,* wherein the court in striking down the Oregon law in question stated, "We think it entirely plain that the Act of 1922 unreasonably interferes with the liberty of parents and guardians to direct the upbringing and education of children under their control."[31]

[29]Statistics from a survey conducted by the Board of Parish Education, Lutheran Church–Missouri Synod, for 1970–71.

[30]See August C. Stellhorn, *Schools of the Lutheran Church–Missouri Synod* (St. Louis: Concordia Publishing House, 1963), tables on pp. 97, 275, 401, 445. These tables reveal an especially rapid growth in schools and enrollment from 1848 to 1869. The statistics pertain to Missouri Synod schools only.

[31]268 U.S. 510 (1925).

But despite this signal constitutional guarantee, Lutheran schools with their bilingualism and German cultural orientation again found themselves embattled in the antiforeign and more specifically anti-German backlash of the First World War and its aftermath. Some Lutheran parochial schools fell victims to the campaign for 100 per cent Americanism; others closed because ecumenically-minded synods turned to the public schools. But many Lutherans remained undaunted in their determination to provide a religious education for their children. It was not until after the Second World War, however, that renewed interest in parish schools led once again to a steady growth in enrollment. Nevertheless, the per cent of eligible Lutheran school-age children in the most populous Lutheran schools—those of the Missouri Synod—has remained virtually unchanged at 33 since the years immediately after World War II.[32] At present the number of schools and the enrollment in elementary and secondary schools are declining slightly from the peak which they reached during the 1960s. The Wisconsin Synod schools, on the other hand, continue to grow slowly but steadily.

Lutherans have been upwardly mobile and swept up in the tide of urbanization for many decades. What effects these changes are having on Lutheran attitudes toward parochial schools is not yet clear. One consequence, noticeable also in Catholic as well as in certain other Protestant schools, is the energetic effort to raise the quality of the educational program of their schools in both the secular and religious departments. Another is the running debate about the church's philosophy of education stimulated by the contemporary crisis of religious faith. Lutheran educators subscribe wholeheartedly to the verse from Proverbs which reads: "The fear of the Lord is the beginning of wisdom." But how this scriptural gem is to be translated into a curriculum of studies for students who will spend most of their lives in the vertiginous physical and moral environments of the twenty-first century remains the big question with which Lutheran as well as other church educators wrestle ceaselessly.

After the Lutherans, the largest group of Protestant denominational schools is the creation of the Seventh-Day Adventists, a numerically small, "third-force" denomination which is known for its international activities in behalf of education, health, the publication of religious literature, and missionary work, all supported by the most generous tithing to be found anywhere in American churches. The various Adventist groups trace their history to the Millerites and the pathetic drama of an unfulfilled prophecy of the second coming of Christ and end of the world which was to take place March 21, 1844. The Seventh-Day Adventists proper owe their inception to the divine visions of Mrs. Ellen G. White, a frail, self-educated woman whose preaching and prodigious output of

[32]Victor C. Krause, ed., *Lutheran Elementary Schools in Action* (St. Louis: Concordia Publishing House, 1963), p. 19.

religious literature were and still remain the inspiration for the vast network of Seventh-Day Adventist enterprises. With her guidance and constant encouragement, the Adventists became an organized evangelistic body in 1863, a step which was formalized at the first general conference in Battle Creek, Michigan.

The Adventist schools owe their founding to Mrs. White's indefatigable efforts also. According to her testimony, in one of her many visions God revealed a plan for the founding of denominational schools and the philosophy which was to guide them. "True education," she wrote, "means more than the pursual of a certain course of study. It means more than a preparation for the life that now is. It has to do with the whole being, and with the whole period of existence possible to man. It is the harmonious development of the physical, the mental, and the spiritual powers. It prepares the student for the joy of service in this world and for the higher joy of wider service in the world to come."[33]

One of the dominant themes in the Adventist philosophy of educating "the whole being" is the extensive health program of Adventism. This too was opened up to Mrs. White in a comprehensive vision revealing the important relationship which exists between good health and godliness and efficiency in service. The vision revealed in some detail the treatment of disease chiefly by assisting nature's way—pure air, sunlight, abstemiousness (no meat, alcohol or tobacco), rest, suitable exercise, proper diet, fresh water, emotional composure, trust in divine power—these were prescribed by Mrs. White as the true remedies. Adventist education stresses these objectives from kindergarten through medical school. The schools are located typically in clear-air, unpolluted locations, in the mountains or open country. Competition and hard body-contact games and sports are discouraged. Adventist higher education places a strong emphasis on nutrition and medical education in association with their own hospitals, sanatoria, and leprosaria, as well as a worldwide network of health food companies in addition to other missionary enterprises.[34]

Beginning with the first academy in 1872, the Adventists now operate an international educational system including elementary and secondary schools, colleges and universities. They maintain over 5,000 elementary and secondary schools the world over. Of these approximately 1,100 are located in the "North American Division." Many of the schools throughout the world are self-supporting in the sense that self-help work opportunities on farms or in furniture factories

---

[33] Ellen G. White, *Education* (Mountain View, Calif.: Pacific Press Publishing Co., 1903), p. 13.

[34] *Seventh-Day Adventist Yearbook, 1968.* The cereal industry in Battle Creek owes its origin largely to the Adventist search for wholesome, nutritious foods. Edwin S. Gaustad could not resist quipping: "While religion since its primitive days has had something to say about food, it has rarely said it so wholeheartedly as in Battle Creek." *Historical Atlas of Religion in America* (New York: Harper and Row, 1962), p. 115.

maintained by the schools enable the students to pay all or a substantial part of the tuition. The work program is regarded not only as a means of developing skills, but as a way of developing character—steady work habits, earning an honest dollar, thrift and tithing. The first Adventist school of this type in the American South was for Negroes, reflecting the origin of the Adventists among the New England abolitionists. It is now Oakwood College near Huntsville, Alabama.[35] Adventists are racially integrated in principle, but in fact they are largely segregated in all-white and all-black conferences, though just recently a movement for integrated conferences has been gaining momentum.[36]

Adventist secondary schools include 92 boarding academies, most of them coeducational. Because the denomination is numerically small and spread thinly over the United States, Adventist elementary schools are for the most part very small. The widely scattered constituency also accounts for the relatively high proportion of boarding academies among Adventist secondary schools. These schools clearly mirror the Adventists' dedication to propagating the true faith, the ideal of service to man, and noncombatant service in war—all proceeding out of a premillenarian vision of the world's end, but coupled with a seemingly contradictory vision of joy in this life. Adventist coeducational boarding schools such as the well-constructed and excellently maintained Auburn Academy at the foot of Mt. Rainier, or the comparable Blue Mountain Academy in the Poconos, both typically healthful locations of the kind the Adventists cherish, are unique in offering, in addition to the customary academic terminal and college preparatory fare, a well-thought-out campus self-help program. This program is required of all, but is pursued by many beyond the required minimum, for it enables needy students to earn up to three-fourths of their tuition under terms paralleling as closely as possible those in the commercial world. These are among the finest of the Adventist schools. There are, besides, many other tiny, poorly financed, struggling schools that are maintained by these remarkably energetic and devout people.

In contrast with the Adventists, the Christian Reformed denomination is an illustration of an offshoot of a relatively small old-church Protestant body that maintains a clear doctrinal identity by integrating religion and education through an extensive day school movement. This church body came into being in 1857 when a group of congregations of orthodox Calvinist persuasion in Holland, Michigan, left the more liberal Reformed Church in America, the lineal descendant of the original Dutch Reformed Church. The secessionists were led by a

[35] Booton Herndon, *The Seventh Day—the Story of the Seventh-day Adventists* (New York, Toronto, London: McGraw-Hill, 1963), pp. 214–16.

[36] See "New Integrated Section Started by Adventists," *Washington Post*, December 12, 1970.

group of conservative ministers who, believing themselves to be the true heirs of Calvinist theology, had migrated from the Netherlands several years before in protest over the state control of the Dutch church. The new group grew by a steady influx of Dutch immigrants until its membership rivaled and eventually exceeded that of the parent body.

While the educational effort of the parent Reformed Church in America now focuses chiefly on the support of three colleges in the Midwest and two schools in the South, the offspring Christian Reformed group maintains 145 elementary and 66 secondary schools in the United States as well as a group of colleges, including Calvin College at Grand Rapids, Michigan, a major teacher training center for several varieties of "Christian" schools.[37] The Christian Reformed schools, resembling the Missouri Synod Lutherans in their generally solid conservative outlook, emerged slowly and sporadically during the last quarter of the nineteenth century; by 1892 there were only about a dozen in existence. The "Society for Christian Education on the Reformed Faith," formed in that year for the purpose of promoting day school education, recommended to the church that the schools be owned, managed and supported by parent "Christian School Associations" established for that purpose. By 1920 the movement had gained sufficient momentum to justify the founding of a National Union of Christian Schools (NUCS) with membership open to any school that subscribes to a statement of the "Reformed Faith," whatever its denominational affiliation. Thus, Congregational and Presbyterian and other denominationally affiliated schools with a Calvinist orientation are eligible to join.

The NUCS is advisory only and does not control the member schools; its function is to assist local schools in such matters as curriculum development, textbook selection, recruitment and placement of teachers, teacher training workshops, conferences and PTA programs and in such business concerns as supplies, insurance and pensions. A daughter organization, the National Association of Christian Schools (NACS), discussed at greater length below, was organized in 1947 as an affiliate of the National Association of Evangelicals. It differs from the NUCS chiefly by the evangelical orientation of its member schools in contrast to the orthodox Calvinist persuasion of the NUCS groups. A few schools are members of both associations.

Considering the complete autonomy of each school in all decisions pertaining to curriculum, faculty, program, textbooks and so on, the Christian Reformed schools exhibit much more uniformity than might be expected. This is attributable partly to the effectiveness of the guidelines and conferences developed by

---

[37]*Statistics of Nonpublic Elementary and Secondary Schools, 1965–66, OE-20111* (Washington, D.C., 1968), p. 7. The 1968–69 *Directory* of the National Union of Christian Schools (Grand Rapids, Michigan) shows 218 schools in the United States and 68 in Canada.

the NUCS, partly to the substantial homogeneity of ethnic and religious background of the patrons and the school people. Virtually all Christian Reformed schools are co-ed day schools. Well over half of the 211 existing "free" schools were founded since 1945.[38] Decades ago when the Dutch language was still the medium of instruction in the early schools, these schools, along with the Lutheran and those of other bilingual ethnic religious groups, were frequently pilloried as "un-American." The fact that even today the Christian Reformed educational leaders, who are determinedly spearheading the battle for state aid to nonpublic schools in Michigan, where most of their schools are concentrated, are running into strong resistance, indicates that the issue of cultural pluralism versus total Americanization is still far from resolved.

The history of schooling among the Presbyterians, another old-line Calvinist denomination, presents a sharp contrast. The Presbyterians' commitment to parochial schools and academies was vigorous before the Civil War, but declined thereafter, a victim chiefly of the rapidly spreading public school ideology and of conflicts within the church. In the 1850s the Presbyterians were not only the third largest Protestant denomination, they could look back on a rich history in school and academy founding beginning in colonial days. Events as various as the rupture of Presbyterianism into "New School" and "Old School" groups, the rumpus in New York over Bishop Hughes' efforts to expel the Protestant bias from the public schools, and the battle with Horace Mann over the alleged godlessness of the public schools all contributed to the incentive to build Presbyterian schools as well as colleges and seminaries for the purpose of raising up an educated clergy and an enlightened laity. As an earnest of its intentions the Presbyterian Assembly of 1847 voted to found a system of parochial schools.[39] Many were established, but not many survived the Civil War. The solid contribution of the Presbyterians to the nineteenth century academy movement, in their home bases and through missionary work in the Ohio Valley and elsewhere, will be touched on later.

Developments in the last decades of the nineteenth century tended to diminish Presbyterian zeal for education. The dynamic thrust of revivalism affected Presbyterianism, as it did, to a greater or lesser extent, all the Protestant denominations. With a heavy emphasis on emotionally charged personal conversion experience, the appeal of the revivals was chiefly to the heart rather than to the intellect. It was essentially a search for personal salvation. Hence in broad effect

[38]"Free" only in the sense of being autonomous and voluntarily Christian; NUCS schools charge fairly substantial tuition fees. The leadership of these schools is virtually unanimous in the belief that they are entitled to state support. Their counterparts in the Netherlands enjoy full government support.

[39]Louis J. Sherrill, *Presbyterian Parochial Schools, 1846–1870* (New Haven: Yale University Press, 1932), pp. 20–30.

and in the first thrust the enthusiasm generated by the revivals was at the expense of the zeal for formal denominational schooling. Moreover, revivalism tended also to erode the formal theological base and ecclesiastical structure of the denominations through which it spread.[40] While the sturdy Calvinism of the Old School Presbyterians was less subject to dissolution than the more volatile theology of the Baptists and Methodists, the effect on the Presbyterian educational effort was nevertheless marked. Other influences worked in the same direction. The slavery issue brought about a sharp division within the church. Then, too, the gradual obsolescence of the academies in the last quarter of the century and the rise of public secondary schools further reduced the Presbyterian commitment to denominational schooling. Finally, the rapid emergency of Presbyterians as an upper-middle class group with access to good suburban public schools or prestigious independent schools also helps account for the decline of Presbyterian schools. Today they number only about 36 elementary and secondary schools, most of them in the South. Their number is slowly diminishing, as one school after another joins the ranks of the nonsectarians.[41] One of the well-known institutions following that course in recent time is the Westminster Schools of Atlanta, Georgia.

The Baptist and Methodist churches, both with huge memberships, but fragmented into many groups each of which maintains a separate sectarian identity, operate a relatively small number of schools. A few of these are survivors of the nineteenth century academy movement, others are carry-overs from a limited commitment to parochial schools in the past, and still others are of quite recent origin. The main energy of Methodism, in the century after its founding in this country in 1784, went into preaching rather than formal education, with the circuit riders appealing to the common man and winning converts in mountain cabins, sod houses and camp meetings along the expanding frontier. However, in the second half of the nineteenth century Methodists began founding parochial schools, academies and colleges in a modest way. But by that time the slavery issue had bisected Methodism into the Methodist Episcopal Church and the Methodist Episcopal Church, South, and in consequence many schools perished, especially those in the South.

Even after the war, founding and maintaining schools were assigned a relatively low priority by the Methodists. The reasons are various. Until recently the Methodist apostolate was chiefly among the poor and people of modest means who could ill afford to pay for separate schools. So the church relied largely on the public schools for secular education and on Sunday schools for religious

---

[40]For a development of this point, see Winthrop S. Hudson, *American Protestantism* (Chicago: University of Chicago Press, 1961), sec. 3.

[41]*Statistics of Nonpublic Elementary and Secondary Schools, 1965-66*, shows that the number of Presbyterian schools dropped from 43 to 36 between 1960-62 and 1965-66.

instruction. Moreover, the evangelical fervor of the Methodists caused them to devote a large share of the church's resources to home and foreign missions for the purpose of winning converts among unbelievers, so that day schools for those who already harbored the true faith seemed less important. The latest available listing shows only 34 elementary and secondary schools under Methodist auspices in the United States, with all but a few in the southern and southwestern states.[42] Among these are several schools conducted by the African Methodist Episcopal Zion Church, such as Lomax-Hannon College boarding school in Greenville, Alabama.

The Baptist commitment in education is somewhat larger, with the major concentration of schools also in the South. Prior to 1860, Baptists founded many academies and hundreds of elementary schools, but most of these expired during the Civil War. A new period of school growth began after Reconstruction and gained momentum at the turn of the century, spurred in part by fear of the "godlessness" of the rapidly spreading public schools and the conflict between science and religion chiefly over the theory of evolution. By 1920 over 50 academies were operating under Southern Baptist auspices, including well over 30 mountain academies supported in large part by the Home Mission Board.[43] But the culmination of the public school movement, coming somewhat later in the South than in other regions, eventually eliminated many of the Baptist schools. The latest available national statistics show 108 elementary and 37 secondary schools under Baptist auspices, a gain of 38 and 15 respectively over a four- and a five-year period.[44]

Many Baptist and some Methodist schools belong to the National Association of Christian Schools (NACS), which embraces schools of 29 distinct denominations with the largest complement consisting of ten varieties of Baptists and kindred pentecostal-holiness groups.[45] Included are schools of the Assembly of God, Free Methodist, Grace Brethren, Foursquare Gospel and Pillar of Fire and other sects which are largely a development of the past half century among the rural poor who felt spirtually disinherited by the prosperity of the established

[42] *Statistics of Nonpublic Elementary and Secondary Schools* shows a total of 46 Methodist schools, a gain of eight elementary schools over the figure for 1961–62, and a loss of four secondary schools since 1960–61. The difference is accounted for in part by the USOE's estimate of the number of existing schools that did not respond to the survey. The larger figures may also reflect some double counting which occurred because, as the USOE explains on p. 3, "institutions offering both elementary and secondary grades are included in both the elementary and secondary school counts."

[43] *Encyclopedia of Southern Baptists* (Nashville, Tenn.: Broadman Press, 1958), p. 389.

[44] *Statistics of Nonpublic Elementary and Secondary Schools, 1965–66*, p. 7. These figures, too, may be slightly inflated for the reasons given in n. 42 above.

[45] National Association of Christian Schools, *School Directory, 1968–69* (Wheaton, Ill., 1969).

churches. As these "third force" evangelical sects, some of which do not readily identify with Protestantism, began moving up the socioeconomic ladder, they built schools in many regions, with a somewhat larger concentration in the South than elsewhere. Typically owned and controlled by parent associations and with coeducational elementary schools predominating, one-half to two-thirds of the NACS schools, it is estimated, are racially integrated in a token way, some are determinedly interracial, while the rest make no bones about their intention to stay "lily-white."[46] An example of a leading NACS elementary school is the Wheaton Christian Grammar School, next-door neighbor in Illinois to Wheaton College, which, together with Calvin College in Michigan, is a chief supplier of teachers for Christian schools of various kinds in the Middle West and South. The Wheaton School welcomed Negroes from its founding in 1942. An illustration of another kind of ethnic interest among NACS schools is the South-west Indian School, Glendale, Arizona, sponsored by the World Gospel Mission.

The origin of Episcopal schools in America is unique in that, unlike the dissenting sects that settled most American colonies, Episcopalians took root on the shores of Chesapeake Bay without a break in polity with the parent Church of England, and so it was taken for granted that the parishes here, as in England, bore the responsibility for educating the young. The first steps in founding schools and colleges awaited direction and financial encouragement from England, since there was no American bishop to guide and facilitate these efforts. That fact probably accounts for the relatively slow, checkered growth of Episcopal schools in colonial times. A further difficulty was the imposition of the English parish system on a population thinly strung out in small settlements along the rivers and bays of Virginia and Maryland. The American Revolution eventually brought about secession of the Episcopal church from the Church of England and the creation of the Protestant Episcopal church in the United States, based on a constitution adopted in 1789.

Once the American church drew away from its English moorings and lived down its Tory sympathies, there began a period of steady growth during which churches, Sunday schools, parish and boarding schools, colleges, seminaries, and guilds for men and women as well as a host of welfare agencies and missionary activities were founded. By 1862, Episcopal parochial schools were operating in at least eleven states.[47] Since the Episcopal church was the only major Protestant denomination that suffered no disruption as a result of the Civil War, the

---

[46] Estimates by Dr. John Blanchard, executive director of the NACS, as quoted in *U.S. News and World Report*, November 10, 1969, p. 52.

[47] Francis X. Curran, *The Churches and the Schools: American Protestantism and Popular Elementary Education* (Chicago: Loyola University Press, 1954), pp. 26–30. For the early history of Episcopal schools, see Clifton H. Brewer, *History of Religious Education in the Episcopal Church to 1835* (New Haven: Yale University Press, 1924), pp. 103ff.

growth of most of its institutions continued with relatively little interruption through the nineteenth and into the twentieth century, except that the growth of Episcopal parochial schools waned in the second half of the nineteenth century as the issue between public and parochial schools was sharply drawn.

Most widely known among the Episcopal schools are the 120 college preparatory academies or high schools, including a number of boarding schools with national reputations.[48] Usually founded by a group of interested clergy and laymen or by a diocese rather than by a local church, most of these are single-sex schools. The early headmasters were usually ordained Episcopal clergymen; not uncommonly headship by a clergyman was a requirement. The founding of Groton illustrates how it was done. The now legendary Endicott Peabody conceived the idea of starting a boarding school for boys and found willing listeners among his Brahmin friends, including the Lawrences of Groton and Phillips Brooks, who became the first chairman of the board of trustees. Since that group embraced in its membership J. Pierpont Morgan also, the financial auguries were all that one could ask. The school opened in 1884 with the stated purpose of cultivating "manly, Christian character" in a family-like atmosphere. While the school aimed to prepare boys for college, Peabody rather deprecated that role and stressed "moral and physical as well as intellectual development," drawing to some extent on his knowledge of the English public school—he had attended Cheltenham for five years—which he believed succeeded better than the typical American prep school in developing maturity and leadership.[49] Before he retired after 56 years as rector of Groton, Peabody had the satisfaction of numbering among his graduates a long list of men in public office and of being the mentor and confidant of Franklin Delano Roosevelt, his most famous pupil.

Less well known but far more numerous are the parish elementary schools on which the Episcopalians have concentrated much attention recently. The 1969 listing shows 265 schools offering at least grade six or higher, and an additional 566 schools offering at the maximum grade five, but consisting more commonly of various combinations of nursery and kindergarten and the first two grades.[50] Episcopal parish day school enrollment is still growing vigorously, while that of the Sunday and released-time schools is declining.[51] The situation reflects a

[48] See The *Episcopal Church Annual, 1968* (New York: Morehouse-Barlow, 1968), p. 39.

[49] Frank D. Ashburn, *Peabody of Groton* (New York: Coward-McCann, 1944), pp. 65–77. The headmaster in Louis Auchincloss's *The Rector of Justin* (New York: Random House, Modern Library, 1965), believed by some to be a fictionalized portrait of Endicott Peabody, displays him in a somewhat different light.

[50] *Directory of Episcopal Church Schools, 1969–1970* (New York: National Association of Episcopal Schools, 1969).

[51] Parish school enrollment grew from 44,075 in 1960 to 72,267 in 1967. The figures for Sunday and released time schools during the same period were 874,550 and 857,931, with a crest of 916,656 in 1964. *The Episcopal Church Annual, 1968.*

growing demand among Episcopalians for a good academic education carried on under religious auspices, through the elementary years at least. Day care centers under Episcopalian auspices are also multiplying, which may portend a further growth of elementary schools since many Episcopal schools that now offer up to grade six began as nursery or kindergarten schools and added grades in response to local demand.

The National Association of Episcopal Schools (NAES), with a voluntary institutional membership of over 600, is a recent outgrowth of several earlier associations. It aims to assist the schools in matters of worship, curriculum, teacher training, in the development of standards and criteria, and in strengthening the relationship between the church and the schools. Most Episcopal schools resemble independent schools more than they do other Protestant schools (with the exception of the Quaker schools, which also feel a strong kinship with the independents), so it is not surprising that many Episcopal schools are members of both the NAES and the National Association of Independent Schools.

Among the numerically small old-church denominations with a long history in education, including elementary and secondary schools as well as colleges, the Quakers are outstanding. "For three centuries," John Hardon says, "the Society of Friends . . . has exerted an influence on American thought out of all proportion to its numbers—less than a quarter of a million."[52] Though the number of existing Quaker schools is small—32 elementary and 24 secondary schools—their influence extends far beyond the bounds of Quakerism and they are sought out by many non-Quakers in search of a good education.[53] Among these schools are some which are models of forward-looking, innovative education, such as the influential William Penn Charter School in Philadelphia, which conducts its affairs under a charter dated 1711 (it had been in operation for 22 years prior to that), and the Germantown Friends School, known for its progressive program and service projects. These and other Quaker schools preeminent in their academic reputations are natural affiliates of the NAIS.

The Quaker mystique with its blend of religious innerness, worldwide social service, pacifism and shrewd business entrepreneurship defies exact characterization. Of all the offspring of the Reformation the Quakers have held most consistently to the principle of individual interpretation and complete freedom from ecclesiastical authority. In the absence of such customary church characteristics as sacraments, ordained clergy and credal affirmations, the Quaker outlook is characterized by an unaffected directness and simplicity and by reliance on the Inner Light—the only trustworthy revelation of spiritual truth by which man is

---

[52] John A. Hardon, *The Protestant Churches of America* (Garden City: Doubleday & Co., 1969), p. 202.

[53] *Statistics of Nonpublic Elementary and Secondary Schools, 1965-66*, p. 7.

placed in a personal relationship with God. With so much latitude given to individual interpretation it is only natural that divisions resulted among American Quakers in the form of variously named "Meetings." These are reflected in the founding of schools designed to perpetuate the special outlook of one or another group.

Quaker schools were among the very earliest in this country. Using homes and meeting houses as classrooms, the first elementary schools were conducted under the general guidance of Quakers in England. Though the charter of William Penn's Pennsylvania provided that education should be at public expense, in practice those who could afford tuition were expected to pay, while the poor were admitted free. Historically, Quaker schools tended to have close ties with the public schools. In many cases schools founded by Quakers received some public support and were eventually taken over by the state. Such transitions worked more smoothly with the Quaker than with other religious schools because the Quaker school day was free of exercises in credal affirmations and formal religious instruction. True, the schools were set apart by the special kind of Quaker spirtuality that permeated the schools and by the plain garb or simple uniform that the Quaker mores commended, a practice that still survives in some schools. But these barriers proved to be far less formidable than insistence on loyalty to a precisely spelled-out creed or confessional, a common requirement among the schools of other denominations. It is not surprising, therefore, that the cosmopolitan studentry of many Quaker schools today is preponderately non-Quaker.

The Quaker reliance on the Inner Light and the consequent rejection of hierarchies, ceremonials or special oracles of truth had a strong equalizing effect among their adherents. In education this manifested itself in the concern for the education of girls as well as boys, and in substantial educational missionary efforts among Indians and Negroes. Some of the earliest nineteenth century coed boarding academies were under Quaker auspices. The concern for racial equality was also inherent in Quakerism from the beginning. "Let your light shine among the Indians, the Blacks and the Whites that ye may answer the truth in them," George Fox exhorted the American Quakers in 1690.[54] The Quaker effort on behalf of the education of Negroes, which was sporadic before the Civil War and drew frequent remonstrances at Yearly Meetings that not enough was being done, gained momentun after the war with the help of the Freedmen's Aid Societies, a largely Protestant interdenominational agency with which many Quakers identified.[55] Negroes were either admitted to Quaker schools or, in

[54] Quoted in Howard H. Brinton, *Quaker Education in Theory and Practice* (Wallingford, Pa.: Pendle Hill Pamphlets, 1949), p. 69.
[55] See W. W. Sweet, *The Story of Religion in America* (New York: Harper and Row, 1950), p. 328.

communities where blacks were numerous, attended separate schools stressing industrial training. These projects often called for great fortitude and demanded costly sacrifices. A notable example was the harrowing experience of Prudence Crandall, a brave Quaker woman in Canterbury, Connecticut, who was jailed and tried in court while a mob wrecked her school because she stubbornly refused to dismiss several Negro girls from her small Female Boarding School. Quaker interest in Negro education and integration is manifest again today in the struggle to integrate schools. The Friends School in Detroit, for example, established in 1965 with the help of local businessmen and educators, aims to provide scholarship aid to 40 per cent of its well-integrated student body.

The very tolerance and broad ecumenicism which are the special glory of the Friends schools are also the source of the problem they now face. As members of one of the oldest religious groups in America, successive generations of prosperous Quakers have been prominent in the nation's business, political and educational establishments. The genius of the Quaker school historically was its capacity to develop in the student the virtues of simplicity, conscientiousness, sincerity and tolerance, along with the love of learning. The aim of the inspired community is to link every individual with the Divinity in a directly personal renewing relationship. Quakers themselves express concern over whether their schools today fulfill this unique mission, or whether they tend rather to bolster the sense of status and material success in their largely middle and upper middle class school constituency. In the words of one Quaker historian and critic, "The Quaker school, traditionally at least, prepares not for the great secular community, but for a specialized religious community attempting to live by higher standards than the world around it. If there is no difference between the standards of the small religious community and the general community, or, if there is a difference and this difference does not appear in the school, then the main reason for Friends' schools has ceased to exist."[56]

The problem is certainly not confined to Quaker schools. Now that all the churches of the West are shaken to their foundations by the crisis of belief, and Catholics and Protestants are struggling to regroup in the rising tension between denominationalism and ecumenicism, church schools of every denomination are bound to ask: What is distinctive about *this* school? What does it do for the young that the public school, given its nature and mission, is unable to do? In later chapters we shall review the answers that the patrons and school people propound in reply.

Besides these major Protestant school groups—Lutheran, Seventh-Day Adventist, Christian Reformed, Presbyterian, Methodist, Baptist, Episcopal and

---

[56] Howard H. Brinton, *Quaker Education*, pp. 73–74. See also Douglas Heath, "The Educative Power of a Quaker Meeting," pt. 2, *Friends Journal*, July 1, 1968, especially pp. 324–26.

Quaker—a group of numerically small sects, less well known because they live in self-chosen separation and reject the ultimate sovereignty of the church as well as the state, contribute substantially to the diversity of Protestant schooling. The Mennonites, like their close spiritual kin, the Amish and the Hutterites, among the oldest Protestant groups in America, conduct not only a few high schools and many elementary schools scattered over the central and middle Atlantic states, the South and Oregon, but colleges also in Goshen, Indiana; Bethel, Kansas; and Bluffton, Ohio. Followers of the martyr John Huss, with an educational tradition stemming from the great John Amos Comenius, the Moravians are another numerically tiny sect with an extraordinarily interesting history. The furtherance of Moravian educational endeavors in North America was the work of the patron Count Nikolaus Ludwig von Zinzendorf of Saxony. His daughter, Countess Benigna, founded in 1742 what is now the Moravian Seminary for Girls, the oldest Protestant boarding school for girls in North America.[57] Because of their open enrollment policies, the influence of the small number of Moravian schools and colleges far exceeds that of the more separatist Mennonites and Amish.

Finally, the Church of Christ, Scientist, a relative newcomer on the religious scene, also has developed schools of its own, which is not surprising in view of the inherently educational tenor of Mary Baker Eddy's emphasis on the healing power of right thinking, which led not only to the founding of schools, but to the extensive program in adult education which the Mother Church carries on through the Christian Science reading rooms and pamphleteering, and by means of the educational objectives of the *Christian Science Monitor.* Best known of the Christian Science schools is the cluster of institutions known as The Principia in St. Louis, Missouri, which offers a Christian Science-oriented academic education from nursery school through college.

The Emergence of Jewish Schools

Jewish education in the United States rests on a venerable tradition going back to biblical times, more particularly to the Book of Deuteronomy. It is therefore remarkable that the major growth of Jewish all-day schools in the United States has occurred only as recently as the past three decades. Although

[57] According to Thomas Woody, this remarkable school opened originally with coeducational classes conducted in the Zinzendorf home at Germantown, and later became a boarding school for girls only, but open to young women of other denominations. *A History of Women's Education in the United States*, 2 vols. (New York: Science Press, 1929), 1: 216. See also James Pyle Wickersham, *A History of Education in Pennsylvania* (Lancaster, Pa.: Inquirer Publishing Co., 1886), pp. 122-77. The oldest boarding school for girls is believed to be the Ursuline Convent established in New Orleans in 1727.

Jews have resided in the United States since early colonial times, their numbers remained very small until the surges of immigration from western and southern Europe beginning in the mid-nineteenth century brought about exponential increases. Records of Hebrew all-day schools go back to 1730, when the Yeshivat Minhat Areb was established in New York City. Yet even after the flood of immigration began, the growth of Hebrew schools was sporadic and vacillating; by 1854 there were only seven Hebrew schools in existence. Not only were the new arrivals too poor to be able to afford private schools, many parents, eager to see their children assimilated quickly to the culture of their new homeland, were happy to send their children to the public schools. But to make sure that the children would not be alienated from their religious heritage, the synagogues supplemented the secular education with religious instruction in part-time Hebrew schools meeting in the afternoon or over weekends. This arrangement proved generally so satisfactory that the number of Hebrew all-day schools in the United States even as recently as 1940 numbered only about 30, all in the Orthodox camp. The Conservative and Reform groups felt no need as yet for Hebrew all-day schools.

But the dramatic world events of the fourth and fifth decades provoked a grave reassessment. The Nazi genocidal war, the resulting influx of Jewish emigré intellectuals to the United States, the founding of the State of Israel, and the rising socioeconomic status of Jews in America, all contributed to a changed outlook. One of the consequences was the swift growth of Hebrew all-day schools. About 90 per cent of the approximately 300 now existing were established after 1940, with about 30 launched under Conservative auspices.[58] Now even some rabbis of American Reform Judaism appear to favor the establishment of all-day schools, though lay leaders remain on the whole firmly opposed.[59] The momentum of growth of the all-day yeshivot is most readily understood as an effort to counteract the indifference to or hostility toward the ancient Jewish heritage by deepening the understanding of the essence of Judaism. Now that over 80 per cent of adult American Jews are native-born there is growing concern over the apostasy of Jewish youth who are tempted not only to reject their religion, but to sever their ties with the Jewish community altogether, since acculturation to America entailed the deculturation of identity-

[58] See Alvin I. Schiff, *The Jewish Day School in America* (New York: Jewish Education Committee Press, 1966), chap. 5. Also, Joseph Kaminetsky, "The Jewish Day Schools," *Phi Delta Kappan*, December 1963, pp. 141–44. An unpublished paper, "Education in the Jewish Tradition," by Rabbi Samuel Rosenblatt of Baltimore was helpful to us in preparing an account of Hebrew schools. Torah Umesorah (National Society for Hebrew Day Schools) publishes annually a *Directory of Day Schools in the United States and Canada* (New York).

[59] See the account of the biennial convention of the Union of American Hebrew Congregations, *New York Times*, October 30, 1969, p. 48.

conferring Jewish traditions. The day schools are a deliberate effort to strike a better balance by enabling American Jews, without sacrifice of their essential Americanism, to recapture the vision of their Jewish origin and destiny.

Since there is no central authority or official hierarchy in the Jewish national community, the day schools are distinct, autonomous, unitary institutions, each governed by a lay board of directors. The schools are for the most part communal in character, drawing students and financial support not from a single congregation, but from the community of variegated Jewish synagogues and agencies. Most schools come into being as the result of organized promotion and encouragement by one of several national organizations. The Torah Umesorah of New York City offers a variety of services to Orthodox day schools, without, however, controlling them. The Commission on Jewish Education of the United Synagogue has a comparable relationship with Conservative day schools. Several school groups are centrally administered, thus constituting small systems. The High Schools of Yeshiva University are a case in point, as are the United Lubavitcher Yeshivoth with a small network of day and other types of schools in the American Northeast and Canada. The unique Hasidic schools in Brooklyn, New York, which imperturbably maintain older cultural and family traditions amidst the welter of the commercial life and distractions of a congested urban environment, provide another illustration.[60]

The modern Hebrew day school is not so much an outgrowth of the Jewish schools of colonial times and the 1800s as it is a new creation in response to the circumstances of Jewish life in twentieth-century America. The curriculum of the earlier schools was usually limited to rote instruction in the Hebrew language, translation of sacred texts and cantillation of the Torah and the Prophets. They were, in other words, essentially parochial in nature. The curriculum of the modern Hebrew all-day school, by contrast, offers, in addition to Hebrew, a special program in Jewish religion, history and culture, as well as a complete general education in the secular subjects taught in public elementary and secondary schools. As a rule, the Hebrew studies take up three or four hours in the morning in a block of time, followed by the "English" studies in the afternoon. It makes for a long, strenuous day that not uncommonly begins at 8 a.m. and closes at 7 p.m. Visitors to the Maimonides School in Brookline, Massachusetts, or the Greater Miami Hebrew Academy in Florida can hardly fail to be impressed by the way these schools propagate the mystique of ancient Jewish

[60]For a delightful picture of life in an all-girl Hasidic school, see Ellen Frankfort, *The Classrooms of Miss Ellen Frankfort—Confessions of a Private School Teacher* (Englewood Cliffs, N.J.: Prentice-Hall, 1970), pp. 1–57. She points out that the Hasidic Jews are as self-sufficient and separatist in their way as the Amish, but in a commercial rather than a rural environment.

learning in the midst of the pragmatic, technological culture of contemporary America.

Compared to public schools, the yeshivot are relatively small, with a mean enrollment of 244 pupils, though the size of individual schools varies from a few pupils to well over a thousand.[61] Prior to 1940 only boys were admitted. Boys and girls are still educated in separate schools for the most part, except at the lower elementary range or in schools located in small communities where it is not feasible to have separate schools, and in the progressive Jewish day schools which aim to achieve a synthesis of progressive and Jewish education. Since 1940 the education of girls has received increasing attention. The number of Beth Jacob all-girl schools has grown and new coed yeshivot have been established. One of the chief reasons for separating boys and girls in the upper grades is the study of the Talmud, which begins usually in grades five to seven. Until quite recently this was regarded as an inappropriate activity for girls, and still is so regarded in most Orthodox schools.

Despite their rapid growth, or more aptly because of it, the Jewish day schools are beset with several critical problems. High on the list is the lack of fully qualified teacher and supervisory personnel, especially for the Hebrew department. Teachers with the requisite scholarly background in Hebrew, Jewish religion and culture, and with good pedagogical training are in short supply. Recently instituted teacher education programs at Yeshiva University and at various seminaries and institutes have contributed significantly, but have not been able to keep pace with the demand. Yeshivot teacher salary scales markedly below those of nearby public schools compound the difficulty.

Serious financial difficulties plague these schools. They suffer the defect of their virtue in that, as communal schools, they lack a single agency, other than the school itself, which is responsible for their financial solvency and welfare—a difficulty which the yeshivot share with many other denominational and all independent schools. The American Jewish community, divided against itself on many basic issues, is ambivalent in its assessment of the yeshivot. Some groups such as the American Council for Judaism and most leaders of the Reform movement oppose the day schools either vehemently or by glacial indifference. Nevertheless, financial assistance to Jewish education from the Federation of Jewish Philanthropies of New York, where until several decades ago most of the educational activities were concentrated, has increased steadily. The fact that Jewish Welfare Fund executives are looking more favorably on the day school is also a good omen. But the battle for recognition of Jewish education, the all-day

[61] In New York City the average enrollment is 346, compared with 142 in Jewish part-time schools. Schools in other communities in the United States enroll on the average 146 pupils. See Schiff, *Jewish Day School*, p. 93.

school in particular, by the major Jewish philanthropic agencies has thus far been disappointing. Now that the issue of state aid for nonpublic schools is joined in one state after another the internecine conflict of Jewish opinion about the day schools emerges as a public debate, with Jewish school educators virtually unanimous and aggressive in favoring such aid, and representatives of the American Jewish Congress and the American Jewish Committee strongly opposed.

A Note on Black Muslim Schools

It would not do to conclude this commentary on the history of religiously affiliated schools without taking note of the newest arrivals, the Black Muslim schools. They are unquestionably religious schools, but quite clearly *sui generis*, a creation of recent years that fits none of the traditional rubrics of American denominationalism. They differ from other Afro-American schools in that the Black Muslim schools are usually conducted in a religio-ethnic mosque-like setting replete with the trappings, vestments, dome and crescent of Mohammedism, the "Nation of Islam." The University of Islam No. 1, founded in Detroit in 1932, is the oldest; No. 2 was established in Chicago two years later. The University of Islam in Harlem, housed in Mosque No. 7, enrolls 650 pupils ranging in age from 3 to 18. Other units of the Muslim educational complex are located in Los Angeles, Washington, and Atlanta.[62]

The chief aim of these schools is to endow the child with a positive, dynamic self-image and a thoroughly disciplined outlook on life. To accomplish this, the schools take a strong antiwhite stance as the quickest and most effective way of reversing the downward cycle of failure and self-denigration among black youth. Discipline in the schools has an almost militaristic cast and the rules regarding dress, grooming and deportment are strict and exacting, with relatively little provision for recreation in the daily schedule. The curriculum sticks to the academic core courses—math, science, history, language, arts and reading—to which, however, instruction in Arabic and French is added. Boys and girls are taught separately, the boys in the morning and the girls in the afternoon, in order that each group can concentrate on learning. The school year is 50 weeks long. "We are 400 years behind," said Minister Louis Farrakhan, head of the Harlem Mosque, "100 years up from slavery. We have a lot of catching up to do. And though we are to enjoy life, we have no time for a lot of play and a lot of sport."[63]

[62]*New York Times*, August 25, 1970, p. 33.

[63]*Ibid.* The literature about Black Muslim schools is sparse indeed. The Illinois study cited earlier mentions (pp. 4–67 to 4–70) several unpublished papers on this topic pre-

The militantly separatist outlook of the Black Muslims raises a question in many minds regarding the limits of freedom to be different in a pluralistic society. "We are striving for total independence from white America," Minister Farrakhan is quoted as saying. In a lecture entitled "The Cultivation of Idiosyncrasy," Harold Benjamin asked: How much uniformity does democratic society need for safety? How much deviation does it require for progress?[64] He made the general point that education in a democracy needs to cultivate idiosyncrasy lest it stagnate from the trend to excessive uniformity. And yet there are limits beyond which idiosyncrasy can endanger social stability, though they are not easy to define. The salient difference between the separation or "deviation" of the Black Muslims and that of the Amish, the Mennonites, the Greek Orthodox or the Hassidic Jews, strongly reflected in their schools, is that Muslim separatism, however understandable it may be in the light of the injustices that blacks have suffered, tends to militancy, in rhetoric at least, while that of the other groups consists of the moral rejection of the state because of its amorality and worldliness, though they propose to live in it peacefully as best they can. But as current experience shows, even the militant avowal of a separate life style is generally tolerated, though uneasily, if it appears to be on a small scale or is seen as an interim phenomenon leading to eventual assimilation from strength. On the other hand, if, hypothetically, the Dukhobors or a contemporary version of the Luddites were to establish schools and teach children to resist the law forcefully or to smash machinery and burn factories, the state would doubtless intervene swiftly and forcefully. We shall dwell on this question of the limits of pluralism and the related issue of state control in chapter 12.

Nonpublic schools functioning within a pluralistic society aim to satisfy a wide variety of needs. But where many choices are open, making a firm choice and living with it entails advantages as well as handicaps. Schools under the control of strongly orthodox or fundamentalist denominations have one conspicuous advantage in that they have a fixed point of reference for their goals, their curriculum, for student conduct, and for the role of the teacher. The schools of the more worldly, latitudinarian denominations, on the other hand, often suffer the defect of their virtue in the form of an enervating skepticism and relativism regarding the proper ends as well as the means of education, particularly with reference to the role of religion in education. The greatest handicap, on the other side, of the orthodox and fundamentalist schools is the

---

sented at the University of Chicago. An article by Clermont E. Vontress, "Black Muslim Schools," published in the *Phi Delta Kappan* 47 (October 1965): 86–90, is still useful though the scene has changed substantially.

[64] *Cultivation of Idiosyncrasy*, Inglis Lecture Genes, 1949 (Cambridge, Mass.: Harvard University Press, 1949).

presence in them of all the old nineteenth-century tensions: science *versus* religion in the specific form of evolutionary theory *versus* a literalistic account of creation; historical criticism *versus* infallible scripture; untrammeled free inquiry *versus* pietistic acceptance of revelation; theological liberalism *versus* fundamentalism. The presence of these tensions and the chance to resolve them gradually may conceivably make these schools a better educational medium than if they were wholly free of them. In any case, the presence of such schools, though they are often viewed with contempt by the intelligentsia and professional avant-gardists, unquestionably adds to the diversity of education as a whole and increases the range of choice, even though the environment within such schools generally lacks the heterogeneity and openendedness of the ideal school. But this is also true of many public schools.

No one is so knowledgeable as to have a corner on ultimate truth, and no one is so wise as to be able to prescribe the education that is best for all. Under the circumstances, the maintenance of alternatives and a range of choice is the best social and educational policy.

3

Independent Schools and Their Antecedents

"The object of the school as stated in the catalogue is to furnish 'the elements of a solid education.' This object the school accomplished well in the main; but there is manifest a tendency to lower its standards, and to regard 'the elements of a solid education' as equivalent to the requirements for admission to college. ... [Exeter] undoubtedly exerts a considerable influence upon schools of its class, and it ought therefore not merely for itself, but as an inspiration elsewhere, to maintain a high level of attainment and efficiency."[1]

Independent Schools as Alternatives

The preceding chapter aimed to set forth the remarkable but little-known or appreciated heterogeneity of church-affiliated schools and how they developed in the United States. We turn now to the unaffiliated or non-sectarian schools and their antecedents. These are the schools people usually have in mind when they speak about "private schools," as distinct from "parochial schools," a term which in the current usage indiscriminately lumps together all the varied types of church-related schools. Private school people, however, prefer to have their institutions called "independent" schools. During the rapid spread of public schools after the Civil War, "public" took on an almost sacred meaning in the minds of

[1] Report on the Phillips Exeter Academy, June 9, 1892, by the Harvard School Examination Board. Quoted in James McLachlan, *American Boarding Schools: A Historical Study* (New York: Scribner, 1970), p. 235.

patriotic Americans while "private" acquired pejorative connotations such as "elitist," "undemocratic" and "un-American." Yet the private schools undeniably perform a public function and represent an important national educational resource. "Independent" is not only a less damning word, it is also a more accurate designation, because it conveys the autonomous, unaffiliated character of the schools in question.

The independent schools nationwide exhibit even greater heterogeneity than the religiously affiliated ones. There are obvious external differences among them such as boarding and day schools; schools in rural, in suburban or urban settings, or ranches, in the desert, in the mountains, by the sea or on northern ski slopes; schools for boys or for girls and coeducational schools. Subtler but significant differences concern the clientele the school is designed to serve. There are schools for students of high, middling and low aptitudes, and for a deliberate mixture of these; racially integrated and segregated schools; schools for the handicapped, the psychologically disturbed; schools for the rich and privileged and for the poor and disadvantaged; schools for the well-motivated and for problem children. The schools differ also as to their educational philosophy and goals. There are college preparatory schools, military schools, tutoring schools, laboratory and demonstration schools, conventional schools and progressive experimental schools, schools specializing in foreign languages, in world-mindedness, in community involvement, in music or fine arts, in choir singing, in athletics, in character building, in work-study programs, in no-nonsense discipline or in an informal, permissive, first-name atmosphere. They are governed in a variety of ways—some by the benevolent dictatorship of the headmaster backed up by the trustees, others by a more democratic rule of the head working in tandem with trustees and faculty, students, and parents working it out together in community "town-meetings." Many of these variations appear also among the church-affiliated schools.

The distinction between the independent and the denominational schools is blurred by the fact that certain denominational schools think of themselves primarily as independent and secondarily as denominational. This is true generally of the Episcopal, Presbyterian, Quaker and the few Catholic schools which belong to the NAIS. It is not so much that they value the religious aspect of education less, though their interdenominational and secularized student bodies pose a problem in this respect; it is rather that their patrons and the public at large think of them primarily as academically superior schools.

Apart from these exceptions, the great bulk of sectarian schools taken together exhibits less diversity than does the independent school domain. The denominational bond and the church organization with its educational service agency exert a standardizing influence which leads naturally to a certain sameness in the schools of a given denomination. Moreover, the church-affiliated schools for the most part are inclined to accept rather unquestioningly the curricula and teaching methods of the public schools in secular subjects, for that way they feel assured that the students are receiving the equivalent of a public school education. By contrast, most independent schools are not all that respectful of the public schools, because they believe the private school can do a superior job academically. Moreover, being autonomous institutions, these schools are free, in theory at least, to be as imaginative and experimental or as traditional or as eccentric as they please. In reality they are conditioned by what is salable in the educational market. But since families differ in their concept of what kind of education is best for their children, the market invites the display of many different independent school models.

This is particularly true just now as we enter the last decades of the twentieth century. Discontent with the conventional school is rife. Inner city public schools in many urban centers are near collapse, not only because of financial stringency, but because of their inability to cope with the problems of poor and disadvantaged children within the framework of the standardized, middle-class–oriented bureaucratic school system. Even in the suburbs with their superior financial resources, many a public school comes off poorly in the competition with the imperatives of the youth culture and the influence of the mass media.[2] What are the alternatives? The traditional ones are the independent and the church-related schools. Except for the few with large scholarship resources, the independent schools provide an alternative to the public schools chiefly for the affluent, while the church schools serve primarily their limited religious constituencies. Recently, however, the emergence of "free" or "community" independent schools has enlarged the range of choice. They are "free" in the sense of being uninhibited by cumbersome bureaucracies or archaic traditions, and free therefore to define themselves in the light of the needs of today's children. Included among these are all sorts of predominantly white experimental schools, black community schools, and a few publicly funded experimental schools operating under what amounts to private, nonbureaucratic control.

The aim of this chapter is to examine the independent school in the perspective of history. For convenience of treatment we divide the approximately 3,200 independent schools in the United States into four groups: the traditional boarding schools, the traditional day schools, progressive and experimental schools, and a special group of new schools devoted chiefly to the education of Afro-Americans. Admittedly, these groups overlap to some extent. Many traditional

---

[2] James S. Coleman documents this general conclusion in his study, *The Adolescent Society* (New York and London: Free Press, 1961).

schools, for example, are in the throes of self-renewal and experimentation. But the suggested types are sufficiently distinct in form and goals to be advanced as representative groupings of private schools.

From the Academy to the Boys' Prep School

The attitude of the American public toward the independent boarding schools is strongly tinctured by the accounts of recent social historians and sociologists—Dixon Wecter, E. Digby Baltzell and C. Wright Mills among them— who portray the elite boarding school as "the most important agency for transmitting the traditions of the upper social classes and regulating the admission of new wealth and talent."[3] Baltzell identified sixteen schools that "set the pace and bore the brunt of the criticism received by private schools."[4] It is an interesting and, in Baltzell's hands, a persuasive thesis. Like most stereotypes it contains a substantial measure of truth. But James McLachlan argues, in *American Boarding Schools*,[5] that it is an oversimplification which obscures both the origin and the goal of these schools. Moreover, as Baltzell himself points out, since 1950 many of these schools have changed "rather radically," so that the stereotype of "old-stock exclusiveness" is less applicable now.[6]

The conventional sociological picture of the private preparatory school portrays it as a creation of the late nineteenth century, based on the model of the English public school and designed to serve an aristocratic or upper class constit-

---

[3]C. Wright Mills, *The Power Elite* (New York: Oxford University Press, Galaxy Books, 1959), pp. 64–65. The other books in question are Dixon Wecter, *The Saga of American Society: A Record of Social Aspiration, 1607-1937* (New York: C. Scribner's Sons, 1937); E. Digby Baltzell, *Philadelphia Gentlemen: The Making of a National Upper Class* (Glencoe, Ill.: Free Press, 1958), and *The Protestant Establishment: Aristocracy and Caste in America* (New York: Random House, 1964). A similar theme is developed in G. William Dornhoff, *Who Rules America?* (Englewood Cliffs, N.J.: Prentice-Hall, 1967).

[4]*Philadelphia Gentlemen*, pp. 293, 305. The sixteen on the select list are all boys' boarding schools, and the dates of their founding given by Baltzell are: Andover (1778), Exeter (1783), Episcopal High School (1839) and Woodberry Forest School (1889) in Virginia, Hill School (1851), St. Paul's (1856), St. Mark's (1865), Lawrenceville (1883), Groton (1884), Taft (1890), Hotchkiss (1892), Choate (1896), St. George's (1896), Middlesex (1901), Deerfield (1903), and Kent School (1906). Baltzell's dates of founding do not agree with those given by the schools in the following instances: Exeter (1781); Lawrenceville (1810); Hotchkiss (1891); Deerfield (1797). The large discrepancies in the cases of Lawrenceville and Deerfield are explained by the fact that both schools had a long history as local academies prior to their emergence as boarding schools. Boarding schools for girls receive precious little attention in all this sociological literature about the role of private schools in "aristocratic assimilation." Male chauvinism, perhaps?

[5]Our account of the independent boarding schools is greatly indebted to McLachlan's perceptive and lively study.

[6]*The Protestant Establishment*, pp. 342–44.

uency. In fact, however, while most of the sixteen schools on Baltzell's list were indeed founded after the Civil War, according to McLachlan's thesis the concept of the boarding school took concrete institutional shape much earlier, as an American adaptation of a continental European model which in its later stages imitated the English public school, but only in superficial respects. Its mission was not so much to raise up an "aristocratic" ruling elite as to educate bourgeois gentlemen.[7] These points become clear only as one delves into the history of the boarding school movement in the United States.

The development of the boarding school is intertwined with the rise and decline of the academy movement of the first half of the nineteenth century. The academies arose early in the federal period in response to the growing need for a more extended formal education for more members of society. The educational developments in colonial times had moved in that direction too, but from very small, informal beginnings. It is worth scouting those developments briefly in order to comprehend what purpose the academies and subsequently the boarding schools were intended to serve.

Formal schooling in the early colonial period was expected to serve only the limited aim of introducing children to the rudiments of learning. Education in its widest sense was not so much a process of deliberate formal instruction as a socially encompassing influence of the family, the community, and the church. It was education by osmosis under various apprenticeship arrangements.[8] Formal instruction was limited to the dame schools (so named because they were conducted typically by an indigent widow or spinster in her own home), evening schools, writing schools, the "old field schools" in the South, and the early parochial schools.[9] Children in isolated homes had to depend on their elders to teach them reading and ciphering and how to scrawl their names. It should be recalled that childhood in colonial times was a brief, foreshortened period ending with early apprenticeships or not infrequently with marriage at age 15 or 16, at which time young men were also subject to militia duty. Paintings of children in early colonial times usually show them dressed as little adults. The span from

---

[7] See McLachlan, *American Boarding Schools*, pp. 5–16.

[8] See Robert Francis Seybolt, *Apprenticeship and Apprenticeship Education in Colonial New England and New York* (New York: Columbia University, Teachers College Press, 1917), especially p. 37.

[9] See Walter H. Small, *Early New England Schools* (Boston and London: Ginn and Co., 1914). Also Louis B. Wright, *The Cultural Life of the American Colonies, 1607–1763* (New York: Harper, 1962), especially chap. 5. For the history of early southern schools, see Philip Alexander Bruce, *Institutional History of Virginia in the Seventeenth Century: An Inquiry into the Religious, Moral, Educational, Legal, Military, and Political Conditions of the People, Based on Original and Contemporary Records*, 2 vols. (New York: G. P. Putnam's Sons, 1910), pp. 293–359. Unfortunately, Lawrence Cremin's definitive interpretation of colonial education came to hand too late to be of use to us: see *American Education: The Colonial Experience, 1607-1783* (New York: Harper & Row, 1970).

birth to the assumption of adult responsibilities was brief and the commitment to formal education was equally so.

But even before the middle of the seventeenth century the hazards of frontier life in small settlements and the fear that the young would become barbarized imposed added responsibilities on formal schooling so that education became gradually more and more "an instrument of deliberate social purpose."[10] The crown of this movement in colonial times was the town Latin grammar school, in form and content classical as well as Christian and supported and controlled variously by public or private agencies. But it was not a popular institution, for it was not so much intended to provide a general education as to prepare the few for admission to Harvard College, or for public service, or for the life of a well-bred gentleman. Moreover, the grammar schools grew slowly and erratically and by the time of the Revolution they were languishing for lack of financial support.

All in all, although the colonial period created many kinds of schools—public, private, and mixed—at the beginning of the Federalist period the educational situation must be described as chaotic. Public common schools were available to most children living in the larger communities, as were free charity schools and a variety of private schools. But little more than an introduction to learning was accessible to most children, and those in sparsely settled country lacked even that. While an elementary education was thus generally available, the big void was the paucity of secondary schools other than the dwindling Latin grammar schools and a few scattered sectarian and private secondary schools. In the late eighteenth century a boy could prepare for college in one of several ways: by private tutoring in the classics and math, usually in the home of a clergyman; by attending either a private or a town Latin grammar school; or by enrolling in a "preparatory department" such as those conducted by Princeton, Columbia and Pennsylvania. Wealthy southern planters not uncommonly sent their sons at the tender age of six or seven to England for schooling. But the training provided through these various arrangements was woefully uneven. This was not as great a handicap as it may appear because the colleges of the developing nation were themselves little more than glorified high schools in comparison with their European counterparts.

It was this vacuum in secondary schooling that the academies were created to fill. The age of the academies, extending roughly from the Revolution to the Civil War, marked a large step in extending the opportunity for more formal, institutionalized education to more young people. As education became "a deliberate instrument of social purpose," it also prolonged the dependency of

---

[10]Bernard Bailyn, *Education in the Forming of American Society* (Chapel Hill: University of North Carolina Press, 1960), p. 22.

young people and increased the number and variety of responsibilities that the family, the community, and the church delegated to the school. This process accelerated during the nineteenth century and has now reached crisis proportions in the advanced technological societies of our time. The greatly prolonged educational dependency of young people, although it frees them more completely from their natal culture and bondage to authority than any earlier generation, has the unhappy psychological effect of extended deferment of admission to fully responsible adulthood. It is widely regarded as one of the chief reasons for the spread of student unrest.

The genesis of the academies lay in the confluence of ideas from many quarters. The word "academy," freighted with classical associations through Plato's Academy, traces its modern history to Milton's essay, *Of Education*, which Benjamin Franklin knew and quoted freely. The name was current among the English and Scottish dissenters who were excluded from the grammar schools as well as the universities of England after the Restoration. The dynamics of dissent provided a strong impetus for the reform and modernization of education manifesting itself in a growing interest in science and a broadening of the curriculum of the grammar school.[11] In America, where dissent was more or less endemic, these new ideas could be tried with impunity. But indigenous religious currents exerted a marked influence also on the development of the academies. The religious revival known as the Great Awakening sparked an intense missionary zeal which led, among other things, to the spread of educational philanthropy. Samuel Phillips, Jr., who founded Phillips Academy, Andover, in 1778, and his uncle, John Phillips, who founded The Phillips Exeter Academy in 1781, had been deeply influenced by the Awakening. Religion, either in the form of nonsectarian Protestantism, or through the surge of competitive denominationalism, was the primary vehicle for the spread of knowledge, secular as well as sacred, until the middle of the nineteenth century.

While the genesis of the academy occurred in Puritan New England, the philosophy of the American academy as a national movement was expressed most coherently by Benjamin Franklin in his *Proposals Relating to the Education of Youth in Pensilvania* and *Idea of the English School*.[12] Franklin saw more clearly than most of his contemporaries that a new democratic, open

---

[11] "The general story of the flow of ideas between the English academies and the American schools and colleges—part of an intimate world of Anglo-American dissent—remains to be told," notes Bailyn (*ibid.*, p. 65). One of the best available sources is Caroline Robbins, *The Eighteenth-Century Commonwealthman: Studies in the Transmission, Development, and Circumstances of English Liberal Thought from the Restoration of Charles II until the War with the Thirteen Colonies* (Cambridge, Mass.: Harvard University Press, 1959).

[12] "English" as used here in contrast to "Latin" or "classical." Franklin was not referring to the schools of England.

society was in the making as well as a new concept of the ends and means of education. He was among the first to recognize that the study of classical languages and literature was fast degenerating into a shibboleth of the educated class and that the Latin grammar school, whose chief beneficiaries were the ministry, the gentleman, and the scholar, was already an anachronism. Young people growing up in the invigorating, expanding world of the eighteenth century confronted a host of unprecedented opportunities for new and as yet undefined careers for which traditional schooling was irrelevant. Franklin's own versatile career was the perfect embodiment of a do-it-yourself education accomplished by making full use of the many opportunities for self-instruction that lay all about. He had tapped fully the educational resources of life outside the schools—the libraries, newspapers, almanacs, lectures, sermons, "how-to" books, accounts of travelers and explorers, the talk in coffee houses, inns and taverns, and self-improvement clubs such as his own famous Junto. What was needed now, Franklin concluded, was a broad general education in subjects "useful" as well as "ornamental" which would help prepare young people to seize the new opportunities. The plan he proposed would make available through formal systematic instruction the kind of education he himself had acquired informally and haphazardly.

The rapid spread of the academies across the land suggests that they were well suited to the character and condition of the people who founded and utilized them. Academies appeared successively everywhere in the Republic, first in the Northeast where they originated and where they long retained a classical cast, then in the South where they grew rapidly, chiefly under Presbyterian auspices; they were multiplying in the Middle Atlantic states by the turn of the century, and reached the Middle West, often with the aid of denominational Home Mission Societies, in a climate charged with Jacksonian politics and the *Sturm und Drang* of Second Awakening revivalism.[13] They reached the Far West last of all, largely with the help of New Englanders who followed the course of empire westward. The academies expanded much more rapidly than the colleges. Henry Barnard counted 6,185 incorporated and unincorporated academies in 1850 compared to only 239 colleges.[14]

The academies developed in great freedom, so that no two were exactly alike. Robert Middlekauff sums up their common characteristics as "a government

[13] See Edgar W. Knight, *Public Education in the South* (Boston: Ginn and Co., 1922), pp. 73–89; James P. Wickersham, *A History of Education in Pennsylvania* (Lancaster, Pa.: Inquirer Publishing Co., 1886), pp. 56–65; Albert Mock, "The Midwestern Academy Movement: A Comprehensive Study of Indiana Academies, 1810–1900" (unpublished manuscript; Cambridge, Mass.: Harvard Graduate School of Education Library, 1949). See also J. O. Grimes, "Early Academies in Michigan," *Michigan History Magazine* 30 (1946): 86–101. For a listing of academies in Iowa, see Clarence Ray Aurner, *History of Education in Iowa* (Iowa City: State Historical Society, 1915).

[14] *American Journal of Education* 1 (1855): 368.

vested in laymen established by a charter issued by the state, a financial status dependent upon both public and private contributions, and a curriculum more or less classical."[15] Outside of the Northeast many were unincorporated, but they were all either private or church-related schools serving a clearly public function, often in close partnership with states or counties which contributed to their support. They did not develop, as the public high school did later, by building up from the elementary or common school curriculum. At the lower level some academies overlapped the common school, though that was not typical. Within the academy, the ages of students varied greatly. In the first class at Andover young Josiah Quincy (later mayor of Boston and president of Harvard), aged six, sat next to 30-year-old James Anderson of Londonderry, New Hampshire.[16] There was little attempt at age-grading. At the upper level most academies accepted college preparation as one of their goals, but some overlapped and rivaled the colleges—indeed, some became colleges eventually. The typical academy was as much concerned with terminal education as with preparation for college. To this end some offered, in addition to the classical curriculum, natural philosophy (general science), history, geography and certain practical arts such as navigation, surveying, agriculture and pedagogy.[17]

Since the academies attracted students not only from the local town but from distant points, educational historians usually characterize them as "boarding schools."[18] If that term is taken to mean an institution at which students are lodged in dormitories under the care and supervision of the master and faculty, then most academies in the northeastern states were day rather than boarding schools. The students generally lived with respectable families in the town, not in campus residential facilities. Phillips Academy, Andover, built its first dormitory fifty years after its founding. The family of Samuel Phillips, Jr., the founder, was among those that took in boarders. The schools tried as best they could to exert a disciplinary influence over students to curb the excesses of youthful ebullience, but it was the family that stood *in loco parentis* rather than the school. The family and town thus became for the academy student an introduction to living in a normal community, rather than the age-segregated grouping that was to prevail later in residential schools and colleges.

Claude M. Fuess' *An Old New England School: A History of Phillips Academy, Andover* portrays the founding ideals and early years of the school that

[15] *Ancients and Axioms: Secondary Education in Eighteenth-Century New England* (New Haven: Yale University Press, 1963), p. 152.

[16] Claude M. Fuess, *An Old New England School: A History of Phillips Academy, Andover* (Boston and New York: Houghton Mifflin Co., 1917), p. 78.

[17] For a further interpretation of the place and function of the academies see Theodore R. Sizer's introduction to *The Age of the Academies* (New York: Columbia University, Teachers College Press, 1964), pp. 1–48.

[18] Sizer, for example, states "most academies were boarding establishments." *Ibid.*, p. 36.

more than any other, along with Exeter, provided the impetus for the academy movement.[19] Samuel Phillips, Jr. was born to a family whose earlier forebears included many Puritan divines. Though his own and his father's generation prospered in business and accumulated large fortunes, the Puritan heritage of bookishness, duty and moral earnestness remained. He received a classical education at the Dummer School (the precursor of Governor Dummer Academy) under the scholarly Samuel Moody, and graduated from Harvard at age 19. A staunch defender of colonial rights and a supporter of the Revolution, he became increasingly concerned nevertheless over "the decay of virtue, public and private . . . owing to the neglect of good instruction." The solution he believed was to found a school which would be led by one of the best men who could be found, "who shall proportion his attention to the various branches of education according to their importance, who shall make it his chief concern to see to the regulation of *morals* of the pupils, and attentively and vigorously to guard them against the first dawnings of depraved nature." The Andover constitution states that "the *first* and *principal* object of this Institution is the promotion of true Piety and Virtue."[20]

His plans were soon implemented once his friend Eliphalet Pearson agreed to serve as "Preceptor," and the school opened in 1778 while the war was in progress. The two men differed on several basic questions. Phillips wanted the school to stress English rather than Latin, which he considered a dead language through which youths were introduced to "heathen writers." Pearson, however, dissuaded him on this point, and so the school's curriculum did not differ significantly from that of the college preparatory Latin grammar school. Exeter's curriculum by contrast had a broader base including besides the classics and mathematics offerings in English studies, music, art and science; it was more widely imitated in the academy world than the narrower Andover curriculum. Samuel Phillips would also have preferred to have no "charity" students, such as he had observed at Dummer, because he considered them a potential source of moral corruption. But on this count too he yielded. Scholarship students with varied backgrounds became a distinctive Andover (and Exeter) tradition which survives to this day.

The corporate form of organization adopted by Andover and Exeter set a pattern, based on that of the colonial colleges, which is still followed by independent boarding and day schools. The schools were incorporated by the state legislatures, in order to assure permanence and stability, and with control vested in a self-perpetuating board of trustees. This device whereby individuals incorpo-

---

[19] Fuess was himself a popular and widely known headmaster of Andover from 1933 to 1948.

[20] Fuess, *An Old New England School*, pp. 55–56, 66. Emphasis in the original.

rate to carry on a socially useful objective proved to be a very efficacious way for the state to encourage the spread of education, while still retaining a measure of control as well as a channel for the state aid which was essential to the survival of many academies.

The transition from the New England academy to the traditional boarding school, as we know it today, and the eventual transformation of many academies into boarding schools involved, besides the obvious shift of student lodging from the community to the campus, a changed philosophy of education. The spearhead of this movement was Joseph Greer Cogswell, the cofounder of the Round Hill School, an influential model in the development of nineteenth-century boarding schools. The story of Cogswell and Round Hill is vital to the understanding of the form and character of many independent boarding and day schools right up to the present. A graduate of Exeter and Harvard, Cogswell was a Federalist intellectual and a social and cultural elitist who was convinced that the spirit and substance of American secondary and higher schooling were too pedestrian and utilitarian to arouse that love of learning which was essential to the development of a high culture in the United States.

Cogswell was joined in this train of thought by the young George Bancroft, whose educational preparation also led from Exeter to Harvard. Both traveled extensively in Europe during the late 1810s and between them visited schools in Germany, Switzerland and England in order to familiarize themselves with the latest continental theories of schooling as well as the best traditional and innovative practices. It was a time of quickening educational theory, the fountainhead of which was Johann Heinrich Pestallozi, the John Dewey of nineteenth century European education. Cogswell visited the aging Pestallozi's school at Yverdun, Switzerland, to observe the new way of developing the child's natural faculties through immediate sense impressions and manual activity instead of the abstractions of the printed page. Cogswell was more impressed, however, by Emmanuel von Fellenberg, a former disciple of Pestalozzi's, whose schools at Hofwyl, near Berne, were a Mecca for interested educators from Europe and America. At Hofwyl he found a new kind of *Landschule*, in this case a cluster of schools based on Fellenberg's concept of the differing educational needs of distinct social classes. Although Cogswell came to observe the famous farm and trade school for the education of poor children, he came away fascinated with Fellenberg's plan for the education of rich children. The goal was defined as the harmonious development of the physical, intellectual and moral faculties by means of a rigorous, detailed schedule covering a liberal curriculum of studies both classical and modern, as well as exercise and play. In the formation of character Hofwyl abjured praise and blame or the incentives of emulation and fear in favor of a close, benevolent parent-like relationship between pupils and tutors. Besides, the rural setting was counted on to exert a benign moral influence. "The great art of educating," Fellenberg emphasized, "consists in knowing how to occupy every moment of life in well-directed and useful activity of the youthful powers, in order that . . . nothing evil may find room to develop itself."[21] That idea became in time the basic strategy of private boarding school education in the United States.

While Cogswell was concentrating his attention on Fellenberg's theory and practice, Bancroft took time from his university studies at Göttingen and Berlin to visit schools in Germany, among them those in Berlin and the famous old Schulpforta boarding school near Naumberg. Through these avenues and in the course of his associations with the Berlin philosopher and theologian, Friedrich Schleiermacher, Bancroft's thoughts about the form and substance of education which was needed in the United States converged with Cogwell's.

After trying unsuccessfully to inoculate Harvard College with their new thought, Cogswell and Bancroft collaborated in founding and staffing the Round Hill School at Northampton, Massachusetts, an institution that was destined to have a brief but exceedingly influential career. In this boarding school Cogswell and Bancroft incorporated many of the theories and practices they had absorbed in Europe. In advertising the school, they stressed the moral benefits of life in bucolic surroundings, with students living under the same roof with their tutors. Though the formal curriculum did not vary greatly from the combination of classical and English studies prevailing in the academies, the teaching methods differed substantially. Instead of competitive recitations in formal classes each student was encouraged to proceed individually at his own pace without the customary inducements in the form of rewards or punishment. Regular physical exercise as well as Episcopal religious devotions were a part of each day's rigorous schedule—"we manage our boys by keeping them employed," said Bancroft.[22] Instead of strict discipline, the school relied on mutual and familial concern. The students who were attracted to Round Hill were uniformly upper class boys from cultivated families residing mostly in large cities, families who were evidently eager to have their children educated in a wholesome environment untainted by the evil influences and pollutions of city life. Mistrust of the city and, conversely, belief in the benign moral and aesthetic influence of bringing up children in secluded innocence amid the beauties of unspoiled nature held a strong appeal for upper class city-dwelling parents. Much later in the century this idea was to assume prominence again in the philosophy of the country day schools. Round Hill marked the practical inception in the United States of an educational philosophy calling for a carefully contrived learning

[21] McLachlan, *American Boarding Schools*, p. 60, quoting from William C. Woodbridge, "Sketches of Hofwyl, and the Institutions of M. de Fellenberg," an appendix to *Letters from Hofwyl* (London, 1842).

[22] Quoted by McLachlan, *American Boarding Schools*, p. 87.

environment combined with the isolation of the young in a unique boarding school subculture under the watchful eye of concerned tutors.

But Round Hill as it was constituted in the 1830s was not long for this academic world. It closed its doors in 1834, chiefly because it was ahead of its time, though administrative and financial difficulties also contributed. Its older graduates, on matriculating in college, were found to be overprepared and often stepped directly into the junior or even the senior class. This early example of advanced placement was unappreciated by the colleges, which at that time had not yet risen much above the standards of the high school. When President Day of Yale College insisted on collecting from his Round Hill matriculants the tuition for the college years they had skipped, Cogswell decided the game was up and departed for greener pastures elsewhere.[23]

The influence of Round Hill as a model for romantic Episcopal boarding schools was enormous. Another Fellenbergian who admired Cogswell's work at Northampton, William Augustus Muhlenberg, founded the Flushing Institute on Long Island in 1828, which also had a relatively brief but exceedingly influential life. The graduates of these two schools had a large part in founding, staffing, supporting and, through successive generations, patronizing the growing list of boarding schools. Muhlenberg's former pupil, the Reverend John Barrett Kerfoot, founded St. James (originally the College and Grammar School of St. James) near Hagerstown, Maryland. George Shattuck, an alumnus of Round Hill, founded St. Paul's in Concord, New Hampshire, and chose as the first rector Henry Augustus Coit, who was a disciple of Muhlenberg's at Flushing and a former tutor at St. James. The first rector of St. Mark's at Southborough, Massachusetts, was an alumnus of Flushing, the second was a graduate of Round Hill. Milton Academy, Milton, Massachusetts, originally incorporated in 1798 as part of a state-wide academy system, carried on a precarious and interrupted existence until it was endowed in 1884 by the family of China trader John Murry Forbes, an alumnus of Round Hill who hoped that the new Milton would be modeled on his old school.[24] The upper-class family names on the Round Hill and Flushing student rosters continued to reappear through successive generations at the major boarding schools in the Northeast.[25]

The further development of the family-type boarding school after the Civil War is best understood in the light of what was happening in the developing colleges. Until late in the nineteenth century the level of work required by the colleges was only a little above that of the academies and it did not compare

---

[23]*Ibid.*, pp. 97–98.

[24]Richard Walden Hale, Jr., *Milton Academy, 1798–1948* (Milton, Mass.: The Academy, 1948), pp. 31–50.

[25]McLachlan, *American Boarding Schools,* pp. 90–91, 181, and *passim.*

with that of the European *Gymnasium*, which prepared young people for the universities. But the growing American thirst for a broader and deeper culture, which fifty years earlier sparked the founding of Round Hill and Flushing, coupled now with the new demands levied by the growth of industry and technology, spurred the colleges to offer a more demanding, thoroughgoing curriculum. As a natural consequence, the colleges evinced a growing concern for more thorough college preparation. Soon a revolution in secondary schooling was in the making. Harvard established the "Schools Examination Board," which offered to have its faculty examine, for a small fee, the instructional program of any school, public or private, of the kind that prepared boys for the college or the Lawrence Scientific School.[26] President Timothy Dwight did some arm-twisting among philanthropists to see that the Hotchkiss School, in Lakeville, Connecticut, was established as a feeder of well-prepared freshmen for Yale College.

Further south, President McCosh of Princeton succeeded in finding a legacy among Princeton benefactors to assist that college in its search for better prepared matriculants. An old academy at Lawrenceville was acquired by purchase, and James Cameron Mackenzie was engaged to draw up plans for a new school, which he did only after visiting Exeter, Andover, St. Paul's and others. He was unimpressed with the quality of the academic work which he found, and drew on his own imagination and his reading about schools in England to establish the Lawrenceville School in 1882 as pre-eminently a nonsectarian college preparatory boarding school. It opened with an excellent faculty and three four-year curricula in classics, in science and in English. The English curriculum, which in the prevailing tradition was considered terminal rather than college preparatory, was soon dropped. A unique feature of Lawrenceville from the beginning was the "house" or home boarding plan whereby new students lodged in groups of not more than twenty-five in houses near the campus under the care of a teacher and his wife, while the more mature students and those of limited means lived in a dormitory.

Lawrenceville's example, and that of other boarding schools founded as or transformed into college preparatory schools, had a pronounced effect. Numerous other traditional prep schools were founded during the eighties and nineties and in the early decades of the twentieth century. After the rich began the migration to the suburbs and exurbs, the unavailability of good public secondary schools in these sparsely settled areas created new opportunities for independent boarding and day schools. The Cranbrook School in Bloomfield Hills, Michigan, founded in 1926 as one of a cluster of institutions devoted to the arts, sciences and education, is an example of a modernized middle-western version of the

[26]*Ibid.*, p. 235.

traditional Episcopal boarding school, set amid the ample estates of millionaire motor-car magnates. The Thacher School in Ojai, California, founded in 1899, is another example of the adaptation of the austere New England model, in this case to the far western environment, resulting in an emphasis on a rugged, horsey outdoor life combined with superior academic opportunities.

A special variant of the academic boarding school is the military school. Its growth was greatly stimulated by the founding of the United States Military Academy at West Point in 1802, and by the establishment of the Naval Academy in 1850. This group, which includes schools steeped in more than a century-old military tradition, expanded steadily both before and after the Civil War and, up to very recent times, in the South especially. The traditional educational philosophy of these institutions with their uniformed cadet corps is the classical concept of total education by means of strict, systematic mental and physical discipline in orderliness, teamwork and leadership training, until these virtues become ingrained and habitual in the form of self-discipline and self-control. A surprising number of military schools are church-related and exist to promote "Sound Learning and the Christian Education of American Youth," as the founder of the Episcopalian Howe Military School in Indiana put it.[27] Culver Military Academy, also in Indiana, one of the best known of its kind, is nonsectarian but requires chapel and church attendance. Enthusiasm for military training is diminishing steadily among today's draft-conscious students who associate the military chiefly with the Vietnam War.[28] The result is apparent in a steady decline in military school applicants in recent years.[29] Most schools with a military tradition tend now to subordinate military training to a general academic and college preparatory education, and a few are considering becoming coeducational or coordinate. Among military schools, as among boys' boarding schools in general, the imperatives of college preparation caused the schools to abandon diverse approaches in favor of preparing a uniform college-admissible product.

The image of the prep school as an institution catering to a wealthy urban clientele for whom the schools provide an elite but thorough academic education and admission to an Ivy League college was well set by the onset of World War I. But as the public high schools prepared ever larger numbers for admission to college, the elitist image of the independent boys' boarding school and the

[27]Porter Sargent, *A Handbook of Private Schools:* An Annual Descriptive Survey of Independent Education (Boston: P.S., 1969), p. 621.

[28]Andrew H. Malcolm, "Military Schools Adjusting to New Irreverence," *New York Times*, March 25, 1970, p. 41.

[29]Seventeen military schools, members of the NAIS, reported an enrollment decrease, on the average, of 10.6 per cent for 1970–71, compared to the previous year. Decreases of smaller magnitude have been reported each year since 1966–67. *NAIS Report*, no. 35 (Boston: National Association of Independent Schools, December 1970), p. 2.

special stature it had achieved began to function as a handicap. Furthermore, the youthful rebellion against authority and restraints places the boarding school, which is still expected to function *in loco parentis*, in an anomalous position, causing it to appear needlessly repressive and rigid compared with the lax discipline in many American homes. We shall explore these matters in subsequent chapters. But these and related questions regarding boys' boarding schools add up to a slackening interest in them, reflected in the fluctuating numbers and intellectual quality of applicants.[30] Whether this is a long-run trend or a temporary phenomenon brought on by the hyperbolic changes of our time it is too early to say. However, the changing fortunes of the boarding schools coupled with recent financial uncertainties have precipitated a thoroughgoing reassessment of the mission and prospects of these institutions.

From the Female Seminary to the Girls' Boarding School

What was happening to the education of girls while so much attention was being lavished on the boys is quite another story, one that offers a fair field for outrage not only by devotees of Women's Lib but for advocates of equal opportunity generally. The belated and hesitant rise of girls' boarding schools reflects the fact that until late in the nineteenth century the formal education of girls took either a back seat or no seat at all compared to the education of boys. "It is not that the need and right of women to education was not recognized," Paul Monroe noted charitably, "but that its nature was considered as determined—whether as a need or as a right—by some consideration of dependency, as that of daughter, sister, wife, mother."[31] The revolutionary Jean Jacques Rousseau, who strongly influenced the education of boys in America both through his writings and indirectly through Pestalozzi, Froebel, and Fellenberg, had only reactionary thoughts to offer about women: "The whole education of women ought to be relative to men. To please them, to be useful to them, to make themselves loved and honored by them, to educate them when young, to care for them when grown, to counsel them, to make life sweet and agreeable for them. . . ."[32] Abigail Adams complained in 1778 about the prevailing fashion "to ridicule female learning." The education of women was regarded as "an attempt to unsex them," Catherine Beecher said in characterizing the strong opposition

[30]The 96 boys' boarding schools reporting to the NAIS averaged an enrollment decrease of 3.3 per cent for 1970–71 compared with the prior year. *Ibid.*

[31]*The Founding of the American Public School System* (New York: The Macmillan Co., 1940), p. 454.

[32]*Emile, or A Treatise on Education*, ed. W. H. Payne (New York and London, 1906), p. 263. Quoted in Kate Millet, *Sexual Politics* (Garden City, N.Y., 1970), p. 74.

she encountered.[33] The struggle to secure for girls an education equal to that available to boys was a slow, uphill battle. If the early champions of women's education are characterized less by the philosophical originality of their ideas of what education should be than by the dogged effort to overcome deeply entrenched prejudices, it is because they had first to be allowed to learn to walk before they could be expected to run.

The history of today's girls' boarding schools is entwined with the academy movement of post-Revolutionary times. Prior to the advent of academies, in the colonial period girls most often learned the rudiments at the dame schools, or if none was available they had to rely on instruction from their fathers, brothers or friends. The town schools and Latin grammar schools were usually closed to them.[34] But proprietary private schools for girls, offering dancing, fencing, singing, plain and ornate needlework and occasionally French were available by the end of the eighteenth century. Of all the colonials, the Quakers in Philadelphia were the most enlightened in their attitude towards the education of girls beyond the household arts. Moreover, the parochial schools of various denominations and other private elementary schools were generally more receptive to the education of girls than were the early town or public schools.

In New England, the academy movement for girls, with a curriculum comparable to those of the boys' academies, began with Timothy Dwight's Greenfield Hill Academy in Connecticut in 1785. Quite independently of this pioneer, the Moravians, as we noted earlier, had founded in 1742 a co-ed day school that became in time a girls' boarding school, now the Moravian Seminary for Girls at Bethlehem, Pennsylvania. Another early champion of women's education, the influential Dr. Benjamin Rush, helped establish an academy for girls in Philadelphia. A variety of institutions for girls or as coeducational academies sprouted in the larger communities before the close of the century and during the early decades of the nineteenth. One of the most renowned of these was the Ipswich Academy in Massachusetts, where Mary Lyon taught for a time before founding her own seminary at South Hadley. But alongside these enlightened ventures was a weedy growth of meagerly staffed and equipped schools taught by poorly educated women for profit. Academies for girls often bore the name "female seminary," and as they developed, they were the first institutions in the United States to provide "higher" education for women.

Above all it was the trio of doughty pioneers, Emma Willard, Catherine Beecher and Mary Lyon, who provided the major impetus. Troy Female Seminary, created by Emma Willard in 1821 and now known as the Emma Willard

[33]"An Essay on the Education of Female Teachers," *American Annals of Education* 5 (1825): 275–78.

[34]Thomas Woody, *A History of Women's Education in the United States*, 2 vols. (New York: Science Press, 1929), 1:137–60.

School; Mt. Holyoke Seminary, later to become Mt. Holyoke College, founded by Mary Lyon in 1836; and Hartford Female Seminary, established by Catherine Beecher in 1828–these three institutions established a tradition in New England which spread rapidly to other sections, especially to the South, where the female seminary became a vogue. By contrast, the academy movement as it spread in the Middle West was overwhelmingly coeducational.[35]

The female seminaries were markedly different from the boys' boarding schools in significant respects. The double standard in sexual mores and the associated parental protection of female children gave a special cast to the education of girls. While the concept of the "gentleman" in the early nineteenth century called for a classical education among other things, the role of the "lady" did not require formal *academic* education, since the looked-for qualities were good breeding, gentleness, charitableness, grace, as well as skill in the domestic realm and–God willing–a bit of wit and charm. Most of the late eighteenth century ladies' proprietary boarding schools were of the finishing school type, stressing dancing, good carriage, how to enter and leave a room properly and how to be seated and to rise gracefully, diction and voice control, some instruction in the household arts and perhaps a smattering of French. It was precisely this concept of the "showy" education of girls that Emma Willard inveighed against in her *Plan for Improving Female Education*, published in 1819 at her own expense.[36]

In place of the finishing school Emma Willard proposed an education in subjects "solid and useful." "It is through the mothers," she declared, "that the government can control the character of its future citizen." Her proposal for the Troy Female Seminary aimed to provide an education which "should seek to bring its subjects to the perfection of their moral, intellectual and physical nature." To this end instruction would be provided in subjects under four heads: religious and moral, literary, domestic, and ornamental.[37] "Literary" was broadly interpreted to include natural philosophy, mathematics and the sciences concerning "the operations of the human mind" and "how they apply to education." One of the public benefits that such an education would provide was to equip able young women for careers in teaching for the benefit of the common schools. Mrs. Willard's concern for the common schools and for the preparation

[35] Mock, "The Midwestern Academy Movement," pp. 165–70.

[36] The plan was composed for delivery to the New York State legislature in the effort to secure a state subsidy for the founding of a female seminary. Though Governor DeWitt Clinton was wholly sympathetic, Mrs. Willard did not succeed in persuading the legislature. But help came from the Common Council of Troy, New York, in the form of a building to be made available to the seminary.

[37] From the reprint of her plan in Willystine Goodsell, *Pioneers of Women's Education in the United States: Emma Willard, Catherine Beecher, Mary Lyon* (New York and London: McGraw-Hill, 1931), pp. 45–81.

of teachers gradually became one of the dominant interests of her career, which she furthered vigorously by lectures and by the writing of many textbooks which were widely used in public and private schools. Chiefly because of her influence, the female seminary became the precursor of the "normal school" of later times.

The female seminaries were a largely indigenous development and less influenced than the boys' boarding schools by European educational philosophies and foreign models. The influence of Pestalozzi among the pioneers in women's education appears to have been marginal. Thomas Woody notes the influence of Mrs. C. M. Thayer, governess of Elizabeth Female Academy, Washington, Mississippi, who combined the method of Pestalozzi with the Lancastrian method of using advanced students as pupil-teachers.[38] When Emma Willard, after retiring from her seminary, finally found time to visit schools in England and France, she found that the education of girls there did not compare with that offered by the newly established seminaries in the United States.[39] The female boarding seminaries grew up quite independent of the boys' boarding schools, and there appears to have been remarkably little communication between them. They were literally two distinct, separate worlds.[40] Unlike the boys' academies, which the girls' seminaries imitated in certain respects, the latter were true boarding schools from the beginning. But the most striking difference of all was the absence of the classical curriculum in the early girls' schools. Since they were happily rid of this course, which weighed like an albatross around the neck of the boys' boarding schools through much of their history, the girls' schools could concentrate on the English program, which was regarded in the boys' schools as a vulgar second track for uncouth terminal students. Moreover, the early girls' school put little stress on athletics and sports, substituting instead much less time-consuming gymnastic exercises and dancing. The time and the curriculum were thus freed for a more thorough grounding in mathematics, natural science, literature, history and the arts. By mid-century the most advanced female seminaries offered work at a level comparable to that of most contemporary colleges.

Mary Lyon's Mt. Holyoke Seminary developed these traits to the highest point. She was deeply influenced during her student days at the Byfield (Massa-

---

[38] Woody, *History of Women's Education*, pp. 282, 424–28.

[39] Alma Lutz, *Emma Willard–Pioneer Educator of American Women* (Boston: Beacon Press, 1964), pp. 81–82.

[40] One boys' boarding school rector who was interested in the education of girls was the Rev. John B. Kerfoot, founder of St. James in Maryland and later president of Trinity College. In speaking at the opening, in 1865, of the Collegiate Institute for Young Ladies in Waterbury, Connecticut, the precursor of St. Margaret's School, he stressed "the double want society begins to feel—an education more truly liberal and freely accessible for its daughters." See Carol Burke Ohmann, *St. Margaret's School, 1865-1965* (Waterbury, Conn.: St. Margaret's School Alumnae Association, 1965), p. 4.

chusetts) Seminary by the Reverend Joseph Emerson, who believed in an academic education as rigorous for women as for men; and she profited by visits with Emma Willard and Catherine Beecher and to Abbot Academy in Andover, an institution founded to offer girls some of the advantages available to boys in the neighboring Phillips Academy.[41] The seminary which Mary Lyon founded differed from others of its kind in two respects: she laid down from the beginning firm entrance requirements and a rigorous curriculum which compared favorably with the English and scientific courses offered by men's colleges at the time. Moreover, she had resolved from the first to found a school that would provide a good education for daughters of the poor farmers and artisans from which she herself sprang. To realize her dream, she campaigned relentlessly among the farmers, villagers, city dwellers and churchgoers of Massachusetts and neighboring states for funds to endow her institution. When her seminary opened in 1837, the charge for lodging and tuition was $64 for the year (compared to $300 at the Round Hill School for boys at nearby Northampton fifteen years earlier).[42] Mary Lyon was united with her sister pioneers, Emma Willard and Catherine Beecher, in stressing the need of financial stability for the female seminaries in order to end the tradition of dependence by these schools on a single founding teacher and reliance on fees so high that only the wealthy could afford them.

The development of female seminaries in the period after the Civil War was conditioned chiefly by the founding of women's colleges and public and private coeducational colleges and universities. As institutions for higher education became progressively available to women and as the aggressive feminism of the Woman's Movement gained momentum during the closing decades of the nineteenth century, many female seminaries were transformed gradually into college prep institutions and, ironically, came to resemble the boys' prep schools more and more. The price that had to be paid in the process was to stress the classical curriculum, and gradually to lessen emphasis on the "showy and ornamental" social graces as well as the domestic arts. The battle over the place of classical studies in secondary education and college admissions proved to be a century long seesaw affair in which the intellectual elite of the college preparatory schools were generally found in the conservative camp. They were deeply and often passionately committed to the defense of classical humanism conceived as the saving cultural antidote to the exploitation of the school and college curricula by commercial and industrial interests and the thrusts of modernism. It was President Charles W. Eliot of Harvard who finally broke the mold with his advocacy of the free elective system.

[41] Arthur Charles Cole, *A Hundred Years of Mt. Holyoke College: The Evolution of an Educational Ideal* (New Haven: Yale University Press, 1940), pp. 1–29.

[42] *Ibid.*, p. 39.

By the closing decades of the nineteenth century two fairly distinct types of girls' boarding schools were recognizable. The first, following generally the academic aspect of the Emma Willard and Mt. Holyoke seminaries, developed predominantly as college preparatory schools. Some were established by the faculties of college or boys' boarding schools who wanted to provide for their daughters the same quality of education available to their sons. Others were established as feeders to certain women's colleges. Thus the Cambridge School of Weston (Massachusetts) was established originally to prepare the daughters of old Cambridge families for Radcliffe, but more recently became coeducational and is now known as a progressive institution. Similarly, one of the aims of founding Baldwin, Shipley, and the Bryn Mawr School was to prepare young women for Bryn Mawr College; and Dana Hall School at its founding had comparable relationships to Wellesley.

The other type of girls' boarding school, while not neglecting intellectual culture, stressed the cultivation of the "feminine" womanly virtues. Miss Porter's, founded in 1843 as a proprietary school in Farmington, Connecticut, was in many respects the prototype for others which were founded or staffed by her graduates. The Westover School, Middlebury, Connecticut, owes its existence to Mary R. Hilard, a graduate of Miss Porter's. Schools of this general type were launched in substantial numbers in the Northeast and South after the Civil War and up to the First World War. It was characteristic of these schools to be founded and to have continued as proprietary schools through many years before they became incorporated as non-profit institutions.

With the sexual revolution in education, beginning in the 1920s, the college preparatory program for girls became increasingly important. The full impact on the girls' boarding schools, however, was not felt until the 1940s. Prior to that time only a minority of upper-class daughters went to college. For them, attendance at the "right" boarding school was conceived as a suitable preparation for the debutante ritual to come. But new headmistresses or headmasters who in the forties and later took over schools whose programs and accepted life styles had been set in the Victorian era brought a new attitude which manifested itself usually in a more demanding academic program and a more liberal social atmosphere. This trend has carried the formerly decorous girls' boarding schools closer to their meritocratic academic sisters, so that they are now no longer as readily distinguishable as before.[43]

[43] *Fortune* magazine undertook in 1936 to identify "Ten Fashionable Boarding Schools for Girls," selecting the following: Foxcroft, St. Timothy's, Ethel Walker, Miss Porter's, Westover, Dobbs (Master's School), Rosemary Hall, Shipley, Madeira, and Katherine Branson. Most of these began as proprietary finishing schools, but by the late 1920s the growing demand for college preparation among girls of the moneyed class, a demand which grew by leaps and bounds in the 1950s, caused these schools to be less concerned about social prowess and the womanly virtues and to stress instead thorough college preparation. The

The recent social revolution has raised many questions about the future of single sex boarding schools, and it is a rare girls' school that is not undertaking a thorough reassessment of ends and means and what options are open. The application lists are not as long and school officials admit privately that the quality has fallen off also.[44] Since the enrollment in girls' day schools is also down very slightly, many are tempted to look to coeducation for answers rather than to a change in the boarding status, though that is under way also. Many former all-boarding schools have become either part-day or day schools simply because of the inability to fill the boarding places satisfactorily. With the expectations of patrons and young people changing so rapidly, the girls' boarding schools, like their counterparts for boys, are reassessing their goals and programs. Many fresh stirrings are evident in the form of more flexible curricula, more scholarships to minority students, increased attention to the arts and to community participation and more student involvement in school governance. We shall explore these developments more thoroughly in subsequent chapters.

The Infinite Variety of Day Schools

Having followed in brief the fortunes of the independent boarding schools, we turn now to an overview of the varied world of day schools. Most boarding schools, except for the few that take boarders for the middle school years,[45] are devoted to preparing for college, a fact which makes for a measure of uniformity among them, apart from obvious differences of location, quality, curricular emphasis, conventional or innovative character, and the boy-girl composition. The independent day school world, on the other hand, embraces a substantial number of elementary schools, and it is among these that the greatest diversity is to be found in educational philosophy, goals and teaching methods.[46] The repressive hand of college admissions requirements is far less constraining in the early

---

emphasis in the *Fortune* article was on the "fashionable" schools of the mid-thirties. Today a list of leading or strong schools would include Brearley, Emma Willard and other schools of the kind that stressed high academic attainments from the beginning.

[44]The annual statistics covering NAIS member schools show declines of 2.2 and 2.9 per cent in 1968–69 and 1970–71, respectively, over the preceding year, in the enrollment of the 42 girls' boarding schools reporting. Prior to 1968–69 they were still growing slightly but at a diminishing rate. The decline has been slightly smaller than for the boys' boarding schools, which are more numerous.

[45]The Fay School in Southboro, Mass., is said to be the oldest elementary boys' boarding school in America. It accepts children at ages 8 to 14. Rumsey Hall in Washington, Conn., a coeducational school, accepts boarders from ages 10 to 15. Many of the graduates of these schools go on to private prep schools.

[46]According to the U.S. Office of Education, statistics for 1965–66 show 1,365 elementary and 1,004 secondary independent schools. The ratio of elementary to secondary among the church schools is far higher—13,975 to 3,602.

elementary years than at the high school level. Moreover, it is much easier to organize a small elementary school around a teacher inspired with an idea or a group of parents who feel that the established schools are failing them than to found a secondary school with costly laboratory and library equipment.

The historical roots of the modern day school can be traced to the proprietary town and church schools in the colonial period. In the beginning, formal instruction in the classroom was expected to provide only a fraction of the child's whole education; the rest would be acquired in the home, the church and the community. But, as we noted earlier, time and circumstances kept enlarging the role that the community expected the school to play. The roles of the church school and of the Latin grammar school were relatively well defined. The church school was to combat illiteracy both in order to facilitate intensive Bible reading as a check on heresy, and to prevent pauperism and destitution. The grammar school, however, was to prepare a select few for the life of public service and the professions. The proprietary schools, on the other hand, were the work of "adventure" masters who appeared in considerable numbers during the half century preceding the Revolution. They offered quite simply to teach whatever somebody wanted to learn—and that included subjects which appeared later in the academies and high schools. Proprietary schools were particularly important to girls who were not admitted to the town schools.[47] While the private venture schools lacked stability and continuity, they enjoyed the virtue of their defect in that they were able to respond rapidly to changing needs.

There followed then, in the nineteenth century, the academies, as another embodiment of the free-wheeling spirit of private venturing in education, with public education growing up alongside and eventually taking over the main burden of schooling. As that happened, the academies, faced with the growing competition of the free public high schools, in some cases became boarding schools, others continued as college preparatory day schools, still others were transformed into high schools, normal schools or colleges, and the rest expired quietly. A few continue to function even today as local public schools under private management. Norwich Free Academy in Connecticut is an example,[48] and there are other scattered examples in Maine, New Hampshire and Vermont.

But the nineteenth century academy was only one of several antecedents of the modern day schools. Others sprang from the early parochial schools. The

[47]Woody, *History of Women's Education*, p. 217.

[48]This academy, enrolling 3,100 students in 1968–69, was founded in 1856, owing chiefly to the chaotic state of public education at the time. It is governed by a self-perpetuating board of trustees, yet serves as the local high school for Norwich and six neighboring towns in Connecticut. The town of Norwich in 1968–69 paid the academy $727 tuition for each town enrollee, the six neighboring towns paid $800. For capital improvements the academy relies chiefly on gifts and the income from the school's approximately $3 million endowment.

history of the Collegiate School in New York City is of special interest in this connection, not only because it is the oldest private day school in the country but because of the way it adjusted to religious, social and educational changes through its more than 330-year history. Founded by the Reformed Protestant Dutch Church in 1638 at the behest of the Dutch West India Company, it began essentially as a coeducational parochial school modeled on those in Holland.[49] From the beginning, children of poor and rich families were admitted without discrimination. As the New Netherlands colony grew, the school was sustained through good years and bad by the sense of obligation felt by the minister and elders of the church.[50] After the British arrived in 1664, it functioned for a time as a city school, but during most of the eighteenth century it returned to its former role as a predominantly charity school. The Lancastrian method, using pupil-teachers or monitors, was employed in the early decades of the nineteenth century as the school was beginning its slow transformation into a charity grammar school. Meanwhile, from 1813 to 1824 it was the recipient of state aid distributed by the Free School Society until aid to denominational schools was withdrawn. By 1870 it was called the Collegiate Grammar School and advertised its new career as a tuition college preparatory school for boys. Beginning in 1893 only boys were enrolled, "because of the growing difficulty of providing . . . a single corps of teachers for thorough collegiate preparation and the finished education of girls. . . ."[51] By that time too the name had changed to "Collegiate School." The history of this school, in undergoing the transitions from a coeducational parochial school to a grammar school and thence to a boys' prep school status, reflects three centuries of changes in American schooling.

Quite another type of school developed in the "country day" pattern, which emerged in the suburbs and exurbs of the larger cities at the end of nineteenth and during the early decades of the twentieth century. Reputed to be the first of its kind is the Gilman School of Baltimore. Founded in 1897 by a group of "prominent Baltimoreans," as they were referred to in the first advertisement, the school was originally housed in the fine old Carroll mansion situated on what was to become later the Homewood campus of Johns Hopkins University. The motivating idea was a school in the country, away from the smoky and vice-laden city environment, where boys could drink in sweet draughts of nature while they received in the classrooms and on playing fields an education comparable to that offered at the best eastern boarding schools. The school was to

[49]William Heard Kilpatrick, *The Dutch Schools of New Netherland and Colonial New York* (Washington, D.C.: Government Printing Office, 1912), pp. 228–30 and *passim.*

[50]Jean Parker Waterbury, *A History of Collegiate School, 1638–1963* (New York: Clarkson N. Potter, 1965), pp. 11ff.

[51]*Ibid.*, p. 117.

exert a "distinctly religious influence," yet remain nonsectarian.[52] In short, the school was to embody some of the best features of the boarding school, yet the boys would be safely in the family nest evenings and weekends, thus averting that "precocious air of sophistication and cosmopolitanism" which vacationing boarding school students affected. There would be time enough later for the boys to see "life." The founders engaged a Bostonian Exeter graduate as the first headmaster, and "The Country School for Boys of Baltimore City" was in business as a college preparatory school. The "open air school" vogue hit Gilman in 1910, compelling the lower school pupils to suffer the vagaries of Baltimore winters in woolen uniforms and mittens. The institution was soon renamed "Gilman Country School for Boys" after Daniel Coit Gilman, the renowned first president of Johns Hopkins. Later, as the growing city engulfed the school in its Roland Park location, the "Country" disappeared in fact and from the name.

The country day school movement became in time sufficiently coherent to produce a special Country Day Headmasters' Association. In 1937 it counted over 100 schools in the United States committed to an education that was to spare the child the perils of the city environment in the form of doubtful companions, questionable amusements, destructive use of leisure and the hazards of city streets. However, as the growing cities grew out to and beyond the original country campuses it became clear that it was not so much the location of the school as a distinctive program that defined the country day school movement. The essential elements were (1) a full day program of academic and extracurricular activities, and (2) close home ties with full involvement of parents. Older schools of various backgrounds joined the movement. The Rye Country Day School, for example, began in 1869 as a proprietary female boarding seminary. At the century's end it was stressing the classical course and college preparation. By merging eventually with a nearby boys' school it became the present coeducational country day school.

The idea of the country school is still very much alive. The Manhattan Country School, now in the sixth year of its existence, lays claim to "Country" by virtue of the fact that the school owns a 200-acre mountain farm in upstate New York, where the children spend occasional weeks communing with nature and learning about farm life. The school proper, located off Fifth Avenue at 96th Street, enrolls a mixture of children, some coming from the crowded East Harlem tenements to the north, others residing in the luxury cooperatives of the fashionable East Side. Not only the students but the faculty and trustees are realistically integrated. Much of the school's pedagogy is straight out of John Dewey but applied without preaching or self-conscious ideology. "I like to

[52] Bradford McE. Jacobs, *Gilman Walls Will Echo—the Story of The Gilman Country School, 1897-1947* (Baltimore: Waverly Press, 1947), pp. 10ff.

think," says Augustus Trowbridge, the founder-director and a Putney alumnus, "that John Dewey would be happy if he saw this place."[53]

A number of day school groups identify with special educational philosophies. One such group espouses the pedagogical theory of Rudolf Steiner, the Austrian philosopher and educator, who inspired an almost religious devotion to his suggestive child-oriented pedagogy. At the urging of a philanthropic manufacturer of Waldorf Astoria cigarettes, Steiner launched in Stuttgart, Germany, in 1919, a privately financed model school called the Waldorf School. The fame of this institution attracted visitors from many western European countries who began Waldorf movements in their homelands. A small but ardent band of American disciples founded eight Waldorf-type schools in the United States, including one in Hawaii, as well as a Rudolf Steiner School Association. Steiner's quasi-mystical animating idea is that the process of education should relate the spiritual life of man harmoniously to the spiritual principle in nature. Finding the pedagogy of his time too intellectualistic, he set out to counterbalance the materialistic conceptions of science by a pedagogy that stresses the child's encounter of the world with his whole being—his mind, his heart and his will. Music, singing, wood carving, rhythmics, training in manual dexterity (including knitting for boys and manual training for girls) are employed as avenues to conceptual learning and to help open the whole child freely to the world. While Steiner's pedagogy embodies some of the elements of progressive education, it differs substantially in that it moves within a metaphysical framework and accepts the need for firm but kindly authority in the school.[54] The Rudolf Steiner School in New York City and the Waldorf School of Adelphi University on Long Island are among the best-known American practitioners of the Steiner method. That method is also adapted to the special therapeutic needs of retarded and handicapped children in the Camphill-Steiner schools.

Felix Adler's Society for Ethical Culture, a small but influential international humanist religious movement seeking to promote human fellowship, service and basic social reforms, was the wellspring for the founding of schools with a positive but flexible philosophy. Within two years after the society had been

[53] Bernard Bard, "A Country School in the City," *Southern Education Report*, April, 1969, pp. 6–11. Also see Peter Schrag, "Experiment on 96th Street," *Saturday Review*, January 20, 1968, p. 59.

[54] Since Steiner was a prolific lecturer and teacher, many of his publications originated as lectures or seminars. Very few of the hundred or more titles of his articles and books have been translated into English. The founding philosophy of the original Waldorf School is developed in his *Erziehungskunst, Seminarbesprechungen und Lehrplanvorträge; Kurs gehalten in Stuttgart vom 21 August bis September, 1919, anlässlich der Gründung der freien Waldorfschule* (Stuttgart: Freies Geistesleben, 1959). A later set of lectures is available in English translation as *The Essentials of Education: five lectures delivered during the Educational Conference at the Waldorf School, Stuttgart, April 1924*, trans. and ed. H. Collison (London: Anthroposophical Publishing Co., 1926). A quarterly *Education as an Art, Bulletin of the Rudolf Steiner School Association* is published in New York City.

established at New York City in 1876, Adler founded the first free kindergarten, known as the Workingman's School. By gradual enlargement it became the present group of Ethical Culture Schools. It was devoted from the first, in the words of the founder, to "active research for ever better educational methods appropriate to the general purpose."[55] At its inception the school was strongly influenced by Friedrich Froebel's pedagogy of "learning by doing"—a cliché now, but at the time a revolutionary approach. However, it was also committed to maintaining an experimental attitude in order to cope with changing needs and fresh problems. "Perhaps the most significant contribution of the Ethical Culture Schools from their very beginnings," says Fred M. Hechinger, "has been their good sense in avoiding extremes."[56] They went part way with the progressive movement but without being distracted by its vagaries. The Ethical Culture schools had their own philosophy which proscribed a permanent commitment to any special one way, no matter how highly touted or fashionable it might be at the moment.

Apart from these illustrations of small school groups based on special educational philosophies, the main stream of private school development, the day school in particular, was most widely influenced by the progressive school movement. The story has been told brilliantly by Lawrence Cremin in *The Transformation of the School.*[57] While private schools were among the leaders in the movement, both public and private schools were drawn into its orbit; it was part of a broader social transformation—"the educational phase of American Progressivism writ large."[58] Cremin describes its genesis in the decades following the Civil War, how it captured the intellectuals and the teaching profession after the turn of the century, its wide impact on the schools and colleges during the interbellum period, and its eventual collapse in the fifties as it failed to keep pace with the continuing transformation of American society. Progressivism was the main concerted effort to cope with the changing problems that were thrust on the school—and wrought in the school—by wave after wave of immigration, and by the accelerating pace of industrialization and urbanization. It meant broadening the school program "to include direct concern for health, vocations, and the quality of family and community life," and beyond that to national and international affairs. It meant "applying in the classroom the pedagogical principles derived from new scientific research in psychology and the social sciences." It meant tailoring instruction more and more not only to the different

[55] Quoted in Fred M. Hechinger, "The Ethical Culture Schools in American Education, 1878-1959," *Teaching and Learning, Journal of the Ethical Culture Schools of New York*, 1959, pp. 5-10.

[56] Hechinger, "Ethical Culture Schools," p. 7.

[57] Subtitled *Progressivism in American Education, 1876-1957* (New York: Alfred A. Knopf, 1961).

[58] *Ibid.*, p. viii.

kinds and classes of children who came to school but to the individual student and his special needs. And it proceeded from the faith "that everyone could share not only in the benefits of the new sciences, but in the pursuit of the arts as well."[59] Although the broad bearings of the movement are clearly discernible, it defies precise definition.

The progressive schools were marked from the beginning by a striking diversity of basic aims, curricula, sponsorship, and style. Francis Wayland Parker, whom Dewey once called "the father of progressive education," began in 1873 to revolutionize the public schools of Quincy, Massachusetts. For the strict formalism and rote learning of the traditional classroom he substituted an informal child-centered program using current materials in place of the well-worn texts, and emphasizing first-hand observation, description and comprehension as approaches to the more conventional studies. Parker, though he was familiar with the newer pedagogical trends in Europe, including the theories of Pestalozzi, Froebel, and Herbart, was more artist than theorist, building the "Quincy Plan" chiefly on his direct observation of children and his intense desire to see them grow and improve.[60]

By contrast, John Dewey, in founding the Laboratory School of the University of Chicago in 1896, began with a well-formed philosophy of education and created the school to test his hypotheses. It was the first progressive private school to be identified as such.[61] The program embodied Dewey's highly influential philosophy of education. He first gave voice to it in a little tract, *The School and Society*, published in 1899, but he was to restate it over and over again in the fresh contexts of a host of major and minor works throughout a long and extraordinarily fruitful life. *Democracy and Education*, hailed as the greatest contribution to pedagogy since Rousseau's *Emile*, was the mature, comprehensive statement of the progressive education movement. Dewey's philosophical response to the radical changes wrought in American life by industrialization was to call for educational reconstruction, in theory and in practice, so that the educative process might serve the end of developing in people the power to meet and master the perennially fresh experience of living. It should be, as Dewey said, "a process of continuous growth, having as its aim at every

[59]*Ibid.*, pp. viii–ix.

[60]Parker's *Talks on Pedagogics* (New York, 1894), while relying heavily on the theories of his European mentors, emerges nevertheless as the first native effort in scientific pedagogy.

[61]For a lively account of this school's early years, see Katherine Camp Mayhew and Anna Camp Edwards, *The Dewey School: The Laboratory School of the University of Chicago, 1896–1903* (New York: D. Appleton-Century Co., 1936). Ida B. DePencier, *The History of the Laboratory Schools–The University of Chicago, 1896–1965* (Chicago: Quadrangle Books, 1967) contains a more prosaic account of subsequent developments.

stage an added capacity of growth." The school was conceived to be society's primary instrument in the cause of social progress.

Spurred by the revolt against "the harsh pedagogy" of the existing schools and by the ferment of change and new thought in the first two decades of the twentieth century, progressive private schools began to emerge in growing numbers. Some were started by teachers who, in seeking to apply a special pedagogical theory, went out and sought the parents. Others were organized by parents who were fed up with public school traditionalism and went out in search of a teacher. Miss Caroline Pratt narrates in her biography how by watching a child at play she came to have a vision of a school in scale with the child which would help him through play acquire a basic understanding of man and nature.[62] It became a reality in 1914 as the Play School—later known as the City and Country School—located in a three-room apartment in Greenwich Village. To her surprise, her clients were not the slum families she had expected, but the children of the Village artists and writers to whom the idea of building on the child's artistic and creative bents held a special appeal. Further uptown and a year later the Walden School—originally known as the Children's School—was founded by Margaret Naumberg. She shifted the focus from preoccupation with the repressive intellectual drill of conventional schooling to a concern for the nonintellectual or affective life of children. This approach became in time something of a vogue which attracted those who believed they found fresh illumination and new clues to the why and what of education in Freudian concepts of the unconscious, repressed emotions, sublimation, fixations and the search for identity. Obviously, the end is not yet for these concepts or their subsequent variants. They are taken far more seriously in the seventies than they were in the first flush of recognition during the 1910s. In the case of the Play School and the Walden School the founding teachers rallied the parents in support of new ideas.[63]

Meanwhile, in Baltimore the Park School was founded by a group of parents and concerned citizens led by European-educated Hans Froelicher, professor of fine arts at Goucher. Several of the founders, including Froelicher, had resigned from the Baltimore City Board of Education as a result of a bitter controversy over the conduct of the public schools. But desirable alternatives were not available; leading Jewish citizens charged discrimination in the private as well as the public schools.[64] They wanted to establish a school free of discrimination

---

[62] *I Learn from Children* (New York: Simon and Schuster, 1948).

[63] For brief but illuminating accounts of these schools and the literature about them see Cremin, *Transformation of the School*, pp. 204-205, 211-14, 278-79.

[64] See Lloyd Marcus, "The Founding of American Private Progressive Schools, 1912-1921" (honors thesis, Department of Social Relations, Harvard University, 1948).

and offering a program based on the actual interests of children. The search for a headmaster ended happily in the choice of Eugene Randolph Smith, a tough-minded Deweyan, under whose guidance the school became known as a center of innovative pedagogy. As one of the founders and an early president of the Progressive Education Association (PEA), Smith exerted a wide influence. In 1921 he went on to head the newly created Beaver Country Day School in Chestnut Hill, Massachusetts, a school founded by parents who had read John and Evelyn Dewey's *Schools of Tomorrow* with deep interest. Under Smith's leadership the school was an instant success and "became not only accepted by discriminating Boston families," Porter Sargent notes with proper Brahmin pride, "but nationally noted as a leader in progressive education."[65]

The story of how progressive schools were founded varied from school to school. In Cambridge, Professor and Mrs. Ernest Hocking and some of their Harvard colleagues, concerned with the overheated, germ-laden air and general inadequacy of the local elementary public schools, created the Shady Hill School in 1915. Under Mrs. Hocking's influence the school took up the European "open air" school practice which was in vogue at the time. Shady Hill was headed for thirteen years by Edward Yeomans, the son of a Chicago manufacturer who through his association with the school board of Winnetka, Illinois, became deeply interested in progressive education. The elder Yeomans' book, *Shackled Youth*,[66] is a sharp indictment of the rigid formalism in public school practice as he knew it. The father also founded in 1923 the Ojai Valley School in California, one of the early progressive schools in the West. In Detroit, Arthur E. Morgan, an engineer who admired Pestalozzi's *Leonard and Gertrude*, was one of the founders of the Moraine Park School. Morgan, president of Antioch College, was also the first president of the PEA. The Putney School in Vermont, a later arrival, was launched by Mrs. Carmelita Hinton's vision of a boarding school that would make school life "more real." The program was designed to give students an opportunity to develop manual skills and a real sense of participation in running the community.

The rise and unexpectedly rapid demise of progressive education is best seen through the brief, meteoric history of the PEA. The main energy of the movement was generated in the 1910s, assisted by a number of influential books such as W. H. Page's *The School of Tomorrow*, and John and Evelyn Dewey's *Schools of Tomorrow*.[67] The association was formally launched in 1919 with 85 members, and with Charles W. Eliot as the honorary president. The influential journal, *Progressive Education*, was launched in 1924. By 1928, with John Dewey

[65] Sargent, *A Handbook of Private Schools*, p. 107.

[66] Boston: Atlantic Monthly Press, 1921.

[67] W. H. Page *et al*, *The School of Tomorrow* (New York: Doubleday Page & Co., 1911); John Dewey and Evelyn Dewey, *Schools of Tomorrow* (New York: E. P. Dutton and Co., 1915).

now the honorary president, the membership had risen to 6,000. In 1930 it set in motion the challenging Eight-Year Study testing the validity of the prevailing college entrance requirements. The membership reached a peak of 10,440 in 1932, but in the midst of the social turmoil wrought by the Great Depression, the PEA began a long, and as it turned out, futile struggle to define its educational philosophy. During the middle and late thirties, reports of various association committees, goaded by the radical critiques of George S. Counts of Teachers College, Columbia, attempted to formulate a social and educational platform for PEA members. But as criticism of progressive education was rising, and as the association became more and more a professional organization, the members could not agree on the ideological direction the movement should take in a time of confusing political, social and educational signposts and rapidly changing priorities. That failure, coupled with the onset of the war, was the *coup de grace*. The surviving organization made feeble efforts after the war to regroup and reform, but they were futile, and the end came in 1955.[68]

"In the end," Lawrence Cremin sums it up, "the PEA's failure was neither financial nor philosophical, but ultimately political: it simply failed to comprehend the fundamental forces that move American education." But the end of the PEA did not spell the end of progressivism in education. Though it went under a cloud of ridicule and abuse during the fifties and early sixties, it has more recently re-emerged in altered form and with the benefit of a new social and political awareness that was lacking in its original embodiment. Its influence on traditional education has been pervasive and profound; there is scarcely a school in the United States which is untouched by the concepts and methods of the progressive education movement.

Beyond Progressivism: New Directions

New private venture schools are virtually limitless in their variety, the form they take depending upon the special purpose and population they set out to serve, the means at hand, and the lights of the founders. Some follow the familiar country day idea in a pastoral setting but with a fresh program. Others are inner-city schools for high school dropouts. Still others, such as the Manhattan Country School described above, or the approach of the Multi-Culture Institute of San Francisco,[69] set out with the idea of an integrated, multi-ethnic education. Free schools show up in all sorts of unlikely places: converted barracks, vacant supermarkets, abandoned storefronts, country barns, deserted churches or the basements of active churches, the homes of teachers or parents.

[68] For a fuller account see Cremin's chapter 7, "The Organization of Dissent," in *Transformation of the School*, pp. 240–73.

[69] See Fred M. Hechinger, "How to Be Very Different Yet Still Get Along," *New York Times*, April 11, 1971, p. E-9.

Some are completely original, others follow one or another model—such as the Montessori, Leicestershire or Summerhill—more or less faithfully. Because many free schools are launched with more enthusiasm than judgment or hard-headed realism, their life expectancy, as we noted earlier, is often relatively brief, though an impressive number of schools showing every sign of stability have come into being during the past five years.

In the Boston area, three recently founded Leicestershire-type nongraded schools illustrate some of the range of differences. The Fayerweather School in Cambridge, drawing its clients chiefly from white upper middle class families in the area, was founded in 1967 "to provide children with an environment in which they can learn for themselves, and in which what they learn is useful to themselves and society."[70] The parents as well as students have a voice in running the school, which is financed chiefly by tuition and gifts. After first opening in an old house five minutes from Harvard Square, it quickly managed to raise enough money to erect a commodious building of its own. In Roxbury, Massachusetts, the Highland Park Free School, housed in a rambling, hundred-year-old former Catholic school and settlement house with an attached chapel, aims to be a true community-run and community-serving school committed to experimentation—whatever works best for the children. Drawing its students chiefly from black, low income neighborhood families, with a few youngsters from socially conscious white families, the school is financially a brinkmanship operation with income pieced together annually from federal and foundation grants and the donations of parents and friends. Highland Park stresses pride in race and early learning of the basic skills, and to that end structures the program of the first years more than do most free schools.[71] The nearby Dorchester School carries on in a former Jewish temple and Hebrew Academy center which is now in a largely black area. This school is supported by the state through the Council for Community Education Development, a private group charged by the state with operating laboratory urban schools. Like its Highland Park neighbor, the Dorchester School tends to review student choices more closely and, if necessary, restricts their freedom somewhat, out of the desire to see them use their time wisely.[72]

Maria Montessori's method has also attracted practitioners among private schools in the United States. One of the first of these, the Whitby School, was founded in 1958 in a renovated carriage house in Greenwich, Connecticut, by

[70] "Notes on a New School," a mimeographed statement issued by the Fayerweather Street School, May 1, 1967.

[71] See Charles Lawrence, "Free Schools: Public and Private and Black and White," *Inequality in Education*, nos. 3 and 4 (Cambridge, Mass.: Harvard Center for Law and Education, n.d.), pp. 8–12.

[72] John Mathews, "Schools for the '70's—Education by Free Choice," *Washington Star*, February 10, 1970.

several Catholic families. Somewhat more structured and sequential than the freer Leicestershire pedagogy, the Montessori method relies on a carefully planned environment and individual or group learning to help the child to become self-motivating and self-directing. Though Whitby began as a lay Catholic school drawing children chiefly from middle and upper middle class families, it believes that the school should mirror modern society, and to that end it recruits children of varied religious and racial backgrounds.

Examples of new schools committed to the Summerhill pedagogy of A. S. Neill abound. The Pinel School, Martinez, California, founded in 1962, is fairly typical. Classes in the standard subjects such as reading and arithmetic are offered, but the children are not compelled to attend. The Summerhillians believe that healthy middle class children will eventually find the motivation to learn the basic skills in school, if they have not already learned them elsewhere. So they let the youngsters discover and pursue their own interests in a stimulating school environment, but without much effort at "aversive control," in B. F. Skinner's phrase, or at disciplinary channeling.[73]

Most of the new community schools involve the elementary or preschool grades only, but here and there parents, teachers, and philanthropists are fired by a vision of building a new kind of secondary school. Founding a private high school in a time when some of the country's oldest and well-endowed schools are in financial straits is an act of rare courage. But it does happen. The Westledge School on the side of Hedgehog Mountain about 30 minutes northwest of Hartford, Connecticut, opened in 1968 with grades 7–9 and a plan to add an additional grade annually up through 12. The brain child of Louis A. Friedman, the headmaster, and 85 Hartford family incorporators, the school is unique in the diversity of its student body, which includes a substantial scholarship group of financially impoverished students as well as youngsters of diverse intellectual and creative capabilities, some of whom are physically handicapped. To find the kind of students who do not ordinarily apply to an expensive country day school, Westledge organized Project LINK, and with the aid of social workers, churches and community leaders combed Hartford's poor and ghetto neighborhoods for students. The project aims not only to involve the community in recruiting these students, but to interest community agencies in supporting them. Once at the school, Westledge students are encouraged to exercise the responsibilities of self-government and are required to share in the labor necessary for the upkeep of the school's facilities and to keep the community functioning. The school makes a point of fitting the program to the individual student, and letter grades and diploma requirements are dispensed with. Though

---

[73] For brief descriptions and commentary regarding free community schools see Bonnie Barrett Stretch, "The Rise of the 'Free School'," *Saturday Review*, June 20, 1970, pp. 76–93.

the school is nondenominational, it stresses instruction in ethics and religion and takes advantages of its unspoiled forest setting to emphasize outdoor sports and nature study.

Another secondary school with aims that distinguish it from the growing list of free, unstructured schools is the Tunbridge School. Still aborning, it consists at the moment of 90 acres of Vermont land and plans to acquire a residence in metropolitan Boston to be used as an urban base. As the primary medium of student learning, the school intends to develop a continuing series of student-negotiated projects, in the form of field study contracts. The faculty is to consist of a small resident staff at the Vermont and Boston bases, complemented by cooperating individuals and organizations drawn from many fields of work who will constitute a network of talent and resources which might be called the floating or dispersed faculty. The plan combines some of the aims of a residential school with John Bremer's concept of "school-without-walls" pedagogy, conceived as a way of assisting adolescents to make the transition from sheltered students to independent adults. The school hopes to receive its first students in the summer of 1973.

The number of children who are involved in free, experimental private schools is of course very small by comparison with those who attend public schools. But the importance of these schools is quite out of proportion to the numbers served because of the impact that they may have on public schools. This is true particularly of two bold experiments designed to retrieve high school dropouts in Harlem: the street academies and the Harlem Preparatory School.

The two levels of street academies and Harlem Prep together comprise a three-stage program which aims to rehabilitate alienated, disadvantaged boys and girls by means of a special educational program radically different from the one that did not work for them. The plan was conceived by Dr. Eugene S. Callender, formerly pastor at Harlem's Church of the Master and later executive director of the New York Urban Coalition, as a competitive alternative to the public schools; the plan was to assume a form such that "the public school system would take up the techniques and incorporate them into their system."[74] But the plan also called for the continued operation of the private alternative. The 14 original street academies, sponsored by the Urban League in 1967 and located in Harlem storefronts, are of two kinds. The beginning level is the street academy proper, taking the form of an induction center staffed by a few teachers and a group of "street workers"—young people who usually live in and know the school's neighborhood intimately. The academies concentrate on remedial work in reading and math, and subjects like African and black history, and a smattering of sociology. But the chief aim is to help the boys or girls by means of individual or group therapy, to arrest the downward spiral of failing and to

---

[74] Dr. Callender as quoted in the *New York Times*, February 16, 1971, pp. 1, 37.

instill the belief, based on self-confidence and hope, that they can make something of themselves, and that a college education offers the way up and out of the morass of dope, hustling, dead-end jobs and squalor. After about six weeks in the academy, if all goes well, the youngster moves on to the next level, another storefront called the academy of transition, which offers more systematic academic training designed to raise the student to about the 8th or 9th grade level of performance.

The graduates of the academies of transition qualify for admission to Harlem Preparatory School, a spin-off from the general academy program but now independent. Until recently another institution known as Newark Prep, a 61-year-old conventional private school, also took academy graduates, but financial ruin caused it to fold in 1969. Harlem Prep carries on in a spacious, largely unpartitioned former supermarket at 8th Avenue near 136th Street under the dynamic headmastership of Edward F. Carpenter, and until recently with the help of several nuns from Manhattanville College of the Sacred Heart. The atmosphere is relaxed and informal, with the head and faculty as deeply concerned with the personal problems and welfare of each student as with his academic progress. The program is extraordinarily flexible and in many ways defies the conventional concept of the prep school. In the groups that assemble in one corner or another with an instructor, the emphasis is not on the coverage of subjects or acquaintance with facts, but on the practice of conceptualization and logical thinking with reference to the discussion of brief position papers on a variety of topics. The curriculum is divided chiefly into English, math and science. "English," however, is so broad as to include almost the whole gamut of the humanities and social sciences. The primary aim of math is not to develop rote skills but to help the student intuit mathematical relationships. Instruction in science ranges over the basic principles of biology, chemistry, physics and psychology, and here again, the aim is not coverage or cookbook laboratory work (there is neither time nor equipment for this) but the comprehension and analysis of basic concepts. The aim is to try to place students in college after two years at Harlem Prep, and so time is of the essence.

The academies and Harlem Prep have run into plenty of problems, foremost among which is funding. Six of the original 14 academies closed at the end of 1970 as several of the corporations which had sponsored and supported them withdrew. The business recession, the unwillingness of most corporate or foundation donors to commit themselves to long-term, continuous funding, and administrative friction within the schools and among the sponsoring organizations all contributed to the closings. Harlem Prep faces similar problems, and it barely manages to survive financially from year to year. In the meantime, plans are afoot under the auspices of the Urban Coalition to open academies in cooperation with the public schools. But as Joseph Featherstone points out, "the more the program ties in with schools, the more it will have to reconsider its narrow aims [i.e., college preparation only]. It is one thing to run street academies aiming to persuade gifted dropouts to go to college; it is quite another to set up an elite program in one part of a dispirited, mutinous city high school. The street academies will have to begin thinking of other challenges besides college to offer to the mass of Harlem's angry youth, and that will not be easy."[75]

Negro suspicion of private schools, attributable in the main to the resort of Southern whites to segregationist academies, appears to be abating steadily. Through much of their history, even after the Civil War, Negroes had to rely on private education primarily, since the public schools were either closed to them or openly hostile.[76] But today as the discontent of minorities with the public ghetto schools increases, black people too are more inclined to experiment with private or community schools as a way of providing for their children an education that will repair the damage and give them a fair chance in life.

[75] "Storefront Schools in Harlem," *The New Republic*, September 7, 1968, p. 27.

[76] See George Washington Williams, *A History of the Negro Race in America*, 2 vols. (1883; reprinted New York: Bergman Publishers, 1968). In the first half of the nineteenth century many states adopted laws making it a crime to instruct black people. Various benevolent and missionary agencies such as the Freedmen's Aid societies and abolitionist groups established schools for Negroes after the Civil War. See George S. Dickerman, "History of Negro Education," *Negro Education*, Department of the Interior, Bureau of Education Bulletin no. 38 (1916); reprint ed. (New York: Negro Universities Press, 1969), 1:244–68.

II

The World of the Private School

4

The Human Input

*"In its deepest
and richest sense
a community must always remain
a matter of face-to-face intercourse.
This is why the family
and neighborhood,
with all their deficiencies,
have always been the chief agencies of nurture,
the means by which dispositions
are stably formed and ideas acquired
which laid hold
on the roots of character."*

John Dewey[1]

Cultural Conditioning and the Private Schools

Until recently it was taken more or less for granted that when young people fail in school, the fault lay not in the school but with the pupil's being unmotivated, cantankerous or stupid. Yet schools that are ready to place the blame for their failure on poor family background or low pupil intelligence do not hesitate to take full credit for their successful graduates. The outcome of recent educational research has had a generally chastening effect on people's expectations or claims of what the formal process of schooling can accomplish. We now know a great deal more about the importance of cultural conditioning of children—by the family, the neighborhood, and the peer group—and the crucial impact that these primary groups have on the education and character formation of the young. Though environmental determinism has been a major theme of sociology for

[1] *The Public and Its Problems* (New York: H. Holt and Co., 1927), p. 211.

91

almost a century, its application to education was never before as clearly documented as in the much discussed Coleman report, named after its principal author, James S. Coleman, professor of social relations at Johns Hopkins University.[2] The conclusions of this massive project, though it dealt only with public schools, indirectly shed new light on why so many private schools succeed despite facilities, per-pupil expenditures, library holdings, average class size, and the education and background of teachers which are in some cases grossly inadequate by public school standards.

The Coleman study, a survey concerning the lack of equal educational opportunity for children of different races, religions, or ethnic origins, found that differences in student achievement in schools of varying quality appear to be attributable not so much to differences in the quality of the schools themselves as to the differences in the students' family backgrounds and the composition of the peer group. Coleman and his collaborators concluded, "One implication stands out above all: That schools bring little influence to bear on a child's achievement that is independent of his background and social context; and that this very lack of an independent effect means that the inequalities imposed on children by their home, neighborhood, and peer environment are carried along to become the inequalities with which they confront adult life at the end of school."[3] The report was greeted with a barrage of criticism, both on methodological and substantive grounds, but time and other studies have vindicated the main conclusion.[4] Surveys conducted for the English Plowden report reached essentially the same conclusion as did a study conducted by Professor Jesse Burkhead of Syracuse University,[5] among others.

The bearing that this conclusion has on private schools will become apparent in this and subsequent chapters where we shall be concerned with the "human input" in the various types of private schools—the patrons, students, teachers, heads, and trustees—their backgrounds and attitudes, and how they affect the output of the schools. Anticipating the general conclusions in a summary way, we can say that as a general rule the home background and socioeconomic status of nonpublic school patrons as a group are clearly above the average for the U.S. population as a whole, although there are, as one would expect, substantial variations in this respect both among and within the various school

---

[2]*Equality of Educational Opportunity* (Washington, D.C.: Government Printing Office, 1966).

[3]*Ibid.*, p. 325. See pp. 217–333 for the evidence supporting this statement.

[4]For a good summary critique of how well Coleman's conclusions stood up three years after the report was issued see Christopher Jencks, "A Reappraisal of the Most Controversial Educational Document of Our Time," *New York Times Magazine*, August 10, 1969.

[5]Jesse Burkhead, Thomas Fox, and John W. Holland, *Input and Output in Large-City High Schools* (Syracuse, N.Y.: Syracuse University Press, 1967).

types. The patrons of independent schools are the most advantaged in socio-economic terms, while the Protestant schools tend to serve a more typically middle-class constituency, except that Episcopal school patrons resemble those of the independent schools, while the patrons of the evangelical "Christian" schools typically include relatively more blue-collar constituents. Patrons of Catholic schools reveal the greatest variation in socioeconomic background, though even here the number who are at or near the poverty level is small. To the extent that a good socioeconomic background is a reliable predictor of children's IQ's and potential academic performance, it is apparent that the children in private schools are with very few exceptions highly educable to begin with.

But the socioeconomic background is neither the only nor the most important factor in the environment of the home or the school. Subtle differences in cultural traditions which pertain to the way children are reared in the home and the extent to which the home and the school are supportive of each other may have a profound effect on the academic performance of children. Though these influences do not lend themselves to precise measurement or exact documentation, abundant evidence came to light, both in our general survey and in school visits, that the home nurture of children in nonpublic schools as well as the home-school relationship is generally conducive to learning and to wholesome student-teacher relationships. This is not surprising in view of the voluntary nature of the "contract" between patrons and schools. The parents choose the school because they believe the environment to be right for the child, and the school chooses the pupil because he is believed to be suited to the school environment; both the patrons and the school have a stake in seeing that the contract is fulfilled satisfactorily. And back of these choices there are usually shared subcultural ethno-religious or class traditions which persist invisibly for long periods even through substantial changes in socioeconomic status or in other aspects of the total environment.

Although the nonpublic school world embraces a remarkably diverse group of institutions, the individual schools tend to be by their very nature homogeneous, unless they make a determined effort, as some have been doing lately, to diversify the student body and staff. The natural tendency for a selective school community is to serve its own kind, so that patrons and students, heads, teachers, trustees, and, inevitably the alumni, tend to have a common ethno-religious or class outlook. This is as true of the elite meritocratic boarding schools as it is of the various kinds of church schools, or of an all-black private school designed to inculcate race pride and "black is beautiful."

The question is raised frequently whether a homogeneous environment composed of like-minded people is a viable educational medium or whether a truly modern education calls for greater heterogeneity of human input, so as better to fit the student to live in a pluralistic society. It is a big question which is not answerable in terms of a simplistic formula. Being educated deeply in a minority viewpoint and its value structure has at least one saving merit in that it equips the student with *a* standard by which to evaluate persons and events in the passing show. On the other hand, being educated in a school situation designed to mirror the "mainstream" in all its complexity has its own hazards, particularly just now when the old WASP standard of values and achievement is increasingly challenged, while no other standard has emerged to take its place.

This issue is not as incriminating of the nonpublic schools as it may seem, chiefly because the public schools, thanks to the sorting out of neighborhoods and schools by income levels, confront much the same problem. A careful rereading of the history of the common school in the United States by recent historians shows that, contrary to the popular American folklore, the public schools never succeeded in being as common as they aspired to be in the philosophy of that uncompromising equalitarian, Horace Mann. Charles E. Silberman points out in *Crisis in the Classroom* that the public school "has always been essentially a middle or upper middle class institution." In communities where a considerable homogeneity of class, ethnic background, religion and race prevailed, the schools, though under public management, resembled class-typed private schools. But schools serving a heterogeneous population not only were controlled by but catered mainly to the upper classes and served the lower classes, and the immigrants in particular, poorly or not at all; youngsters from most minority groups were made to feel alien and estranged, just as black Americans have been up until very recently.[6]

The new awareness that the public schools are intended to serve all children, including those from racial or ethnic minorities, and should provide equal educational opportunities, impinges on the private schools also. Whatever social issues affect American society as a whole deeply and pervasively also influence the nonpublic schools, for they are part of the nation's social conscience, part of the means by which the promise of American life seeks fulfillment. Thus many private schools are seeking ways and means to serve the disadvantaged youth in city slums, and to increase the participation of their students and staff in the most pressing social problems of our time.

The Patrons: Backgrounds and Outlook

What, then, are the characteristic differences in the complex subcultures of the various groups which make up the nonpublic school world—differences in

[6]Charles E. Silberman, *Crisis in the Classroom: The Remaking of American Education* (New York: Random House, 1970), pp. 53–61. See also Lawrence A. Cremin, *The Genius of American Education* (New York: Random House, Vintage Books, 1965), and Michael B. Katz, *The Irony of Early School Reform* (Cambridge, Mass.: Harvard University Press, 1968).

social origins, income and occupations, educational backgrounds, political orientations, and religious and moral commitments? These are the interlocking background factors which influence decisively the parents' choice of school for their children and make up the human input of the school.[7]

The social and economic backgrounds of the parents clearly reveal that there are relatively few children from poor families in nonpublic schools (see table 2 and figure 1). A negligible number of all parents have combined annual incomes

Table 2

CHILDREN FROM POVERTY-LEVEL FAMILIES
IN NONPUBLIC SCHOOLS (1968)

School Type	Total Students in Sample	"Poor" Children[a] in Sample	Per Cent "Poor" of Total Sample
All elementary	47,348	2,023	4.3
All secondary	100,005	3,376	3.4
Catholic schools	85,645	4,450	5.2
Northeast	34,750	2,423	7.0
South	22,402	1,142	5.1
Midwest & Far West	28,493	885	3.1
Protestant schools	18,720	271	1.4
Lutheran	6,631	65	1.0
Seventh-Day Adventist	2,791	100	3.6
Christian Reformed	6,533	93	1.4
National Association of Christian Schools	2,765	13	0.5
Episcopal schools	5,305	252	4.8
Independent schools	34,455	296	0.9
Northeast secondary	12,310	174	1.4
South secondary	7,484	70	0.9
Midwest & Far West secondary	12,244	49	0.4

[a]The questionnaire stated, "Poverty defined by the Federal Government as $3,500 for a family of four" (1968). In 1970 the Bureau of the Census defined 15.3 per cent of all children under 18 as "poor" (*Statistical Abstract of the United States, 1970* [Washington, D.C., 1970], table no. 499).

of less than $6,000. But the income levels of patrons of the various school types differ widely. The patrons of independent schools, as a group, are economically far better off that the parents whose offspring attend Catholic or Lutheran schools. Over two-thirds of the independent school patrons enjoy incomes of

[7]A word about the location or setting of the schools which were included in our survey. Most are located in metropolitan areas, with suburban locations favored over those in central cities. But about a fifth of the independent schools—mainly the boarding schools—are located in farm or open country, while many of the Lutheran, Seventh-Day Adventist and Christian Reformed schools are scattered among the smaller communities (with populations of 50,000 or less) or across rural areas.

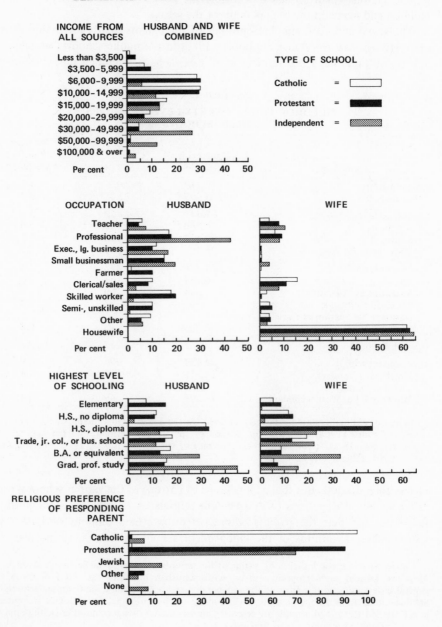

Figure 1

SOCIOECONOMIC PROFILE OF PARENTS OF NONPUBLIC
ELEMENTARY AND SECONDARY SCHOOL CHILDREN

$20,000 or over (almost three-fourths of the patrons of National Association of Independent Schools members fall into that bracket), while a fifth of the total have incomes of $50,000 or more. Among the patrons of the religiously affiliated schools, the Episcopalians are the highest, almost half having incomes of $20,000 or more. By contrast, only about one out of seven of other Protestant school parents has a family income in this category. The differences at the lower end of the scale are equally striking. There we find 38 per cent of Catholic and 44 per cent of Protestant parents (except Episcopalians) reporting incomes of $10,000 or less, compared with only a negligible fraction of NAIS or unaffiliated independent school parents at that level.[8]

These striking differences in the material prosperity of various groups are borne out by the school head's impression of the social class composition of his student body. The independent school heads describe their students overall as predominantly upper middle class or upper class, while only a tiny number have a student body with chiefly working or lower class backgrounds. By contrast, well over three-fourths of the Catholic school heads characterize their students as middle class or lower, while a majority of the Protestant heads see their students as predominantly middle class. Not a single Protestant and less than two per cent of the Catholic heads claim an upper class constituency.

With these figures in mind, it is interesting to review the school head's impression of the extent of the socioeconomic mixture of students within his school. The independent schools that draw their students, as we noted, preponderately from upper and upper middle class families with high incomes, nevertheless believe they have a better student mixture than either the Catholics or Protestants claim for their schools. Of the independents, well over two-thirds think they have a "fair" mixture, but with the majority of students belonging to the same social class. The Protestant secondary school heads are the most modest in their claims, with almost half judging that in their school there is "little or no mixture—almost all students from the same social class." The Catholic position is in between, but nearer the Protestants' than the independents'.

It appears probable that the church-school heads made the judgment about the relative homogeneity of their studentry by reference to a religious rather than a social criterion. However that may be, the Catholic schools as a group clearly exhibit the greatest social diversity, with the Protestant schools next, followed by the independents. It is doubtless true that some Catholic schools have fairly homogeneous student bodies, though this is far less likely to be the case than in specific independent schools. The claim by the independents of relatively more social diversity than exists in fact might also be based on a

---

[8]Throughout this chapter, except where otherwise stated, reference to "Protestants" excludes both Episcopalians and Quakers, whose socioeconomic profile resembles closely that of the independents.

religious instead of a social criterion. Most independent schools accept students with a variety of religious backgrounds, whereas the appeal of most church schools is largely denominational. There is also the fact that many independents, recognizing that their appeal is predominantly to upper and upper middle class families, often make strenuous efforts to broaden the social base of their student body by means of scholarship funds.

Another measure of the differences in student mixture among the three school groups is the enrollment of students from families at or below the poverty level. Roughly somewhat less than half of all private schools enroll at least some such students. The Catholic schools are in the lead, followed by the Protestants and the independents. Just over half of all Catholic schools reported having such students. Of the Protestant schools about a third of the elementaries and about half of the secondaries enroll students from poverty level families. Among the independents less than a tenth of the elementaries enroll such students, while in the secondaries the figure rises to well over a third. The latter doubtless includes high-tuition schools that recruit poverty level students with the aid of scholarship funds. But all in all, the percentage of poor students who attend nonpublic schools is small in comparison with the percentage of poor children in the population at large (table 2), even in the low-tuition Catholic schools. Various reasons such as denominational loyalties, the unavailability of nonpublic schools in poor areas, and, above all, the tuition cost and economic pinch prevent most poor children from enrolling in nonpublic schools.

The educational achievements of nonpublic school parents are such as to enhance the academic potential of the student input of these schools. As a group they have had considerably more formal education than the national average of persons over 25. Of all the responding parents (mothers and fathers combined), substantially over a third hold bachelors' degrees; taking the fathers alone, almost half are college graduates.[9] But when these composite figures are broken down by school types, a pattern of differences paralleling that of the socioeconomic backgrounds of parents comes to light. Wheras slightly less than a quarter of Catholic and Protestant school parents possess B.A. degrees or the equivalent, this level has been reached by just over half of the Episcopal parents and by almost two-thirds of the parents of children in independent schools, while almost three-fourths of all NAIS fathers hold that degree. Moreover, whereas well over a fourth of the fathers in all groups have engaged in graduate or professional study, the figure for NAIS fathers is about 50 per cent.

Well educated themselves, the parents evidently have undiminished confidence in the power of education, a confidence which is reflected in the high

---

[9]In the United States population at large, 10.5 per cent of persons over age 25 have completed four years or more of college. U.S. Bureau of the Census, *Statistical Abstract of the U.S., 1969* (Washington, D.C., 1969), table 152, p. 106.

percentage of those who wish their offspring to obtain at least a B.A. degree: 64 per cent of the Protestant, 71 per cent of the Catholic, 89 per cent of the independent group as a whole, and 93 per cent of the NAIS parents state that they have this goal in mind for their children. But whether their children will want to go to college is now the growing question. With every year more young people are unsure that more formal education is worth all that effort and expense. And so the dialogue between the upset parent and the skeptical son or daughter is a lively one.

To what extent are these parents sending sons and daughters to the kind of school they themselves attended out of desire for their children to perpetuate family tradition or to enjoy as good an education as the parents felt that they had received? To those who maintain that nonpublic schools serve an "ingrown" segment of the population it will come as a surprise that a substantial majority of fathers of nonpublic school children received all or most of their schooling in public schools.[10] Ranking the fathers in ascending percentages of schooling obtained wholly in public schools we find the following: Catholic 57, Protestant 75, NAIS 77, and other independent 79. Comparable figures for mothers are somewhat lower, with Catholic mothers falling slightly under 50 per cent. That more mothers than fathers obtained all or part of their schooling in private schools may be significant, for it is commonly assumed that mothers are generally more deeply involved in decisions regarding the education of children and choosing a school.

The closest family-school ties appear to prevail in the Catholic and in the Christian Reformed groups. Family continuity in attending nonpublic schools is much less pronounced in all other Protestant as well as in Jewish and independent schools, in part because the church schools in question were unavailable to the parents, since the founding of many Protestant evangelical schools and the Jewish all-day schools came only after 1950. An interesting sidelight is the fact that the families of most nonpublic secondary school students have somewhat closer ties to private schools than do the families of private elementary school students. In other words, by and large, family tradition is a somewhat stronger influence in seeking a private secondary than an elementary education.

That the Catholic schools should have the lowest percentage of public-school–educated parents is understandable, since the Catholic system has the highest ratio of school places to eligible children. Moreover, it is well known that

[10]C. Wright Mills, for example, commented on the "tendency for given upper class families to send all their sons to the same schools that the father, or even the grandfather, attended." *The Power Elite* (New York: Oxford University Press, Galaxy Books, 1959), p. 66. Doubtless there are traditions of that sort in some families, and the schools, like the private colleges, have encouraged them. But our point is that the number of such families is restricted, so that most students who attend independent schools nowadays are the first representatives ever, or in several generations, to enroll in a private school.

in decades past the church brought firm pressure on its members to educate their children in Catholic schools. The very high percentage of Protestant public-school-educated parents can be explained in part by the fact that Protestant schools were few and far between during the 1940s, just prior to their upsurge in the 1950s and early 1960s.

The occupations of nonpublic school patrons correlate closely with the socio-economic differences already noted. Overall, the parents are engaged chiefly in one of four types of occupation: professional (other than education) or scientific; manager, executive or proprietor of large business; small business owner or manager; skilled worker or foreman. The distribution of these occupations among the parents of children enrolled in various nonpublic school groups is generally consistent with the other characteristics already noted.

Again in this connection Catholic and Protestant fathers show a strong resemblance in that they are spread fairly evenly over professional, skilled worker and large and small business managership occupations, with a noticeable list toward business, divided about evenly between large and small. As between various Protestant denominations, Lutheran fathers present a norm of balance between professional, skilled worker and business occupations, with an appreciable jump in the percentage of professionals among secondary school fathers, a pattern which is repeated by the Seventh-Day Adventist school fathers. Among the Episcopalians, however, over half of the elementary school fathers are in professional work, compared to only about 39 per cent of secondary school fathers. Another noteworthy variation within the Protestant framework is the fact that about a fourth of the fathers of Christian Reformed elementary and secondary school students and almost a fifth of the National Association of Christian Schools secondary fathers are farmers—the only school groups to show anything more than negligible per cents of tillers of the soil. But these two groups differ in other respects. The NACS fathers include a strong complement of skilled workers and an appreciable per cent of professionals, while the Christian Reformed fathers, with the smallest percentage overall of professionals, incline more toward small business management. Teaching and school administration are poorly represented among all the father groups except the Jewish, seldom rising even to one-tenth of the total.

Among the independent school fathers the distribution of occupations is markedly different. The percentage of professionals rises steeply, in the South and Northeast especially; business managers increase somewhat, while the number of skilled workers drops to a negligible fraction. The same pattern holds for the NAIS, Episcopal and Friends schools.

The characteristic difference between the occupations of Catholic and Protestant parents on the one side and the independents on the other comes to light again in the matter of labor union membership. In about a fourth of all Roman

Catholic school parents either the husband or wife is a member of a union; among Protestants the number is only slightly less. But among the independent school parents it plummets to a minute fraction.

Noteworthy also is the number of working mothers in the families of private school youngsters. Here Catholic, Protestant and independent parents are not far apart. About four out of ten of the Catholic, Protestant, and independent schools mothers have some form of remunerated employment, compared with a national figure, for 1968, of 27.9 per cent of all married women with children between the ages 6 and 17.[11]

Middle and lower class working mothers are doubtless motivated in part by the need of additional family income to meet private school tuition bills. For example, 62 per cent of the Seventh-Day Adventist mothers work; tithing and school support are particularly high among the objectives of this group's mothers of secondary school students. By contrast, a much smaller number of Christian Reformed mothers are in the labor force; but since this group contains a substantial number of families living on farms and in small towns, their record of outside employment may not be really comparable. That the spur to work is not only financial need is plain from the fact that a sturdy 39 per cent of the more affluent independent secondary school mothers in the Northeast are also in the labor force. However, even here the necessarily high tuition costs in independent schools may be a motive.

Though in socioeconomic characteristics Catholic and Protestant parents have much in common, both differing materially from independent school parents, the resemblance does not extend to their political party affiliations. Almost two-thirds of Catholic parents affiliate with the Democrats, while not quite a fourth identify with the Republicans. By contrast, a strong majority of Protestant parents identify with the Republican party. Independent school parents also affiliate chiefly with the Republican party, but by a smaller majority.

If we judge by the way nonpublic school parents rate themselves on a six-point scale between the poles "liberal" and "conservative," Catholic parents can be characterized as moderately conservative, with relatively little regional variation. Protestant parents, on the other hand, lay claim to a strong conservative outlook, with the Christian Reformed parents furthest to the right, the Seventh-Day Adventists nearer the center, and the Lutherans between. The position of Episcopal and independent school parents is much like the Catholics'—moderately conservative—except for the independent school parents in the South, who are firmly on the right, while the Northeast parents land just to the left of center. Only the Jewish patrons place a strong majority on the liberal side.

[11] See U.S. Bureau of the Census, *Statistical Abstract, 1969*, pp. 38–39.

Why Families Choose Private Schools

One of the significant differences between private and public schools, as we noted in the opening chapter, is the fact that the private school is chosen by family patrons because it is thought to be particularly suited to their children's needs, while public school patrons, whether out of choice or necessity, accept whatever education the state, acting through its political subdivisions, manages to deliver in the local school. It can be argued, of course, that public school patrons are not without recourse to change the schools, either through the political process, or through organizations such as the PTA, or by direct "community control." But in practice, these alternatives are not only cumbersome and frustrating, they are largely illusory as long as budgetary control remains centralized in the higher administrative echelons rather than in local hands. Private schools, on the other hand, are under the necessity of competing for the custom of buyers, and this process places the power of decision in the hands of families which function in effect as a school district for the purpose of assigning children to specific schools. And since the "buyer" pays the tuition directly to the school, the budget is locally controlled, with families having a voice, in that support is forthcoming only as long as the family is satisfied with the school.

Trusting the responsibility for decisions about children's education to the user or client rather than to the dictates of a neutral statutory formula raises a fundamental question regarding the fitness of parents to exercise such choices intelligently in the best interests of the child. The answer depends in part on how well the parent is informed about the possible alternatives, and it depends above all upon one's estimate of the common man's conscientiousness and his capacity to reach wise decisions. "What the best and wisest parent wants for his child," John Dewey observed in *The School and Society*, "that must the community want for all its children." But are parents in fact wise enough to be trusted with the decision?

The degree of information available to parents about possible alternatives, as matters stand, is generally inadequate. How much do private school patrons know about what really goes on inside the *public* school? According to the Gallup poll cited earlier the public as a whole admits to knowing very little about the public schools. Lacking reliable descriptions about the schools, most people are left to form impressions on the basis of hearsay and the news coverage of sensational incidents. Newspapers should play a far more prominent part than they do in the vital task of interpreting the public schools to the community. Information about private schools, on the other hand, is available in various handbooks, the most comprehensive of which is Porter Sargent's *A Handbook of*

Private Schools.[12] Books of this kind, though they contain much useful information, are primarily public-relations-oriented and are thus of limited usefulness as guides. However, this cavil is not as serious as it may seem. Most parents, in choosing a school, do not rest the decision on an objective exploration of various alternatives; the choice is usually conditioned *a priori* by religious, social or academic family interests which greatly narrow the range of choice to start with; and the advice of friends, relatives, and perhaps a few of school visits lay the ground work for the final decision.

The question of whether families are capable of making wise choices regarding the education of their children has been raised recently in connection with various voucher plans which propose to eliminate the financial and legal barriers to a wider range of options for all families embracing public as well as private schools. John E. Coons, one of the codrafters of a statutory model of a "family power equalizing" plan,[13] says, "My own prediction is that a family's choices for its children on the whole would be no less appropriate than those neutrally dictated by statutory formula," and he quotes a passage from Blackstone to the effect that "At common law the principle duty of parents to their legitimate children consisted in their maintenance, their protection, and their education. . . . Providence has done it more effectively than any law by implanting in the breast of every parent that natural insuperable degree of affection which not even the deformity of mind, not even the wickedness, ingratitude, and rebellion of children, can totally suppress, or extinguish."[14] E. G. West's *Education and the State*[15] is a sustained argument designed to show, particularly with reference to the experience of the English people, that the parent is generally in a far better position to select an appropriate education for his children than is the political state with its mandated common education for all.

The question of the fitness of private school parents to choose the best education for their children is answered in large measure by the relatively high

---

[12] Subtitled *An Annual Descriptive Survey of Independent Education* (Boston: Porter Sargent, 1971). Two other handbooks are in fairly wide use also: Bunting and Lyon Staff, *Private Independent Schools* (Wallingford, Conn.: Bunting and Lyon Inc., 1971); and C.E. Lovejoy, *Prep School Guide*, 3rd ed. (New York: Simon and Schuster, 1968). Less well known is *The Vincent-Curtis Educational Register* (Boston: Vincent Curtis Co., 1970).

[13] With William Clune and Stephen Sugarman. The plan is briefly described in *Inequality in Education*, nos. 3 and 4 (Cambridge, Mass.: Harvard Center for Law and Education, n.d.), pp. 1–5. The economic and legal aspects of this plan are developed by the same three authors in *Private Wealth and Public Education* (Cambridge, Mass.: Harvard University Press, Belknap Press, 1970).

[14] 1 Blackstone, sec. 447.

[15] London: Institute for Economic Affairs, 1965. See especially chap. 14, "Are Twentieth Century Parents Competent to Choose?"

socioeconomic characteristics and educational levels of private school parents which were reviewed above. Private school parents are generally better informed about the chosen school than are most public school parents about the school their child attends. The typical nonpublic school is founded to serve and is supported by a cohesive ideological community based on religious, social, academic, or racial interests, rather than to serve a neighborhood or district of the general community as the public school does. Moreover, the typical private school is relatively small and familial and thus in a good position to establish direct cordial relations with parents as well as to keep them informed.

Most important of all is the way the felt identification of the family with a close-knit ideological community conditions the choice of this or that nonpublic school. Figure 2 shows that strong majorities of Catholic, Protestant, and independent school parents concur in believing that the private school of their choice offers better training in diligence and study habits, "better" presumably than the alternative public school. But that reason was the only one which drew concurring majorities in all three groups. Other suggested reasons tend to differentiate the church and independent schools along quite characteristic lines. Naturally, the school's religious program counts heavily in the Catholic and Protestant parent choices, noticeably more strongly so among the Protestants; the same holds for the other religio-moral reasons such as "stricter discipline," "values and attitudes or customs closer to those in the home," and "atmosphere free from problems of drugs, delinquency, and turmoil."[16] By contrast, independent school parents put greater stress on reasons having to do largely with the quality of the school's academic program, such as "better teachers," "smaller classes," "greater likelihood of admission to college," and "more academically challenging curriculum."

While Protestant and Catholic school parents are certainly not unappreciative of the importance of an academically challenging curriculum, good teachers, and other indices of superior scholastic quality, they leave no doubt that these are not to be preferred above an education in religiously rooted values. These parents want "a Christ-centered education," and as a teacher at the Delaware County Christian School in Pennsylvania said, "Home, school and church all work together toward the same goal. Parents can feel that the school and church teach the same philosophy that is taught at home." In addition to this positive mutual reinforcement, there is also present in the minds of parents a negative motivation—fear of the competing influences to which their children might be

[16]Parental concern over drug abuse appears to be inversely proportional to the actual use of drugs in the school. Parents in the South, where, at the time of our survey (spring, 1969), drug use appeared to be lowest, showed the highest concern; while the independent school parents of the Northeast, where drug use appeared to be highest, showed the least concern. See chap. 5 for more details.

Figure 2

WHY PARENTS CHOOSE NONPUBLIC SECONDARY SCHOOLS

(Reasons endorsed as important or very important by at least 40 per cent of the parents)

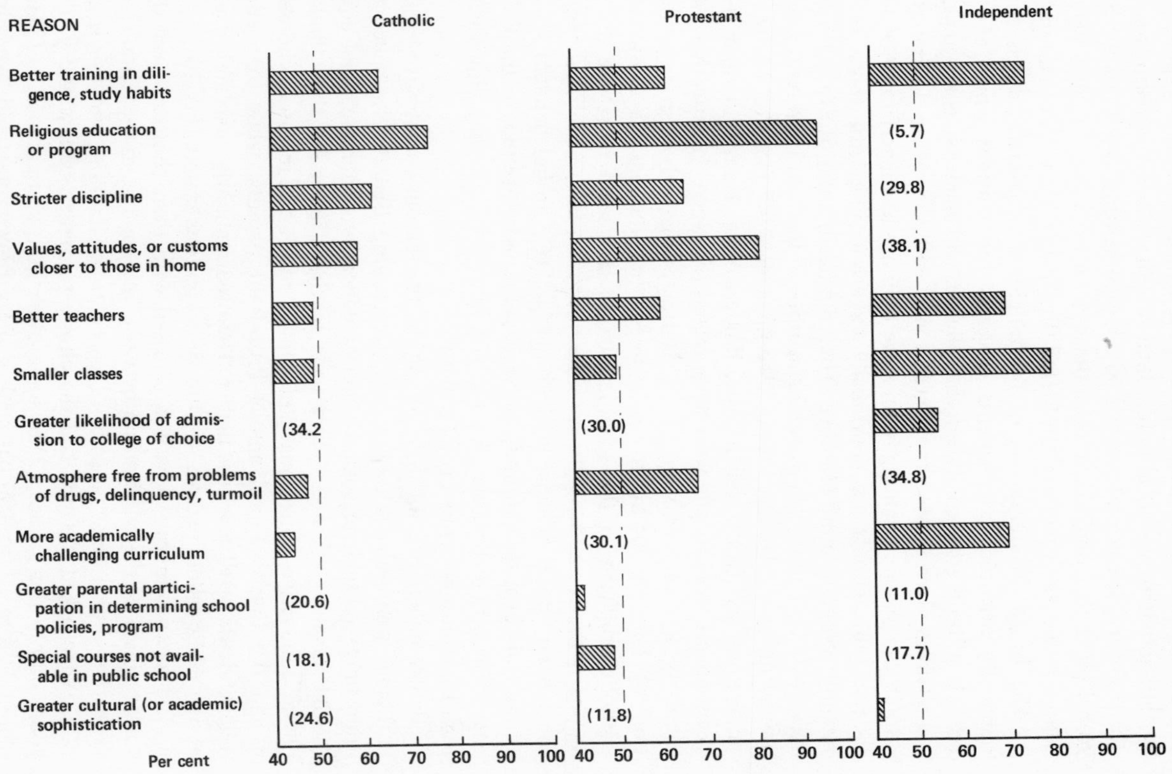

exposed in the public school. The principal of a Christian high school in a large city in the Pacific Northwest showed the visitors a recent newspaper "exposing" certain activities in a local public high school including experiments with sensitivity groups, sex education, and so on, commenting that it was the best promotional piece that could have been devised for his school. And as students in his school noted, their parents considered this "a safe place" for them to be.

The broad differentiation of the religio-moral church schools and the academically oriented independents obscures the tensions which exist in many schools of both groups between the religious and academic goals—tensions which are resolved often in ways that parents view with skepticism or disapproval. Most church schools are straining to improve their academic performance, while many independent schools are continually experimenting with ways to make their religious program more effective. Thus the headmaster of Stony Brook, a Christian School on Long Island belonging both to the NAIS and NACS, writes in his annual report of January, 1969, "We must face the fact that Stony Brook isn't understood by all its constituents. For example, I am told there have always been sincere evangelicals who have feared our open, investigative curriculum." Similarly, a teacher at Monsignor O'Rafferty High School in a middle-class section of Lansing, Michigan, complained that the parents wanted a stronger Catholic emphasis in the school, but did not seem to realize the change in emphasis that came with the introduction of an innovative curriculum. On the other hand, at St. Albans, in Washington, D.C., an independent school with a strong Episcopal background, the teachers noted, "We like to think the parents chose this school because of its Christian values, but they choose it to assure their boys' admission to a good college."

Before concluding this brief survey of the reasons parents give for choosing a particular nonpublic school, it is worth noting that they attached very little importance to such reasons as "better educational buildings and equipment," "social advantages," and "more male teachers." Nor did they think "a more liberal, innovative educational philosophy" much of a reason to choose a school; it had the lowest appeal among Protestant parents, while the Catholics and independents rated it a little higher. The predominantly conservative orientation of nonpublic school parents in educational matters is unmistakable.

The parents appear to be well satisfied with their choices. Given the mutual voluntariness of the relationship between the family and the schools, one would expect to find a large measure of parental satisfaction, and this is indeed the case. When asked, "If you had the choice to make again, would you (1) enroll your child in this school, (2) in some other nonpublic school, or (3) in a public school," from 87 to 100 per cent in the various groups said "yes" to the first option. The Christian Reformed parents turned out to be the only one hundred percenters, equally enthusiastic over their elementary and secondary schools. On the lower side were parents of Jewish and of independent secondary schools of the Northeast, the heartland of those who think otherwise on many school issues, but even in these cases the level of satisfaction was very high. If all the fractional parent minorities having second thoughts followed through on them, the public schools would get slightly over half the elementary school transfers, while other private schools would get the lion's share of the secondary level transfers.

Given this very high level of satisfaction with the school as a whole, what are the parents' opinions regarding aspects of the school that stand in need of improvement? Figure 3 presents the parents' "report card" on the schools' performance in 19 different areas. The greatest measure of dissatisfaction (though it nowhere rises above one out of five parents in any group) is with the following: (1) foreign language instruction; (2) the program in the arts, studio or creative work; (3) vocational, technical and business training; (4) the school's capacity to give the child an exposure to and understanding of the larger world outside the school; (5) the lack of parental voice and influence in determining the school's policies and programs. The relatively high number of "no opinion" responses to the first and third items probably means that the programs in question either do not exist in the school or are so marginal that parents have little or no knowledge of them. The low score they give the arts program reflects, we believe, a serious indictment of the narrow insistence of many schools on verbal-intellectual instruction and neglect of the sensory and affective needs of the developing child. The reaction to the fourth item is ironic in that many parents enroll their children in nonpublic schools *because* they desire a familiar and somewhat protective environment; moreover, although Protestant parents score their schools as satisfactory in this respect, these schools tend to be more separatist than do either the Catholic or independent schools. And as for the responses, or lack of them, to the fifth item they seem to bespeak, besides a sense of dissatisfaction with the fact that they do not have more voice, some uncertainty also on the part of parents who are not sure just what the role of parents should be in shaping the school's policies.

Parents give different reasons for believing the school of their choice to be superior to the public school, depending upon the *kind* of school they have chosen. Church-school parents freely concede that the public schools are in a better position to offer breadth and variety in the curriculum, and that they put the graduate in a stronger position for college admission. But they are convinced that their school offers a superior education in character and values, and that it does a better job in motivating their children for learning over the long run. Independent school parents, on the other hand, are convinced that their school is academically superior to the public school, even though it may lack curricular breadth; and they are persuaded, moreover, that the school increases the

Figure 3

PARENTAL SATISFACTION (OR DISSATISFACTION) WITH VARIOUS ASPECTS OF THEIR CHILDREN'S EDUCATION IN NONPUBLIC SCHOOLS

LEGEND

+ = Greater than average parental satisfaction
− = Greater than average parental dissatisfaction
0 = Greater than average "no opinion" or "no response"

How satisfied are you with	Elementary Cath.	Prot.	Indep.	Secondary Cath.	Prot.	Indep.
The progress your child is making in his studies?	+	+ −	+	+	+ −	+ −
The way your child is getting along in other activities?	+	+	+	+	+	+
The friends that you child has made in school?	+	+	+	+	+	+
The amount of voice and influence you as a parent have in determining school policies and programs?	− 0	+	− 0	− 0	− 0	− 0
The school's effectiveness in giving your child confidence and a sense of his importance as an individual?	+ −	+ −	+	+	+	+
The grading or evaluating policies and practice?	+ −	+	+	+ −	+	+
The general communication between school and parent about your child's education?	+	+	+	+ −	+ −	+ −
Your child's opportunity to develop independence and autonomy while at this school?	+ −	+	+	+	+	+
The guidance and counseling which your child receives?	+ −	+ −	− 0	−	+ −	−
The influence of the school on your child's character and moral values?	+	+	+	+	+	+
The extent to which your child is challenged and stimulated by the school?	+ −	+ −	+ −	+ −	+	+ −
The math and science instruction?	+ −	+ −	+ −	+ −	+	+ −
The English or language arts instruction?	+	+	+	+	+	+
The foreign language instruction?	− 0	− 0	− 0	−	− 0	
The social studies instruction?	0	+	+	+ 0	+ 0	+ 0
The vocational, technical or business training?	− 0	− 0	0	− 0	− 0	0
The teaching skills of your child's teachers?	+	+ −	+ −	+	+ 0	+ 0
The program in the arts, studio or creative work?	− 0	− 0	− 0	− 0	− 0	− 0
The school's capacity to give your child an exposure to and understanding of the larger world outside school?	−	+	−	−	− 0	−
Average percentage for all items	72.1 14.8 13.1	81.2 6.9 12.0	81.6 9.5 8.8	81.6 8.6 9.8	86.6 6.8 6.6	76.2 11.7 12.2

Note: The average percentage for all items is given at the bottom of each column, e.g., parents of children enrolled in Catholic elementary schools showed a 72.1 per cent "satisfactory" rating as the average of all 19 items, compared with 14.8 per cent "unsatisfactory" and 13.1 per cent "no opinion."

student's chance for admission to college. These same parents also believe their school does better than the public school in developing in the student the character traits of independence and autonomy, while the church-school parents think the public school does better in engendering these traits which the orthodox probably regard as of dubious value in any case. And finally, on the question of whether private or public schools are best in fostering democratic attitudes and values, private school parents overall are about evenly divided. It is hard to say to what extent this attitude reflects a measure of parental defensiveness against the charge of divisiveness and counter-democratic influence which is so often laid at the door of private schools by public school advocates. Not to be overlooked, however, is the fact that practicing Christians sincerely believe that democratic ideals rest ultimately on a religious foundation, and that therefore the schools which exert a Christian influence serve the ultimate ends of a democratic society best of all.

Backgrounds of Teachers, Heads, and Trustees

What now of the economic, social, and educational backgrounds of the teachers, heads, and trustees of these nonpublic schools?

Estimates by teachers and heads of the economic circumstances of their parents depend on childhood impressions, so they are only general approximations at best. They clearly reveal, however, a characteristic difference between independent and church-school heads and teachers (see figure 4). As for the teachers, almost half the Catholic and well over half the Protestant teachers grew up in homes where the family income was in the next to lowest quartile of the community, whereas well over half of the independent school teachers came from families whose income was in either the top or second highest quartile. Among the teachers in Jewish schools (not shown in the table), a large majority grew up in families whose income was in the lowest or next to the lowest quartile, the poorest overall of all groups. Yet it turns out that the educational level achieved by these fathers is highest of all.

These characteristic differences are repeated in the economic status of the school heads' childhood home. Only a little over a third of the Catholic heads grew up in a family whose income status was average or better than average compared to that of other families in the community, while the comparable figure for the Protestant groups is even a little lower. In the independent schools, in this respect there is a sharp difference between elementary and secondary school heads. While only about a fourth of the former grew up in families whose income was better than average, two-thirds of the secondary school heads were reared in families so favored—quite the most affluent of all groups. Almost a third of all independent school heads and half of the southern NAIS school

Figure 4

SOCIOECONOMIC PROFILES OF NONPUBLIC SCHOOL HEADS AND FACULTY
(Elementary and Secondary Schools Combined)

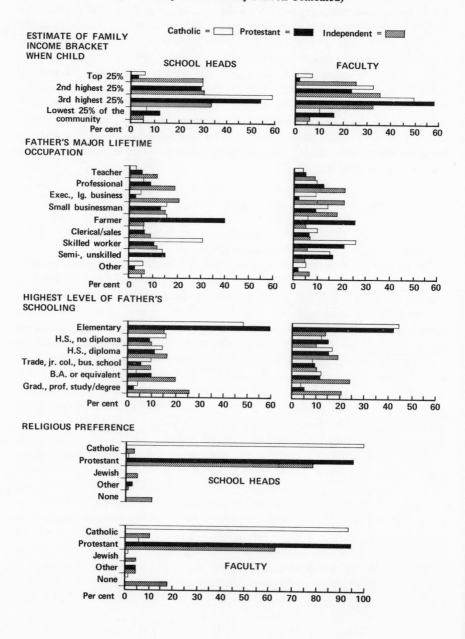

headmasters were brought up in families enjoying an income ranking in the top quarter of the community, while only a negligible fraction of the Catholic heads and not a single Protestant claims so affluent a family background. All told, with the exception noted, nonpublic school leaders have not come from wealthy families.

The differences in the home background of teachers in the various private school groups are indicative also of characteristic occupational, educational, and religious variations among the schools. The Protestant heads and teachers are unique in that a substantial majority were reared on farms or in small-town America. Over 90 per cent of the teachers in Jewish schools, by contrast, are city-bred. Teachers in Catholic schools, however, show a greater diversity in place of origin: about a fourth are from rural areas and small towns, almost half grew up in populous centers of 100,000 or more or in adjacent suburbs, while the remainder come from middle-sized towns. As for the independent school teachers, the largest cluster claims rural and small town homes as their place of origin.

The migratory pattern of school heads also reveals some characteristic differences among the main school groups. Catholic school heads have migrated in substantial numbers from the "home region" in which they grew up (largely North, Midwest or Far West) to the South, while, with few exceptions, heads of Protestant schools have stayed close to their home locality, predominantly the Midwest and Far West. The pattern of independent school heads is mixed, with elementary heads tending to move west, while the secondary school heads turn in great numbers to the Northeast, traditionally the stronghold of independent secondary education.

A word about the economic circumstances of the governing board members. Since many are drawn from the ranks of parents, they generally reflect the income and social patterns of the more affluent parents, but with more trustees richer, and fewer poorer, than the parents overall. But again the characteristic differences among the various school groups come to light. For example, while only a fourth of the Catholic and a fifth of the Protestant board members reported a yearly income in excess of $20,000, just over half the governing board members of NAIS schools enjoy incomes of $50,000 or more.

The educational level attained by the parents of nonpublic school teachers and heads affords an insight into the generational social mobility which these school people have enjoyed. The level of schooling attained by the fathers of school heads and teachers is roughly similar. About half of the fathers of Protestant and Catholic school principals received no more than an elementary school education, while only about one of seven of the independent school teachers' parents failed to go beyond that level. And at the other end of the range, the number of Catholic and Protestant fathers of school heads who achieved a bachelor's, doctorate or professional degree is low, it rises to almost half for the fathers of the independent secondary school heads.

The criticism of private schools over alleged inbreeding is made not only with reference to the clients but to the staff as well. Catholic teachers, it is said, are products of all-Catholic schooling, Lutherans likewise draw from their own schools, independents from theirs, and so on. So sweeping an allegation is not borne out by the facts (see table 3). It is true that over two-thirds of the Catholic school teachers and an even larger percentage of heads attended

Table 3

PUBLIC-PRIVATE EDUCATION OF PRIVATE
SCHOOL CONSTITUENCIES

In per cent

Constituency	All in Public Schools	Mostly in Public Schools	All in Nonpublic Schools
Catholic			
Parents			
Elementary schooling	44.7	5.0	50.3
Secondary schooling	59.0	3.7	37.3
Faculty			
Elementary schooling	27.1	5.5	67.4
Secondary schooling	27.3	2.2	70.5
Head			
Elementary schooling	12.9	9.1	78.0
Secondary schooling	12.9	3.8	83.3
Protestant			
Parents			
Elementary schooling	64.1	5.5	30.3
Secondary schooling	77.7	2.9	19.4
Faculty			
Elementary schooling	43.9	5.8	50.4
Secondary schooling	54.3	2.9	42.9
Head			
Elementary schooling	49.0	4.0	52.0
Secondary schooling	50.0	3.1	46.9
Independent			
Parents			
Elementary schooling	79.5	4.3	16.2
Secondary schooling	69.3	5.4	25.3
Faculty			
Elementary schooling	73.4	5.2	21.3
Secondary schooling	67.7	3.3	29.0
Head			
Elementary schooling	75.7	3.5	20.9
Secondary schooling	54.4	6.1	39.5

Catholic schools. The Protestant teachers and heads, however, are roughly about evenly divided between those who attended Protestant and public schools. As for the independent school teachers, almost three out of four attended public elementary schools, a ratio which diminishes somewhat for the secondary school years as an appreciable but still small number transferred to private schools.

That a substantial majority of Catholic teachers should have taken all or most of their schooling in Catholic schools is to be expected because of the predominance, in the past, of religious on Catholic faculties. Moreover, although the church's plan to establish a religious alternative to public education all the way from kindergarten to graduate school fell far short of fulfillment, Catholic schools were, nevertheless, widely accessible. The education of Protestant school teachers, on the other hand, doubtless reflects the unavailability of Protestant secondary schools in many localities. The fact that so large a majority of independent school teachers and heads attended public schools is noteworthy. However, when the record of nonpublic school attendance by these constituencies is compared with the United States "norm" in this respect over the time span covering the age of these constituents—people ranging in age from the twenties to the sixties—*all* the private school groups show a greater attendance at nonpublic schools than is true of the adult population at large.[17] Moreover, as the involvement with and responsibility for the school increases, from parent to faculty to head, the likelihood of prior nonpublic schooling increases, dramatically so among Catholic and Protestant heads and faculty where, compared with parents, two times as many received nonpublic secondary schooling.

The level of higher education achieved by teachers in the various types of private schools affords still another insight into the basic difference between independent and church-related schools. The independents come closest to making the bachelor's degree a minimum professional requirement. Only about four per cent of their teachers hold no college degree—probably instructors in the arts, foreign languages, or other subjects where talent, experience, and mastery are perhaps more important than a college degree. The percentages of

[17]The national norms are as follows:

	Number	Per Cent of Total
Attendance at nonpublic elementary schools	8,382,023	10.0
Attendance at nonpublic secondary schools	2,506,535	9.0
Total attendance at nonpublic schools	10,888,558	9.7

Note: National figures of private school enrollment taken at ten-year intervals from 1919 to 1950 for elementary schools and from 1929 to 1960 for secondary schools.

113

Protestant, Catholic and Jewish school teachers who hold no college degree are respectively 13, 14 and 21. In the case of Jewish schools, the very demanding program in Hebrew language, religion, and culture calls for rabbinical training rather than a college degree, and that probably accounts for the substantial minority of clerics teaching in those schools.

Independent school faculties are distinguished also by the fact that they list substantially more advanced degrees than do either the Catholic or Protestant staffs, though they are more than matched in this respect by teachers in Jewish schools, who to some extent make up in advanced degrees what they lack in B.A.s on the staff. About 44 per cent of the independent school faculty hold some kind of master's degree as compared to 33 and 26 per cent among Catholic and Protestant teachers. The independent schools have been forehanded also in recruiting holders of the Master of Arts in Teaching, a relatively new degree based on a fresh concept of teacher preparation that suits these schools very well. Some of the wealthier schools provide incentives and financial support also for their teachers to undertake graduate studies, a practice which is to be found among the better church schools also.

As for the education of heads of nonpublic schools, most hold the bachelor's degree, though there are exceptions among Protestant elementary heads, particularly the Seventh-Day Adventists. A slim majority of Catholic elementary school heads hold master's degrees of one kind or another, the most popular being the M.Ed., while among heads of Protestant and independent elementary schools fewer than a third hold an advanced degree, although many heads have taken graduate courses from time to time to meet special needs. On the other hand, a high percentage of secondary school heads hold master's degrees, in some cases more than one kind, but only about one in twenty school heads pursued graduate work through the doctorate.

Ordained ministers are a minority among the heads of schools, particularly at the elementary level. At the secondary level, however, about two-fifths of the Catholic heads are clergymen, while a little over a fourth of the Protestant heads are men of the cloth. Surprisingly, 16.7 per cent of the NAIS schools have clergymen as heads, but the number in the independent school groups as a whole is minuscule.

The educational attainments of governing board members are best compared with those of the parents. The trustees echo, and in some groups quite surpass, the parents in this respect. Whereas the educational level of independent school trustees exceeds that of the parents only slightly, twice as many Protestant trustees (42%) and three times as many members of Catholic governing boards (66%) have completed college at least, compared to the parents who patronize their schools.

The occupational backgrounds of faculty, heads, and trustees closely parallel the other socioeconomic patterns already examined. Only a negligible fraction of the fathers of Catholic and Protestant school heads and teachers were educators or professional men compared with upward of a third of the fathers of independent school heads. The Catholics show the widest occupational diversity, with a range covering professional work and business management but with the largest cluster (41%) in skilled, semiskilled or unskilled labor, with skilled workers making up well over half that total. The background of Protestant teachers and heads is different chiefly in that a fourth give farming as their fathers' occupation; almost half of Lutheran school heads had such a background. The most marked difference in the background of the independent school teachers is that over half their fathers were engaged in professional or business executive work, occupations which also require advanced education and more capital resources.

Noteworthy about the occupational characteristics of the trustees of the nonpublic schools is the fact that the governing boards of the three major school groups have much in common: business and professional people constitute the majority on most boards of Catholic, Protestant and independent schools, particularly so among the independents. "Educator" is given as the occupation of a fourth of the Catholic trustees, while farmers and skilled workers make up a fourth of the Protestant board membership. As one would expect, more women serve on elementary than on secondary boards. Yet taking elementary and secondary boards together, women comprise only 12 per cent of the Protestant membership, whereas almost a third of the Catholic trustees are women. Independent school trustees are split roughly in the ratio of three-quarters male to one-quarter female.

These composite profiles of nonpublic school teachers and heads would be incomplete without some identification of their political views. They differ somewhat, though not very significantly, from those of the parents. About two-thirds of the Catholic teachers identify with the Democrats, much as Catholic parents do, while over two-thirds of the Protestant teachers say they affiliate with the Republicans, which places them right in line with Protestant parents. Independent school teachers show a more balanced distribution, with most, though not a majority, identifying with the Republicans, and with the rest almost evenly divided between Democrats and political independents. Teachers in Jewish schools resemble the Catholics in their political loyalties, though the Jewish group includes a higher percentage of independents, and of all the major groups they show the least sympathy for the Republicans.

In view of the general similarity of the political outlook of parents and teachers in each group, it is interesting to note that parents tend to see their

115

children's teachers as somewhat, though not disturbingly, more politically liberal than themselves. This is true of the attitude of Lutheran parents regarding the teachers in Lutheran secondary schools, as it is of the parents of Episcopal, independent and Catholic school students. The parent-teacher gap is most noticeable in the southern independent schools where only 17 per cent of the parents view themselves as liberal but 32 per cent think the faculty is liberal. Jewish school parents, on the other hand, consider themselves to be much more liberal than Jewish teachers, a relationship which prevails also, but to a lesser degree, between NAIS elementary school parents and teachers.

The political orientation of the school heads is roughly similar to that of parents and teachers. A substantial majority of Catholic heads are Democrats; an equally impressive majority of Protestant heads accept the label of Republican; the independents, true to their name, are a mixture of Republican, Democratic and independent with independent registering the highest affiliation. But such labels, often only nominal and unrevealing, become more meaningful in the light of the way the heads position themselves on a liberal-conservative scale, whence the following blends of political-ideological orientations emerge:

Catholic elementary . . . . Conservative Democratic
Catholic secondary . . . . Liberal Democratic

Protestant elementary . . . . Conservative Republican
Protestant secondary . . . . Conservative Republican

Independent elementary . . . . Conservative Republican
Independent secondary . . . . Liberal independent-Republican

On the question of unionizing nonpublic school teachers, a majority of those who voiced an opinion among Catholic faculty approve, while the Protestant teachers are most firmly opposed. The independents are closer to straddling the issue, but a majority is opposed. The attitudes of the school heads toward unionization of teachers rather surprisingly tends to follow the same patterns as that of the teachers.

From the above profiles of the various private school communities it is clear that any such thing as a distinctive private school subculture embracing all types of private schools has no existence in reality. It may in truth be said that the main school communities—Catholic, Protestant, and independent—have little in common besides having students whose parents have had considerably more formal education than the national average of adult persons and who, in substantial majorities, are educationally ambitious for their children. In other respects, the patterns of differences are striking, the chief one lying in the contrasting socioeconomic backgrounds of the families who support the schools. The

Catholic schools show the greatest social class mixture and in this as well as other respects most closely resemble the urban public schools. While the Protestant schools are chiefly a middle-class phenomenon but with an appreciable lower class complement, the independent schools draw their students predominantly from upper and middle class families with high incomes and more formal education than is to be found among the parents of Protestant and Catholic school children.

How Religious Preferences Affect the Composition of Schools

We turn now to examine briefly the bearing that the religious factor has on the composition of the school's student body and staff. To what extent do religiously affiliated and nonaffiliated private schools limit their enrollments to students of certain denominations, and what specifically is the attitude toward the enrollment, in a given school, of Roman Catholic, Protestant, Jewish or students of other faiths or of no church affiliation?

Naturally, students in Catholic schools come largely from Catholic families, but not wholly so. These schools enroll a small percentage of students from Protestant homes, but virtually none with a Jewish background and few from religiously unaffiliated families, except in the case of recently founded inner-city Catholic schools, where the student body is not uncommonly half or more non-Catholic. Students with non-Catholic backgrounds presumably do not apply to Roman Catholic schools in sizable numbers. Regarding the racial minority enrollment, reported in more detail in a later chapter, Catholic schools enroll an appreciable number of black students, especially in the South. However, some parents of these students list their religious preference as Catholic.

The practice of Protestant schools respecting religious mixture varies. Lutheran and Christian Reformed schools, including members of the NUCS, are attended largely by children of parents affiliated with those deminations. The same is true, incidentally, of Jewish schools. Some Lutheran schools in urban locations also have a significant complement of black Americans, some of these are non-Lutheran while others identify themselves with that faith. A small percentage of parents with children in NACS schools report no religious affiliation, but it is safe to guess that they are Protestant in the most general sense. Among the Protestant groups it is the Episcopal and Friends schools that turn out to be the most latitudinarian. Slightly over a fifth of the enrollment of Episcopal secondary schools is made up of children of other faiths or with no particular religious background.

Parents of children attending independent schools are predominantly Protestant, overwhelmingly so in the South. In schools of this type located in the

Northeast and West, students of Jewish background make up about a fifth of the enrollment, and Catholic students are also well represented; the Protestant matriculants are reduced proportionally, though they are still well in the majority. In the South, however, only a negligible percentage of independent school students have a Jewish background. All in all, the number of independent school students whose parents claim no religious affiliation never rises over a tenth—additional proof, if any were needed, of the pervasiveness of religious identification, however tenuous it may be, among parents who enroll their children in these largely nondenominational schools.

Parents react in various ways to this religious mixture, or lack of it, in the schools. Regarding the admission of students or the employment of teachers of other faiths, independent school parents express few if any restrictions except that a negligible number favor excluding Jewish students and teachers, and a faint trace has reservations about employing Catholic teachers. If these responses are taken at face value, it appears that the old residual anti-Semitic and anti-Romanist prejudices have relaxed their grip in this sector of private education, where a quarter of a century ago both were strong. Parents of Catholic students do not quite match that degree of tolerance, but they strongly favor accepting both Protestant and Jewish students and teachers, though they show a slightly greater receptivity to Protestants than to Jews, and are more favorably disposed to students rather than teachers of those faiths. The Catholic parents' willingness to accommodate students and teachers of other denominations suggests the degree to which these schools have become ecumenicized, a point which is confirmed by the eagerness of many Roman Catholic educators and parents to accept state aid, even at the cost of submitting to a measure of state control over the "secular" part of the school program. By contrast, Protestant school parents, while favoring the admission of Jewish and Roman Catholic students, are largely opposed to employing either Jewish or Catholic teachers.

It is apparent, then, that while the church schools continue to limit admission largely to children coming from families of the same faith, yet the barriers are lowered somewhat, particularly in schools of churches that are most susceptible to the new ecumenical spirit that is abroad. We shall return to this point in later chapters, since it has a direct bearing on the contribution which the church schools can make to the education of black and other minorities, and a bearing also on the issue of state aid to nonpublic schools.

5

The Emerging Student Outlook

From Complacency to Unrest

The abrupt change in student attitudes from the complacency of the nineteen fifties to the militancy of the late sixties is to adults the world over one of the most arresting and perplexing phenomena of our time. It is the more dramatic because it came so suddenly. A widely read study summarized the changing values of college students in the 1950s as follows:

A dominant characteristic of students in the current generation is that they are *gloriously contented* both in regard to their present day-to-day activity and their outlook for the future. Few of them are worried—about their health, their prospective careers, their family relations, the state of national or international society or the likelihood of their enjoying secure and happy lives. They are

[1] "You Have to Grow Up in Scarsdale to Know How Bad Things Really Are," *New York Times Magazine*, April 27, 1969, p. 125.

119

supremely confident that their destinies lie within their own control rather than in the grip of external circumstances.[2]

In view of the surging discontent that characterized the school and college worlds of the sixties, the above quotation seems scarcely credible. Yet the statement was a faithful reflection of the outlook of college students as it was perceived in the middle 1950s. At that time no one could have foreseen that the halcyon student outlook was a passing phase that had already matured and reached the point of demise. As Hegel said about larger, cosmological concerns: The owl of Minerva launches its flight only as the evening sun is setting.

The shift in the student outlook from the "glorious contentment" of the fifties to the questioning, unrest, and militancy of the sixties is a familiar story to everyone over thirty. The new student movement teethed itself in the battles over civil rights, which ended, so it seemed at the time, in an exhilarating victory. In those first skirmishes the students enjoyed the sympathy and encouragement of an older public which was eager to expiate a guilt-laden conscience. Student activists saw themselves as the vanguard pressing for national reforms long overdue. The prompt passage of civil rights legislation and the promise of a concerted war on poverty lent support to the electrifying hope that the time for remedying basic and longstanding injustices was at hand at last.

But the events that followed quickly blunted the newborn optimism. The war in Vietnam, the next target of student involvement, brought the activists up hard against a deeply divided public opinion and the bristling police and military power of the government establishment. Day-to-day developments made it painfully clear, moreover, that the new legal guarantees of civil rights, far from remedying ancient injustices promptly, succeeded only in exposing the abyss of the problems of Black America, a problem that could not be remedied by legislation alone because it called for profound psychological changes in the hearts and minds of white people, as well as fundamental political and economic alterations in the social order. Moreover, the determined self-reliance of black student activists, causing them to spurn the help proffered by white cohorts eager to enlist in their cause, was another distressing development. The war on poverty, too, begun on a wave of hope and optimism, turned into a frustrating wrangle. These events, transpiring against a background of anxiety over the many confusing signposts to utopia and to oblivion in a technological world adrift, led the hard core of student radicals to the conclusion that the modern establishment itself is on trial, that there is no hope short of "changing the System." Though an alarmed older generation is frequently assured that the radicals are only a minute fraction of all college and school students, the militant

[2] Philip E. Jacob, *Changing Values in College: An Exploratory Study of the Impact of College Teaching* (New York: Harper, 1957), p. 1 (emphasis in the original).

stance of the few has nevertheless induced a mood of alienation which deeply affects the outlook of the whole youth population.

While college and university campuses were the primary scene of these startling developments, there were swift repercussions in public and private schools. The time lag between the onset of disturbances on college campuses and their echoes in the schools grew steadily shorter. Instant transmission by television quickly propagates every fresh departure from yesterday's norms, styles, slogans and causes—every novelty of the inventive youth culture. But the college happenings that the news media exploit so eagerly reverberate in the schools only selectively. School boys and girls are a little younger and closer to home still, so their outlook and reactions to events differ in certain respects from those of their collegiate brothers and sisters. They are less inclined to protest against the large social, economic and political injustices in the world at large, for at this stage in life they are seeking to identify themselves, to build a bridge between their private and social worlds, and to frame their own personal declaration of independence from adult authority in the home, the school, the community. And in consequence they tend to be highly sensitive to plans or expectations that prolong their dependence or act as a brake on their progress to independent manhood or womanhood.

In the school world it is the unrest and rebellion in public high schools that have been making most of the headlines, but private school students too are caught up in the new vivid awareness of a world in the throes of a revolutionary change. Yet unrest in private schools has reached nothing like the degree of turbulence in the high schools, either in militant dissatisfaction with the educational process or the feeling of profound disenchantment with American society and its institutions. Though there is ample evidence of underlying frustrations and tensions among private school students, they result only rarely in overt protest, demonstration, or militancy. The reason appears to be the smallness, the familial atmosphere, the selectivity of most private schools, and, in the church schools, the adherence to religious principles as guides to conduct—conditions which are conducive to good communication and acceptance of mutual responsibilities, based on trust and warm, supportive human relationships.

We shall be concerned in this chapter with how students in various types of private schools—church-related and independent—react to their school world and to the adult authority in it, discussing some of their grievances and problems, their career hopes and outlook.

The Students on Schools, Morals, and Life Goals

It should be remembered that we are dealing with a group of young people coming predominantly from good homes, with parents educated well above the level of the national average and educationally ambitious for their children.[3] All but a tenth of the students come from families in which religious beliefs and values are influential, and the concern for the transmission of a special religious heritage is high among the reasons why they chose a private school. And even among the remaining tenth—those who tend to give greater weight to academic than to religious concerns—the fact that a predominantly secular private school can, if it so desires, instill respect for religious faith and principles is an added attraction to many.

Based on the school heads' estimate of the average SAT scores of seniors and the juniors' report of their own verbal and mathematical test scores, they are a highly educable group that should, in the normal course of events, produce more than its share of leaders. The test-wise and relatively highly selected independent school students outdistance those in most church schools in this respect, chiefly because they come from families which have long been education-oriented for social, occupational and cultural reasons. The youngsters in the church schools, we suspect, are not intrinsically less bright, but they are intellectually somewhat less sophisticated. What this signifies educationally is that the selected independent school graduates gravitate more readily toward the Ivy League colleges,

[3] Regarding our student respondents, several facts should be noted. The large majority (83.2 per cent) were by design eleventh graders, and 85.6 per cent were between ages 16 and 17. They were almost exactly evenly divided by sex. But significant differences in the composition of the student sample in the various types of schools should be noted. (All figures in the tables below are percentages.)

	Catholic	Protestant	Independent
Boys	36.3	43.9	56.7
Girls	63.7	56.1	43.3

These variations have a bearing on the student responses at certain points. It is generally assumed that girls tend to be somewhat more docile and can be expected to reply differently from boys to questions about life choices and career plans.

Most (56.1 per cent) of the respondents were in coeducational schools:

	Catholic	Protestant	Independent
All-boy schools	15.7	2.0	40.9
All-girl schools	30.6	9.8	20.9
Coeducational schools	53.7	88.2	39.2

The independent group has a larger percentage of boarding students than the others. Boarders are more prone to express grievances because of their total immersion in a confining environment to which they become highly sensitive.

	Catholic	Protestant	Independent
Boarding students	15.5	20.2	35.1
Day students	84.5	79.8	64.9

while a fairly high proportion of the church school young people matriculate in either their own denominational or in state colleges.

What do these relatively favored young people want of their school? Judging from their reactions to a list of six possible educational outcomes or goals (see figure 5), these youthful nonpublic school students say they want most of all to have the school assist them "to learn to think clearly and independently," and they care least of all about "developing the skills necessary to earn a good living and compete." This outcome is as surprising in its strong endorsement of a purely intellectual, academic goal as it is in rejecting another that many adults regard as one of the chief and essential aims of education. While the reasons why they chose "thinking clearly and independently" over the other distinctly academic goal—"gaining in understanding of the main areas of knowledge"—can only be guessed at, conversations with students lead us to believe that they appreciate the general usefulness of learning to think clearly for all life situations, while "the main areas of knowledge" option smacks of curricular requirements concerned more with the acquisition of knowledge rather than its use, and justified by the abstract ideal of "general education" which has only a limited appeal to the young.

Students generally assigned a low place to the presumed nonacademic school goals, the lowest place on the totem pole being reserved for "learning to make a living." It is not surprising to see the relatively affluent independent school students treating this aim so cavalierly, but that the still upwardly mobile Protestant and Catholic students should so regard it is a surprise. However, one should not press this explanation too far. The students have better reason than anyone else to be aware that most of these schools, as now constituted, do not in fact attempt to develop the vocational skills, other than proficiency in basic communication, that would enable students to earn a living. In other words, many upwardly mobile young people who are quite innocent of any antiestablishment learnings, and they are unquestionably in the majority, expect to learn the needed vocational skills elsewhere than in the academic secondary schools.

Another presumed nonacademic goal—"becoming an interesting individual to yourself and others"—evidently does not so much differentiate students in various types of schools, as it distinguishes the Cavaliers from the Roundheads in otherwise fairly homogeneous student bodies in the same type of school. For example, for many Catholic students that option was a clear second choice, but even more in the same group chose this as their second least valued goal. The Protestant students, however, strongly reject it, while among independent school students this goal, with its egotistical-hedonistic overtones, is a clear second choice.

The goal that sharply differentiates the Protestant school students from all others is the importance they attach to "developing sound moral standards and

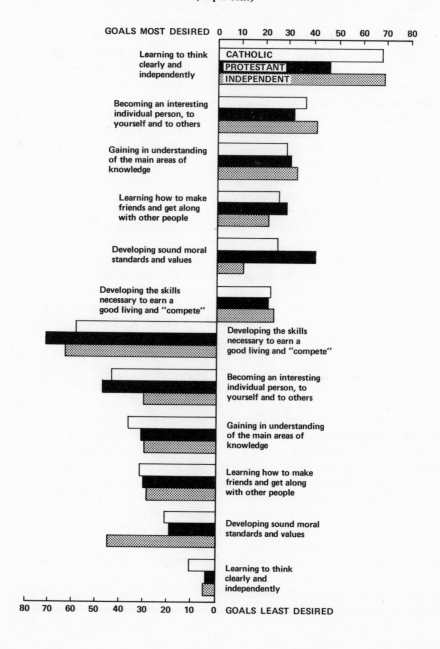

Figure 5

WHAT THE STUDENTS WANT FROM THEIR SCHOOLS
(Students were asked to check the two goals they
"most" desired and the two they "least" desired)
(In per cent)

values." When we consider that these are predominantly junior-year students, it is remarkable that so many Protestant youngsters agree with their parents in assigning so high a place to moral education. Catholic students attach much less importance than do the Protestants to this end in this context of educational goals, but in another connection, in comparing the advantages that nonpublic and public schools offer, Catholic students cite stronger moral education as the greatest benefit that Catholic schools confer.[4] By contrast, independent school students, in any and all contexts, consistently assign only a small role to moral education.

Nowhere is the differentiation of the church-related schools and the nonsectarian independent schools sharper than in this matter of student attitudes toward moral education. The close association of religion and ethics in most of the church schools leads in many cases to a predominantly prescriptive, authoritarian approach to moral conduct, under which some students chafe while a majority appears to accept the state of affairs, and some defend it vigorously. Prescriptive, Bible-centered ethics is characteristic particularly of the Protestant schools, especially those of the Calvinist and evangelical persuasion, though it is also observable in Lutheran and to some extent in the stricter Catholic schools. At its worst, school principals, often with the consent of parents and sometimes after consultation with students, see fit to legislate on all the minutiae of the student's daily deportment, dress, and manners, all incorporated in thick, detailed "student handbooks" wherein virtually nothing is left to the student's imagination or his "still, small voice." But at its best, the practice of Christian ethics helps students, teachers, and principals not only to choose the "right" course, but to put their hearts into it, and generates a community humbly dedicated to the pursuit of justice and truth.

Though few of the church schools show overt signs of student unrest, the subsurface tension between the school's prescriptive ethics and the desire of students for more freedom and personal responsibility frequently surfaced during interviews with students. "Authority is God-given," said a teacher at a Christian Academy (NUCS) in the Philadelphia area. "Thus it is our duty to obey authority. The rebel is the person who has not yet been brought under the Holy Spirit." This classic Puritan precept was being quietly questioned by students in the school who were forming their own views. "Since the first grade," said a junior, "I've been in a Christian home and a Christian school and doing a lot in a Christian church. I'm just beginning to get out now—to reach out. It's hard to wait so long." And then she added, "Yet, I'll probably go to a Christian college because there are so many problems in the world, you need all the Christian

---

[4] See Andrew M. Greeley and Peter N. Rossi, *The Education of Catholic Americans* (Chicago: Aldine Publishing Co., 1966), especially chaps. 6 and 7.

buttressing you can get." But a classmate who had reached out on his own initiative to work in a ghetto recreational program was more skeptical. "They're trying to protect us from being exposed to the outside world," he said. "They figure that if they teach you the right way, you'll be all right. But it could be that we're evading the real problems that we'll get into." Some church school teachers and principals welcome this "reaching out." "There's a healthier attitude to us sisters," said the principal of a Catholic girls' day school in Pennsylvania in describing today's teacher-student relations. "We used to be looked at without question, as law. Now there's an opportunity to talk and question and explore things with us." But for every church school where such a new spirit has taken hold, there are others where students not only do not complain about the strictness of behavior codes but demand with the brutal consistency of the young that they be enforced uniformly and firmly, even though their teachers are disposed to relax the barriers a bit. As a junior girl in a Lutheran high school in St. Louis said, "The school should be more like a school."

Independent school students, on the other hand, have little doubt that they believe the school's main business is academic and not moral education. Whereas most Catholic school students maintain that moral education is the chief advantage that their school offers compared to the public school, most independent school students put moral education far down on the list of potential advantages offered by the private school. Do they mean that they think poorly of the moral education their school provides, or that it is not properly the school's business, or that moral education is really not important? Conversations with these students about drug abuse, cheating, and problems of racial and social justice show them to be often advanced and penetrating in discussing the moral dilemmas of school life and in the world at large. They do care. What they dislike intensely is the moral ambiguity and hypocrisy, the double-talk of public relations that they encounter in school life and in public life, and the fact that they continue to be treated as children who have to be guided along the path of rectitude by adults who often seem not to practice what they preach. So it is not that they believe moral education to be superfluous, but that they do question the effectiveness of the school as a moral educator.[5] The problem is particularly acute in the traditional boarding schools where the students speak of being "cabined, cribbed and confined" in an artificial environment under the watchful eye of masters standing *in loco parentis.*

[5] A study including students in a public and independent school consortium found that "the majority of students said their school had *either* hindered their progress *or* neither hindered nor helped in two areas: developing skills useful for many kinds of jobs, and learning how to make better ethical or moral distinctions." Leonard L. Baird, "Schools in Transition: Report on the Trial Administration of Questa II" (Andover, Mass.: Secondary School Research Program, 1970), p. 34.

Despite these and other complaints which we shall examine later in this chapter, the level of satisfaction that students find in nonpublic schools is extraordinarily high. The great majority is convinced that they receive more individual attention than they would in the public school and that the teachers really care about them. While they recognize that the public schools often have superior facilities, equipment, and a broader, more comprehensive curriculum, nevertheless they believe their school to be academically superior. The vast majority of Catholic, Protestant, and independent school students who were interviewed and canvassed agreed in this respect. "Public schools sometimes have better facilities," said a student at the John Carroll School in Alabama, "but we have a great principal, and the school is small and he listens." About seven out of ten students in both the church-affiliated and independent schools rank the education they are receiving in basic studies—math, science, English, and social science—as either good or excellent. The satisfaction in foreign language instruction is somewhat lower, fluctuating from school to school, but remains generally high. They think well also of the guidance and counseling they receive. But the level of satisfaction drops sharply in respect to the program in the arts, notably in the church schools, indicative of the fact that offerings in art are either poor or nonexistent in many schools. In such imponderables as the school's effectiveness in stimulating the student to learn, encouraging him to think for himself, and helping him gain confidence and a sense of importance as an individual, most students rate their schools good to excellent. Students in the Northeast are consistently more critical of their schools than are those in the South, despite the fact that the institutions they attend include elite schools of considerable stature commanding high respect in academic circles.

However, a different and less reassuring light is shed on the students' rather generous appraisal of their schools by the reaction to the statement, "Except for getting a diploma or getting into college, I don't see much point to the work I am asked to do in this school." Roughly about a fifth of the church school students and over a fourth of independent school students agree with the statement. It suggests that, although these students generally think well of their school, a substantial minority sees "school" as a rather tedious means to an end, and that it may be the concept of school itself, rather than their particular school, that they are unhappy about.

The texture of the students' hopes and aspirations for later life is indicated by what these junior-year young people have in mind as life goals, selected from the following list:

1. To earn a decent living.
2. To achieve wealth and power.
3. To have a happy marriage and family life.

4. To develop my own interests and abilities to the fullest wherever this may lead.
5. To enjoy the pleasures of life.
6. To work for the improvement of society and the benefit of other people.
7. To become well known and respected in my community, work, or profession.

The striking feature of the goals these students choose (see table 4) is the fact that they are reaching primarily for personal happiness and a life of social service, rather than for power, riches, fame, or success. At this stage of their lives they idealistically seek wholesome, largely noncompetitive forms of self-realization such as a happy married life, opportunity to develop their own interests and abilities, and to work for the improvement of society. Students in all school groups overwhelmingly spurn the goal "to achieve wealth and power," and they show little, though varying, interest in entering the competitive business or financial race, in becoming well known or "successful," or in living a life devoted to pleasure-seeking. The arrival of the consumer culture has apparently freed most of these young people from the financial anxiety or economic ambition

Table 4

LIFE GOALS OF STUDENTS
(Listed in order of frequency of response)[a]

In per cent

Catholic (Boys, 36.3; Girls, 63.7)	Protestant (Boys, 43.9; Girls, 56.1)	Independent (Boys, 56.7; Girls, 43.3)
To have a happy marriage and family life (53.8)	To have a happy marriage and family life (68.8)	To have a happy marriage and family life (50.9)
To develop my own interests and abilities to the fullest wherever this may lead (53.8)	To work for the improvement of society and the benefit of other people (59.5)	To develop my own interests and abilities to the fullest wherever this may lead (50.6)
To work for the improvement of society and the benefit of other people (49.7)	To develop my own interests and abilities to the fullest wherever this may lead (36.3)	To work for the improvement of society and the benefit of other people (38.1)
To earn a decent living (17.6)	To earn a decent living (17.7)	To enjoy the pleasures of life (24.2)
To become well known and respected in my community, work or profession (12.5)	To become well known and respected in my community, work or profession (8.4)	To become well known and respected in my community, work or profession (17.6)
To enjoy the pleasures of life (9.3)	To enjoy the pleasures of life (7.4)	To earn a decent living (12.9)
To achieve wealth and power (3.2)	To achieve wealth and power (1.9)	To achieve wealth and power (5.7)

[a]Respondents were instructed to choose two goals only.

which was normal a generation ago. What many see as a growing privateness among the young may be reflected in the relatively low value they place on being "known and respected." While concerned with helping their fellows, they appear to be looking for a humane, live-and-let-live life built on personal ties and sharable values, a life idea that would obviate in their adulthood the invidious competition and comparisons that plague them in adolescence.

The students in the church-related schools appear to be somewhat more altruistically inclined than those in the independent schools, who are appreciably more status- and success-oriented. Thus, Catholic and Protestant school students assign a higher priority to "working for the improvement of society and the benefit of other people," but very few opt for "enjoying the pleasures of life" as a life goal; while the independent school students give the former goal a somewhat lower and the latter goal a somewhat higher priority. Respect, wealth, and power also mean more to the independent student since many come from families where those goals are imbedded in family traditions. These differences are not great, perhaps, but, like the weatherman, they show which way the wind is blowing.

Young people today find themselves in an adult American society which appears to them to be increasingly committed to material, commercial values and status anxiety, while it professes, at the same time, the highest loyalty to the ideals of justice, equality, and freedom. Endowed with a large measure of youthful idealism, they view askance the adult competitive world of money and status, with each competing group—capital, labor, technicians, specialists, intellectuals—seeking to increase their income and prestige at the expense of the general well-being. Young people see more quickly than their elders that the bright future that scientific expertise was supposed to bring is not materializing. They are the first to sense acutely the serious threat of a retrogressive destruction of the environment and the dehumanization and depersonalization of life.

And yet, despite the generation gap that the students' low-toned life goals may indicate, there appears to be no serious communications gap with their parents. For the overwhelming majority of students the parents are the strongest influence; Catholic, Protestant and independent students agree in this respect. Friends and fellow students are a strong second among persons who are admired and influential, followed somewhat more distantly by the admired teachers. Clergymen are a distant last, for the independent school student especially, though they exert a somewhat stronger influence among Protestant students. Given the generally good family backgrounds of most of these young people, it should come as no surprise that they are confident that they have as much opportunity to get ahead in life as the majority of Americans. The characteristically critical skepticism of the independent school students of the Northeast causes them to feel slightly less bullish about their chances, but their counter-parts in the South are unmitigated optimists.

However much students in various private schools differ in family back-ground, ethnic origin, economic level, or intellectual aptitude, they are remark-ably similar in their career ambitions. The occupations favored by the largest number are not those that were popular even a few decades ago. Reflecting the current youthful antimaterialism and apparent scorn of conventional economic success, the respondents give careers in business management, whether large or small, very short shrift; such a career appeals to less than one per cent of the Protestant students and to only 12 per cent of the independent school students, with the Catholic students in between. There is small comfort in these figures for future business interests who might hope to recruit executives from this rela-tively bright pool of the youth population. The occupational shift indicated by the plans of these young people is heavily toward education and the professions. Catholic students lead with just half having such career goals, while Protes-tant and independent school students are not far behind.

The School Environment: Stress, Grievances, and Other Problems

Although many nonpublic-school students find general satisfaction in their program of studies, other aspects of life in the school and the school environ-ment draw complaints and criticisms. The first of these concerns is the competi-tion and stress that became increasingly noticeable in the late fifties and early sixties, as the schools responded to the chorus of critics who maintained that they did not sufficiently challenge the student intellectually, and what they offered was too easy and contained too many "frill" subjects. With the public schools bearing the brunt of the clamor, by the mid-fifties both public and private schools were taking thought of ways and means to develop a more demanding, tightly-paced curriculum in basic academic subjects. Though the *Sputnik* launching was widely credited with providing the needle of reform, the process had begun some years before. First the advanced placement program and later the Conant study of the public schools spurred the schools to extend the quality and range of the "hard" academic subjects and to make the students work harder. The focus was on the academically talented and the manpower needs of the military-industrial complex of an advanced technological society.

But once the leading schools and colleges were in hot pursuit of academic excellence, a new issue emerged: Were the new demands so rigorous as to inter-fere with the balanced development of the total personality of some, perhaps many, students? Was *human* excellence being sacrificed in the race to achieve academic excellence and trained, specialized manpower? Had the schools, abandoning the traditional goal of preparation for life, trapped students in a regimen of systematic age-grading, testing, pitilessly competitive college prepping and rigid credentialism?

To ascertain how private school students feel about this aspect of schooling we queried them about their study loads, the grading system, pressure for grades and for college admission, and related attitudes and practices that potentially generate special stress.

With respect to the student work load we found little evidence suggesting that most students in any of the school groups, except a substantial number in the NAIS schools of the Northeast, feel greatly overworked. One would think it not unreasonable for secondary school students to spend as much as two hours a day, five days a week, on homework. Yet only a little over half of the Catholic boys and girls and even fewer Protestant students say they study as much as from ten to fifteen hours or more per week outside of class. Independent school students, in particular those in the Northeast, do more homework, most students maintaining that they work at least ten to fifteen hours, and some claiming they study from fifteen to over twenty-five hours weekly. With few exceptions southern schools appear to make lighter academic demands on their students than do those of other regions.

But homework is only one measure. Although the church school students spend less time on homework, they tend to spend more in class. It should be kept in mind that most church schools add religious education to the usual academic curriculum, thus making for a longer day. Jewish schools, for example, require a heavy program in Hebrew religion, language, and culture, in addition to a basic secular academic curriculum. Thus, there appears to be little or no significant difference in the students' total work load in the various schools, except as noted.

Most students themselves think the total work load expected of them is about right, though about one in five thought it was too much, a feeling that was particularly evident among students in Lutheran schools. By contrast, about three out of ten Jewish school students think not enough is expected of them!

What about family pressure to make good marks and excel? On the whole, complaints about family stress on obtaining good grades or winning acceptance by a college of their choice are remarkably few among students in church-related schools. Catholic students are the most relaxed, with fewer than a fifth saying that such pressure is excessive. It rises to a little over a fifth among Protestant students. But over a third of the boys and girls in independent schools experience the urging and cajoling from home as either "too much" or "far too much." The latter figure seems somewhat higher than is desirable, especially when one remembers that the responding students are largely juniors, still a year away from the zero hour in the competitive college admissions race.

Another sensitive indicator of academic stresses and strains is the student attitude toward grades and the grading system. Most private school students appear to be relatively complacent regarding this issue, which continues to be a lively topic of debate on many college campuses. A comfortable majority of students in the church schools favor retention of the conventional letter grades instead of a new scheme such as some form of honors-pass-fail, or teachers' comments instead of grades. But about a fifth of the students in the more highly competitive independent schools in the Northeast and West lean toward teacher comments in lieu of grades. Whatever the students' feelings may be about grades and the grading system, these respondents are not about to wage a major war on this aspect of their schooling. The sharp controversies about grades on college campuses appear to have had as yet only slight repercussions in private schools.

All in all, the picture that emerges from these responses is one of general student satisfaction with their programs rather than of tense, overworked boys and girls who chafe under the goads of competition. The students in church-related institutions reveal a more relaxed attitude than do those in the independent schools, especially in the meritocratic schools of the Northeast, where the tension is considerable. While those who believe the stress to be excessive are in the minority, their number is too substantial to be ignored.

The intricacies and contradictions of the student's experience of school life, so well portrayed in J. D. Salinger's *Catcher in the Rye*, are nowhere so obvious as in the phenomenon of student unrest which has so alarmed and perplexed adult society. Of overt confrontations, demonstrations, and militancy there has been relatively little on private school campuses. But though the visitor finds them outwardly calm, he soon learns from talking with school heads, teachers, and students and by scanning student newspapers that some schools are seething with unrest beneath the surface. That there are fewer such in 1971 than in 1968–69 is a gratifying result which is attributable, we believe, to imaginative responses by some schools to the deeper sources of student discontent.[6] But in schools that stress student selectivity and scholastic achievement particularly, students continue vigorously to question "the school's authority, its standards, rules and traditions," as a housemaster noted, "demanding justification in all areas of school life, and resisting the old take-it-for-granted, if-you-say-so-it-must-be-true-Sir line of non-reasoning."[7] Student unrest in schools and colleges differs chiefly in the degree of boldness and assurance that the more mature

[6] See Alan R. Blackmer, *An Inquiry into Student Unrest in Independent Secondary Schools* (Boston: National Association of Independent Schools, 1970), pp. 33–72.

[7] *The Lawrence* (Lawrenceville School, N.J.), June 9, 1969.

college student brings to his radical stance. But the seeds are germinating in many a school boy and girl, awaiting only the freer environment of the college or university to spring into flower.

Three points stand out in surveying the nature and sources of student discontent with their schools. The first is the relative uniformity or lack of wide variation among the grievances voiced most frequently by students in Catholic, Protestant, and independent schools. While there are significant and predictable variations in the frequency with which certain grievances are expressed by young people in the religious as compared with the purely academic schools, the range of fluctuation remains, with minor exceptions, astonishingly narrow.[8] The second point is the widespread faculty awareness of the extent of student grievances in their schools. In some cases, the teachers rate the frequency of expressed grievances higher than the students do. The third point is the distressingly small number of parents who are aware of the grievances that their children express in considerable volume. Either the children do not gripe at home or the parents do not listen.

Among the grievances voiced most frequently, "lack of student voice or influence in shaping school rules and policy" heads the list. Roughly half or more of Catholic, Protestant, and independent school students vent this criticism, with the independents in the van, and with strong faculty confirmation that the complaint is justified backing up the students in all groups (see figure 6). Student complaints and school conflicts regarding "overly strict regulations of dress codes and hair styles" continue to make news in many communities; it is a frequently vented student grievance in all types of private school, with the young people attending independent schools again in the forefront. But this grievance has less support from both faculty and students as "justified" than has the issue about "student voice" in school policies. It suggests that a vocal minority of students wants more freedom of dress, but that for the majority it is not a burning issue. As for the parents, they hear very little about it, and those that do hear have precious little sympathy. There is unfortunately no way of determining a baseline which would enable one to discern, with reference to this question, whether the student protest in this or that school is made against a highly repressive, authoritarian school administration or a tolerant, permissive one. But taking the results as a whole, there is little question that in most private schools the well-scrubbed, neat, and conforming youngster is favored overwhelmingly,

---

[8] There are, however, somewhat larger variations within each group, both regionally and denominationally. Generally speaking, they follow the familiar pattern which finds students in Northeast NAIS schools more prone to complain and criticize than those in, say, southern schools or those with a Protestant fundamentalist religious affiliation. Likewise, boarding school students tend to be more critical than those in day schools. See Blackmer, *Student Unrest*, table A, p. 86.

Figure 6

STUDENT GRIEVANCES AS HEARD BY
STUDENTS (S), FACULTY (F), AND PARENTS (P)

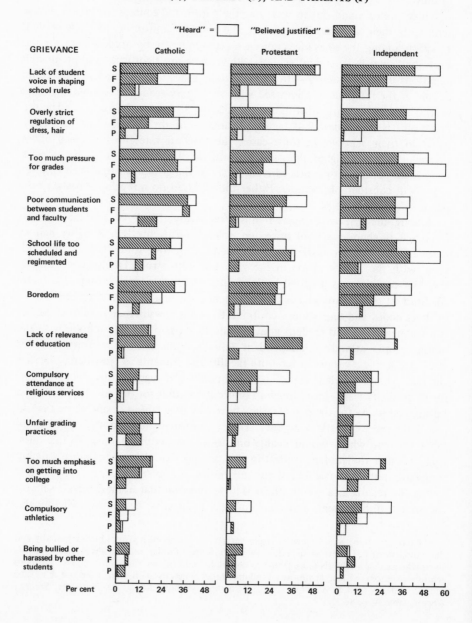

and that the would-be barefoot, hairy, bearded rebel must run the gamut of varying degrees of disapproval.

Fairly high on the list of student complaints is just plain boredom. Grievances centering in "lack of voice," "poor communication," "too much pressure for grades," and "too much regimentation" or "lack of relevance" are part of the stock in trade of today's impatient young, though the volume of dissatisfaction expressed on these counts is far too strong to be ignored. But educators and parents should note with some concern the fact that well over a fourth of the students in all three school groups believe that the complaints about boredom are justified and that, moreover, about a fifth of Catholic and independent school teachers and a fourth of their Protestant colleagues agree with that judgment. In this case even the parents of Catholic and independent school students show some concern, though Protestant parents appear to be largely unnoticing or unconvinced.

As in the experience of American colleges and universities, student discontent, apart from the demands of black students who present a special case, appears to correlate fairly closely with scholastic aptitude and with prime educational and economic advantages. The brighter the students, the more critical they tend to be. As a general rule, students in schools practicing highly selective admissions are more prone to disenchantment than those who enroll in schools that have no such pretensions. As we have seen, a significant number of those in the elite independent boarding schools of the Northeast are restive and questioning. What are their main complaints? Essentially, they are of two main kinds and spring from two sources.

First, these students quarrel with the older generation about the central purpose of education. To many an intelligent school boy or girl the goals of college preparatory schools today are too limited and narrow, too dominantly scholastic. This student seriously questions whether the standard academic education of today is worth it. What such students seek is an education directed toward the heart and senses as well as toward the intellect. They wish to reinstate the historic emphasis on the achievement of *human* excellence, of which academic excellence is only a part. They wish to be addressed as whole human beings, and so they are concerned about the effect of the school environment and its impact upon the life of the student.

The second cause of complaint is inherent in the boarding school situation as traditionally conceived—a sheltered home away from home, with life lived in a total educational hothouse. Whereas in earlier times boarding life was looked on as an adventure and an opportunity, today's young people, conditioned to look repeatedly for experiences in a new key and with easier access to new thrills, find boarding school life artificial, confining, and boring.

One of the irritating restrictions, which is not limited to the boarding schools, in confinement to an environment limited to one sex. Many students find such confinement an acute personal deprivation.[9] The majorities among Catholic and independent school boys and girls opting for coeducation are substantial, except in the South, where the desire for coeducation in Catholic schools is more moderate. Protestant school students, however (other than Episcopal and Quaker), show only a bare majority in favor of such a shift (Protestant schools are overwhelmingly coed to begin with). The strong desire for coeducation among students of single sex schools may help explain why a fairly substantial number of young people, particularly those in the Northeast, where boarding schools abound, rated the social life in their school as unsatisfactory, though they found much to praise in the academic fare.

What this implies for the future of single sex schools is not altogether clear. A wholesale shift to coeducation would have the regrettable outcome of increasing by that much more the uniformity and standardization of schools at a time when many deplore the lack of diversity and the steady constriction of choices to fewer and fewer really different options. As it is, single sex schools, many with distinguished records, serve as a counter-cyclical force resisting the rush toward the standardization of education in this respect. For many such schools, however, the issue is now or may soon be defined as a struggle for bare survival. Unfortunately, there is no assurance that turning to coeducation is in itself a guarantee of survival. For example, a school for girls that has built a distinguished reputation among its kind could well turn out, in the process of becoming coeducational, to be just another school. But there may be no satisfactory alternative, except perhaps for a small number of prestigious, well-endowed single sex schools that could continue to attract a sufficient number of clients who prefer that kind of an environment or feel they need it. Some students indicated a desire to change from coeducational to single sex schools, and some in single sex schools express satisfaction with their school as it is. But their number is very small. The steady growth of sentiment, over the past century, in favor of coeducational education makes it seem unlikely that the trend will be reversed or arrested in the foreseeable future. Indeed, many traditionally single sex schools of national prominence are now in the process of change to co-ordinate or coeducation. Yet a number of single sex colleges have let it be known recently that after a careful study of various alternatives they have decided to stand pat in this respect.

As for the boarding schools, no one aspect of their environment stands out as the chief target of the protest from the students. It is the totality of the boarding situation which engenders the sense of confinement and unreality. It is in part the restriction on freedom for senior students, in maturity, or at least in sophistication, the equivalent of a college freshman or sophomore a generation ago: compulsory attendance in each of the school's activities, rules and check-ins

[9]*Ibid.*, pp. 47–48.

which seem to the impatient ones the customs and conventions of another age. The frustration in part also comes from a sense of being overprotected, over-sheltered from the stormy blast. The mature student is eager to widen his experience, to "bust loose" and get where the action is. Examples of such feeling are legion. The following is typical:

What is to be done about the sheltering hills and valley land and the invisible gates created by a narrow academic environment? . . . How can the student who has to live in this isolation during four of the most critical years of his adolescent growth be helped? . . . There are so many rules to guide you and people to help you that all you have to do is stick a book in your face and walk. The path has been walled in and family style meals have been provided three times a day along the way. At 9:30 everyone becomes quiet and is guided into his own bed for a good night's sleep. The problem is personal. You must find the confidence in yourself to break the bubble and breathe not necessarily fresh air but real air.[10]

It points up a problem as well as a dilemma. Such frustration is an effective damper on academic learning. Yet the idea behind private education is to create a special learning environment by bringing together a group that is relatively selected and homogeneous in respect to ability, or religious, ethnic, or social background. But today's questioning, restive students want to break the mold in order to enter a new and as yet undefined world that is waiting to be born. The problem is not, of course, peculiar to private schools. Judging from the extent of the militancy which is reported in the news media, public school students, black as well as white, appear to be showing signs of growing tension over the adult world which they will someday inherit. The problem is to some extent inherent in the notion of "school," conceived as a carefully contrived and regimented learning environment from which real life relationships and responsibilities have been expunged. In the student view, schools have not helped as they should to bridge the gap between the student's private and social worlds, or between the adolescent and the adult worlds. He remains too long—or too unremittingly without interruption or opportunity for creative breaks—in the rites of puberty, trapped in a childish limbo of prolonged dependence.

Militancy, Drugs, and Drinking

No single phenomenon of the behavior and outlook of young people is more deeply symptomatic of the way radical environmental changes are affecting the psyche of the young than the present-day drug scene. Just as the distrust and rejection of authority as such and the aggressive militancy of the reforming zeal of young radicals are unparalleled in modern social history, so is their resort to

[10]*The Kent News* (Kent School, Conn.), May 12, 1969.

drugs as a means, evidently, of expanding experience or escaping from reality into a world of dreams and fantasy. To what extent are the young people in private schools caught up in these perplexing developments?

To begin with, what is the "political" outlook of these students, their attitudes toward the formal political process, toward protests, militancy and violence as means to effect change? Indicative of their attitude toward politics is the reaction to the statement, "I don't expect ever to be concerned about politics." Seven out of ten Catholic and independent school students disagree. The strongest disagreement is voiced by students in southern Catholic schools, who evidently expect to be more concerned about politics than students in any other regional or denominational groups. Among the Protestant school groups, about three-fourths of the students in the Christian Reformed and NACS groups expect to take an interest in politics, but the more quietistically inclined Lutherans show noticeably less interest and the Seventh-Day Adventists much less.

With so much interest expressed in the normal political channels, it is a foregone conclusion that not many of these young people believe in resorting to militancy or violence. And this is indeed the case. Asked for their reaction to the statement, "To accomplish significant change or reform it is necessary to use militant tactics and confrontation, even with the possible risk of violence," upward of seven out of ten students in Catholic and independent schools disagree, and the Protestants showed an even higher number disagreeing. Numbers of Seventh-Day Adventist students failed to respond to the statement, despite that denomination's known stand of noncombatancy in war and firm commitment to peaceful means of settling disputes. Running true to form, the students of the Northeast independent schools, including those of the NAIS, show the highest level agreeing—just over 22 per cent. It seems an ominously strong minority of young people who are—or were in 1969—ready to resort to violence if necessary.

Another key to student attitudes regarding peaceful versus violent change is contained in their reactions to the statement, "Most accounts of police brutality are exaggerated." Since the hard facts regarding alleged police brutality are usually subject to dispute because of the conflicting testimony of different eye witnesses, student reactions to this statement can do no more than reveal where their sympathies lie: with "law and order," or with the rebels. The Protestant school youngsters show almost three-fourths agreeing with the statement; Catholic students are somewhat more skeptical, but still well over 60 per cent agree, with little regional variation. But the independent school students are sharply split between the South where almost three-fourths of the students agree, while only about 37 per cent of young people in the Northeast agree.

Even more indicative of where these students stand on the issue of militancy is the issue raised by the statement, "I do not support the tactics of most

138

militant student protestors." Here the Protestant school students again come up strongly supportive, while the Catholics are in the middle, and the independent group shows itself to be the most sympathetic to militant protestors, though there is again the characteristic cleavage between southern and northeastern schools.

The common pattern of these four sets of responses stands out clearly. Protestant students (other than the Episcopalians and Friends) take the most conservative position. Within the Protestant group, however, the Lutheran students are revealed as somewhat more inclined to question the status quo than are the other subgroups, while the Seventh-Day Adventist students appear to have separate terms of reference that largely negate for them the meaningfulness of the political turmoil within the present student generation. Catholic students are characteristically in the middle, with the young Catholics in the South influenced more by the church's outlook on social questions than by prevailing regional sentiments. The independent school students of the Northeast and, to some extent, those in the West contain the avant-garde of the private school world, with a strong minority that is outspoken in its disenchantment with the world and the school as they find it.

Given the public's deep concern over the alarming spread of drug addiction among teenagers, the facts about drug use in private secondary schools, or rather student awareness of it, are bound to be disturbing. The following discussion is based on student responses to the statement, "Student use of drugs is a problem at this school." One must assume that this statement was subject to varying interpretations. "Drugs" includes everything from marijuana to various hard drugs. To some, the fact that a few young people are experimenting with pot might be regarded as a campus problem, others might take it in stride. Despite this lack of definiteness, the responses provide at least a rough clue to the magnitude and dispersion of the problem as the students themselves saw it in 1969.

The range of those who "strongly agree" or "tend to agree" with this statement varies enormously between a minute fraction of the Protestant school students and to almost a third of those in independent schools. The breakdown by regions, however, shows that well over a third of the independent students in the Northeast and West saw student drug use as a problem, though it had not hit those in the South to the same degree. It did not appear to be a large problem in the Catholic schools, and seemed to be almost nonexistent in most Protestant schools, except in the Episcopal, where over 40 per cent of the students considered drug use a problem.

It is instructive to see student awareness of the drug problem in relationship to drinking. Roughly speaking, where drug use is deemed to be a serious problem, drinking is less so; narcotics tend to be a substitute for alcohol. Drinking, however, is a more pervasive as well as an older problem which is both more widely and more evenly distributed among young people in the various school types. Student reactions to the statement, "Drinking is not a problem among students at this school," show that roughly about a third or more of students in all three school groups regard drinking as a problem. But the same caveat applies here as above: a few cases of student drunkenness or a recent beer party that got out of hand might cause very straight-laced souls to consider drinking a campus problem, while others might judge these happenings more lightly as outlets for youthful ebullience. In any case, the number of Catholic students who say that drinking is a problem in their school is somewhat higher than the Protestant and independent school students who so reply. But among the Protestant subgroups, the highest concern is expressed by Lutheran students, with just under half saying that drinking is a school problem, while the lowest concern is expressed by the abstemious Seventh-Day Adventist students. Judged by these responses, student drinking shows no such sharp regional differences between Northeast and South as are apparent in drug use, though in this case southern independent school students consider drinking more of a school problem than do those in the Northeast.

The drug problem, or the student recognition of it, being a fairly recent development, is thus seen to be spottier and less widespread than drinking, which has long had a measure of social acceptance. In the private school world drug use has caught on fastest in the most competitive academic schools enrolling high-ability students with largely upper and upper middle class backgrounds. Tensions, basic uncertainties about career directions and life's meaning, boredom with the pettiness of school regulations and the drip-drip of school learning may conceivably exact a heavier toll in the lives of very bright, brittle students than in those of more average youngsters. Yet the fact that the youthful drug culture flourishes in suburban middle class high schools in the Northeast and West as well as among young people in urban high schools and the children of the urban poor and in ghettos casts doubt on such reasoning. From general observation it seems apparent that drug use is probably much more prevalent in metropolitan and urban than in rural environments, a fact that may help to explain the low concern over drug use among most Protestant students.

A more plausible explanation for the great variations in drug use among private school students is to be found, we believe, in the character of different types of schools and the religious and value orientation of the families from which they draw their students. Thus, judging from what the students had to say in the spring of 1969, in most Catholic schools the problem was minimal, while in most Protestant schools—with exceptions as noted—it was all but nonexistent. While to the unchurched, traditional religion appears to be fighting a losing rear-guard action against the forces of modernism and secularism, yet it evidently continues to be a factor in the salient influence exerted by many homes and schools wherein religion provides the basis of authoritative values as effective guides to personal and social conduct.

Concluding Remarks

By and large, the students did not articulate any radical notions of what they ask from their schools' academic program. The great majority in all types of schools want to be helped to think clearly and independently. The Protestants are most concerned with moral education, and independent school students with self-development and fulfillment. On the whole they find their academic education generally good as well as their training in independent thinking and self-confidence. They believe that their school is superior chiefly because the teachers care and give them individual attention. Except for a sizable minority of independent school students from the Northeast, they appear relatively untroubled by excessive scholastic demands, except that the pressure for grades is strong in some schools. The expressed life and career goals of the great majority are idealistic, personal, noncompetitive and altruistic. The great majority expect to go to college.

As for grievances over their schooling, they pertain chiefly to the school environment taken as a whole. Substantial numbers (the brighter and more affluent being the more critical) vigorously seek a larger voice in the decisions that affect their lives and resent restrictions on dress and hair styles, poor communication between faculty and students, and excessive regimentation. Many profess to be bored by school, even though they think well of their school. There is more evidence of frustration and discontent and basic questioning of educational goals among independent school students than in those from the church-related schools, and student unrest is most concentrated in the elite boarding schools of the Northeast. Yet few signs of political and social militancy appear among these students overall. However, drug use appears to be a problem in the independent schools of the country except in the South, but is not yet a serious problem in the church-affiliated schools.

Given these outcomes, one is tempted to conclude, on the one hand, that many if not most private schools are islands of serenity in a frightfully turbulent world. The students on the whole reveal a self-image based upon confidence in themselves and pride in their school in which they generally find considerable satisfaction. Especially in the church-related schools, they seem in the main a contented, relaxed, conventional, even complacent group of young people. Most students in private schools believe their own school to be academically superior to other nonpublic and public schools in the country. Catholic students rate their school well above average, and Protestant students give their own schools a comparably high mark. Students in Jewish schools also think well of theirs. As for the students in independent schools, though they tend to be more critical of aspects of their schooling, yet when they think comparatively, they are convinced that their own school is clearly superior.

But there is another, far less reassuring side. Consider the substantial number of these same students who say that except for getting a diploma, they do not see much point to the work they are asked to do at their school. That feeling, weighed in the light of other evidence of discontent with their schooling, leads one to suspect that they share with their generation much of the discontent with things as they are. But the unhappiness is not so much with their own school as with the way education is traditionally conceived, or more fundamentally, with the shape of the established world and the mode of life which the school is designed to serve. Are the students—this questioning minority—saying in effect: My school is better than most, but the idea of the conventional school and the kind of education it provides are somehow inadequate for our lives and our future?

Their clichés about nonrelevance, their clamor to have a voice in school affairs, the fact that they sense that more learning goes on outside the classroom than in it, and their rebellion against the cut-and-dried methods of rote learning—these are clear signs that today's schools are more than normally out of phase with the life and needs of students, living in a time of frenetic change. Besides, now that the ubiquitous TV tube brings the whole world, with all its miracles, violence, eroticism and grotesquery right into the youngster's bedroom, the well-ordered conventional school with its inflexible goals, set routines, competitiveness, and petty rules must seem to the sensitive young not only tepid by comparison, but a frustrating throwback to days long gone.

Whether or not these questioning young people, who though still in the minority comprise a far larger segment of the young population than ever before, are to be seen as a new breed remains an open question. Many close observers argue that their discontent cannot be explained merely in terms of the normal generational conflict. They see it as something deeper and more pervasive. Maturation comes earlier than it used to, and the young evince a strong desire to identify with their peers by the time they have reached their early teens. At the same time school and college are held up to them as a prolonged but nonetheless required probation for life's responsibilities which they may assume only after an elaborate preparation. The response of the young to this combination of precocity and dependency is to foster a separate youth culture, the creation of a world of their own with its own ideals, mores, heroes, life styles, music, and language—a standing repudiation of the adult world which keeps them at arm's length.

6

Teachers and Teaching in Private Schools

*"But education is too significant
and dynamic an enterprise
to be left to mere technicians;
and we might as well
begin now the prodigious task
of preparing men and women
who understand not only the substance
of what they are teaching
but also the theories
behind the particular strategies
they employ to convey that substance.
A society committed
to the continuing intellectual,
aesthetic, and moral growth
of all its members
can ill afford less on the part
of those who undertake to teach."*

Lawrence A. Cremin[1]

Profiles of Private School Teachers

Teaching in private and in public schools differs in essential respects. Public school teachers are accountable through their principals to city-wide or state-wide centralized bureaucracies comprising many echelons of specialists and co-ordinators. Roughly ten per cent of public school staffs in metropolitan population centers are engaged in full-time supervision. The aim is to achieve efficiently uniform qualitative standards by means of central planning, direction, and control and by standardizing techniques and procedures.[2] What and how the teacher

[1] *The Genius of American Education* (New York: Random House, Vintage Books, 1965), p. 57.

[2] "The administration of a large American high school," notes Martin Mayer, "is an exercise in logistics. Often there is a room . . . set aside for 'scheduling,' its walls covered, floor to ceiling, with cards to show who is teaching what, when and to whom. The secretaries . . . have 'ditto sheets' to show where teachers and children may be found at any time

143

teaches day by day is usually pretty well prescribed, with relatively little left to his initiative and judgment. Salaries are generally based on seniority rather than on merit, with fixed increments awarded for advanced degrees. Except in schools that have instituted team teaching, there tends to be little or no differentiation of the job or added responsibility for the experienced or meritorious teacher. It is said that the beginning teacher starts with a classroom of thirty children, and twenty years later she is still teaching thirty children—it adds up not so much to twenty years of experience as a year's experience repeated twenty times. The surest way to advance professionally is to leave the classroom and become an administrator. Yet, despite the degree of standardization and uniformity under which most public school teachers function, many remain dedicated, productive, helpful, and admired by young people.

The private school teacher's world is very different. He is more likely to be working in a small, unitary school run by a headmaster or principal who as a rule enjoys a generous delegation of authority by his governing board, to which he is solely accountable. He is the captain of the ship. Relationships within the school tend to be informal and familial, and the teacher is allowed considerable leeway in what and how he teaches. The private school teacher is generally poorly paid, sometimes way below his public school colleague. Yet his salary level, such as it is, is more likely to reflect both experience and merit; and he may be asked to assume part-time administrative duties while still remaining, in fact and in spirit, a member of the faculty. If he works in a boarding school, his duties are likely to be multiple, including housemastering and coaching, and his day a long one. The day school teacher too, in addition to teaching a variety of subjects each requiring separate preparation, is likely to be called on to take on a spate of extra-curricular duties such as athletic coaching and directing other activities.

Some Catholic schools, however, resemble the public schools in certain respects. Diocesan schools, for example, are linked generally into a system, one for each diocese. But the central supervision is generally lax and free-wheeling by public school standards, and nothing like the public school ratio of administrative to teaching personnel is generally available.

Another noteworthy difference between private and public schools is the proportion of men and women teachers. While women far outnumber men, overall, in both public and private elementary schools, in the Protestant elementaries the proportion of men teachers is twice that in the public schools. Similarly, at the secondary school level, slightly over half of the public school teachers compared to three-quarters of the Protestant teachers are men. In the

in the day. . . . The principal is usually too busy to teach—and so are half a dozen deans, co-ordinators, assistant principals and so forth. They are the most highly paid people in the school." *The Schools* (Garden City, N.Y.: Doubleday and Co., Anchor Books, 1963), p. 11.

independent schools—elementary and secondary—the per cent of male teachers exceeds that in the public schools.[3] But in the Catholic schools less than half are men. As one would expect, the female complement of Catholic faculties consists largely of nuns, but in all other private school types married women teachers predominate, with a higher ratio of marrieds in secondary than in elementary schools.

With these general differences between public and private school teachers in mind, we can begin to draw profiles of teachers in various types of private schools. The profile of the independent school teacher, emerging out of a welter of individual differences, is that of the dedicated amateur—a man or woman broadly educated in the humanistic liberal arts tradition, not highly specialized, and but lightly burdened, if at all, with the pedagogical formalism of professional education. More than likely he is of Protestant background (Episcopal, Presbyterian, or Congregational), wears his religion lightly, but believes firmly in the importance of character education. At the same time, since he is aware of the youth counter-culture, he is less certain now just how the development of character is to be accomplished. And even if his background is Catholic or Jewish—and their number is increasing—he tends to accept the traditional WASP moral and social standards, though perhaps with growing doubts. Whatever the ethnic origin or religious loyalties of the independent school teacher, he is uncomfortably aware that the assimilation of students of heterogeneous origins to the old Anglo-Saxon standards is not working as it once did, except possibly in a few of the prestigious bastions of meritocracy concentrated in New England and in scattered replications elsewhere, particularly in the South. And even there, the old confidence and self-assurance are being eroded by the young radicals with their insistent questioning of authority, assumption of eccentric life-styles, and the spreading drug culture.

The profiles of the Catholic, Protestant, and Jewish teachers are delineated primarily by their religious commitment, which takes varying forms because of the disparate backgrounds of priests, brothers, nuns, ministers, pastors, and rabbis, not to mention the lay teachers in church schools. The religious personnel on the teaching staffs of Catholic schools, for example, are drawn from a host of different national and international teaching orders and "congregations" ranging from the worldly Jesuits to the humble Trinitarian Fathers, from the Society of the Sacred Heart to the Daughters of Charity of St. Vincent de Paul. But members of the elite as well as the humble orders receive about the same median preparation for teaching, usually in Catholic colleges and universities. In recent years Catholic school teacher preparation for lay as well as religious

---

[3] Public school statistics from "Estimate of School Statistics, 1968–69," *Research Report 1968-R16* (Washington, D.C.: National Education Association 1968), p. 14.

teachers has been guided largely by public school standards. The sisters have progressed a little farther into graduate studies than have the priests, and the same is true of the laywomen as compared with teaching laymen.[4] The religious teachers migrate among the Catholic schools in response to canonical rules and the practices of various orders which call for a change of scene at intervals. The turnover among the lay teachers is also considerable, chiefly because the career opportunities in most Catholic schools are usually not comparable, in terms of salaries and teaching loads, to those offered in public or independent schools. Since the lay teachers are engaged primarily to take up the slack caused by the decrease in available religious teachers, they tend to be a heterogeneous group.[5] The Catholic schools thus have on their hands the special problem of welding their itinerant lay and religious pedagogues into a coordinated team.

Protestant teachers, in this as in most other respects, pursue their separate denominational ways. One thing they all have in common, however, is the willingness to meet public school teacher preparation standards. One gets the impression that the college background of many Protestant teachers is more pedagogical-utilitarian than liberal-humanistic. But the fact that many of the male teachers and administrators have had either full or partial seminary training, and that they along with the women teachers have acquired bachelor's degrees in the religious environment of Protestant colleges, means that they approach their teaching duties with a special sense of religious dedication. Yet their college training is often narrowly orthodox in a religious sense. Their characterization of schooling as God-, Christ-, or Bible-centered comes readily to their lips, naturally and unaggressively. As the resident intellectual in a NUCS academy in Pennsylvania said (an English teacher with a Ph.D.—he was a rarity), "We are doing the work of the Holy Spirit—this is His curriculum." The visitor is struck by the readiness of Protestant teachers to articulate such beliefs and to attest the divine sanctions under which the school operates. These are seldom mentioned by teachers in Catholic schools, where the teachers are more disposed to discuss the problems and needs of education per se and how education should relate to the mounting social problems of our time.

---

[4] See George N. Shuster, *Catholic Education in a Changing World* (New York: Holt, Rinehart and Winston, 1967). The data on which this study relies (the "Notre Dame Study") were gathered in 1962–63. The levels of education of all types of Catholic teachers have risen since then, according to the National Catholic Educational Association survey in 1969–70.

[5] In 1950 lay teachers comprised only 7 per cent of the total elementary and 16 per cent of the total secondary Catholic school staff in the United States. By 1970 more than half (52 per cent) of all Catholic school teachers were lay. According to The National Catholic Educational Association's *Report on U.S. Catholic Schools, 1970–71* (Washington, D.C.: Research Department, NCEA, 1971), ". . . in the light of more positive lay theology of the recent second Vatican Council, this growing presence of the Catholic lay teacher could be considered in many ways a desirable and long overdue development" (p. 16).

In the schools of the Lutheran Church–Missouri Synod, the male teachers, who predominate, are "called" by means of a formal "Diploma of Vocation," which enjoins the teacher to perform his duties "faithfully according to the Word of God and the confessional standards of the Evangelical Lutheran Church as drawn from the Sacred Scriptures and found in the Book of Concord."[6] Women teachers, however, whose special status often suggests second-class citizenship, are merely called under a "solemn agreement" which exhorts them to "set a good example of Christian character and living to young and old." The agreement can be dissolved by reason of matrimony or for other "good and valid reasons."

Teachers in Lutheran and Seventh-Day Adventist schools come nearest to being exclusively one denominational, respectively, but those in NUCS and NACS schools are interdenominationally Protestant. Nevertheless, they generally resemble the Lutherans in the religious zeal that imbues their teaching. Teachers in the coeducational Seventh-Day Adventist boarding academies tend to stress the nonacademic aspects of teaching—the teacher's role as a counselor in student value formation and in shaping a philosophy of life, his part as friendly guide in the students' social development and a source of beneficial adult influence on the lives of young people. But like the teachers in the Lutheran, NUCS, and NACS schools, they are fully committed to being competent instructors of academic subjects as well. In their view, the dual mission of academic and religious-moral instruction neither is incompatible nor does it bifurcate the educational program. On the contrary, they believe these concerns to be related inextricably and that there can be no true education without that linkage. "Religion," they maintain over and over, "permeates the entire curriculum." Or as a Lutheran high school teacher in Indiana put it, "Everything is spiritual—not denominational, but spiritual."

The Teacher on Education and Teaching

With the opening of schools in September, 1970, many college graduates looking for teaching jobs were astonished to find that the schools had quietly put up "no vacancy" signs. The teacher shortage which began soon after the end of the Second World War was for so long a part of the educational landscape, it was assumed by all except those who study educational statistics that it would go on indefinitely, and that any reasonably intelligent young person whose career plans were not fully set or who desired to avoid the draft could always find a place as a teacher. During the height of the shortage, the well-qualified

---

[6]Victor C. Krause, ed., *Lutheran Elementary Schools in Action* (St. Louis: Concordia Publishing House, 1963), pp. 390–91.

teacher was in a position to be selective about where and in what type of school he chose to teach. Now it is the schools that are in a position to be selective, and principals and headmasters are rejoicing that the long drought is over at last.

During the two preceding decades, most certified nonpublic school teachers could have done better, in terms of salary and work-load, by shifting to the public schools. Salaries there rose much faster than in most private schools, save only the small circle of well-endowed independents. It is true that in the period of rapid expansion many urban public schools were plagued by large classes, double shifts, and other expedients. But the church schools also grew rapidly during the same period, and for financial reasons not a few had to cope with student-teacher ratios on the upper side of 35 to one. These factors, and others to be explored below, tended to balance out in such a way that no sudden or heavy shift of teachers from private to public schools, or the reverse, occurred. Most private schools, though they became progressively disadvantaged in the salary competition with public schools, managed somehow, even through the height of the shortage, to hold together teaching staffs for their growing schools. Furthermore, the appeal of teaching in private schools was such as to permit the founding of a substantial number of new church-related and independent schools since the close of the Second World War.

The reasons that lead a prospective teacher to choose one type of school rather than another are of course many and varied. Salary is only one among many factors that influence the choice. A desired location; a special type of school; institutional prestige; an intellectually stimulating environment; an exciting experiment or innovation under way; an opportunity to serve a constituency with a special religious, ethnic, or social background; congenial colleagues; modest teaching loads; good parent-school relationships; or just plan lack of ambition or initiative—these and many other considerations compete with salary in influencing a candidate's choice to go to or remain at a given school.

We found Catholic, Protestant, and independent school teachers agreeing most closely on the following reasons for preferring a private school: the educational philosophy of the school; a greater sense of community and freedom from impersonal bureaucracy; the freedom to design and teach courses; the quality of the faculty and of the school head. The weight and priority assigned to these reasons vary appreciably among teachers in different types of schools (see figure 7). The school's philosophy is important to over 90 per cent of the Protestant secondary school teachers, but to noticeably fewer of their elementary colleagues. No other group reaches so high a level of approbation on this point, though the teachers in independent elementary schools come close. The philosophy of these two groups is, of course, strikingly different. The position of Protestant teachers is confirmed by other known facts which together point to the strong sway of religious commitments in Lutheran, Christian Reformed, Seventh-Day Adventist, evangelical and other "Christian" schools.

Figure 7

WHY TEACHERS TEACH IN NONPUBLIC SCHOOLS

(Reasons checked by faculty as either "important" or "very important")

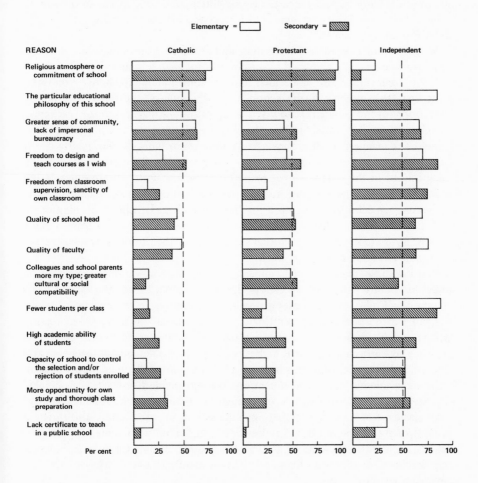

Why teachers in the independent elementaries attach so much importance to the school's philosophy became apparent in interviews with teachers. Their reasoning parallels that of the parents who say they chose the school chiefly because of the quality of the educational program, the greater degree of personal attention given to the child, and the better training in diligence and study habits that these schools are thought to provide. The generally middle and upper class outlook of these schools and their clientele is doubtless another aspect of their

149

"philosophy" which makes parents and teachers feel at home. The importance that this group attaches to the school's philosophy may also reflect the growing interest in new experimental schools based either on foreign models, such as the Summerhill, Montessori, or Leicestershire "integrated day" plans, or on original designs. Schools of this sort naturally attract teachers who are eager to try new and different approaches.

Why "a greater sense of community and freedom from impersonal bureaucracy" is more strongly endorsed by teachers of independent and Catholic schools than by their Protestant colleagues is not immediately apparent. Not unexpectedly, "the quality of the school's faculty and of the head" are potent attractions for independent school teachers, but noticeably less so for teachers in the church schools which reflect the duality of religious and academic aims. Elementary teachers in all groups attach more importance to the quality of the faculty than do their secondary peers. It may be that the elementary teacher, being locked in the classroom for many hours on end with immature minds, has a special need for the companionship of good adult colleagues, while his peer in the secondary schools finds more intellectual and social outlets in his subject field and in the company of maturing young people. The parochialism of many elementary schools may be another reason why the teachers emphasize the importance of good colleagues.

Besides these reasons which appeal strongly but in varying degrees to all groups, there are others which clearly differentiate teachers in the various types of schools. Chief among these is the great variation in the reactions to the "religious atmosphere or commitment of the school" as a suggested reason. Understandably, teachers in the church schools, the Protestants noticeably more so than the Catholics, rank this highest of all, while independent teachers naturally find this a negligible reason. Instead, consonant with their preoccupation with the academic aspect of education, the independents attach considerable importance to attributes which are thought to be indices of academic quality: small classes, freedom from classroom supervision, selective admissions (favored more strongly in the South than elsewhere), high ability students, opportunity for thorough class preparation, and related reasons. Among Catholic and Protestant teachers, on the other hand, all these academic characteristics are rated as somewhat less important.

One negative "reason" that evidently influences the choice of some independent elementary and secondary school teachers is the fact that, unlike the public schools, most independent schools do not require a teacher certificate. The implications of this relative lack of interest in "professional" preparation for teaching will be examined in a later chapter.

School characteristics which appear to have surprisingly little influence on teachers' choices in all groups are such considerations as the degree of faculty voice in determining school policy, salary, coeducation or lack of it, quality of library facilities, prestige of private as compared with public schools (except among the southern independents), and the racial or socioeconomic diversity of the students.

Further light is shed on the teacher's attitudes toward the school's philosophy by his views concerning what is most and what is least important among various aims of education selected from the following suggested list of ten: to help students (1) develop basic skills of language and mathematics; (2) learn to think clearly and independently; (3) learn how to become good citizens in a democratic society; (4) gain an understanding of the main areas of knowledge; (5) develop sound moral standards and values; (6) become interesting individual people; (7) learn how to make friends and get along with other people; (8) develop the skills necessary to earn a good living and "compete"; (9) prepare to work for the improvement of society and the benefit of other people; (10) develop a lifetime love of learning.

All teacher groups agree in attaching the greatest importance to the academic goal of helping students "learn to think clearly and independently." It functions as a common denominator, an aim inherent in the very idea of "school" conceived as something more than a means of indoctrinating the young in the ways of the tribe. But the responses to other suggested goals fall into the familiar pattern that differentiates the church and independent schools. Church-school teachers see as the second and third most important goals the broadly moral and humanitarian ones of helping students "develop sound moral standards and values" and "prepare to work for the improvement of society and the benefit of other people"—goals which independent school teachers rate very low; they declare instead for intellectual ends—"an understanding of the main areas of knowledge" and "developing a lifetime love of learning."

This pattern of divergence is repeated in the teachers' ranking of goals they consider least important. Church-school teachers give a low place to helping students "become interesting individual people," an objective which fares somewhat better among independent school teachers, but not much. It probably sounds too egotistical, self-indulgent and frivolous to church-school teachers, who as a group stress the importance of moral and humanitarian education; and we suspect it lacks academic respectability with the academically oriented independents.

Both groups also give short shrift to the goal of helping students "develop the skills necessary to earn a good living and 'compete,' " the independents more so than the church schools. One can only speculate as to the reasons. With supermarkets and appliance shops piled high with consumer goods and with unsolicited credit cards clogging the family mail, it is small wonder that these predominantly middle class teachers and upper class students show a diminishing concern for the purely economic problem of making a living. Moreover, the word "compete" may have turned off some respondents, especially among the avant-garde independent school population. Competition has strong pejorative overtones for today's young and this attitude is evidently rubbing off on their teachers. Another possible explanation of why learning how "to earn a good living" is crowded out by other objectives, particularly in the eyes of independent school faculties, lies in the socioeconomic composition of the various groups. The independents come from well-educated and financially comfortable families where concern for the mere learning of skills is minimal and where competing for a living is often sublimated in the satisfactions of professional or other status-conferring activities. By comparison, the socioeconomic background of church-school teachers and students includes a substantial contingent from lower middle and some lower class families who are upwardly mobile and not in a position to be quite so cavalier about the economic facts of life.

There are also sharp differences as well as similarities between the teachers' and students' views of the goals of education. Both groups agree in giving the highest emphasis to "learning to think clearly and independently." But when it comes to the goal chosen as the next most important, the two groups differ strikingly, particularly in the independent schools. Students there give a high place to "becoming interesting individual people" whereas, as we noted, their teachers rank it among the least important goals. The disagreement reveals, we believe, a significant incompatibility between the educational philosophy of students and their teachers: the student is concerned with the development of his whole person, while the teacher is concentrating rather single-mindedly on the development of the student's mind.

On the other hand, when it comes to their evaluation of the school's achievement in accomplishing its aims, teachers and students show a relatively high degree of agreement. Teachers in all types of private schools give high marks to their school's instruction in basic academic subjects—mathematics, science, and English—and the students agree. Both groups are less satisfied with the offerings in foreign languages and social studies, and with regard to the school's program in the arts, the level of satisfaction drops sharply, especially in the church schools, and most noticeably among the Protestants—evidence of the fact that this aspect of schooling is poorly developed in many church schools. Teachers in independent elementary schools are better satisfied in this area. But the overall assessment of the schools' academic achievement by the teachers closely parallels that of the students.

There is generally less concurrence, however, in the appraisal of the school's influence in the noncognitive, affective, and behavioral dimensions. In such imponderables as the school's success in challenging and stimulating its students and helping them to think for themselves, the teachers think the school is doing only a fair job, with the Protestants being most self-critical, while most students, it will be recalled, rate the school good to excellent in this respect. In matters affecting student behavior and character formation—guidance, moral and religious education—Protestant teachers, in particular, give their schools high marks, the Catholics are less sure, and the independent school teachers are divided over whether their schools are satisfactory or deficient in respect to moral education. The students, on the other hand, especially those in the independent schools, are generally doubtful whether the school has a legitimate role in moral and religious education, and tend to be skeptical of the school's influence on this score.

The conflicting claims and doubts regarding the effectiveness of moral and religious education have spurred some research recently that raises serious doubts about the religious programs in church schools and what they accomplish. Joseph Fichter found, on the basis of a longitudinal survey of Jesuit high schools, that "in terms of Christian formation, ethical behavior, and moral attitudes the schools that have the best religion courses achieve no better results than the schools with the worst religion courses." And he concludes, "It raises doubts about the traditional assumptions that an authentic character formation of young people must be undergirded by religious motives and convictions."[7] Similarly, one of the main conclusions of Andrew M. Greeley and Peter H. Rossi in *The Education of Catholic Americans* is that Catholic schools do not produce better adult Catholics; at best they reinforce the parental and home influence in young people from homes that are strongly supportive of religious life to begin with.[8] A controversial study of the effects of Lutheran parochial schooling seems to raise similar doubts.[9] The visitor gathers the impression that church-school principals and religious teachers attach much more importance to the

[7]Joseph H. Fichter, S.J., *Jesuit High Schools Revisited* (Washington, D.C.: Jesuit Educational Association, 1969), pp. 180–82.

[8]*The Education of Catholic Americans* (Chicago: Aldine Publishing Co., 1966), pp. 77–113.

[9]Ronald L. Johnstone, *The Effectiveness of Lutheran Elementary and Secondary Schools as Agencies of Christian Education* (St. Louis: Concordia Publishing House, 1966), and William A. Kramer, ed., *Eight Critiques of the Johnstone Study on the Effectiveness of Lutheran Schools* (St. Louis: Board of Parish Education, The Lutheran Church—Missouri Synod, 1967). Donald A. Erickson's "Contradictory Studies of Parochial Schooling: An Essay Review" (in *Eight Critiques*) suggests on p. 8 that careful analysis of the Johnstone data "seems to support rather than challenge the interpretation provided by Greeley and Rossi: In general, the religious attitudes of students who receive virtually all of their elementary and secondary schooling in parochial schools are affected perceptibly, regardless of home backgrounds. The immediate consequences for students from devout homes are slight, but these students tend, perhaps partly because they often acquire pious spouses, to maintain a notably higher level of religious commitment as adults than confreres with similar backgrounds but a different educational experience. The immediate consequences for students from marginal homes are pronounced, but in later life these effects tend to disappear."

contribution of religious teaching in student character and value formation than do the students themselves. The evidence mounts that instruction in religion as such is not nearly as influential in the life of the present-day church-school student as are the home, the mores and expectations of the religious community as a whole, and the relative homogeneity in outlook of the student's family and social class background.

One aspect of the school's program that most teachers, like their students, are unhappy about is the controversial subject of sex education. The prevalence of "no opinion" and "no response" to a question concerning it probably indicates the lack of an identifiable sex education program in many schools. Several years ago the NAIS developed a well-conceived program in sex education for member and other interested schools, public and private.[10] Judging by our survey, its impact upon the private school world appears to be modest as yet—a casualty, perhaps, of the heavy flak of conservative and fundamentalist criticism which aims to discredit the very idea of sex education in the schools.

The self-evaluation of nonpublic school teachers—the assessment of their own strengths and weaknesses in various aspects of the teaching function—affords a valuable insight into the teachers and the schools that employ them (see figure 8). Of all the varied competences on which the teachers were asked to rate themselves they scored highest in their ability to achieve good rapport with young people. Four out of five listed their ability in this area as strong or very strong. By contrast, the teachers rate their own ability in the purely pedagogical skills (use of teaching materials and aids, direction of independent student work, testing, measurement and evaluation) strikingly lower. For example, only three of ten think they are capable of using teaching materials and aids effectively. If the teachers are indeed as empathic and friendly with students as they think they are, this fact may help explain the relatively high degree of satisfaction that the students find in private schooling, especially in those institutions that are obliged to make do with salary and facility inputs that seem quite inadequate by public school standards.

While there is no way of determining the accuracy of these self-appraisals, the impressions gathered during school visits strongly confirm the generally good rapport with students in most schools. Moreover, in rating the presumed advantages of private over public schools students generally give first place to "more individual attention from teachers." This suggests that, even after allowing for some human exaggeration, the teachers have a valid point in stressing their generally good empathy with students. The opportunity to be in such a relation-

---

[10] *Planning a Program of Sex Education, Talks Presented at the NAIS Annual Conference* (Boston: National Association of Independent Schools, 1967); and Edward Yeomans, *NAIS Institute on Sex Education, A Summary Report* (Boston: National Association of Independent Schools, 1966).

Figure 8

TEACHERS' SELF-RATING OF TEACHING EFFECTIVENESS
(Abilities rated "very strong" and "strong" combined)

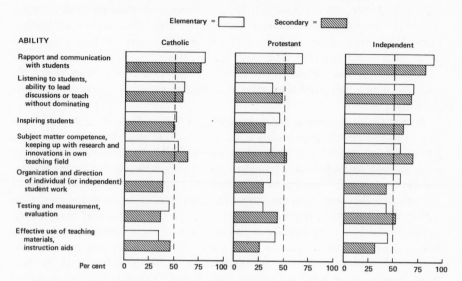

ship with young people is evidently high among the reasons why the teachers choose a private school.

More difficult to credit is the claim by over half the teachers of independent schools and almost as many Catholic teachers that they are good at "inspiring students." We noted earlier that over a fourth of the students in all school groups complained of boredom, with independent school students more vocal about this than the other groups. There is no way of knowing whether this is high or low in comparison with, say, the public schools; but whatever may be true comparatively, the boredom index is too high for schools that claim to be educationally effective.

But this point aside, further confirmation of the generally good student-teacher relations in nonpublic schools is to be found in the very nature of the private school. The teachers are usually rather carefully selected for personal characteristics and group loyalties which are in tune with the philosophy and personnel of the school. Lutheran principals look first of all for sound, right-thinking Lutheran teachers. Headmasters of elite prep schools search for candidates with character, versatile talents, and good academic background in the liberal humanistic tradition. By contrast, public school superintendents are confronted with the need of filling numerous vacancies, and rarely have the opportunity to "fit" the teacher to the school in the same degree as does the head of a small, relatively homogeneous private school. So the public school places greater reliance on certification as a general measure of the fitness of the teacher for the "typical" public school situation. It is the source of widespread disaffection among ghetto parents who complain that white middle class teachers are hired to teach black lower class children, with few qualifications for that special task other than the possession of a teaching certificate. Advocates of community control, such as the parents of the Bedford-Stuyvesant area of New York City, leave no doubt that what they value in a teacher above all else is rapport with students.

Rapport with the young, however important that is, does not make up for the lack of competence in pedagogical skills. The fact that elementary and secondary private school teachers rate themselves lowest of all in "effective use of teaching materials and instruction aids," and low also in "organizing and directing student independent work," should be a matter of concern to all types of private schools. Whether and to what extent these teachers differ in this respect from public school teachers there is no way of knowing. But at a time when educational reform is moving steadily in the direction of more individualized instruction, independent work, and the use of audio-visual and electronic teaching aids, the fact that so many private school teachers admit to feeling weak in these techniques is not a good augury for their future. The situation points up the critical need not only for greatly improved in-service training programs but for a more thorough training of apprentice teachers in the new techniques.

Curiously, how well or poorly teachers rate their own effectiveness appears to bear no relationship whatever to whether or not they are certified. The independent school teachers, who as a group have the lowest per cent of certified teachers, show the highest per cent of those believing themselves to be strong. The Protestants as a group are the most modest in assessing their competences in all aspects of the teaching function, yet they have an appreciably higher percentage of certified teachers. Conceivably this could be traceable to their youth; they happen to be the youngest of the three groups of teachers. The Catholics have the highest per cent of certified teachers but take a middle position in appraising their competences. Naturally, many factors contribute to this result. For example, the independent schools draw much of their teacher talent from Ivy league colleges and universities, populated by relatively sophisticated, self-confident young people, while the church schools depend largely for their teacher supply on denominational institutions of lesser renown.

In general, the private school teachers appear as a relatively relaxed, untroubled group of people. Yet it would be quite unrealistic to conclude that all is sweetness and light or that the oft-alleged "dedication" of the private school teacher, in the church school in particular, triumphs over all personality conflicts and the paucity of human and economic resources. They do indeed have their problems—problems which vary considerably from school to school within wide limits, depending upon local circumstances, resources, the quality of leadership, the character of the school, its reputation and traditions, and many related factors.

Concern over the meager faculty salaries comes closest to being a universal problem for teachers in nonpublic schools of all types (see figure 9). Yet it is far

Figure 9

PROBLEMS NONPUBLIC TEACHERS FACE
(Aspects of teaching rated "a problem" or "a serious problem")

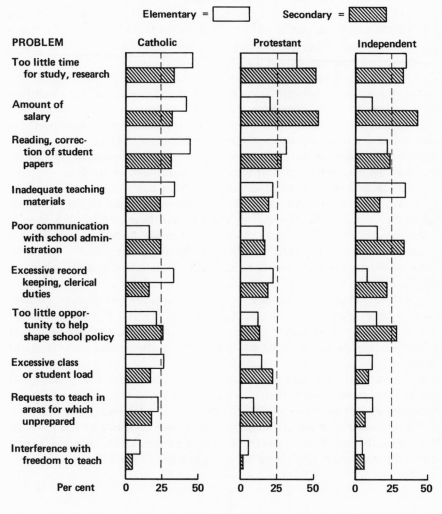

from being a uniform complaint. The degree of unhappiness expressed by various groups of teachers is not, as one might expect it to be, inversely proportional to the amount of the salary received. For example, the elementary teachers, who are lowest on the salary totem pole, complain less than the secondary teachers do. While well over half the Protestants, who on the average are least well paid, rate this a problem or a serious problem, the number of independents who think so is not far behind, despite the fact that their salaries are the best of the three major groups. Even fewer Catholic teachers see salary as a major problem, though theirs are usually far lower than those of the independents. This is partly accounted for by the substantial number of religious among Catholic teachers, for whom financial reward is usually not a major consideration.

Another aspect of private school teaching that troubles the teachers—though the complaints seldom rise to half of any group—is the amount of work that is expected of them. Many feel too much is expected by way of student load in classes, record keeping, clerical duties, and correction of student papers. Some teachers—the number is small in the aggregate but varies considerably from school to school—are unhappy over being asked to teach in areas in which they are not prepared. These complaints are usually most pronounced in schools with high student-teacher ratios. Others vent their concern over the multiplicity of time-consuming duties by saying there is too little time for study and their own research. In general, elementary teachers appear to feel the pressure of long days and manifold responsibilities more heavily than do secondary faculty.

Most teachers feel that communication between teachers and administration is good on the whole. An appreciable number of Catholic faculty, however, record this as a problem. Conceivably the reason is the relative heterogeneity of Catholic school teaching staffs, since they include both lay and religious teachers, and not infrequently members of diverse teaching orders. Moreover, many of the religious teachers are assigned to their teaching posts instead of being specifically selected by the principal, and are subject to frequent reassignment. These practices are changing. As a nun remarked to the visitor of a private Catholic girls' school in suburban Philadelphia, "Vatican II started a lot of things!" But as matters stand, all these factors increase the Catholic principal's difficulties in welding the varied and peripatetic teachers into a well-integrated staff.

One aspect of the private school teacher's professional life that seems by his own admission remarkably satisfactory, whether he be teaching in a Catholic, Protestant or independent school, is his freedom to teach and design courses as he wishes. Fewer than one in ten record interference on this score as a problem. It is evidently one of the substantial sources of satisfaction to many private school teachers which helps to offset partially some of the deficiencies in other respects.

Salaries, Tenure, and Other Conditions of Employment

Salary scales are widely regarded as a significant index of the quality of instruction: the higher the teacher's pay, the better the chance of a qualitatively superior school outcome. But while money is obviously important, it is not everything. If salary were indeed the all-powerful magnet to the teacher candidate, private schools would find it next to impossible to staff their classrooms and laboratories. Operating a private school is typically an exercise in financial brinkmanship, with the perennial threat of expenditures outrunning the income. In consequence, low faculty salaries in effect subsidize the education of the pupils. The great majority of private school teachers evidently find their greatest satisfaction not in the pay check they draw or whatever status they may enjoy, but in the satisfaction they can take in the performance of a useful social service. This is true of most school teachers, but particularly so of those in most private schools. The job calls for unending optimism in the task of helping others, with but small expectations of tangible rewards, monetary or otherwise.

The facts about faculty salaries can be readily summarized. The medians of cash salaries (exclusive of benefits) of lay teachers in elementary day schools during 1968-69 were as follows: Catholic schools averaged from $3,400 in the South to $4,014 in the Midwest and Far West,[11] the Protestants ranged from $4,800 to $5,357, the average for the independents was $5,600, and for teachers in NAIS schools, $6,200. These sums compare with an average salary of $7,854 for public elementary school teachers in the spring of 1969. Salaries in nonpublic secondary day schools were somewhat higher, with Catholic lay teachers averaging from $6,292 in the Northeast to $8,868 in the Midwest and Far West, Protestants from $4,060 to $6,560, and independents from $6,052 in the South to $8,931 in the Northeast. The national average for public school teachers was $8,467.[12]

[11] These averages are unquestionably on the low side. One cannot be absolutely sure that the Catholic responses included only figures for full-time lay teachers and excluded all the religious personnel, who are not paid a salary but usually receive maintenance and a cash allowance which generally adds up to less than a full-time lay salary.

[12] Public school average salaries are from *Financial Status of the Public Schools, 1970* (Washington, D.C.: Committee on Educational Finance, National Education Association, 1970), p. 19. Data obtained from salary studies conducted by three national nonpublic school associations are available for 1969-70, a year later than our study data:

| | Catholic[a] | | Lutheran[b] | NAIS Day Coed[c] | |
	Elementary	Secondary	Elementary Only	Elementary	Secondary
Median	$5,000-5,999	$6,000-6,999	$5,496	$6,800	$7,400
Range	n.a.	n.a.	$1,250-16,716	$3,500-15,000	$3,500-16,380

(Table notes are on p. 160.)

Annual fringe benefits and perquisites (including social security, retirement plans, medical insurance and health services, family allowance, housing and meals, if applicable) improve the compensation of the nonpublic school teacher by more than 20 per cent on the average. There is an appreciable increment for those who teach in boarding schools, where the average cash salary is somewhat lower than in the day schools, but where housing and maintenance boost the total compensation by as much as 50 per cent.

A big gap between the salaries of elementary and secondary teachers is evident in all types of private schools. This is true also of the public schools, even though they are committed in theory to the principle of equal pay. The higher salary for secondary teachers is often justified by the longer training required of secondary teachers, partly also because the overwhelming majority of elementary teachers are women. Neither argument should go unchallenged. Elementary teachers ought to have, if anything, even more training than teachers in secondary schools in fields such as psychology, anthropology and learning theory, as well as in appropriate subject-matter fields. And as to sex discrimination, the basic justice of equal pay for equal work is generally honored in the breach. Sex discrimination in salaries, while not generally admitted, is widely practiced by private schools which are hard pressed to meet the faculty salary budget. Many elementary teachers are married women who want to be usefully and gainfully employed; others teach under an arrangement which admits their children to the school tuition-free—an illustration of the kind of accommodation that a small private school can arrange. In Protestant schools some of the women teachers are ministers' wives, who are forbidden in some denominations to take other kinds of jobs, but for whom school teaching is approved as a dignified and appropriate occupation.

Private school teacher salaries vary enormously by states and regions, just as public school salaries do. But from the figures cited it is obvious that most private schools do not pay their teachers as well or nearly as well as do the neighboring public schools. Two-thirds of all private elementary school and one-half of all secondary school heads estimate that their schools pay faculty members on the average (with benefits) from $500 to $2000 less than do the public schools, while only among the NAIS secondary school heads is there any appreciable number who estimate that their schools pay more.

---

[a]*A Statistical Report on Catholic Elementary and Secondary Schools for the Years 1967-68 to 1969-70* (Washington, D.C.: National Catholic Education Association 1970), p. 22 (salary information available only for 1969–70).

[b]"Supplement" to *Teacher Salary Study, Elementary Schools* (St. Louis: Board of Parish Education, The Lutheran Church—Missouri Synod, July 1970).

[c]*Annual Statistics, NAIS Member Schools*, no. 31 (Boston: National Association of Independent Schools, December 1969), p. 4.

An even more striking difference between public and private school salary policy lies in the criteria employed to determine salary levels. Whereas public school teachers in general support fixed salary scales determined by seniority and the amount of education, a solid majority of the teachers and heads of private schools believe that greater weight should be given to merit than to seniority. In keeping with this belief, the current practice of independent schools is to weight merit more heavily than any other factor. On the other hand, although Protestant and Catholic teachers favor merit over experience, in practice their heads reverse the order. The difference between the independents and the church schools is attributable chiefly to the relative affluence of independent schools compared to the chronic impecuniousness of many church schools. Schools capable of paying only low or modest salaries struggle to provide a living wage for every teacher, and there is little latitude to recognize either seniority or meritorious service except within very narrow limits.[13] However, the better-heeled schools are in a position to stretch out the scale by establishing a substantial differential between a living wage and a reward for experience or merit or both.

One of the reasons why private schools are responsive to the claims of merit while most public schools are not lies in the characteristic difference in their institutional structure. It is the difference between what is possible in a small unitary organization as against a large bureaucratic system. "Merit" entails qualitative measures based on normative and admittedly subjective judgments. In the intimate environment of a small school with close human relationships, the school and department heads are in a position usually to make evaluative judgments about the teachers on the basis of fairly extensive direct observation. But a large system relies on uniformity, standardization, and spelled-out procedures, rather than subjective evaluations, as the best guarantee of fair and equitable treatment.[14]

If this is true of public schools, one would expect to find variations in the world of private schools between schools that are autonomous and those that are systemic. And in general this is the case. The independent schools, which are for the most part purely unitary, tend to stress merit pay. Catholic schools, on the other hand, include the more or less autonomous parochials as well as the diocesan and order schools, which are grouped into loosely knit systems. To the extent that these schools rely on interchangeable personnel they tend to give

[13]The Lutheran position, as stated in the *Teacher Salary Study*, is that "merit pay is not practical until all teachers receive adequate salaries for their basic work" (p. 21). A "Merit Pay Report" in the NUCS *Directory 1968–69* includes a teacher evaluation inventory (pp. 195–96).

[14]Parenthetically, parents of public school students favor merit pay. The percentages of responses of a broad cross-section of parents to a Gallup poll question, "Should each teacher

weight to seniority and thus resemble the public schools in their salary policies. The Protestant schools, however, vary considerably. For example, the Lutheran Church—Missouri Synod and its 35 district school offices publish salary guidelines that put only a moderate stress on merit pay. Since Lutheran teacher candidates receive their first appointment from the synod and thereafter are under district jurisdiction, the stress on uniformity and seniority in the salary policy is reminiscent of that of the public schools.

Another factor which strongly affects the salary expectations of certain church-school teachers is the concept of teaching as a religious mission or "calling," giving primary emphasis on "service to children . . . 'not for gain or glory,' but rendered with a sense of divine compulsion."[15] The beliefs of the Catholic monastic orders in this respect are well known—they do not expect and do not receive competitive salaries. While there is nothing quite comparable to formal monastic service among Protestant teachers (except in the Episcopal church), yet they too enter teaching usually with a strong sense of religious dedication. Hence they are less expectant of and less concerned about monetary rewards than independent school teachers. For example, a Lutheran high school teacher replied typically to a question about why the teachers remain at the school, "Whatever our reasons, they are not monetary." The present financial crisis of the Catholic schools is attributable in large measure to the fact that since the religious teaching orders no longer attract sufficient numbers to staff the schools, the places are filled by lay teachers who expect to earn a living wage.

How do nonpublic school teachers manage to support themselves and their families on the appallingly low wages—not much above the poverty level—that some schools pay? The question is most acute for Protestant secondary school teachers, who are mostly married men. The answers are various. The moonlighting teachers do everything from driving school buses to painting houses or operating a filling station. Four out of ten of all responding teachers have paying

---

be paid on the basis of the quality of his work or should all teachers be paid on a standard scale basis?" were as follows:

	National Total	Public School Parents	Parochial School Parents
Quality of work	58	61	52
Standard scale	36	35	43

Data were obtained in a Gallup poll sponsored by CFK, Ltd. From "The Public's Attitude toward Public Schools," *Phi Delta Kappan*, October 1970.

[15] *Teacher Preparation and Professional Growth, 1969 ACCESS Report* (Wheaton, Ill.: National Association of Christian Schools, 1969), p. 56.

summer jobs, and excluding the Catholic religious, over half the teachers find gainful summer employment in jobs which are for the most part unrelated to the school or teaching. This despite the fact that they badly need the time to attend summer school or to do some prolonged and intensive reading for their own professional improvement. Better than six out of ten of those who work summers earn over $500, and almost a quarter earn over $1500, a higher rate of pay in some cases than their teaching job offers. Another way of eking out the pitifully low salaries is the by now common practice of having spouses work and bring home a second pay check. Some schools employ husband and wife teams, thus getting in effect two teachers for the price of one and a half. Married women make up well over half of the teaching staffs in independent and Episcopal elementary schools, and nearly that number in the Lutheran and Seventh-Day Adventist schools. Many of these women work at paying jobs in the summer as well. Not all of them, of course, work out of sheer economic necessity. But given the generally inadequate salaries in all but a small group of private schools, it is safe to conclude that the spur of financial need is the compelling reason.

In view of the generally low salaries it is hardly surprising to find that a substantial majority of our private school respondents want a stronger voice in determining salary policies. Yet the poorest paid are not necessarily the most eager to have their say. As a group, the Protestant school teachers are the least insistent on the right to help shape salary policy even though their salaries are often gallingly low. On the other hand, the independent school teachers, who are the best paid in the nonpublic school domain, join the poorly paid Catholic teachers in demanding a voice in salary policy decisions. Obviously, other than purely economic motives are at work here. But the discontent over salaries surfaces in the complaint by one-third of the Catholic teachers and well over half of the independent secondary school teachers that they do not have adequate information about policies regarding salary, promotion, and tenure. Again, the Protestants are by far the most accepting of the status quo.

The same informal, individualized, unsystematic approach that distinguishes private from public school salary policies also characterizes the attitude of private school teachers and heads toward tenure. Unlike college teachers, for whom tenure has been a professional sacred cow for many decades, protecting an enormous amount of mediocre teaching and mindless research, private school teachers for the most part show a surprising lack of interest in the topic. Only about one out of four Catholic and Protestant and only one out of five independent secondary school teachers favor having a formal written tenure policy. Oddly enough, school heads support that practice somewhat more strongly. Most teachers and heads believe there should be no permanent tenure, and that the school should be free to dismiss teachers if their work becomes unsatisfactory even after three or more years of service. However, in most schools, except

163

those with automatic turnover by means of teacher reassignments, a "presumption of tenure" sets in after about three to five years of service. Nevertheless, the recognition of the school's right to weed out the incompetents stands in sharp contrast to the unrelenting demand of public school and college teachers for tenure.

Yet there may be good reasons why public school and college teachers stand more in need of the protection of tenure than private school teachers do. Given the religious and ethnic heterogeneity of the teaching personnel in some public schools, the low threshold in tolerance of individual differences (especially for teachers) in many American communities, and the fact that many public schools must administer their affairs in an atmosphere of political chicanery and conflicting social pressures—in view of these circumstances, a formal tenure policy guaranteeing job security is a way of protecting the personal and professional freedom and security of the public school teacher.[16] In the college world uniform tenure policies are commonly defended as the best protection of the teacher's freedom of utterance against incursions by censorious public officials, conservative trustees, or hot-headed presidents. The fact that private school teachers do not feel the need of this kind of protection says much about the prevailing quiescent climate in those schools. Tenure is a two-edged sword. Whatever the benefits that flow from strict adherence to a formal tenure policy, and they are undeniable, these are purchased at the cost of erecting heavy obstacles against the removal of mediocre and incompetent teachers—the "deadwood" which the public schools and colleges are obliged to work around.[17]

[16] The vice principal of a Los Angeles high school is quoted as saying, "Teaching is one of the few fields where you can fail, if you don't fail too badly, and you're all right. You're protected." Myron Brenton notes that the attitude of the wider community has brought on the protectionist security-minded unionism of public school teachers by trying to purchase education at bargain rates, with the teacher vulnerable to salary manipulations, mass layoffs, and the like. *What's Happened to Teacher?* (New York: Avon Books, 1971), p. 91. In a number of dioceses Catholic lay teachers have organized independent locals affiliated with the American Federation of Teachers to back up their demands for higher salaries and better working conditions. The Archdiocese of New York is an example. *New York Times*, December 9, 1970.

[17] Judging from the nationwide Gallup poll referred to in n. 14 above, a majority of parents oppose tenure. They responded to the question, "Are you for giving teachers tenure or are you against tenure?" as follows (responses in per cent):

	National Total	Public School Parents	Parochial School Parents
For	35	29	28
Against	53	60	62

Poor salaries are part of a syndrome that includes heavier teaching loads. Thus, the church-school teacher tends to have a somewhat heavier load than the better paid independent school teacher. It may be that the latter spends more time in coaching athletics and in other extracurricular duties, but in the crucial matter of class size, a major component in figuring the teaching load, the independent teachers are firmly committed to the mystique of small classes at a time when this practice is being questioned on educational as well as economic grounds. Larger classes, or even a mixture of large and small classes, they maintain, would impair the educational effectiveness and distinctiveness of their schools. As the head of a girls' boarding school in Massachusetts put it, "Small classes aren't the end-all, but we have to retain this distinction to be competitive with public schools." And as for the academically oriented NAIS teachers, who on the average already enjoy the smallest class size, they are strongly opposed to any increase.

The question of class size is of vital importance to the future of all schools, public and private. Unlike industry, which in the pursuit of profits strives constantly to increase productivity per man-hour of work, education in pursuit of excellence works the other way: the better the school, the smaller the classes and the student-teacher ratio, and the higher the salaries and the cost per student. In consequence, the spiraling cost of public education is provoking taxpayer revolts, while many independent and church schools feel they have about reached the limit of escalating tuition. Finding ways of teaching more students with fewer teachers but without lowering the quality is one of the paramount problems of education. No simple solution is in sight. The best hope lies in combining a judicious mixture of large and small classes, wider use of paraprofessional personnel, and the selective introduction of mechanical, electronic, and other types of teaching aids enabling the teacher to direct the education of more learners. That such steps will cut the cost of education without impairing its quality is as yet only a hope. By the gauge of past experience, the introduction of special teaching devices has generally *added* to the cost of education, though the devices may bring significant educational benefits in the form of more intensive, enriched, or accelerated learning.

The Teacher's Role in School Governance

One of the much discussed questions of school policy and practice nowadays is how much voice or power the various school constituencies should have in shaping policies. It is commonly supposed that most private schools are structured to place the decision-making power almost entirely in the hands of the school head and governing board. This is true of some, but by no means of all. In fact, there is considerable variation in the degree of influence accorded to faculty, students, and parents in different types of private schools. The general bearings of this issue are developed in chapter 10. At this point we should like to comment briefly on certain aspects of how faculties see themselves in relation to school administration and what they perceive to be the students' role in the decision-making process of their schools.

Although the church schools are commonly regarded as being more authoritarian and less democratic in their governance than independent schools, we cannot support such a view without important distinctions and reservations. For example, a far larger per cent of Protestant than independent school teachers agree with the statement, "In this school the faculty has as much voice in determining school policy as does the school head or administration," this despite the fact that in other connections Protestant teachers see the head and especially the governing board as quite properly exercising much more administrative power than the faculty does or should. This seeming contradiction may be resolved by taking into account the nature and functioning of certain Protestant religious communities. The school head functions, in principle at least, as *primus inter pares* of a group engaged in a common educational-religious endeavor pursued in an atmosphere of fraternal respect and trust, all are equal before God. Most Protestant teachers evidently feel they have all the influence they need or should have and are glad to concentrate on their teaching. When asked whether they had "too little opportunity to help shape school policy" only a negligible number agreed, compared to about a third of NAIS teachers who agreed. But the nonsectarian school teacher, undeterred by an overarching religious authority, behaves like an individualist who desires to make his voice heard in school affairs. Independent school teachers already have far more voice in the decision-making process than Protestant teachers do, but they want more. The evidence appears to support the generalization that schools whose primary goal is academic excellence generate demands for progressively increasing faculty influence.[18]

But there are other factors at work also, as may be seen from the relationship of faculty and administration in Catholic schools. The position of the Catholic teacher in respect to voice or influence is characteristically nearer the independents' than the Protestants'. Catholic secondary school teachers, however, are less sure than either the independents or the Protestants that they have a sufficient voice in determining the school's educational policies. Yet, many Catholic secondary schools already accord their faculties a considerable degree of influence

---

[18] A corollary of this demand is a more emphatic insistence on freedom of teaching and expression. A clear majority (60 per cent) of independent school teachers believe they should have the right to express their opinions about any issue they wish in the classroom, student newspaper, and elsewhere. Catholic teachers as a group muster only a bare majority (51 per cent) for such a stand, while among the Protestants only 31 per cent agree.

in policy formulation. These schools tend to be more sensitive also than other schools to "client power," that is, the combined influence of parents and students.

Private school teachers think they are a more significant influence in shaping school policies than either the governing board, the parents, or the students, but a lesser one than the school head. As for the board, most private school teachers believe that it should confine itself to such matters as selecting a new head, setting faculty salary policy (though the teachers think they too should have a strong voice here) and effecting any significant changes in admissions policy, such as admitting more minority students or children from poor families. For the rest, they think the board should keep hands off educational policy matters as well as most other aspects of school life. Only among Protestant teachers is there a relatively high acceptance of a directly educational role for the board. When one considers that most governing boards are empowered legally (or ecclesiastically) to take any and all steps that they deem wise or necessary, the offhand way in which teachers dismiss the educational influence that the board might exert is a commentary on the now generally accepted concept of a restricted role for trustees. Though some trustees are tempted to "interfere" in the affairs of the school, more perhaps out of a proprietary interest than in a meddlesome spirit, most are content to play a ceremonial, financial, and public relations role. It is a far cry from the concept of the trusteeship in days gone by, when trustees had few compunctions about taking a direct hand in guiding the affairs of the institution in all its aspects. But in the meantime education has become the province of professional educators to whom the trustees defer as "experts."

On the whole, private school teachers evince no overweening desire to have a significant influence in most policy decisions—nothing approximating the degree of faculty control that prevails in most colleges or universities. There are exceptions, of course. In the elite prep schools, such as Andover, Exeter, and the St. Grottlesex fraternity, one finds a high degree of faculty self-government. But in most others, when teachers do seek to make their influence felt, it is only on matters closely concerned with what they teach and with their students' daily lives, school work, and dress and behavior problems. For the rest, vast numbers of teachers are content to teach and let it go at that, leaving the running of the school to the administrators.

With respect to student rights, though the teachers generally agree in principle that students should have a voice in school affairs, they are chary of making any real concessions to "student power." They are inclined to regard student participation in school policy formulation as a privilege granted by the school rather than a student right. Teachers in Protestant secondary schools endorse this view overwhelmingly. Only among Catholic teachers is there an appreciable number—about a third—who see this as the students' right, a surprisingly liberal view on the part of church schools toward adolescents. The confident adult authoritarianism of Protestant schools is further confirmed by the strong majority of its teachers who believe that the school head should have, as a matter of school policy, the power to revoke the selection of particular student leaders. But substantial majorities of teachers in all other types of schools take the same position.

What is the attitude of these teachers about how best to deal with the student counter-culture and the questioning and confrontations which it precipitates? Most elementary school teachers, for whom the problem is minimal, would cope with it by applying firm discipline, with the Protestants surest that this is the right way and the Catholics least sure. But a smaller per cent of secondary teachers, for many of whom the issue is real and daily, are inclined to recommend that course. Surprisingly, however, secondary teachers overall are more inclined to believe in firm discipline than are the secondary school heads.

Why should the teachers be more disposed than the heads to fall back on the traditional simplistic formula for handling the complex problem of student unrest? Perhaps it is because of the teacher's view of his job. He thinks of himself as a subject-matter specialist responsible for what goes on in the classroom, an obligation which does not concern to any larger extent the wider psychological, behavioral aspects of his charges. Relatively isolated in his own sphere of action, he is characteristically inclined to minimize and underestimate the array of influences with which administrators must cope in school governance, including student behavior. On the other hand, the school head is less isolated than the average teacher, with the result that his relationships with the world beyond the classroom help to bring greater insight into the complex forces that influence the youth culture. He is responsible not only to the individual student for fair and constructive treatment but to the students' parents, and he must concern himself with the repercussions of his action on both faculty and student morale. Furthermore, it is he, not the teacher, who must face whatever consequences ensue from his choice. For all these reasons he does not easily permit himself the luxury of simple "firm discipline" decisions.

However much their attitudes toward student rights differ in the various schools, a large majority of teachers are united in believing that "due process" in case of serious student discipline or dismissal is important. Since no precise definition of "due process" was before them, it was easy to assent to proper procedures in principle, for it is equivalent to being for virtue and against vice. However, given the other known characteristics of these teachers, one would expect them to stand for fair, conscientious treatment and respect for the persons of young people. School heads are in substantial agreement with teachers on this point, although those in the academically strong independent schools show noticeably less enthusiasm. Why is this? One would suppose that the heads of these sophisticated institutions would be keenest of all for due process.

A possible clue emerges in the teachers' appraisal of the state of discipline in their schools. A majority of teachers in the church-related and independent elementary schools think it is about right. But in the independent secondary schools a slight majority of teachers, except in the South, are dissatisfied and think there is not enough discipline. The regional difference in this respect is marked. The explanation which appears to be most compatible with known facts is that the southern schools are able to maintain a rather strict discipline based on student acceptance of southern traditions of honor, courtesy, and respect for authority while the academically elite schools of the Northeast are much harder pressed to restrain a questioning, critical student body which is straining at the leash in their demand for more latitude in personal conduct, self-expression, and life-styles. It is a situation that places the northern headmaster in an embattled position between his studnets who demand more freedom, and the teachers and parents who are for clamping down harder.

The Responsibility of the School to Its Teachers

We have emphasized repeatedly that the chief problem of the schools, as such, is the expectation of society that they must somehow make up for all the shortcomings of the other institutions that slough off responsibility for the upbringing of children. So the school is saddled with responsibility for everything from education for life in tomorrow's world of vertiginous change to imparting the skills necessary to earn a living or preparing for college; everything from educating the child in religious, ethical, and civic dimensions, to teaching him about sex, about how to drive a car, and to build in him the perspicacity to see behind the deluge of false advertising and extravagant claims; and everything from opening his eyes to the evils of racism to building up safeguards against drug addiction. And the teacher, in addition to carrying the multifarious responsibilities of classroom instructor, patrolman, friend, patriot, scholar, disciplinarian, and baby-sitter, is expected also to be a model citizen and a personal example to young people.

Within the ranks of private school faculties one finds highly perceptive, gifted, strongly motivated, and skillful teachers, and their number appears to be increasing. But the rank and file are ordinary people of whom too much is expected, people who are severely underpaid and overworked, and people who, while they derive their major satisfactions from serving as guides to the young, also experience many discouragements. Teaching requires a continual act of faith, of trust, and of patience, and few people are blessed with inexhaustible reserves of these virtues. After five or ten years in the classroom, the enthusiasm for teaching inevitably wanes and its rewards pall, except for the rare few who remain young in spirit. A study of public school teacher drop-outs supports the disquieting conclusion that "those who depart are rated as better teachers than those who stay."[19]

Although some private schools offer a career ladder which beckons to the enlarged responsibilities and better salaries of the master teacher, while others offer at least some incentive in the form of merit pay, there is no way of knowing whether or to what extent the overall quality of teaching differs significantly as between public and nonpublic schools. Moreover, though public school teachers include a large number of graduates of state teachers' colleges recently transformed into general colleges, while the nonpublic school teachers come from Catholic, Protestant, private, and state colleges, the differences, except in the case of the religious teachers, are not very significant. True, the independent school teachers have had the advantage of a somewhat more liberal education, some at universities of high repute. But even an Ivy League education is no guarantee of long-maintained intellectual vigor, effective teaching, or the capacity to think penetratingly about the ends and means of education. "The weakness of teacher education," says Charles Silberman, "is the weakness of liberal education as a whole; if teachers are educated badly, . . . it is in large measure because almost everyone else is educated badly, too."[20]

Examples of the new, more flexible, diversified pedagogy are multiplying just now among private schools, particularly among the independents and to some extent among Catholic schools; but what the teachers themselves have to say about their ability to apply new methods is not reassuring for the future improvement of nonpublic schools. Fortunately, most faculties embrace a few young insurgents or undiminished older radicals—persons whom conservative headmasters often think of as "trouble makers." But the main impression is one of people who are content to do the conventional teaching job in the traditional way, people who lack the time and the inclination to seek a deeper understanding of the learning process. They read very little in the literature of educational research, professional journals, or books on education. "There are in all departments," a science teacher at Choate is quoted as saying, "men who freely admit they have not read a book outside of their course reading in years, as well as men who admit their commitment to academics to be secondary to that for [sic] athletics."[21] There is no reason to believe that Choate is an exception in this respect.

Not only is there a need for thorough-going reform of teacher education (we return to this subject in chapter 12); most schools do precious little by way of

[19]Brenton, *What's Happened to Teacher?* p. 27.

[20]*Crisis in the Classroom: The Remaking of American Education* (New York: Random House, 1970), pp. 380–81.

[21]Peter S. Prescott, *A World of Our Own: Notes on Life and Learning in a Boys' Preparatory School* (New York: Coward-McCann, 1970), p. 366.

inservice training of young teachers, let alone the re-education of the older ones who have become bogged down. Here or there in larger secondary schools a department chairman takes a continuing interest in the improvement of instructional techniques, but they are the exceptions rather than the rule. Generous sabbatical policies and financial assistance for summer study are available in the better-off schools, but these are utilized usually for the individual's professional improvement rather than as a means to improve the total learning environment of the entire school. Certain of the church schools—the Missouri Synod Lutherans come to mind—conduct a continuing program of in-service training through state and district offices including visits to classrooms, discussion of curriculum materials, and setting goals for improved patterns of performance. And each of the nonpublic school educational associations is committed to helping member schools with advice, with illustrations of what other schools are doing, and with national and regional conferences which aim to inspire as well as to instruct. The NAIS staff, for example, conducts a comprehensive program including the publication of how-to-do-it booklets, a quarterly *Bulletin* covering a wide range of interests, and conferences and numerous workshops addressed to the urgent problems of member schools. The activities of the associations are unquestionably an immense help and stimulus.

The weak link in the process of producing effective teachers is not, however, the lack of outside agencies and associations to provide necessary support. The central weakness lies in the failure of individual schools to provide necessary sustenance for the continuing professional development of young teachers. The education that counts for most in shaping a teacher is what he learns about children, teaching strategies, and the learning process in his classroom from nine to three every Monday through Friday. Such on-the-job experience is potentially more influential and lasting than his college education and all his courses in education, workshops, and institutes taken together. But this is true only if he has sympathetic encouragement and guidance from able and experienced colleagues. Without such help, his very independence, his freedom to design his own courses and teach them in his own way, which is often cited as the glory of the private schools, can be a severe liability. As a teacher in a midwestern suburban country day school observed, the teacher, wrapped up in his own courses and with the classroom as his private sanctum, can make the same mistakes over and over until they become habitual. The only answer is a new awareness on the part of individual schools of the importance of steady, constructive efforts to help young teachers grow as professionals and as people.

7

Styles in Leadership: Headmasters and Principals

*"The head of a school . . .
need not choose between
being an absolute boss
or only a sweeper of floors
and payer of bills.
What the good teacher
can do for children,
the good administrator
can do for his teachers—
create and maintain
an environment in the highest degree
favorable to their learning
and growth."*

John Holt[1]

The Changing Conception of Leadership

The success or failure of private schools depends to a large extent upon the quality of the school head's leadership. Whereas the public school principal characteristically is subject to the control of a central administration and guided by detailed, carefully spelled out procedures,[2] the private school head works within an autonomous domain. In principle at least, the private school is directed

[1] Introduction by Nat Henthoff, to *Our Children Are Dying/The Headmaster*, by Henthoff and John McPhee (New York: Four Winds Press, 1967), p. 17.

[2] Bernard Bard, in reporting on the year-long study of high school principals in New York City undertaken by Arthur J. Vidich and Charles W. McReynolds for the U.S. Office of Education, notes some of the frustrations of the job: "If the union has emasculated the principal as boss, the bureaucracy has emasculated him as administrator. It gives the orders on teacher assignments, controls the flow of substitutes, shapes the curriculum, dispenses the budget, promulgates 'circulars' by the hundreds, and demands reports in volume. . . . . Badgered by the union and the board, bludgeoned by the critics, buffeted by the community and its spokesmen, baffled by student militancy of a style and vehemence they never experienced, the principals' occupational psychology . . . is to defend the status quo and their own expertise." *Saturday Review*, January 24, 1970, pp. 59, 71.

173

from within and is responsible only to its own board, its clients and supporters, not to government bureaus or to the public at large. And since most governing boards of private schools customarily delegate broad powers to the head—powers that reside legally in the trustees—it is the quality of the head or succession of heads that makes or breaks a school. In bygone days the head more often than not exercised these powers autocratically, either gently and benevolently, or ruthlessly and harshly, depending upon his style and his conception of the best way to get the desired results. He was secure in the knowledge that he could be shorn of his authority only by the intervention of the governing board or the reigning ecclesiastical authorities, or *in extremis* by a total rebellion of all the school's constituencies; this happened only rarely, in response to gross mismanagement or glaring insensitivity to the principles of elementary justice.

But now that the teachers have become professional and power-conscious while the students tend to question not only the wisdom but the legitimacy of autocratic authority, the dictatorial stance is considered an anachronism. In modern times the etiquette of administration calls for a wise head to share certain of his powers not only with his coadministrators, but with the faculty as well; and more recently he is obliged to ponder the extent to which it is either expedient or wise to hear the student voice in decision-making. The sensible head also listens to the views of parents and alumni—but without neglecting his main task with reference to these constituencies, which is to educate them about the ends and means of a good education and what that entails by way of academic freedom and responsibility.

People who are disposed to think of times past as the "good old days" often bemoan the fact that the era of the great college and university presidents and of great headmasters is past. Where are today's Daniel Coit Gilman, William Rainey Harper, Charles Eliot, Nicholas Murray Butler, William Allan Neilson, and Alexander Meiklejohn—giants who were innovators as well as leaders? What headmasters today are surrounded with the aura of a Mackenzie of Lawrenceville, Peabody of Groton, Drury of St. Paul's, Stearns of Andover, or Perry of Exeter? Comparisons of this sort are manifestly loaded in that they pit the best of several generations of leadership in the past, seen in the saving perspective of time and distance, against the unfinished careers of those currently laboring in the vineyard. Legends are not made overnight, least of all in today's flamboyant world of communications, which exploits every chink in the armor of anyone who rises to prominence. Moreover, the public has come to expect that prominence is usually achieved only with a supporting cast of public-relations men, fund-raisers and assistants, so that when fame comes it has a suspiciously synthetic cast. Educators are no exception. Yesterday's educator-heroes had the advantage of working under relatively uncomplicated conditions in which a gifted man with strength of character and personality and the power of convictions could be a

174

dominating centripetal influence, while placing the seal of his personal leadership firmly on a school or college enterprise.

But now we have entered the age of consensus with its competing centers of power and influence, each of which must be consulted, persuaded, or placated about a proposed plan of action. It is standing operating procedure for a school head who runs hard up against a problem to ascertain first what other schools of his kind are doing about it. Like as not his letters will cross theirs asking the same question of him. It usually leads to a conference or a "workshop" for the discussion of common problems. There are obvious advantages in such a procedure. Several heads may indeed be better than one, and reflections on pooled experience should yield more circumspect decisions than each one picking his way through on his own. But the need of eliciting a consensus obviously marks out a new role for the school head or college president. Unlike the dictator of old who knew what he wanted and who enjoyed the power to command, the modern head does not decide on a course of action by consulting his own intuitions and the advice of a few confidants; he is expected instead to canvass the opinions of interested constituencies, so that his role becomes that of a negotiator, mediator, balancer, and compromiser, instead of a charismatic leader whose word is law within his fiefdom. The style of leadership that results is therefore characterized more by prudence, circumspection, balancing of conflicting influences, and caution rather than by the boldness and swiftness born of the self-confident exercise of sole control.

But there are exceptions. While it is true that the trend in modern times and modern techniques of administration have led to a growing democratization of private school governance, some of the old-line independent schools retain much of the flavor of the nineteenth-century authority structure under which the head is invested by the governing board with virtually absolute power, while the faculty has very little to say except in an advisory way or insofar as it is permitted some elbow-room in carrying out the headmaster's mandate. Though such a scheme of governance is condemned nowadays as dictatorial and anachronistic, in the hands of a wise and gifted headmaster it has been known to achieve great results. The unique accomplishments of Deerfield's Frank Boyden, who bridges both eras, are a case in point. Without pretense of power-sharing or any semblance of faculty committees or student government—not even a business manager—he not only violated all the accepted rules regarding the proper delegation and distribution of power and responsibility but ignored the claims of participatory democracy—yet with a splendid outcome.[3] But the point is that Boyden's way—total reliance on his own intuition and judgment—seems in retrospect like a happy but clearly dated exception that proves the rule.

[3] See John McPhee, *Our Children Are Dying/The Headmaster*, pp. 163–253.

In private school leadership there is no single style or way of leading that can serve as a model for all schools—no single educational pathway, no special previous career or class background that spells success or failure as a school head. Everything depends upon the personal and professional qualities that the head brings to his work and his ability to establish a relationship of mutual trust and respect with the constituencies within and outside of the school. Just as in teaching, there are many different ways of being good and many ways to fail, and no two successes or failures are identical.

Despite the fact that the modern private school head is more consensus-minded than his predecessor of a half century ago, still, compared with a high school principal he is in many respects "on his own." His job is that of an educational entrepreneur who should be shrewd enough to perceive, in the words of the old hymn, that "new occasions teach new duties, time makes ancient good uncouth"; and he should be imaginative enough as circumstances require to revalue the ends or to devise better means to their realization, and persuasive enough to lead his constituencies in the process of revaluation and reform. The job of administering the ongoing affairs of the school is the easiest part. Where the head is put to the test is in responding to situations not of his own making that close in on him, new currents that render hitherto workable assumptions obsolete. He is less free than was his precursor of even two decades ago to plot his own course. He is drawn willy-nilly into the search for better, more effective education, into the battle for equality of opportunity and against racism, into the religious dilemmas of our time, and as many heads see it, into a struggle for economic survival. Most school heads unite in emphatic agreement that their job today is radically different from what it was ten or even five years ago. It is vastly more complex. As the head of a well-known school in Washington, D.C., said to visitors: "The old certainties are gone. . . . We must build on new values and recast the old."

These strong currents of change convey to many private school heads an acute awareness of the uncertain and unpredictable future not only of their own school but of nonpublic schools as a whole. Contradictory and opposing forces are at work. On the one hand, though boarding schools are suffering a decline in applications, the independent schools as a whole are still growing in numbers. The high-fee institutions survive chiefly because parents are prepared to make sacrifices to give their children an opportunity for what they consider to be the best education within their means. As long as the public schools in many localities are in deep trouble and turmoil, the demand for places in private schools, especially in day schools, will increase. But what the headmasters worry about is that, given the already top-heavy fee structure of expensive schools, along with the heavy capital cost of plant expansion and inflated operating costs, there is little area for maneuver in the event of contingencies such as the unionization of the faculty and service staffs, or the need for increased funds to improve the student ethnic mix, or to finance new ventures generated by Black Power issues and militancy. And in the background is the threat of loss of income because of conservative shifts in the public's expectations of the school in everything from the treatment of radical teachers to the petty vagaries of dress codes and hair.

Nor is the position of the church schools an enviable one, as the school heads are well aware. In these days of ceaseless and largely unpredictable change and with ecumenicism in the air, the future of institutionalized religion is fraught with uncertainty. In the Catholic world the combination of the subsidence of anti-Catholicism in the public schools, the increased cost of Catholic schooling because of the decrease in the religious personnel, and the participation of Catholics in the migration from city to suburb with consequent access to better public schools—all combine to reduce the margin of possible benefits to be reaped from enrolling children in Catholic schools. The results are evident in the widely publicized closings and mergers which have reduced Catholic school enrollment by about 23 per cent since 1965, and the end is not yet in sight.[4] There is little optimism of growth among the heads of the Lutheran, Seventh-Day Adventist and Christian Reformed school groups, though there is no evidence either of a serious decline. It is the school heads of the evangelical groups who are most optimistic. One can only speculate regarding the reasons. Evidently the growth of these schools is in part a backlash among middle and lower middle class social and ethnic groups against modernism in religion, politics, education, and the spread of the hedonistic-pagan lifestyle; in part it seems to be a manifestation of the desire to overcome the jagged disjunctions of modern life by means of a total spiritual commitment as a witness to the truth revealed directly in Scripture. But the schools that serve these ends are not without their strong internal tensions between the academic ambitions of teachers and heads and the fundamentalist convictions of parents, or between the idea of Christian brotherhood and inherited racial prejudice.

The Religious and Moral Orientation of School Heads

The feature which most sharply differentiates the various nonpublic schools of the nation is their view of the role of religion in the educational process. Until very recently almost all school heads as well as most of the teachers in Catholic schools were drawn from the clergy and religious orders. The growing dearth of the religious personnel for teaching apostolates is a matter of grave concern to Catholic leaders, though some see in it an opportunity for a salutary academic

[4] Enrollment declined from 5.6 million in 1965 to 4.3 million in 1970-71. *A Statistical Report on Catholic Elementary and Secondary Schools for the Years 1967-68 to 1969-70* (Washington, D.C.: National Catholic Educational Association, 1970); and *New York Times*, April 7, 1971.

renewal and the opening of more windows upon the world. Be that as it may, Catholic school leadership remains largely in the hands of men and women who received a liberal education and formal teacher training (if any) largely within the confines of Catholic colleges, seminaries, and universities, with perhaps some additional graduate work here or there in non-Catholic institutions. Notre Dame and Fordham Universities, Hunter College, Boston College, Holy Cross, the string of Loyola colleges and universities, and a host of other Catholic institutions of higher education operated by various teaching orders are the chief sources of teacher supply. The Lutheran schools rely primarily on the midwestern Concordia colleges of the Missouri Synod and to some extent on the graduates of Capitol University, Valparaiso University, Muhlenberg College, Pacific-Lutheran University, Wartburg College and others operated by various Lutheran bodies. The Seventh-Day Adventists have their own teacher-training centers, among which Walla Walla University in Washington state and Andrews University, Michigan, are prominent. And the Christian schools of Calvinist, evangelical, and pentecostal bodies look chiefly to Calvin College in Michigan and Wheaton College in Illinois for their teachers.

So it is that upbringing, education, and a host of churchly influences combine to shape the values and outlook of these church-school educators. Religion, along with philosophy, is preeminently a concern with life goals and transcendent ideals—salvation in religious terms, the good life in philosophical terms. However much religion is suspect in the eyes of secular educators because of its reliance on supernatural powers and transcendent values, it moves within a framework of concern for first and last things and explicit convictions about the nature and destiny of man. The orthodox church-school educator, therefore, finds the major premise of the educational syllogism in the theological doctrine of his communion, and his task as an educator is to devise the minor premise and the conclusion in the form of an educational program that will implant and nurture the faith in the lives of the young.

In practice, however, this is far from being either a neat or a simple step. Even seemingly entrenched doctrinal positions undergo reinterpretation and change. Who would have thought in 1950 that by 1970 Catholics would be openly challenging the doctrines of papal infallibility, sacerdotal celibacy and other seemingly fixed and irrevocable cornerstones of Catholic belief? Moreover, it is far from simple to translate religious ideals into educational goals or, having done so, to find the appropriate means to attain them. Spiritual ideals are usually open to a variety of interpretations and do not point unequivocally or consistently in a single direction. Even if one were to reduce the educational goal to purely behavioral terms, such as "to make better Catholics," or "to make better Lutherans," there would still be ample latitude for debate because of varying conceptions of the meaning of "better" in these contexts. Thus, though the church school educator appears to have an advantage over the secular private school head in that he works within an apparent community consensus regarding religious and moral goals, his mandate as an educator is far from clear. Not only must he bridge the dualism of religious and academic ends, he must do it in a way such that conservatively minded church authorities, boards, and clients, as well as liberally minded constituents—the faculty and students in particular—do not feel undercut, co-opted or sold out in the process.

In probing further into the religiously rooted goals as these are conceived by the heads of church schools, our school visitors found a singular lack of imagination and enlivening thought. For example, in certain of the Protestant schools which stress religion heavily—Lutheran, Christian Reformed and schools of the evangelical sects—the effort to elicit from the head his conception of how religion influences the goals as well as the content of education seldom led to anything more than the repetition of denominational rhetoric to the effect that education is to be "Christ-centered" or "Bible-centered" or "for the greater glory of God." In many schools religion appears to be not so much the invigorating nucleus of a humane education as a protective facade which facilitates the perpetuation of ethnic subcultural traditions. Yet the evidence is substantial that despite the inability of most religious educators to articulate their guiding principles in anything but pedestrian ways, the religious setting of the school does make an important difference. It is not what the teachers say, but what they do; not the content of religious and moral instruction, but the life within the school. The atmosphere, the outlook and expectations, the dedication of the staff, the warmth of the relationship between the young and adults in most schools in which religion is a vital influence, are unmistakable. Perhaps much of this atmosphere is attributable to the cultural homogeneity of ethnic background, class, or religion which is characteristic of most of these schools. But however one explains it, there is no doubt that the presence in the school of pastors, nuns and priests, or rabbis exerts, seemingly more by example than by precept, a pervasive influence over the young. As William James once remarked, if one had the choice between associating with a rich religious personality or a "sterile scientific prig," it would not be a difficult decision. Many young people in the church schools feel that the presence of the religious teachers adds a special dimension to their schooling.

The public's conception of the place of religion in the church schools tends to exaggerate the stress on formal religious exercises, indoctrination, and more or less overt preaching. As the principal of a Catholic high school in New York City said, "You don't push dogma down children's throats. At this level, religion should be an opening up process and no more." Rigid, routinized, mindless observances of traditional religion do not go down well with the generation now in school. As a teacher in a Catholic middle school in Cleveland said, "The students don't go for religion with a capital R." Yet it remains a vital force for many students, not as a set of observances, but as a spirit that pervades the entire environment. In many schools the course in religion or the "meeting" in Quaker schools is the one point where students and teachers can come to grips more candidly than anywhere else in the curriculum with the problems of sex, alcohol, and narcotics, abortion and birth control that beset young people.

By contrast, in most nonsectarian schools religion in the traditional sense, when it is not totally absent, plays an ambivalent role. Though in times past many heads of independent schools were clergymen, today very few have had theological training, or even much college work in religion. In these schools religion survives in the form of an ecumenical humanism tinctured with liberal Protestantism. Their primary concern is the student's academic development, and religious education plays a subordinate role. However, because they do stress the development of character and the student's growth in moral values, doctrinal religion survives usually as a shadowy presence serving as the handmaiden of morality. Many Episcopal and Friends schools, even though denominationally affiliated, are in this respect essentially akin to nondenominational independent schools. In such schools, whether church-affiliated or not, the relationship of religion and morality is vague and the place of religion in the school is often ambiguous: the headmaster strives to maintain a semblance at least of continuity with the school's liberal Protestant charter while the younger faculty are generally indifferent and most of the students are either apathetic or hostile to formal religion. The continuation of compulsory chapel, where it still exists, is a topic of perennial debate. As academic concerns become all-engrossing and traditional religion is relegated to a marginal or largely ceremonial role, the chaplain is obliged to operate far from his theological base if he expects to command the attention of students and exert any influence on their lives. Often the headmaster, the chaplain, a few older faculty, and a handful of students are the only ones who seem concerned about the survival of traditional religion on the campus. The headmaster of a nonsectarian boys' boarding school in Massachusetts told our visitors that although he knew most of his boys neither prayed nor sang in the school's splendid, costly chapel, he would insist that they attend its services as long as he remained as headmaster. Six months later, yielding to student pressure, compulsory chapel was abolished; the head is still there.

The traditional model that young people in independent schools were expected to emulate was the WASP gentleman: the versatile, clean-cut, well-mannered, prudent man of affairs, who, favored by the circumstances of his birth, plans his life and invests his time and money carefully with the goal of becoming rich, respected, and influential—a pillar of society. It was the ideal of the ruling class that set the tone and standard of success in American politics, business and industry, society, education, and the professions from colonial times until well into the twentieth century. It is also the ideal that a growing segment of young people, including those who are to the manor born, are questioning vigorously today. The fact that this life-style is being viewed with growing misgivings or outright disdain (and in some cases flatly rejected) by some of the brightest and most advantaged students deeply troubles their parents and perplexes the headmasters of the prestigious schools, most particularly the boys' boarding schools. They sense that their traditional mission—forwarding their graduates to the Ivy League colleges—is in danger of losing its validity, while there is no clear vision of a fresh goal that is viable under the existing pattern of private school support. It is not surprising, therefore, to find in *The Independent School Bulletin* and at conferences of the NAIS concerned discussions by headmasters about the prospects for survival of their schools. The fact that such searching reappraisals are taking place may mean that the prospect for a renewal with new goals is brightening. However much these schools are censored as having been in the past exclusively the servants of a select class, they represent an educational resource which the nation can ill afford to abandon.

The Head: The Ideal and the Reality

"Not long ago a faculty friend in a college searching for a president," wrote E. Wilson Lyon, former president of Pomona College, "asked me to suggest a candidate. 'If you run across a six star man,' he wrote, 'with the hide of a rhinoceros, the patience of Job, the power of an atomic bomb, the missionary zeal of a Livingstone, the money-making proclivities of a Carnegie, all combined with infinite tact, sound educational policies, magnificent appearance, and a knock-out wife, let us know.' "[5] The private school headship or principalship is usually of a smaller order of magnitude, but the problems inherent in the office are comparable. The range of activity that the head may be properly expected to engage in is so considerable as to defy the powers of any one man to cover it satisfactorily. He deals with at least six constituencies: the faculty, the trustees, the students, the parents, the alumni, and the public, each of which could claim much of his time. And there is always the hazard, as Robert M. Hutchins once remarked, that he will spend just enough time with each of the six to irritate the other five.

The magnitude and scope of the head's responsibilities vary enormously depending upon the size and type of school as well as the kind and volume of financial support it enjoys. The administrative and other problems of elementary schools are usually simpler than those of the secondaries, and the same should be said of day in comparison with boarding schools, all other things being equal.

[5] "On Being a College President," *American Oxonian* 38 (July 1951): 137.

But apart from these and other evident variations, the inherent difficulty of the job is the versatility that is expected of the incumbent: he must be a competent administrator who can evoke cooperation from people who often have little taste for it and prefer "to think otherwise"; he should have a good head for budget-making and running a business enterprise; he should be himself a competent teacher and a good judge of the teaching capacity in others; he should know how to interpret the school to the community and win for it moral and financial support; and above all else he should combine in his person the philosopher of education who can think penetratingly about ends, and the man of action who can translate a vision of what should be into the means for its fulfillment. It is a tall order, and it is small wonder, therefore, that there are many journeymen but few masters. Since such paragons of virtuous versatility are few and far between, most schools in choosing a new head settle for a person who appears to embody as many of the desired characteristics or potentialities as possible.

The leadership style of private school heads differs significantly from that of public school superintendents and principals in that the private schools pay much less attention than do the public schools to administrative skills and techniques per se, and much more to personal and moral traits, including an interest in the young and related characteristics. Neither the private nor the public schools appear to pay much attention, in considering the qualifications for school leadership, to scholarly attainments or to interest in educational research or academic innovation. Trustees of private schools prefer personable, likable men and women of sterling character to stand for their school in the public eye.

While opportunities for the formal training of public school administrators are available in abundance in public and private universities, programs tailored to the special requirements of private school headships are few and far between. Apart from the valuable inservice summer workshops and seminars in educational leadership and administration conducted by the NAIS, the NCEA, and other denominational bodies, and the occasional summer courses offered by the Universities of Chicago, Virginia, and elsewhere, the only nonsectarian graduate center that presently concerns itself to any significant degree with the special needs of private school leadership training is the University of Massachusetts at Amherst, where a doctoral program in educational administration is sufficiently flexible to take into account the special concerns of private school administrators.[6] Trustees and patrons of private schools still tend to assume that leaders

[6] The NAIS-sponsored summer seminars on school administration, which began in 1960, were developed and are conducted by Professors John B. Matthews, Jr., and John Seiler of the Harvard Business School, using as a model the Institute for College and University Administrators conceived by Professor Robert M. Merry. The workshops, which go back to 1968, are conducted by invited school heads and NAIS staff members. The doctoral program at the University of Massachusetts has existed only a few years, and it is as yet too early to assess its effectiveness.

are born and not made, a view that is not easily disputed because the able leaders of the past, in the absence of opportunities for leadership training other than by example or by understudying a great headmaster or principal, rose usually from the ranks of teachers and learned what was learned about leadership on the job and by "instinct." But as the acceleration of change and the attendant complexity and involvement of the head's job increase, the time for learning the hard way is foreshortened as the costliness of the mistakes of inexperience rise. And so the national private school associations, recognizing the supreme importance of creative leadership in both academic and business affairs, are giving more thought to leadership training programs designed to speed the maturation of potential leaders by schooling them in the knowledge, insight and skills which will enable them to make sound judgments and circumspect plans. These efforts by the associations are restricted, unfortunately, by the paucity of their financial and planning resources.

Most heads of private schools, at both the elementary and secondary levels, are teaching heads, an arrangement which is made possible by the relatively small size of these schools.[7] In this respect the heads of American private schools resemble those of the English state schools as described by the Plowden committee. The teaching head in American church-affiliated schools is usually selected for his teaching ability and interest in children as well as for his leadership and administrative potential. The various criteria are weighted somewhat differently in the selection of the heads of independent secondary schools in that the leadership potential is of greater concern than teaching ability. But this exception aside, in most private schools administrative matters are held to a minimum by delegating some of them to experienced secretarial assistants and by sharing others informally with the teaching staff. This contrasts sharply with the public school practice in the United States, where about 50 per cent of the elementary school administrators do no teaching at all and evidently prefer it that way.[8]

[7]Some statistics on the average size of schools in the United States are given below:

Year	Elementary		Secondary	
	Public	Nonpublic	Public	Nonpublic
1963–64	380	354	413	297
1965–66	420	326	438	296

Source: Digest of Educational Statistics, 1967, table 2; and *Digest of Educational Statistics, 1969*, table 7 (Washington, D.C.: U.S. Office of Education, Department of Health, Education and Welfare, 1967, 1969). The steady trend towards consolidation among public schools has probably enlarged this difference by now.

[8]*The Elementary School Principalship in 1968* (Washington, D.C.: National Education Association, 1968), p. 44. Of the elementary school administrators sampled, 19 per cent termed themselves "head teacher" or "teaching principal" and 82 per cent called themselves "principal" or "supervising principal." In the latter group 69.8 per cent claimed they spent no time in regular classroom teaching in an average work week.

The small school led by a teaching head has certain advantages in that it minimizes the distinction between "administrators" and "teachers" as well as the higher status which is usually accorded the former to the detriment of the teachers. Moreover, the teaching head is more likely to prevent administration from developing a life and empire of its own, as it so often does once those responsibilities are separated wholly from teaching. John Dewey commented long ago on the fact that so many teachers and administrators succumb to the temptation to become submerged in the mindless routines and details of their calling, to expend most of their energies upon forms and regulations, reports and percentages. He saw this as evidence of a lack of intellectual vitality and serious commitment to the continuing study of education.

The faculties of elementary and secondary nonpublic schools do not see their school heads primarily as scholars or philosophers of education nor as administrators or chief executives; neither do they admire them for business and financial expertise. Rather, the heads are appreciated for their personal qualities and for their moral and spiritual leadership, for their interest in and understanding of young people, and because they are approachable leaders who work well with other teachers—as the first among equals—and with the public. Only among the faculties of the Catholic elementaries, which group includes some larger schools, is the head characterized as predominantly an administrator.

The way the faculties assesses private school leadership is instructive in both what it reveals and what it omits. In general, the traits that they see as most characteristic, in addition to moral leadership, are those conducive to making the school function harmoniously—informality, approachableness, understanding, personableness, liking for young people. No sensible person would underrate the importance of good human relations and mutual respect in the school situation. But if the school is to be educationally effective, it should be a center of ceaseless inquiry into the ends and means of education. Given the structure of the private school, the head is in the best position to provide the spark of renewal and invigoration. Yet the majority of teachers seldom see the head as most characteristically an educational philosopher, or an inventive, imaginative leader who stimulates fresh inquiry or provokes enthusiasm for trying new ways.

The teachers' views of the head's qualities are, in the main, confirmed by the opinion of governing board respondents, who are charged usually with the selection of the head. Evidently, the qualities of leadership they search for reflect what they consider to be characteristic of the heads now employed, for the trustees also emphasize the personal qualities which serve as an example to the young, over and above academic expertise, or the capacity to stimulate inventive, imaginative solutions to educational problems facing the schools. Only the Catholic secondary school governing boards—a group with a high proportion of educators—showed a strong tendency to characterize the head as one who gives much attention to philosophical goals of education and practical ways in which to achieve them.

This evidence suggests that one of the chief reasons why many established private schools are content to carry on the educational fundamentalism of the three R's, taught in the time-honored way, is the failure of trustees or other selection groups to search for the kind of leadership that would challenge the conventional way and the accepted order of things.

Today's school heads, more than those of the past, depend upon others for ideas and support in planning for needed changes. The source of ideas and inspirations they value most is the resources of imagination, analysis, and experience which they find among their faculty colleagues. This fact points up the great importance, in filling faculty vacancies, to look not only for persons who qualify for a particular teaching slot, but for young teachers who have knowledge of and can generate enthusiasm for experimental approaches. A few such can improve the whole tenor of faculty discussions, and through leadership of faculty committees and special study groups gifted teachers can exert a considerable influence. Most heads count among their most instructive, enlightening sources of new thought the deliberations and reports of faculty committees addressed to problems as varied as teaching methods, curricular reform, discipline, religious life, coeducation, the grading system, off-campus learning activities, and a reassessment of the school's goals and prospects.

Among Catholic schools reassessments have been prompted recently both by the calamitous financial outlook of some, and in the interest of strengthening the capacity of schools, diocese by diocese, to develop a rational plan which is within the church's financial capabilities. Studies of this sort are common, too, among independent schools either individually or in groups. Given the ferment in education today, with long-held assumptions called into question, with the future shrouded in uncertainties and unpredictables, and with survival at stake for many institutions, it is to be expected that the governing boards and heads of private schools will tap all the expertise available to study the course that the school should pursue. The Choate–Rosemary Hall study and that of Exeter are two of several entered into by single-sex schools to explore the possibility of conversion to coordinate education or coeducation. The Four-School study (Andover, Exeter, Lawrenceville, Hill) probed various possibilities of a new mission for these institutions, such as the establishment of a four-year senior-high–junior-college combination, similar in its structural arrangement to Simon's Rock, in Great Barrington, Massachusetts. The "Turning-Point Committee" at the Ethel Walker School is a good illustration of the type of reassessment which is going on in many schools.

Because of the distractions of their job, most heads devote relatively little time to continuing self-education by studying educational journals, research reports, or books on education. If the test of a good education is the degree to which it sparks a lifelong desire for the continuance of learning, the colleges have failed these heads, the denominational colleges even more so than the others. But then, the multifarious responsibilities of the job are so time-consuming and distracting, the habit of study and reflection even if once acquired rapidly falls into disuse.

One formerly untapped resource of ideas and inspirations is the students themselves. They are beginning to be heard, sometimes in a big way.[9] It is the young who have the future in their bones. It is they who perceive, however dimly and confusedly, if not the shape of things to come, at least the irrelevance, the outwornness, the betrayal of the dream which is implicit in things as they are. It is particularly important that they be listened to about education, for the school is their world, or rather, the world that adults have made for them. As such it is bound to incorporate visions of the past rather than a fresh appraisal of new possibilities that the young discern, as they see the world with eyes as yet unencumbered by the rationalizations, compromises, hypocrisies, accumulated guilt feelings, and frustrations that older people collect along life's way. The major dilemmas of "school" stem from the fact that it is conceived as a place where the young are told what to see and believe and study and value by adults who, in the fast-changing world of the present, are prone to live in a receding and already obsolete world. When this happens, what the adults think the school is doing for the young often bears little or no resemblance to what the young actually get from the school.

The authoritarian outlook, exemplified in some Protestant school heads by the "father knows best" and "children should be in their place" attitudes, is often oppressive in the largely unquestioned matter-of-factness with which it is accepted. Outwardly it works, to the satisfaction of the adults at least. These schools have fewer behavior problems and seemingly lower levels of dissent and expression of grievances than is the case in progressive independent schools where students are more likely to be consulted and encouraged to make their views known.[10] Nevertheless, the visitor finds the relationship in the Protestant

[9]See Alan R. Blackmer, *An Inquiry into Student Unrest in Independent Secondary Schools* (Boston, Mass.: National Association of Independent Schools, 1970), pp. 29–39, for an account of the varied and constructive responses made by NAIS schools in 1968–69 to student desire for a voice in the decisions affecting their lives.

[10]Yet some of the same doubts and resentments that flourish in other schools also surface among the students in Protestant schools. Visitors to a Christian academy found the faculty generally agreeing that there was no student unrest, just "some negative attitudes." "Authority is God-given . . . the rebel is the person who has not yet been brought under the Holy Spirit," they explained. But a student later expressed his own version: "This is a small Christian school and the kids want to rebel. . . . Sometimes they want to be like the cool kids in the public school. . . . There is a lot of unrest in Christianity itself. . . . Some don't want all this big relationship with God."

schools between head and students to be generally a cordial one. The explanation appears to lie in the sense of community centering in a shared religious faith which, by infusing both the school and the home, leads to a mutual reinforcement of accepted standards of behavior and roles. But however satisfactory this relationship is for avoiding "trouble," whatever insights the young may have regarding the process of education and how it may be improved remain largely untapped and unappreciated. Only in framing the petty regulations regarding dress and grooming and the bland agenda of student government are students in many of these schools encouraged to participate.

A number of independent schools, on the other hand, have profited by student-initiated general school evaluations aimed not only at specific issues but at deeper reforms. Students at Deerfield, St. Paul's, Exeter, and Choate recently drew up comprehensive proposals which precipitated extensive faculty-student conferences that are likely to have far-reaching effects.[11] The NAIS, recognizing the growing student interest in educational change, held four conferences in 1969–70 on "Student Concerns and Institutional Response" attended by faculty, administrators, and students. At one of these, student spokesmen drew up a ten-point list of desiderata toward which student-faculty discussion groups should work.[12]

"Without external pressures or alliances," wrote Anthony G. Oettinger about the public schools, "the schools themselves rarely initiate change."[13] Private schools too are cast in a durable mold and are resistant to change. But the prospects for change appear brighter now, especially among the independent schools, than for some time. And the primary influence in bringing about the improved prospect is the aroused interest of students. An alliance of students working in tandem with a headmaster and a faculty who are willing to listen—yes, even to learn—holds out hope that a new day is dawning for the schools.

The Head as Administrator

The thing that makes the private school head's job so rewarding as well as so taxing is the variety of activities that he is supposed to be knowledgeable about, engaged in, overseeing, or leading. A good head must be something of a Renaissance man, a jack-of-all trades; and he must learn to live with the fact that his day, like "woman's work," is never done. Schools that are both small and

[11]Blackmer, *Inquiry into Student Unrest*, chaps. 5–7.

[12]For a sensitive report on these conferences see David Mallery's *Toward a More Human School* (Boston, Mass.: National Association of Independent Schools, 1970).

[13]*Run, Computer, Run: The Mythology of Educational Innovation—an Essay* (Cambridge, Mass.: Harvard University Press, 1969), p. 61.

impecunious—the description fits most elementary and many secondary private schools—have little to spend on administration, so that the head not uncommonly is the whole administration and must be many things to his varied constituencies. To the students he is not only a teacher among others, he is also a father confessor, a counselor, tutor, coach and fellow athlete, a morale builder, the number one rooter at all school activities, as well as the symbol of authority, a disciplinarian, and, when the going is rough, the scapegoat. To his teaching colleagues he is the faculty builder, the chief of curriculum planning, a teaching guide, and a student of methods and theories, a general trouble-shooter, a stimulator and enlivener of lagging projects, who must also project the proper ceremonial image. In addition to all that, he is the immediate controller of the school's purse-strings and as such the man to see about promotions, pay increases, benefits and other vital statistics. He is, in short, "the boss." Few jobs call on the same person to be a friendly colleague, the judge, and, if need be, the executioner also; but this is all in the day's work of most school heads. Beyond that, to the parents he is the symbol of the school's integrity and its chief spokesman and interpreter, and a pleader for support in the community. More importantly in the eyes of some parents he is expected to function also as an advisor and amateur psychologist who is called on to diagnose their children's progress or lack of it, personality problems, and emotional hang-ups. To the trustees he is the man in charge, accountable to them for the operation of the school in all its detailed functioning; and they expect him to be the school's chief public relations officer and money raiser. It is a formidable list that even the most versatile man or woman can cope with only partially at best. The sensible head soon learns to shape the office to his own special strengths and abilities.

The principal of a small elementary school—with, say, a hundred or fewer students—may be obliged to carry on with only one man or woman Friday who functions ostensibly as a secretary, but is actually the principal's sixth sense as well as an extra pair of eyes and ears and hands. Such a functionary may bear any one of several titles in name or in effect: secretary, assistant, dean, registrar, business manager, admissions officer—a sort of academic ombudsman who collaborates with the head on some or all these functions and acts as a buffer between him and the plethora of daily happenings and perplexities. Or these functions may be divided among various members of the faculty who are paid a little extra and gain some administrative experience which may help to prepare them for a headship later. Many church-affiliated elementary schools are administratively understaffed just as they are underbudgeted, whereas the more prosperous independent schools and the larger, higher fee secondary schools of all kinds generally provide considerable administrative assistance for the head. The atmosphere of the small school—and increasingly that of the large school as well—is conducive to informal relations between teachers and administrators and thus tends to tone down the status distinctions between teachers and administrators.

In the larger private schools, the head is usually a full-time administrator with a staff set up in accordance with a more or less formal table of organization, and with the separate officers each possessing a measure of special expertise, learned, more often than not, as teachers on the job. But even here full-time administrators appear to be relatively rare. The dean, the registrar, the director of admissions of a secondary school enrolling upwards of 500 students usually keeps his hand in also as a teacher, so that here too the status distinction between teacher and administrator is not sharp. But the business, public relations, and fund-raising functions are more likely to be held by full-time practitioners who in many cases have been recruited from occupations other than teaching. These positions are sought after by, among others, Army colonels and Navy commanders who have reached early retirement, as well as by an occasional businessman who is fed up with the venality and money-grubbing of the commercial world and is looking for socially significant work. The business managership calls for an able, imaginative, far-sighted person, but too frequently the position is filled by bookkeepers who merely record transactions rather than see the job as an opportunity to help creatively mold the institution's future.

In trying to ascertain how the heads divide their time among a plenitude of functions, we found that heads of all types of private schools, particularly the smaller ones, say they devote more of their time to working with students directly than to any other responsibility. This is true particularly of Catholic and Protestant elementary school heads, most of whom carry substantial teaching loads, while they also carry their share of advising and counseling duties and cope with special situations arising from student conduct. The next most time-consuming responsibility is the head's activities with the faculty—discussing curricular questions, meetings with committees and chairing faculty meetings, interviewing candidates and making appointments, discussing teaching problems and questions pertaining to salaries and related matters. The heads of Catholic schools devote almost all their time to these two primary responsibilities—students and faculty—in comparison with independent heads who spread a share of their time over a variety of other activities, such as admissions work, alumni relations, and long-range planning. The Protestant heads, on the other hand, devote more time to their governing boards who, as we have noted in several connections, play a more prominent role in these schools.

The one activity to which most heads admit devoting relatively little time is fund-raising. The reluctance to spend much time on this activity points up a dilemma in the prevailing concept of the head's manifold responsibilities. If he is to be an effective educational leader, he should be above all a student of the

189

psychology and philosophy of learning, and if he is to keep abreast of new developments in education his week ought to include some quiet hours for study and reflection and the exchange of ideas with colleagues.[14] But the hard facts of life intrude in the form of the continual financial brinksmanship required to keep the operation solvent and running. The church school heads have an advantage in that local congregations and, to some extent, the local dioceses or religious orders fend for them. These schools are inclined to cling to the faith that the Lord will somehow provide, which means practically that congregational tithing will make up the difference between the school's operating cost and income from the relatively modest tuition payments. The independents, however, have to rely on their clients, alumni, and such others as they can manage to interest in supporting the school. The alternative is the repeated escalation of tuition and fees which in some independent schools have reached dizzying heights. Now that all but a few well-endowed private schools face a deepening financial crisis, heads must find ways to devote more time to the urgent business of keeping the schools not only solvent but operating with a financial margin sufficient to enable them to maintain an effective, decently-paid teaching corps and to create some elbow-room for improvements and experimenting.

But where is the time to be found in the head's busy schedule for this, to most people, somewhat distasteful business of beating the bushes for financial support? There is talk in some of the larger schools of experimenting with a two-man headship—bisecting the job—with Young Aristotle in the study concerned wholly with academic leadership and administration, while Mr. Brisk is on the road giving his undivided attention to business management, fund raising, and public relations.[15] It is easier said than done. The various constituencies as well as the general public are accustomed to look to one person as the head, and it is difficult to achieve complete equality in a divided headship. Potential donors usually want to talk with *the* head man and tend to think of him, in accordance with past traditions, as the academic head of the school. But sometimes it happens, in both schools and colleges, that the appointed head or president, who has made his way up the required academic ladder, turns out to have a greater flair for business management and entrepreneurship than for academics and is content to delegate educational leadership to a dean or a

[14] Rabbi Cohn, the headmaster of the Maimonides School in Brookline, Massachusetts, when asked how he might better spend his time, replied that he would like to spend 20 per cent of it thinking, 40 per cent in give-and-take discussion between students, teachers and himself, 10 per cent as a supervisor, and leave 30 per cent for those bits and pieces such as the repair of the boiler.

[15] Edward T. Hall, "Two Heads are Better," *The Independent School Bulletin*, October 1968, pp. 12–14.

vice-principal, while he devotes his time chiefly to building the buildings, increasing the endowment, augmenting the annual operating income, and working with the alumni, the governing board, and in the community.

A similar division of leadership is not uncommon among church schools, especially in the Catholic parochials, where the local pastor often assumes the major responsibility for the school's finances while a nun takes over the academic principalship. In Protestant schools, particularly those owned by parents, the governing board usually plays a more aggressive part in school governance than is the case in other nonpublic schools, though this does not necessarily mean that the board assumes full responsibility for the school's financial solvency.[16] In the last analysis the extent to which governing board members— whether in church or independent schools—pitch in and free the school head of gnawing financial worries depends not so much on the form of organization and formal division of responsibilities as on the school's tradition and the ability of the head to persuade the natural community of support of the unique value and benefits of the school's work.

How Can a Head's Performance Be Measured?

How does the head determine whether or not he is doing an effective job? A school is not a business enterprise, the success or failure of which is revealed by a profit and loss statement in annual reports. The school's profit is in what its graduates carry away in terms of improved skills, heightened awareness, an enlarged sense of appreciation, and a deepened comprehension of man and his place in nature and society. These are obviously not measurable either in the process of acquiring them or in their ultimate effects. But the head and those who judge the quality of his leadership are not without important clues, though each of them needs to be interpreted with care and circumspection. They concern chiefly the stature that the school attains or maintains. For example, continued pressure for admissions to the school is commonly regarded as a measure of success, though taken alone it can be deceptive. Schools are sought after—and rejected—for spurious as well as for sound reasons. Another gauge commonly used to measure the stature of secondary schools and their heads is the college

---

[16]For example, in some Protestant schools, governing board members serve on the schools' admissions committees. A visitor to a "Christian" high school found that the admissions committee consisted of a group of men from the board plus the headmaster and a teacher coordinator. Admission was not based chiefly on academic ability, but rather on special guidelines having to do with family faith, the composition of the class into which the student was to be admitted, and so on. Independent school boards, by contrast, set admissions policy but seldom take part in the screening of applicants.

performance of their graduates. But who can determine whether a good college record is attributable chiefly to high native intelligence, to family and home influences that provided strong incentives, to preparatory schooling, or to other special influences and circumstances such as the fact that some young people turn out to be "late bloomers"? Moreover, there are schools that regard college prepping as only one aspect of their total mission, which also includes a terminal education designed to equip students to live in the modern world. Formal evaluations by accrediting agencies are another index, but as everyone who has followed this activity knows, the standards employed are more often than not strongly establishment oriented, so that an unorthodox or off-beat school is likely to be viewed askance.

The ability to attract and hold a good faculty is another conventional measure of the head's success, but "good" here as elsewhere rests on a subjective judgment. Does it mean a properly certified faculty, teachers with solid Ivy League degrees, a faculty chosen for its liveliness and provocativeness but with a mixed educational background, a faculty chosen with an eye to the kind of personal influence each teacher exerts, a "safe" faculty that will not rock the boat, or a mixture of several of these characteristics? And as to faculty turnover, many church-affiliated schools shift nonlay teachers from post to post at intervals of three or four years by "assignment" or "calling" as a matter of policy, while some independent schools regard a certain amount of turnover at the lower level a desirable thing.

Or is the head to be judged, by himself and his constituencies, by the extent to which he succeeds in introducing creative innovations or in coping with change? Whether his activity in this area raises or lowers his stature depends upon many factors, including the specific character of the reforms, school traditions, the cooperation of the faculty and the response of students, and the reaction of trustees, parents, and alumni. Timing is an important factor. A young headmaster taking over after a long preceding regime, during the latter stages of which nothing much changed, is rather expected to challenge established practices and policies. Some schools, on the other hand, are seen admiringly in the eyes of their supporters as pockets of stability which are counted on to remain unchanged in an unstable world. "Just because there is change everywhere else, we must make sure nothing changes here," said an alumnus of Choate, overlooking the fact that many things had indeed changed.[17] It is not uncommon for church-school leaders, accustomed to appealing to the eternal verities, to support such a view. While some private school educators take the coming and going of hair styles, student demands, and rising faculty expectations in stride, others take these phenomena as symptoms of deeper disturbances that challenge the

[17]Peter S. Prescott, *A World of Our Own* (New York: Coward-McCann, 1970), p. 381.

validity of the very goals and traditions of the school, without which the school would lose its *raison d'être*. The school visitors gained the impression that some heads are waging a prolonged quixotic battle to suppress the symptoms, for fear of opening up a Pandora's box of questions about goals and fundamental assumptions.

Another gauge of the head's effectiveness is that intangible, the morale of the school: an indefinable blend of loyalty, pride, and emotional attachment. Although there is no objective measure of morale, even sophisticated observers voice confident judgments about it based on the belief that the difference between schools with high and low morale is readily apparent. But it is far from easy to assess morale, because the means by which it is expressed have changed drastically during the last decade. Exuberant "school spirit" is largely a thing of the past, and its disappearance worries many of the elders. To the Now generation it is square to express enthusiasm for anything connected with adult-managed institutions, except perhaps at football, basketball, or hockey games. Today's critical students express their approbation in strange ways. As a senior in the Cambridge School of Weston, Massachusetts, put it: "If you ask me anything specific about this school, I'd have to say it stinks. But if you ask me is it a good school, I'd have to say yes."[18] Naturally, many things besides the influence and achievements of the head coalesce to produce good morale. But to a marked degree in the independent schools, and to some extent in the other types, the head provides the vital presence that holds students, teachers and administration in a constructive working relationship. He is the bond that makes things work by giving both spirit and direction to the enterprise. "The headmaster is a crucial figure. His style and personality inevitably define and lend either clarity or confusion to the polarities and paradoxes [that] schools try to balance."[19] But no matter how capable or charismatic the head, he alone cannot build good morale in the absence of a generally empathic response from faculty, students, and trustees. Yet this too depends in large measure on the head's personality and approaches. It is a virtual certainty that the spirit pervading a school will not be vigorous and sustained unless the head lends vitality and direction to all its endeavors.

There are also the more obvious gauges of a head's success: buildings, enrollment growth, campus expansion, growing prestige, alumni satisfaction, enlarged financial support. Few school heads are content to be known as great builders in

---

[18]Richard H. de Lone and Susan T. de Lone, "John Dewey is Alive and Well in New England," *Saturday Review*, November 21, 1970, p. 83. This article contains a lively appraisal of the Windsor Mountain School in Lenox, the Cambridge School of Weston, and the Stockbridge School in Stockbridge, all in Massachusetts; the Woodstock County School in South Woodstock, and the Putney School, both in Vermont.

[19]*Ibid.*, p. 84.

bricks and mortar only or for filling the coffers of the endowment fund. Being the special breed that they are, they prefer to be known for the faculties they developed, for their success in working with teachers and students and, as one of them commented, "presiding over the whole show and constantly trying to continue things so the school will be in first-class shape ten or twenty years on."[20] They desire above all to see their lives and careers as having contributed to a fundamental social endeavor which is vital to human welfare.

How Long the Tenure?

How long, ideally, should the head's term of office be? If he takes over his duties with a mind full of ideas, it may take three or four years of adjustments to put these into effect, and unless he is willing to be a new broom that sweeps clean, it may take even longer. Beyond that at some point in most administrations things level off and a period of stability ensues. This usually suits the trustees and parents as well as older faculty who grow weary of the yeast of change and are grateful for a steady pace and a period of relative calm and stability. But the students and young Turks on the faculty may begin to grow restive as the school becomes more settled in its ways.

We asked the constituencies of schools of different types—head, faculty and trustees—what they consider the ideal length of tenure for the head. Their judgment appears to be affected to some extent by what they have observed to be the normal span between the coming and going of heads. In the church schools the general expectation of a relatively short tenure prevails—about seven to nine years, with some believing the head should move on after three or four years. Very few of those questioned show any enthusiasm for a tenure extending beyond twelve years. In the independent schools, however, our respondents see merit in a longer tenure, with some favoring fifteen years or more. These norms conform roughly to the realities. Independent school headmasters (including their colleagues among the Episcopal and Friends schools) tend to have longer tours of duty than do the heads of most church schools.

This divergence affords an insight into a basic difference in the conception of the role of leadership in the two types of schools. Although it would be a mistake to underestimate the extent to which district or conference officers of the church schools work with local educational councils to find "the right man," heads of church schools, except as noted, tend to be regarded as interchangeable administrators within the denomination or religious community, people who can be shifted readily from one post to another. The common character and similar

[20]Francis V. Lloyd, Jr., "The Secondary School Principal or Headmaster: How He Got There and How He Finds It." *The School Review* 76 (March 1968): 92.

structure of schools of the same denomination make it possible for a knowledge-able, experienced administrator to move relatively easily from one to another, secure in the knowledge that he will be working, in a new situation, with people who share his basic assumptions about goals and beliefs. The search for "a new man" is restricted usually to a circumscribed list of those who are eligible on religious and educational grounds. The sense of being subject to a larger, all-encompassing authority—the Catholic, the Lutheran, or the Seventh-Day Adventist Churches—supports the idea of carrying out God's mandate. "God wants us to do this work," said the head of a Christian academy in Pennsylvania. "It's as simple as that." It matters most that he be doing this work; where, apart from considerations of private convenience, matters less.

Independent schools, by contrast, cast a larger net, so that the search for "the right man" usually takes months and sometimes years. Since the successful candidate is to be the head of a fully autonomous school, the trustees and the faculty, and nowadays in some cases the students, want to make sure he has not only the right academic and administrative qualifications, but above all that his personality and approach be such as to merit the confidence of faculty and respect and affection of the students, as well as to win friends and support for the institution, and to establish a cordial working relationship with the trustees. "I am fully aware, how rare such men are," wrote Judge Samuel H. Huntington, midway through the long search for the first rector of St. Paul's School. "Still I would postpone the opening of the school even a year, rather than to begin with a teacher who did not come pretty nearly to the standard which I have briefly indicated."[21] For the independent school the choice of a new head is a critical decision which can make or break all but the strongest institutions within a decade.

There is much to be said for the practice of some schools in appointing a head for a specific term, near the end of which the performance is assessed in order to determine whether or not the contract should be renewed. Original appointment with indefinite tenure, unless it provides for evaluation and review at stated intervals, easily leads to prolonged tenure even for a head who is doing no better than a routine job, while the need for a fresh assessment and vigorous leadership piles up ominously. As long as some independent school headships carry with them the pomp and imperiousness of a small independent barony, it is embarrassing all around to raise the question of the headmaster's competence, unless an understanding to that effect is made a part of the original appointment. We noted above that, contrary to what is commonly believed, the length of tenure of independent school headmasters is increasing rather than diminishing. Some

[21] From a letter to George C. Shattuck, Jr., quoted in James McLachlan, *American Boarding Schools: A Historical Study* (New York: Scribner, 1970), p. 146.

see this as a good thing, because it lends stability and continuity to the school's functioning. But there is no way of knowing how many heads are overstaying the period of their maximum effectiveness. Too often, well-intentioned protocol, hopes for a second wind, trustee timidity before the professional's expertise, or the plain fact that most trustees are uncertain about when they ought to speak out and when they should remain silent cause an indefinite postponement of the evil day for raising the difficult issue.

The Leadership Role of the Governing Board

It is at such a point of decision that the role of the governing board is crucial. However the appropriate area of jurisdiction of the governing board is conceived—it varies greatly among schools of different types—everyone agrees that the choice of a new head, or the evaluation of an incumbent's leadership, is preeminently a trustee function. Whether it is also uniquely a trustee function is increasingly questioned by teachers and more recently by students of the more advanced secondary schools. It is not uncommon for enlightened trustees to involve the faculty and, to some extent, the students in the search. But under the governing statutes of most schools they cannot yield even a fraction of their empowerment to reach the final decision without inexcusably abdicating their responsibility.

How well are the governing boards equipped to tackle this as well as other problems that come under their purview? There is truth in John Kenneth Galbraith's sarcasm that "the governing board is not yet a harmless anachronism. In many respects, it remains a barrier to rational progress."[22] Recent studies leave no doubt that college and university trustees are drawn from a very narrow spectrum of society, and that they are selected more for their donorship potential or their "name" than for any capacity to carry out the duties and responsibilities of the office. School trustees, by comparison, are drawn from a somewhat broader spectrum, though here too certain strata are neglected.

For example, in the matter of age, though almost a third of the adult American population was between 20 and 34 years of age in 1968, we found that this group is only fractionally represented on the boards of Catholic, Protestant, and independent schools, with the elementary schools somewhat more hospitable to youth. In respect to income, though about two-thirds of the population earned less than $10,000 in 1967, this group is totally unrepresented on the independent school boards sampled,[23] and a little over a third of Protestant

[22]Quoted by Morton A. Rauh, "Putting the Trust in Trustees," *The Independent School Bulletin*, October 1969, p. 66.

[23]There are some exceptions. For example, the board of directors of the New Lincoln School in New York City granted permission for two students to attend board meetings, but

elementary school boards come from this group. Occupationally, it is the business and professional (other than education) people who sit on the boards, while educators are only fractionally represented, except on the boards of Catholic secondary schools, where they comprise two-fifths of the whole.

We found also that the typical pattern of trustee participation is such that their relation to the school is in many cases tenuous and distant. Most involved are the governing board members of Protestant secondary schools, with a participation that averages almost two hours per week, devoted largely to periodic board and committee meetings. The pattern of Catholic secondary school board participation averages out to about an hour and a quarter per week but differs from the Protestant pattern in that it gives less stress to board meetings, and more to conferences with school personnel and talks with students. The typical independent secondary school trustee spends about the same amount of time per week as the Catholic, but spends more time on fund raising. The amount of time devoted by elementary school trustees is only slightly less. Overall, the level of participation of elementary and secondary school trustees is about equal to that of college trustees (about one and a half hours per week on the average). It is questionable whether it is enough to give trustees the grasp they need to reach well-founded decisions. But most headmasters interviewed thought it was about right and expressed the fear that overinvolvement might sorely tempt the board to preempt the managerial functions that ought properly to be exercised by the head.

In fact, the heads of several parent-owned and operated NACS and NUCS schools complained bitterly to school visitors about the intervention of certain board members who call the tune in school affairs while other trustees remain indifferent to the school. Evidently, these were not isolated cases. The NUCS House of Delegates, concerned over the number of principals and administrators leaving their positions, authorized in 1968 a "Principal Mortality Study" which found that, next to low salaries and heavy work loads, the defecting principals attributed the high turnover to "too much responsibility and too little control" and "relationships with the school board."[24] The seeds of misunderstanding, lack of communication, and meddling are always present in institutions controlled de jure by a board which must of necessity delegate most of its powers to appointed administrators who are accountable to the board.

Morton A. Rauh of Antioch College holds that board-school relations might be improved by taking several radical steps. Though he is speaking of college trustees, one should keep in mind that secondary schools, especially those in the

without voting privileges. The membership of the board includes, in addition to twelve public figures, eight parents and four members of the staff.

[24] *Directory: 1968–69* (Grand Rapids, Mich.: National Union of Christian Schools, 1969), pp. 192, 214–215.

independent sector, tend to imitate the colleges with a time lag of a few years. He suggests, first, that the trustees be brought out of their seclusion and anonymity and that trustee meetings be opened to the academic community. He reasons that "while some open meetings about controversial items would be uncomfortable, trustees would quickly learn to adapt to the new setting." Second, he suggests enlarging the franchise by permitting other constituencies, the faculty in particular, to have a voice in the election of trustees just as alumni do. Third, he recommends that trustees be drawn from a wider spectrum of society as regards age, income, and occupation so that more diverse views are represented on the board. Fourth, he suggests that trustee responsibility be more widely shared in answer to "the clear need for faculty and students to join with management and trustees in joint solutions to common problems," instead of carving out separate areas of jurisdiction. And fifth, he recommends that greater trustee participation be encouraged in order to increase their understanding of the institution.[25]

In the college world, certain of these steps have been urged for some time and in the upheavals of the last few years forward-looking institutions have been experimenting actively in opening up the decision-making process to the academic community by creating various kinds of advisory joint committees of trustees, faculty, students, and alumni. Faculty representation on the governing board, efforts to diversify board membership, a broader sharing of the responsibilities of college governance, and, perforce, a larger investment of trustees' time in instituting and participating in these developments together define a trend that may in time lead to a substantial revision of the concept of the governance of private educational institutions.

Rauh's first suggestion—opening trustee meetings to the academic community—will set many administrative and trustee teeth on edge, and we too question its advisability. If the end is to inform the school community about who the trustees really are and to give assurance that they are sufficiently knowledgeable about the attitudes of various constituencies to reach wise, just, and impartial decisions, this can be accomplished by carefully structured committees with adequate faculty, student, and trustee representation. Not the least of the benefits that would flow from such an arrangement is the insight that older and younger people gain by listening to points of view other than their own and learning in the process the art of working together as partners in a common enterprise. These encounters have often led to setting aside a day or several days for an all-school meeting just before the fall opening or during the school year,

[25] Morton A. Rauh, *The Trusteeship of Colleges and Universities* (New York: McGraw-Hill, 1969), p. 67.

such as the Middlesex School's Evaluation Day[26] or the weekend student-organized retreat at the Delaware County, Pennsylvania, Christian School. It is an eye-opening experience for trustees who become involved in these activities. The Germantown Friends School draws on its Quaker heritage of the Meeting to bring all school administrators and representatives of faculty, students, parents, and alumni together into a "school committee" which sits from time to time in order to distill "the sense of the meeting." But the hazard of open trustee meetings in some institutional settings is that they might become an endless forum for many voices, or a kind of adversary proceedings which might not only divide the community but seriously impede the decision-making process and undercut both the trustees and the school head in the exercise of their responsibilities.

Many alert schools are already exploring or trying various possibilities of broadening the base of the advisory bodies that contribute to decision-making. By virtue of their relatively small size and closer relationship of students and teachers, many private schools are in a position to move more freely than the colleges into a more open and shared responsibility in school governance. There is a strong likelihood that the voices of responsible young people will be listened to, and that it will challenge the inventiveness of old and young to find the means of involving the student's whole person in the process of learning and in the conduct of the school. In the process, old assumptions will inevitably be put to the test and some may prove to be obsolete. As Cary Potter, president of the NAIS, said: "If schools are going to respond in major ways to the needs of the times, they are probably going to emerge as quite different institutions from those with which many of their constituents are familiar."[27]

[26] Blackmer, *Inquiry into Student Unrest*, pp. 75 ff.

[27] "Student Concerns and Institutional Response," *Report of the National Association of Independent Schools*, May 1969 (Boston: NAIS, 1969), p. 3.

8

Making Ends Meet: The Crisis in School Finance

"The time for action,
whether of a broad
or specific nature, is extremely late.
Our historic partnership
of public and private commonweal endeavor
is in grave danger
because of the state of apathy
that is permitting the decline
of private institutions.
Unless this decline is arrested
and reversed, we
and our children after us, will almost
certainly be living in a society
where the idea of private initiative
for the common good has become
little but a quaint anachronism
largely associated with the mores
of an earlier age."

Alan Pifer[1]

The Fat Years and the Lean Years

All along we have stressed the diversity that characterizes the private school world as a whole. But there is one respect in which nonpublic schools are all alike, and that is in their concern over how to make ends meet. There is little or no diversity in respect to this well-nigh universal financial plight. And beyond the immediate concern over how to meet this year's unavoidable expenses, the long-run outlook, in view of the present economic uncertainties, is anything but reassuring. The combined thrust of long-run inflation, the current recession, and steeply rising teacher salaries has precipitated a deepening crisis so serious that private school leaders openly speculate about the capacity of many schools to survive, not only the new experimental schools, but long-established ones. The

---

[1] Alan Pifer, "The Jeopardy of Private Institutions," reprinted from the *1970 Annual Report of the Carnegie Corporation* (New York, 1970), pp. 14–15.

basic problem is twofold: (1) how can income from various sources be increased on a scale sufficient to meet the constantly increasing costs; and (2) what can be done to control the escalating costs? As long as costs increase faster than income, all private institutions—schools, colleges, universities, hospitals, museums, symphony orchestras—are headed for trouble, and their survival is imperiled.

The sudden economic down-turn, coming after two relatively prosperous decades, has caught all private institutions overcommitted and unprepared. The schools are no exception. In good times the schools tend to spend right up to their annual income or a little beyond, figuring that small deficits can always be covered in ensuing years by tuition increases or periodically by an organized campaign for funds. In this spirit many schools took on during the good years commitments to a step-by-step program of faculty salary increases, curriculum diversification, improved student services in counseling, health and off-campus opportunities, scholarships for a better ethnico-economic mix of students, and renovations and additions to physical facilities. Growth, constantly increasing annual budgets, and occasional deficits came to be accepted as part of the school's normal operation and expectations. But now that the lean years are here, the needed tuition increases, which were counted on in the past to balance the books, loom as a risky step. Moreover, to some heads and trustees the times seem inauspicious for intensive fund raising and the energetic pursuit of financial aid. Nevertheless, costs keep rising relentlessly in the continuing inflation, while the sources of income grow at a much slower rate. "The result," in the words of Cary Potter, "is that the schools start the 1970s having used up much if not all the income growth potential, while faced with all the upward pressures of the last five years, further compounded for private institutions by the decline in both the tuition and gift potential brought on by the 'recession.' "[2]

In this chapter we shall have something to say about what can be done about this financial plight. It is indeed perilous for many private schools, but it is certainly not hopeless. We doubt that the climate which was so favorable to large-scale philanthropy to private education in the 1950s and 1960s is changing drastically for the worse. The summary figures for gifts to education do not bear out such a gloomy prediction. We believe, however, that the new and tougher situation calls for more careful long-range planning, a hard look at expenditures and the budget-making process, far greater cooperation with other schools both to diversify life within the schools and to effect economies, more aggressive and

---

[2] "Independent Schools and Public Aid," a Statement for the Panel on Nonpublic Schools—President's Commission on School Finance, November 25, 1970, p. 2. The statement notes that for the NAIS member schools during the 1960s, "despite major increases in giving and other income and nearly double tuition, there was not only no gain in the financial viability of institutions, but actually a decline with more than half of the schools reporting operating deficits in 1969–70 as opposed to about one-third in 1960."

persistent student recruitment as well as fund raising, and above all the kind of leadership that sees the changing times and the changing human outlook not as a threat but as an opportunity.

As a prelude to developing these points about what can be done, we propose first to come to grips with the present financial situation and practices of nonpublic schools, a task which is rendered extraordinarily difficult because there is nothing even approximating a uniform accounting system among them. There are also many variables. Many church schools, for example, receive substantial contributed teaching and other services upon which they do not even attempt to place a dollar value, or they do not count the cost of the use and maintenance of the school's facilities, expenses which are often defrayed directly by the congregation or parish, which also contributes money in support of the school. For these and other reasons, published figures on the per pupil cost of educating young people in church schools—usually reported as being much lower than the cost of comparable grade levels in the public schools within the same community—are often quite misleading and should not be taken at their face value.

Where the Money Comes From

The sources of income of nonpublic schools vary greatly. Tuition has always been a major source of operating revenue, but the extent to which different types of schools depend on this source varies considerably. Just as there are few nonpublic schools which are altogether "free," in the financial sense, so there are very few at the other extreme wherein tuition pays the full cost of the child's education. Whereas most nonpublic schools raise much or most of their operating revenue by tuition and fees, they are aided also by funds from other sources: by gifts, grants, and the proceeds from bazaars, fairs, dinners, and other enterprises designed to raise money for current expenses; by income from endowment enjoyed by a favored few schools; by parish or church contributions functioning as a "living endowment"; by a great variety of projects and auxiliary enterprises, such as summer camps, profits from book store and food service operations, rental of facilities and services, and so on. A few forehanded schools avail themselves of public assistance from federal funds disbursed under titles of the Elementary and Secondary Education Act (ESEA); others qualify by virtue of their location for one or another kind of state or local aid, such as equipment grants, bus services, food subsidies, health services, textbook loans, aid for pupil accounting and mandated services, shared-time programs, and a variety of other forms of public assistance. Of major benefit to the Catholic schools are the contributed services of the nuns and priests of the religious teaching orders. These would add up to a staggering sum expressed in terms of the cost of equivalent teaching services by laymen paid at going faculty salary rates. As a result, many Catholic schools have only the vaguest notion of the true cost, or conversely, the true financial input of the school.

In considering the income pattern and financial practices of the church-related schools it is well to take note first of the considerable differences in the per-pupil cost among schools of different denominations, using as a bench mark the national average expenditure per pupil in 1968 of $594 in public elementary and secondary schools.[3]

Turning first to the Catholic schools, we note that the decade of the sixties began on a note of high optimism but ended in pessimistic reappraisals. "Because of teacher salary pressure and the necessity of going into the open market to recruit teachers," writes Professor Ernest Bartell, C.S.C., an economist at Notre Dame University, "the per-pupil costs of Catholic schools have increased far more rapidly than per-pupil costs in other sections of education. In the Ohio diocese . . . costs were a meager $65 per pupil in 1958, they had gone up to $92 . . . by 1963, and were up to about $200 per pupil in 1969. . . . Three hundred per cent increases over a ten-year period are fairly typical in the operating cost of Catholic schools."[4] By comparison, the increase in per-pupil expenditures in public schools during the decade 1957–58 to 1967–68 was 85.9 per cent.[5]

The reported per-pupil cost in Protestant schools is appreciably higher than in the Catholic schools of the same level and comparable quality, chiefly because the contributed services of the teaching orders reduce the reported cost for Catholic schools. For example, in the Lutheran elementary schools the per-pupil cost was reported to be $364 for 1970, an increase of 48 per cent since 1964, while the secondary schools spent $669 in the same year, an increase of 46 per cent over the five-year period. The average tuition charge in 26 Lutheran high schools for 1970 was $390.[6]

How much of the per-pupil cost is covered by tuition charges?[7] We found that most Catholic elementary schools receive from one-fourth to one-half of

[3]*Estimates of School Statistics, 1968–69*, NEA Research Report 1968–R16 (Washington, D.C.: National Education Association, 1969), p. 21.

[4]*Public Monies for Nonpublic Schools?* (Washington, D.C.: National Committee for Support of Public Schools, 1970), p. 5. The increase in the example given figures out to 207 per cent.

[5]*Estimates of School Statistics*, p. 21.

[6]*Newsletter for the Schools of the Lutheran Church—Missouri Synod* (St. Louis: Board of Parish Education, March 15, 1971).

[7]Responses to questions designed to probe the financial situation of schools were in many cases so spotty and internally inconsistent as to rule out overall comparisons in terms of means or averages or longitudinal comparisons. Schools which did answer all or most of the questions turned out to be a small and probably unrepresentative sample. Therefore, we

their income from tuition with the rest coming mostly from parish, diocesan, and other contributions (see table 5).[8] The Lutheran elementaries derive only about a fifth of their income from tuition (which is typically higher than that in Catholic schools), with the balance coming largely from church contributions. The pattern of the Christian Reformed and NACS schools differs in that they derive about two-thirds of their income from tuition. The Jewish elementaries present a different pattern still in that about half of the operating income is derived from tuition, with the other half coming largely from nonchurch donations.

The relationship of tuition fees to church donations is well illustrated by the experience of the parochial schools of the Baltimore archdiocese. While tuition ranged in 1970 from $50 to $250, with many parishes offering so-called family rates (progressively lower tuition for the second, third, and fourth child), the average tuition was $74. On the other hand, the average cost of operating the parochial schools was reported to be $181 per child. Of this cost, 48 per cent was covered by parish funds, 41 per cent by tuition, and the remainder came from miscellaneous sources.[9]

Among Catholic groups, in a few cases as much as 90 per cent or more of the parish's income is expended on the parochial school.[10] One of the unfortunate consequences of this pattern of finance is that tuition charges are lower in affluent suburban parishes where parish donations provide a large subsidy, and higher in less affluent inner-city schools where the subsidies are smaller—a situation which led Monsignor O'Neil D'Amour to say, "Our pattern of support is an unconscionable mess."[11] Since averages and composites tell only part of the story,

---

have used our data in this connection only as a basis for generalizations which are supported also by observation during school visits and by various reports, and to highlight the range of differences within and among school types by comparing the financial patterns (as revealed by questionnaire responses) of selected individual schools.

[8] Professor Ernest Bartell says about the tuition policies of Catholic schools: "The first Plenary Council of Baltimore established the norm of tuition-free schooling in American Catholic schools. Had the norm been observed universally the parochial and diocesan school systems would have been financed entirely from general revenues of the Church and would have financially resembled a public-school system for the Catholic community. However, today only about 25 per cent of the Catholic elementary schools and less than ten per cent of the secondary schools are tuition free." "Efficiency, Equity and the Economics of Catholic Schools," a position paper prepared for The Washington Symposium of the NCEA, November 10, 1967. Judging from the trend in school finances, the per cent of tuition free schools has diminished since 1967.

[9] Commission to Study State Aid to Nonpublic Eduation, *Report to the Governor and General Assembly of Maryland*, January, 1971, pp. 9-10.

[10] *The Catholic Review*, August 28, 1970, p. 1.

[11] *Report to the Governor and General Assembly of Maryland*, pp. 9-10; quotation from C. Albert Koob, O. Praem., ed., *What is Happening to Catholic Education* (Washington, D.C.: National Catholic Educational Association, 1966), p. 34.

Table 5

SOURCES OF ANNUAL OPERATING INCOME, NONPUBLIC SCHOOLS, 1967–68
(Day Schools Only)

School Group	Elementary Schools — Per cent of income derived from				Secondary Schools — Per Cent of income derived from			
	Tuition & fees	Church subsidies	Individual or corporation donations	Other[a]	Tuition & fees	Church subsidies	Individual or corporation donations	Other[a]
Catholic Northeast	23.8	66.4	–	1.0	48.3	25.9	2.2	20.1
Catholic South	46.9	41.9	0.2	8.8	59.7	26.6	1.9	9.1
Catholic Midwest/Far West	35.0	62.2	0.8	2.2	60.8	26.1	3.9	7.4
Lutheran	18.3	81.5	0.2	0.06	65.3	32.0	1.7	0.6
Seventh-day Adventist	59.8	37.3	2.9	–	67.9	23.9	0.5	6.7
Christian Reformed	67.4	19.6	4.1	2.6	36.4	9.9	50.2	4.3
National Association of Christian Schools	66.0	–	27.4	6.6	54.8	25.2	16.4	22.4
Independent	90.1	–	5.6	4.9				
Northeast					90.1	0.03	4.5	6.0
South					100.9	–	3.9	6.8
Midwest/Far West					82.9	–	7.1	9.1
Episcopal	80.7	0.2	3.7	1.2	81.3	0.3	7.2	6.8
Jewish	48.0	–	47.0	1.7	54.7	–	16.4	22.0

[a]Other sources include income from endowment, reserve funds, and other investments; government grants, scholarships, or contracts; and miscellaneous sources identified by the schools.

Note: The finance section of the general questionnaire asked the schools first to report their total operating income (in dollars) for the academic year 1967–68, and then asked how much of the operating income (in dollars) came from each of the sources listed above. The sums reported by the schools in the second instance add up (and average out) in most cases to less than 100 per cent of the operating income and in a number of cases to more. Evidently the former are reporting the fact that their realized income fell short of the budgeted income, while the latter reported all their realized income and gifts for the year regardless of whether or not they were applicable to operating funds.

it is more instructive to review the contrasting experiences of a few specific schools. Although Catholic schools in general ask for the lower payments by parents and also show the lowest per-pupil expenditure, there are striking variations. A diocesan high school in the Philadelphia archdiocese enrolling about 650 boys derived only 13.6 per cent of its total support from tuition and fees in 1967–68, while the bulk of its operating funds were provided by the archdiocese. On the other hand, a Catholic order school in the New York metropolitan area enrolling upwards of 200 girls obtained 72.2 per cent of its income from tuition. The tuition charge at the former was $310, at the latter $800.

The pattern of support for Protestant schools differs from that of their Catholic counterparts chiefly in relying more heavily on tuition. Yet here too there are pronounced variations. For instance, a Lutheran parochial school in a middle-sized California city raised only 20.8 per cent of its $200 per-student cost by means of tuition, with the rest contributed by the parish and miscellaneous sources; while a Lutheran parochial in suburban Chicago raised 70.2 per cent of its $300 per-student cost by tuition, with the balance coming from the parish and auxiliary sources. The NUCS and NACS schools tend to rely heavily on tuition payments and expect less assistance from local churches. These schools, as we noted earlier, are to a large extent parent-owned and controlled and draw students inter-congregationally and inter-denominationally from evangelically oriented congregations, so that there is in many cases no well-defined supporting community; hence, each school must stand more completely on its own financial bottom.

Independent schools present a distinctly different pattern of support. The accounting methods of most well-established institutions of this type are generally more sophisticated than those of the church schools, and many publish annual financial statements of income and expenses, assets and liabilities, similar to those issued by private colleges. The cost per student in the more expensive NAIS schools is substantially above that in the public schools, and the tuition in some cases equals or exceeds that charged by some of the most expensive private colleges and universities. Nevertheless, the parent who pays the full tuition seldom pays the full cost of the education of his son or daughter.[12] The difference—usually a fractional one, but a crucial fraction to the school—must be obtained from other sources. A handful of the member schools of the NAIS have substantial endowments, placing them in a strong position financially. But contrary to a widespread belief, the vast majority of independent schools either have no endowment whatever or one so small that it contributes only marginally to

[12]This is true except in schools that draw heavily on tuition income to support a substantial scholarship program. In such cases the parent paying the full tuition helps support other children who are on full or part scholarships.

the school's annual income.[13] The crucial gap between tuition income and operating costs is covered by endowment earnings (if any), gifts, and miscellaneous revenue (rental of facilities, summer camps and other projects, auxiliary services run at a profit, interest, sale of property, and the like). The degree to which NAIS schools depend on tuition payments varies substantially. Compare, for example, three New England boarding schools. School A, a well-known school enrolling over 800 boys and blessed with an endowment well in excess of $50 million, needed to obtain only 34.5 per cent of its annual operating income from tuition and fees in 1967–68 (but incurred a deficit of $151,000). School B, on the other hand, which enrolled upwards of 200 boys and had an endowment of less than a million dollars, obtained 94.4 per cent of its income from tuition (and incurred a deficit of $14,000). The cost per student in the former was $5,045; in the latter, $2,900. School C, enrolling about 350 girls and equipped with an endowment of about $2.25 million, spent that year $4,125 per student, of which 72.8 per cent was derived from tuition (and showed a surplus of $32,000 at year's end).[14]

The independent elementary schools, including Episcopal and Friends schools, obtain on the average about 80 to 90 per cent of their income from tuition, though here again the averages conceal substantial variations. Since these relatively high-fee schools generally serve an affluent clientele, their potential for acquiring funds by means of fund-raising campaigns directed to parents, alumni and friends is often high. On the other hand, endowment funds are rare among independent day schools, and so they rely largely on tuition and fees, while the cost per student is naturally much lower than that in the boarding schools.

[13] Secondary schools with endowments of over $10 million at market value in 1969, as reported in the American Alumni Council *Reports* were the following:

Exeter.	$63,476,588	Northfield &	
Andover	51,745,868	Mt. Hermon	$12,638,251
St. Paul's	39,386,052	Lawrenceville	12,453,935
Groton	18,319,116	Western Reserve	12,098,422
Punahou	16,511,473	Culver	11,468,941
Principia	14,906,986	Deerfield	11,329,145
Milton	14,110,590	Loomis	10,725,707
Choate	12,988,000		

Among the schools in our survey, only one in six reported any endowment whatever, and only one in nine had invested funds exceeding $200,000. All but a few of these are independent schools.

[14] In the *Annual Statistics of Member Schools, 1970* (Boston: National Association of Independent Schools, 1970), the NAIS reports that the percentage of its schools which derived all their operating income from tuition dropped from 19.4 per cent in 1967–68 to 9.7 per cent in 1969–70. There was no appreciable difference between elementary and secondary schools' percentage of income from tuition.

School D, a K-6 co-ed day school located in a large Missouri Valley city, enrolled about 200 in 1967-68, with a per-pupil cost of $837, of which 93.2 per cent was obtained from tuition; the rest, in the absence of endowment funds, came from gifts. School E, a K-12 day school located in a medium sized middle western city, enrolled over 500 boys and spent $1,600 per student, of which 88.8 per cent was derived from tuition, with the balance obtained mainly from the yield of a modest endowment of less than a half million. It closed the year with the budget in balance. By contrast, school F, a twenty-year-old K-12 coed day school enrolling about 350, located in the suburb of a large city in Southern California, in the year in question had an operating cost of $1100 per student, and derived 87.5 per cent of its total income from tuition and about 10 per cent from gifts and grants. This school, which has no endowment, at the close of the year showed a whopping operating surplus of $139,300 out of a total income $525,900, a very exceptional situation.

An examination of the tuition-increase policies of randomly selected independent schools of the Northeast shows a growing trend, in the second half of the sixties, toward small annual tuition increases instead of more substantial jumps taken every other or every third year, which were the rule in the first half of the decade. In good times, schools such as these increased fees only every two or three years, figuring on a surplus in the first year of a three-year cycle (part of which might be used to retire past deficits), a balanced budget in the second, and a manageable deficit in the third, covered either by the first year surplus of the same or the next cycle. The two-year cycle was projected to produce a surplus the first year, a deficit the second. Escalating costs and the financial uncertainties dictated the trend toward smaller but annual increases. The generally cautious fee pattern reflects the fear, voiced by many headmasters, that they are dangerously close to "pricing themselves out of the market."

School officials as well as parents are giving thought to ways and means of softening the impact of the heavy tuition charges. The practice of billing the annual tuition fee in two chunky installments—usually at the opening and again mid-way through the school year—creates a hardship for patrons who are obliged to pay the tuition bills out of current income. Certain banks and other credit agencies have developed programs which spread payments over monthly installments, and a number of schools have developed their own twelve-month or longer payment plan under similar terms and conditions.[15] This is a convenience

---

[15] Installment plans are not limited to independent schools. A not uncommon practice among Catholic inner-city schools, where tuition is often of necessity high because parish donations are either nonexistent or so low as to pay only a fractional cost of school operations, is to pay the tuition charge in weekly installments. For example, an inner-city school in Baltimore with a largely black clientele in 1969-70 charged an annual tuition of $200 payable in 40 weekly installments of $5 each.

to parents whose current income or other assets are sufficient to cover the annual tuition charge, but it obviously does not help those who truly need scholarship assistance or loans spread over a longer period.

Loan programs, while long a commonplace in colleges and universities, are relatively new in nonpublic schools. But as the pressure on limited scholarship funds in high-tuition schools increases, some schools are striving to interest parents in long-term loans that shift at least part of the burden from the scholarship program to the parent, thus enabling the school to stretch scholarship funds farther. Among the serious obstacles to the wider use of loans is the compelling fact that parents who face the financial need of borrowing for their son's or daughter's four-year college education are reluctant to begin borrowing while the child is still in secondary school, years away from realizing on his earning potential. So far only a very small number of nonpublic school parents are taking advantage of existing long-term loan programs. Conceivably the terms might be made more inviting if the schools were to work out a tuition-deferment plan similar to that proposed by President Kingman Brewster of Yale, under which adults would pay for the cost of their education by a kind of voluntary private tax on their income over a thirty- or forty-year period.

The foregoing account has concentrated on the standard sources of operating income, but nothing has been said as yet about supplementary support produced by fund campaigns, including those waged for capital funds. The experience of schools in raising money by this means is so extraordinarily diverse that few significant generalizations emerge. Apart from annual giving campaigns soliciting support from alumni, parents, and friends, nonpublic schools wage larger campaigns only intermittently, as they decide to increase faculty salaries and scholarship aid, to augment or improve their physical facilites, or to increase their invested funds. The rule that applies with very few exceptions in such campaigns appears to be: "Them as has, gits." The larger, well-endowed independent schools easily outstrip all others in the dollar volume of capital gifts and bequests received during the five-year period of 1963-1968. Thus, the heavily endowed school A received just short of $10 million in capital gifts during that period, far and away the largest amount.[16] By comparison, the struggling school B received only about $320,000 during the same period. Apart from some Catholic order schools, very few church schools of any kind reported substantial capital contributions. The cost of augmenting or improving physical facilities is evidently covered usually by parish and church donations and by means of inter-parish diocesan loans amortizable over a period of years out of parish donations.

[16]This school completed a five-year campaign in 1971 that realized a grand total of $26.6 million in gifts, quite the largest sum ever raised by a private school.

Where the Money Goes

Where the money goes is no mystery. With respect to the two major categories of expense, administration and instruction, the schools differ in what they include under these rubrics, so that precise comparisons are ruled out. Nevertheless, some general differences come to light regarding the expenditure patterns of different schools (see table 6).[17]

Among the day schools, the Protestant institutions at all levels in 1967–68 devoted the lowest percentage of the total outlay to administrative cost,[18] the Catholic schools were next lowest, while the independent schools show the highest expenditure on administration. One might expect the percentage of administrative costs to be lower in elementary than in secondary schools, but no consistent pattern to that effect is disclosed.

One would assume that boarding schools, on the other hand, with their responsibilities of twenty-four hour and seven-day week surveillance of students, would allocate proportionally more for administrative staff. Many do, but a few show a very low percentage devoted to that function. Since schools comprising 90 per cent or more boarders spent roughly half their total operating income (less in the South) on the school's "hotel" operation or what in college finance is usually accounted as "auxiliary enterprises," the administrative cost factor bears a different relationship to the total budget than is true of day schools.

One of the key items in the administrative budget is the salary of the school head. In most schools it bears a fairly definite and stable relationship to the level of faculty salaries in the same school, being usually about 20 to 40 per cent above the highest faculty salary level and, in the case of boarding school heads, involving superior benefits also, in the form of such perquisites as housing and services. But since the head's salary is set in relation to faculty salaries, which in chapter 6 were seen to be deplorably low in most non-public schools, it too is generally far below the salary paid for comparable responsibilities in public

---

[17]"Administration" costs, as we conceive them, are taken to include the salaries of the school head, dean, director of admissions, business manager, and other related officers and their clerical staff. Comparisons with public school policies and practices are not possible because "administration" is there defined to embrace only the superintendents and their staffs, that is, the personnel charged with running the system as a whole and its several subdivisions. Other costs which in nonpublic schools are commonly denominated "administrative," such as principals and their supporting administrative and clerical staff, are included under instructional expense in statistics published by the U.S. Office of Education. See, for example, *Digest of Educational Statistics, 1969* (Washington, D.C.: U.S. Office of Education, Department of Health, Education and Welfare, 1969).

[18]The findings reported here are for the year 1967–68 and are based on a selected group of schools of each type responding to all or most questions in the "Finance" section of our general questionnarie. It may be assumed that these are among the stabler, more developed, relatively more sophisticated schools, which suggests that the percentage of administrative costs might be somewhat higher than that for the general average of schools in each group.

Table 6

ANNUAL OPERATING EXPENDITURES OF NONPUBLIC DAY SCHOOLS, 1967–68

Number of Schools Reporting	School Group	Mean Annual Operating Expenditure,[a] 1967–68	Per Cent Annual Operating Expend. for Admin.	Per Cent Annual Operating Expend. for Instruc.[b]	Mean of Average Annual Operating Expend./Student,[c] 1967–68	Mean Enrollment, October 1, 1968
		Elementary (K–8)				
9	Catholic Northeast	$63,356	16.2	65.3	($133)	478
10	Catholic South	$42,670	10.8	54.1	($155)	276
8	Catholic Midwest & Far West	$50,213	13.1	68.5	($161)	312
15	Lutheran	$45,360	9.9	71.4	$260	164
1	Seventh-Day Adventist	$10,200	–	83.4	$200	36
7	Christian Reformed	$67,671	12.0	73.4	$414	186
2	National Association of Christian Schools	$91,550	11.2	49.5	$550	189
7	Episcopal	$61,343	13.4	79.3	($451)	136
3	Jewish	$96,667	13.7	72.9	$900	108
7	Independent	$132,914	14.4	55.8	($791)	168

Secondary (9–12)

14	Catholic Northeast	$211,986	13.3	52.9	($333)	634
15	Catholic South	$110,447	12.5	56.9	($240)	461
23	Catholic Midwest & Far West	$229,317	10.3	51.9	($348)	659
4	Lutheran	$208,175	11.4	65.3	$450	486
5	Seventh-Day Adventist	$224,760	8.6	54.9	($709)	317
4	Christian Reformed	$322,000	5.4	80.0	($438)	735
3	National Association of Christian Schools	$105,000	11.8	70.0	$433	293
4	Episcopal	$348,350	23.1	43.7	($1,489)	234
3	Jewish	$301,567	16.7	64.9	$1,300	374
21	Independent Northeast	$566,324	16.2	59.3	($1,483)	382
12	Independent South	$205,842	16.5	63.6	($780)	264
25	Independent Midwest & Far West	$505,404	13.1	59.6	($1,260)	401

[a]Excluding depreciation reserve for buildings.

[b]Instruction includes only faculty salaries, grants, benefits, and leaves; educational materials, supplies, and equipment; and library operation.

[c]Where not all schools in a group reported cost per student, it was computed on the basis of 1967–68 operating expenditure divided by October 1968 enrollment (figures in parentheses).

213

schools and decidedly less than the normal return from a business enterprise requiring an entrepreneurship comparable to that called for in the private school head. It seems scarcely credible that many private school heads received in 1968–69 salaries of less than $5,000. Most of these are in Catholic schools, where, as we have noted earlier, the averages tend to be depressed by the substantial number of schools headed by nuns, priests, and brothers who do not receive a regular salary; moreover, in parochial schools not infrequently the pastor serves as the principal, and few if any administrative expenses are recorded. In any case, over 90 per cent of all elementary and over 70 per cent of all secondary heads of Catholic schools received less than $5,000 during the year in question. This compares with averages of $11,957 for elementary and $12,348 for public secondary school heads in the same year.[19] About half of the Protestant principals received $5,000 or less, with the other half ranging up to a maximum of $15,000. Independent schools show the greatest range—from under $5,000 to $25,000, with the largest group falling into the $15,000 to $18,000 range. In all school groups, salaries for elementary heads and for women are consistently lower than those for secondary school principals and for men.

It is obvious that financial or material considerations play only a small part in motivating a man or woman to accept the headship of a church-affiliated day school, whether Catholic or Protestant. Such a position, considering the multifarious responsibilities which the incumbent bears, is poorly paid by any standard. On the other hand, many independent schools pay their headmasters somewhat higher salaries than those received by their public school counterparts. This is particularly true of the boarding schools where perquisites of office usually add substantially to the total compensation. But the boarding school headmaster is also expected to sacrifice much of his private life to the round-the-clock needs of his charges.

With respect to the cost of faculty salaries, benefits, and other outlays for instruction, we are concerned here only with the per cent of the whole budget devoted to this purpose, not with faculty salary scales as such, since these are covered in chapter 6. In elementary and secondary day schools the per cent of total operating expense devoted to instruction varies within a wide range. The Protestant groups, which spend least on administration, devote from 50 to over 80 per cent of the total budget to instruction, while Catholic schools spend on the average somewhat over half on this item. The independent day schools taken together devote on the average about 60 per cent to instruction. Boarding schools present quite another picture. Reflecting the many operating expenses

[19]Attributed to an official of the National Association of Secondary School Principals in an article by Timothy D. Schellhardt, "Principals' Rule Erodes as Students, Teachers, Parents Attack Them," *The New England Association Review*, Summer 1970, p. 34.

incurred in connection with student dormitory operation and comprehensive recreation programs, boarding schools expend on academic instruction only from about 20 to 30 per cent of the total budget.

Of crucial importance in this connection is the student-teacher ratio. As the figures above show, in all but the boarding schools, expenditures on instruction—mainly faculty salaries—account for from 50 to over 80 per cent of the outlays. Those figures most probably have increased since 1967-68, the year of our data, since faculty salaries had been for several years prior gathering momentum in a spiral of increases, rising faster than any other major category of school expense, and showing no signs of a let-up until 1970, when teacher supply began to outstrip demand. The pupil-teacher ratio is customarily regarded as a quick index of the quality of a school's program: the nearer the ratio approaches 1:1, the better the school (whether it is, in fact, all that sure an indicator is a question which we reserve for later comment). At the moment we are concerned about the relation of the pupil-teacher ratio to the financial crisis in the schools. A ratio of 10:1 is obviously twice as expensive as 20:1, as Beardsley Ruml pointed out to the colleges in the 1950s. At the time, he was urging a change to the higher ratio as the way to finance a dramatic increase in faculty salaries, which were lagging badly. Today the ratio is again being examined as a possible way of cutting back in order to close the gap between income and expenditures.

What makes the plight of many of the church schools so serious is the fact that there is little or no "give" in their pupil-teacher ratios, since most of them have for too long labored with what are generally regarded as unfavorable ratios of 30 or 35:1 or worse, and only recently struggled—with some success—to achieve a better position. For example, Catholic elementary schools between 1964 and 1969 improved their overall pupil-teacher ratio from 38:1 to 29:1, while the Catholic secondaries recorded in the same period a gain of from 20:1 to 18:1; meanwhile the per cent of the religious personnel on the professional teaching staffs dropped from approximately two-thirds to just over a half, and is still dropping, thus saddling teacher salary budgets with still another heavy additional cost factor.[20]

Not all private schools have been hit as hard as the Catholic by these developments, but their impact has been powerful to the point of being devastating in some schools of every type. We found that among the Protestant groups ratios of 30:1 or above are the rule in Christian Reformed and NUCS secondary schools, while their elementaries show ratios of about 25:1; the Lutheran schools are better off, with the elementaries showing a ratio of 23:1, an improvement of

[20]*A Statistical Report on Catholic Elementary and Secondary Schools for the Years 1967-68 to 1969-70* (Washington, D.C.: National Catholic Education Association, 1970), pp. 5, 13, 14.

about 20 per cent over the past decade, while the secondaries held steady at 19:1.[21] As the ratios improved, the cost per student rose steeply.

It is the independent schools above all others who have been instrumental in associating low pupil-teacher ratios with quality in education. These schools show an overall ratio of 13:1 for elementary and 12:1 for secondary schools. The financial pattern of these schools, separating them quite distinctly from all but a few church-affiliated ones, involves both higher per-pupil costs and higher faculty salaries.

A high per-student cost has many ramifications, not the least of which is the effect on the scholarship policies of schools. In the absence of income from endowment, a high per-student cost necessitates high tuition charges. These in turn both increase the need and reduce the value of scholarship funds, for the higher the tuition the more costly the scholarship has to be. Adequate scholarship resources are critically important educationally for independent schools in particular, for without them the student body is bound to reflect a financially sorted-out uniformity based on the ability to pay, thus depriving the campus of much of its potential human diversity. The church schools too have to be concerned about their scholarship resources, but their problem is less acute, partly because the tuition is usually much lower, partly because they attract students from a somewhat broader socioeconomic range to begin with. Yet it is a rare private school, whether denominational or independent, that does not take steps to help equalize, at least to some extent, the opportunities of the poor and the rich child.

In church schools this is usually done very informally, without entering in the school accounts an income and expense item for scholarships. "They come in free if they can't pay," said the principal of a Catholic elementary school quite simply in response to a query about the number and amounts of scholarship awards; or as the principal of a diocesan high school put it, "If a poor family want to send their child, the school will go easy on the bill." This policy seems on the face of it generous to poor children; yet many Catholic leaders express concern, and justly so, that the low tuition policies of their schools actually subsidize the education of children from affluent families more than they help the poor. Apparently the Jewish schools lead all others in scholarship aid in that over half the students in their institutions have a substantial part of the tuition cost underwritten by scholarships. The scholarship policies of Episcopal schools are noteworthy in that they make more awards to students needing large scholarships, while the other Protestant groups tend to use the available resources

[21]*Newsletter for the Schools of the Lutheran Church–Missouri Synod*, March 15, 1971, p. 2.

chiefly to support young people needing only a small amount of financial aid to remain in the school.

Most independent schools tend to divide scholarship awards roughly into thirds, with one part awarded to the very needy, the second going to students who can pay about half of the fees, and the third allocated to those who need only a little aid. But as the table on scholarship aid among NAIS schools shows (chapter 9, page 249), the average grant per pupil has almost doubled during the 1960s—a growth-rate faster than that of fee increases.

Since scholarship funds are intended above all to assist the student who needs help to defray the tuition, it is important to determine as exactly as possible the financial need of his family. The School Scholarship Service (SSS), sponsored in 1957 by the National Council of Independent Schools, precursor of the NAIS, was designed to help the school determine how much the family can contribute annually to the student's overall school expenses. Using a form that was adapted from the older College Scholarship Service's "Parent's Confidental Statement," the SSS utilizes the expertise of the Educational Testing Service in processing the forms. Members of the SSS agree to support certain principles in the award of scholarships, chiefly to avert the temptation to engage in competitive bidding for the best talent. The service has succeeded in bringing greater uniformity and fairness in the administration of scholarship programs in independent schools. Church schools are also finding this service useful.[22]

Some schools charge a differential tuition in lieu of a scholarship program. The Kent School in Connecticut is one of several that have a sliding scale of tuition fees under which the patrons are assessed according to their ability to pay.

What effect the financial crisis will have on scholarship allocations remains to be seen. The temptation will be strong to cut the costly scholarships to the very needy and to offer moderate assistance to more families who are able to pay a part of the tuition. The price of following such a course would be to curtail not only the schools' contribution to the most profound social problem of our time, but more directly to diminish the quality and diversity of the education which the school offers its students. The recent steps taken by many private schools in reaching out to disadvantaged minorities has done much to increase their stature. Difficult as it is to afford generous scholarship funds in a time of recession, it may be even more difficult to cope later with the problems which would be entailed by laying the axe of economy heavily to that section of the budget, which in most schools is only a small part of the total to begin with.

[22]See the account of how St. Joseph's, a large Cleveland diocesan high school, uses the SSS "to distribute aid according to ideals of charity and justice," in *Momentum*, February 1970, pp. 27ff.

Another measure of the financial stringency which the schools face is the amount of indebtedness they carry. As of 1969, for 331 schools reporting, a third were free of debt, another third reported debts of a magnitude that could be considered modest, while the remaining third reported debts in excess of $100,000. Many of these are relatively small schools, and a debt of that size is a grave impairment. Since the financial prospect for many private schools has deteriorated rapidly since 1969, and school after school has incurred substantial annual operating deficits for 1970 and 1971, the amount of indebtedness and the number of schools in debt most certainly have increased rapidly. The fact that the highest percentage of "modest" indebtedness (under $100,000) was reported by the independent school group indicates that the above figures do not fully reveal the present worsening plight of the nonpublic schools. In most church schools, indebtedness occasioned by capital improvements is normally carried by a congregation, parish, or diocese; and the same is true in some cases of past operating deficits. Debts so held, which are probably considerable, are not included in the above figures. All in all, there is little solace to be found in this picture.

A word about the proprietary schools. Now generally suspect among private and public school educators and the knowledgeable public, the proprietary school has had nontheless an honorable place in the history of private schooling. Many a well-established nonprofit institution traces its history to an inspired and inspiring teacher who began with a small group of students and managed so shrewdly that over the years a thriving school emerged, built up by means of surplus income, until eventually the fully fledged institution became incorporated as one not operated for profit. Few academic proprietary schools remain, and these only under special circumstances. In these days when most schools find it impossible to close the gap between income and expense except with the help of tax deductible gifts or other sources of revenue, the proprietary school has hard sledding to stay in the compeitition, much less to show a profit.

But as long as a proprietary school can pay its way, there seems to be no convincing moral or educational argument why it should be suspect simply because it is proprietary. Many educators fear that the profit motive is subversive of all education, and indeed that does happen in the case of furtive, "fly-by-night" schools. Yet there are many proprietaries—the thousands of nonacademic private vocational schools are cases in point—which give fair measure for the tuition paid; and on the other hand, there are ample illustrations of nonprofit public and private schools which are ill-managed and squander their resources ineffectively. Now that the critics of present-day education are reexamining the structure of schools and colleges with an eye to generating some inter-institutional competition as an incentive to improvement, the profit motive is seen in a new light as a possible way of overcoming the built-in inefficiencies resulting from the bland acceptance of the prevailing academic mythology.[23] Among the various alternatives, "teacher accountability," that is, paying teachers on the basis of what students actually and demonstrably learn, is being widely discussed.

What Can Be Done?

As a first step in exploring what can be done about the financial crisis in nonpublic schools, it is instructive to review briefly what the trustees and school heads—persons directly responsible for planning and administering the school's financial affairs—thought about various possible ways of closing the gap between income and expenditures in the spring of 1969, shortly before the full impact of the business recession was felt. What seemed to them the most promising course or courses?

Theoretically, the gap can be closed either by finding ways to increase income, or ways to reduce expenses, or both. Looking, first, to possible ways of increasing income, characteristic differences appear among the trustees of various types of schools. The time-honored method of increasing tuition and fees, which for over two decades has been the major recourse in keeping private schools abreast of rising costs, remains in the eyes of independent school people the best hope. The church school trustees, however, see this as a less hopeful or less desirable possibility, and tend to look elsewhere for the needed support. The Catholics pin their chief hope on federal or state aid, while to Protestant trustees, who join the independents in expecting relatively less assistance from that source, increased giving by the parents, individually and through the churches, seems the best hope. Private philanthropy from other sources, such as alumni

---

[23] A strong hint of a possible change in attitude toward the profit motive in education is contained in the recent suit brought by the proprietary Marjorie Webster Junior College, Washington Junior College, Washington, D.C., against the Middle States Association of Colleges and Secondary Schools over the regional accrediting agency's refusal to review the college for accreditation. In the opinion of Judge Smith of the trial court, "Educational excellence is determined not by the method of financing but by the quality of the program. Middle States' position, moreover, ignores the alternative possibility that the profit motive might result in a more efficient use of resources, producing a better product at a lower price." Quoted in James D. Koerner, "The Case of Marjorie Webster," *The Public Interest* 20 (Summer 1970): 53. Koerner's article is admittedly partisan, favoring strongly the plaintiff's case, and it contains a number of dubious allegations about the practices and motives of Middle States. Yet his general thesis, and the judge's opinion, seem to this author to be better founded than the Middle States' position.

The Middle States appealed Judge Smith's decision to the U.S. Court of Appeals, which ruled against the college. On appeal by the college, the U.S. Supreme Court declined to review the case, thus upholding the right of the Middle States Association to limit its accrediting function to nonprofit institutions.

gifts, corporation and foundation grants, bequests, and annuities is regarded optimistically as a good but secondary source of additional support by trustees of all types of secondary schools, though those serving the elementaries are less sanguine of help from that quarter.

Looking, next, to the possibility of solving the school's financial problems by cutting costs, we find that most trustees in all types of schools believe such a course is generally less desirable than increasing income in one way or another. Nevertheless, many trustees and school heads believe that potential economies are possible and acceptable in the following areas, arranged in a rough order of priority.

1. More efficient operation of the school's physical plant received cumulatively the strongest endorsement as a source of potential economies, especially among the officials of independent schools. Over half the NACS secondary schools, however, believe they are already down to rock-bottom in this respect.

2. Consortia with other schools to share facilities, costly equipment, personnel, and the cost of services and supplies also drew a cumulatively strong endorsement, except among Christian Reformed schools where consortia of numbers of elementary and secondary units already exist to some extent. The seven-unit system in Holland, Michigan, is an illustration.

3. A less costly student-teacher ratio is heavily favored by Protestant secondary school heads; Catholic heads also see much potential in such a course, but the independents are cooler to it. In all types of schools the heads of the secondaries see more possibilities here than do the elementary heads. Most faculty people, as we noted earlier, are firmly opposed to this course.

4. Increased enrollment to produce a more efficient operating unit is regarded by Protestant elementary and secondary school representatives as a hopeful course. The independent school people, however, are less favorably inclined, and the Catholics see little hope in it.

5. Pruning the curriculum to eliminate small, marginal, expensive courses is not regarded as having much potential for economies. Most school heads evidently feel that the school's offerings are spare enough as it is and that trimming is not needed or unacceptable. The trustees tend to agree.

6. Bolder policies of investment and use of endowment funds are favored by half of the independent schools, the only ones to whom it pertains, since only very few denominational schools own invested funds.

7. Cutting or holding the line on administration costs, as one would expect, has little appeal to school administrators, most of whom feel that the allocations in this category are now satisfactory and cuts would be unacceptable. This view is prevalent particularly among the elementary church

schools, which tend to be administratively lean. The independent second-aries, on the other hand, admit that there might be some potential for savings in this area.

8. Cost analysis surveys by experts drew a mixed reaction. Elementary school heads are generally least persuaded that these would be helpful, but Catholic and independent secondary school heads believe they hold some potential for producing financial benefits.

Against this backdrop of reactions by the school authorities about what can be done to close the gap between rising costs and lagging income we venture some judgments and recommendations of our own.

The challenge, as we see it, is not merely to close the inflationary gap so that the school remains solvent and able to engage in business as usual. That is at best a counsel of "thrifty mediocrity." The challenge is to push ahead to new levels, to incorporate in the private schools the constantly improving educational opportunities which one should expect will characterize all good schools in the future, just as they are typical of the best schools today. For if the private school is to prevail as a viable alternative to good tax-supported public schools—and we believe that all nonpublic schools, whether church-affiliated or independent, will be measured increasingly by that standard—then it must plan its financial course not merely to survive; it must aim at bold and imaginative solutions of educational as well as financial problems. And to that end it should aim not only to increase its income, but also to reassess its practices in order to get the greatest educational value out of every dollar.

To remind the schools that much more is at stake than immediate survival, essential as that is, may seem like a hard saying in a time of mounting deficits. But deficits can be beneficial in one respect: they provide a sharp stimulus for a total reassessment of goals and practices. As John Gardner once said, institutions don't move unless they are shoved. The fact that an institution no longer can make ends meet is a hard shove toward doing things differently. In prosperous times the tendency to take on all sorts of attractive functions and services is well-nigh ungovernable, and they usually get built solidly into the annual budget. And given the mindless way in which successive annual expenditure budgets are usually prepared—by adding x per cent to the various categories of the preceding year's expenditures—the school contracts to pay annually, over and over again, for all kinds of obsolete and inefficient accretions as well as for services which are essential, relevant, and well performed. To some extent this is inherent in the nature of institutions. But it is also true that institutions die, and deservedly, when the load of unexamined accretions seriously impairs their ability to meet the new challenges of changing times.

We turn first to a review of various ways of increasing income which are particularly applicable to nonpublic schools. One of the major uncertainties that keeps Catholic school financial planning off balance is the as yet undetermined fate of state and federal aid projects, the outcome of which hinges on the Supreme Court's interpretation of the constitutional questions raised by various specific state aid enactments. These are surveyed in chapter 11. Given these uncertainties, which are bound to recur from time to time in new forms, we believe nonpublic schools of all types are well advised to base their financial planning and projections on the assumption that little more than the prevailing forms of auxiliary state and federal assistance (food subsidy, transportation, health services, ESEA library assistance, shared time programs, etc., which some eligible schools do not yet fully utilize) will be forthcoming in the immediate future. The schools will do well, therefore, to take energetic steps to increase their income from other sources, while doing what they can to influence the course of public opinion so that eventually the state aid, which many believe to be essential to the long-run survival and improvement of large numbers of nonpublic schools, becomes a reality.

Increasing income by raising tuition has become virtually a conditioned reflex among independent school leaders, while church school leaders have also resorted to it, but to a lesser extent. With the onset of the recession, however, many independent schools approach fee increases with growing caution. Most increases in the recent past have been pegged at points fixed by trustees and heads on the basis of informed guesses about what the traffic could bear. A study of the fee structure of 24 independent schools (see figure 10) reveals that the average (mean) tuition of day schools, in terms of the purchasing power of the dollar, rose only slightly between 1940 and 1969, more slowly than did the per-pupil cost in public schools. Boarding school tuition, on the other hand, measured in constant dollars, was markedly cheaper at the end than at the beginning of the same period, and since 1960 has held about even with the inflation. It is evident from the low fees (measured in constant dollars) charged by day and boarding schools during the 1950s that the education of children of the rich was being subsidized in part by the low faculty salaries prevailing at that time.

One hopeful sign is the fact that families with an annual income of $15,000 and over—potential clients of day and boarding schools—are now the fastest growing income bracket.[24] The pool of those who are able to afford independent schools—or church schools— is increasing.

Despite the fact that these statistics taken by themselves support an optimistic outlook, the cautious approach of independent school leaders to fee increases is probably justified. Factors other than financial influence the decision to

[24] U.S. Bureau of the Census, *Current Population Reports*, series P–60, no. 75, "Income in 1969 of Families and Persons in the U.S." (Washington, D.C.: Government Printing Office, 1970), p. 23, table 7.

Figure 10

AVERAGE TUITION CHARGES IN CONSTANT AND CURRENT DOLLARS, 1940-69
(Comparison of 12 independent boarding and 12 independent day schools
with average daily attendance expenditure in public schools)

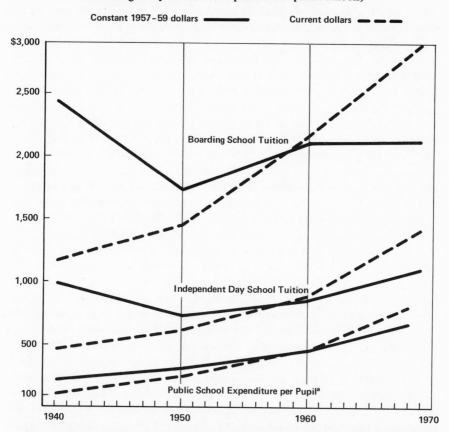

Sources: Data on tuition in 24 independent schools are from Porter Sargent, *Handbook of Private Schools* (Boston, 1940–41, 1950–51, 1960, 1969). Data on public school expenditure are from U.S. Bureau of the Census, *Statistical Abstract of the United States: 1970* (Washington, D.C.: Government Printing Office, 1970), table 165, p. 114; table 516, p. 338, "Purchasing Power of the Dollar: 1940 to 1969," was used to express current dollar value in 1957–59 dollars.

[a]Based on current expenditure allocable to pupil costs, capital outlay, and interest.

choose a nonpublic school. Though a boarding school education actually costs less now in constant dollars than in 1940, boarding schools are finding it increasingly difficult to fill their places. This difficulty suggests that it is not so much high fees as the declining marginal utility of boarding education which is the root of the problem. The ills from which independent boarding schools are currently suffering, in addition to steadily rising tuitions, are pinpointed by

Headmaster Frank Ashburn of Brooks School, North Andover, Massachusetts, as both loss of a favored position in respect to college admission and student resentment of the isolation, confinement, and restrictive rules of boarding school life, resulting in a conviction that "real life" lies elsewhere. Ways must be found to make this form of schooling more attractive and less confining and to persuade potential clients that a boarding education is worth the difference in cost.

Private day schools, on the other hand, are in a position to continue to meet much of the mounting cost by fee increases scaled to keep pace with the inflation of money. This is true of the church schools as well as of the independents. Though lack of adequate data precludes an analysis of the fee history of church schools, it is our impression that these schools could realize much more income by experimenting with increased tuition combined with a carefully advertised and administered scholarship program for those who cannot pay any or only a part of the full fee. Too many church schools subsidize the education of affluent members of the parish by not charging enough.[25] There is a limit, naturally, to tuition charges, but we doubt that most church schools are anywhere near it. The limit is set by what parents take to be the marginal utility of a church school education for a given tuition charge as over against a free education in the available public school. The fact that many public schools, particularly those in suburbia, have improved in recent years, combined with the spread of ecumenism which makes a denominationally oriented religious education appear to be less essential in the eyes of some parents, has doubtless acted as a brake on tuition increases in church schools. This state of affairs coupled with persistence of the traditional view that church schools ought to be free—deeply rooted in the Catholic Church in particular—makes many church school leaders timid about loading a large share of school costs on the tuition charge for those who are able to pay it. As matters stand, notes Ernest Bartell, both the tuition charges and the fund-raising techniques in support of Catholic schools are regressive, that is, they fall more heavily on the poor than on the rich.[26]

Apart from reliance on tuition to close the gap between income and expenditures, far too many nonpublic schools fail to realize their fund-raising potential. Only a minority of independent schools have engaged systematically in the kind

[25]Neil G. McCluskey, S.J., concludes that "the present system of financing Catholic schools is unbelievably archaic, obsolete and inefficient." *Catholic Education Faces Its Future* (Garden City, N.Y.: Doubleday and Co., 1969), p. 264. But McCluskey advises the schools to move in the opposite direction, that is, to abolish tuition, and in its place levy a school tax on every adult member of the diocese. He would also have the parish schools brought under much firmer diocesan control, using the public school system as a model (pp. 263–70).

[26]Ernest Bartell, "Efficiency, Equity and Economics," pp. 5–7. "In effect the fiscal policy of the Church becomes responsible for an ethically incongruous redistribution away from the poor in favor of the rich."

of aggressive, many-sided, persistent pursuit of philanthropy that is essential for the survival of all kinds of private institutions that contribute to the common good. Very few schools have developed strong programs for raising annual funds, capital gifts, bequests, and deferred giving. The common reason given is that schools lack the means to engage specially qualified personnel to conduct such programs. In this respect many schools are penny-wise and pound-foolish. The employment of a development officer and, in the larger schools, an adequate staff of paid and volunteer workers, is an investment that usually pays dividends many times the amount of the dollars paid in salaries. As in other types of investments, the return is not always immediate, because it takes time to assess and develop the best sources of gifts and to establish the regular habit of giving to annual funds supported by alumni and parents.[27] Smaller schools with a limited outreach in the community may find it feasible to employ a part-time development officer who is shared with other small schools in the community. Many church schools have not realized on the potential to enlist support from other than parish or general church donations. Since these schools serve the community, the possibilities of support from individuals and corporations should be explored fully.

It is the trustees above all who should lead the way in this activity. Numbered among the trustees of many schools are businessmen and lawyers who are in a position to help not only in identifying and approaching potential donors but in advising regarding tax questions that arise. The religious head of a small, struggling Catholic boys' day school in the Boston metropolitan area told visitors that when the school's fund-raising drive was turned over from the clergy to the lay board of advisors, the proceeds quadrupled in a single year. He believed this course may be a saving pattern for other Catholic schools. As more lay boards take over governing responsibilities of Catholic schools, one should expect that the schools will increase their community outreach in a variety of ways, and as this happens the fund-raising potential of the schools is bound to increase.

Some independent boarding schools supplement their income appreciably by a variety of auxiliary enterprises ranging from summer conferences, institutes, and camps to year-round school operation, adult education programs, leasing of facilities, and farming. Schools which own substantial tracts of real estate might

---

[27]For the independent schools there is sound advice in William J. McMillan's "Improving Financial Management in Independent Schools," *The Independent School Bulletin*, October 1968, pp. 7–11. McMillan is headmaster of the Pine Crest School, Fort Lauderdale, Florida, which was incorporated as a nonprofit school in 1959, after operating successfully for the 25 years preceding as a proprietary school. See also "A Young School Ponders the Long Pull at a Crucial Time" by Edgar L. Sanford, Headmaster, Charles Wright Academy, Tacoma, Washington, in *Financing the Independent School of the Future* (Boston: National Association of Independent Schools, August 1968).

explore ways of putting some of the land to use to use for income-producing projects which are compatible with the educational purposes of the school. To conceive of and further projects of this kind requires the services of an imaginative, resourceful business manager who has an eye for realizing the income-producing potential of the school's total resources.

Another source of additional income for schools fortunate enough to have endowment funds is to take steps to increase the yield on investments. In the past most schools relied on a trustee finance committee to manage the portfolio, but experience shows that the highly conservative "safe" investment policies pursued by most trustees usually resulted in disappointingly low levels of yield and capital growth. The Ford Foundation, long interested in this problem on behalf of the colleges and universities, recently announced the formation of the Common Fund for Nonprofit Organizations to provide professional investment management in which secondary schools are invited to participate. A member institution may place all or part of its funds in the Common Fund in amounts ranging from $100,000 to $10 million. Member institutions may elect either a fixed rate of distribution based on average market value under the "total return" concept, or the distribution only of income from interest and dividends, with capital gains being reinvested. The Fund should be particularly valuable to institutions with small endowment funds.

This brief review of possible ways of increasing income covers only those that are of relatively wide applicability, and it does not pretend to be complete. The most important consideration of all—one that is too complex for extensive treatment here—is the steps that can be taken to make the school and its program more attractive, and to attain an optimum size so that the interrelated factors of tuition income and other resources can be brought into an economic balance with expeditures for staff, facilities, and maintenance. Countless studies have been made of the ideal or optimum size of schools, but no two agree. Yet the optimum size of a given school in relation to its actual or potential resources has a strong bearing on the institution's viability, and the vigor of the student recruitment effort and fund raising programs have much to do with the size that the school can attain.[28]

Looking to the other way of closing the gap—the painful process of paring expenditures—the chief problem is to find ways of cutting back without sacrificing academic quality or institutional morale. The Academy for Educational Development recently published a checklist entitled "148 Ways Colleges and Universities are Meeting the Finance Pinch"—32 ways to increase income, 116 ways

---

[28] An NUCS K-12 coed academy in Pennsylvania, finding that it needed about 60 additional students to attain an optimum size, engaged a salaried patron as a recruiter. Through his efforts the school acquired not 60 but 99 additional students.

to reduce expenditures. Many of these apply to schools also. We wish to touch here on only a few of the main potential sources of lowering costs which are applicable to most nonpublic schools, both elementary and secondary.

The first concerns the largest single category of expenditure in most schools and the one that is, moreover, central to the schools' work—the instructional budget. The professionalization of teachers and increased faculty control have produced a syndrome of higher faculty salaries and lower student-teacher ratios—all in the name of academic excellence—which has sent the cost of education skyrocketing. In the university world the rule is: the more highly trained and better paid the professor, the lighter his teaching load and the fewer his contacts with undergraduates. Fortunately this is not true of the school world, since school teachers are not siphoned off into research. But the schools have their own version of the syndrome in the fetishism of small classes. Whereas industry measures its profitability chiefly in terms of the increase in productivity per man-hour, in education it works the other way: the better the school and the more highly selected the students, the lower the teacher's productivity as measured in terms of numbers of students taught. As a result, per-pupil costs have soared each year in both public and private schools. A survey of 1200 school districts, sponsored by *School Management Magazine,* showed that the per-pupil cost in the average public school jumped 13 per cent in 1970 over 1969. Inflation accounted for part of the increase, but most of the remainder went into increased costs of instruction. At the same time, "drastically increased spending in recent years," commented a public school official, "has probably had little effect on the quality and quantity of education that children receive."[29] There is no reliable evidence of a high correlation between the per-pupil cost and the quality of education in either public or private schools. On the contrary, the Coleman Report leads one to suspect that if there is indeed a correlation, it is a very low one. Yet the efforts of trustees and administrators to change this state of affairs are regularly nullified by strong faculty resistance.

But now that many nonpublic schools are in severe financial stress, the issue of per-pupil cost is raised with renewed urgency. Fortunately, some schools have been experimenting with ways of reducing teaching costs that appear to hold promise of improving rather than diminishing the quality of education. Edward Yeomans, in describing the "integrated day" or "informal classroom" as an outgrowth of the Leicestershire plan in English primary schools, notes that "it is something of a revelation to see 40 or 45 children going about their work with little need of direction or restraint from the teacher."[30] And Charles Silberman

---

[29] As reported in the *New York Times,* January 11, 1970.

[30] *Education for Initiative and Responsibility* (Boston: National Association of Independent Schools, 1967), p. 21.

227

shows that informal education is already working in the United States, either as indigenous developments or adaptations of English experience, in public and private schools as diverse as those of New York's Harlem; in the cities and hamlets of North Dakota; Philadelphia, Pennsylvania; Tucson, Arizona; Cambridge, Massachusetts; Washington, D.C.; Paterson, New Jersey; San Antonio, Texas; and Johnson County, North Carolina, not to mention the rash of recently founded free or community schools.[31]

The tendency to overteach grew strong in the conventional schools once the "pursuit of academic excellence" was in full sway, and it is only recently that second thoughts have set in. The shibboleths of coverage of subject-matter, time-serving, inflexible requirements, fixed courses, and small classes, have cost schools enormous sums without demonstrably improving the quality of the outcome. As one headmaster put it, "We are wedded to the concept of 'small' classes, which means that a master is likely to go over the same material three or four times when he might well accomplish the same results, equally effectively, in a single meeting with a larger group of students. Is the small class always best for the student, and the best utilization of faculty time and energy? We all talk about 'large group, small group teaching,' but in all honesty, how many of us have done much about it?"[32] Too little serious attention is given to planning an effective mixture of class sizes suited to the nature of the learning tasks at hand. Even so-called independent work by students, when it results in frequent tutorial sessions, often ends up consuming more teaching time than the conventional class sessions, without appreciably facilitating learning.

A careful analysis of teacher utilization may also disclose areas and tasks which can be turned over to teacher aides. Public and private schools which have experimented with so-called paraprofessionals are learning that certain teaching functions can be well performed by intelligent, concerned adults with special teacher training. The aides are usually married women living in the school's neighborhood and paid on an hourly basis. A recent evaluation by the Institute of Educational Development of the use of over fourteen thousand aides in the New York City schools reported "overwhelming evidence" of the success of the program, wherein the aides, over half of them black, were used chiefly to provide more individual and remedial instruction and to help cope with certain disciplinary problems. Aides are used freely in the Individually Prescribed Instruction curriculum (such as that in the McAnnulty Elementary School in Pittsburgh, Pennsylvania, and the Nova Schools in Ft. Lauderdale, Florida). This

[31] *Crisis in the Classroom: The Remaking of American Education* (New York: Random House, 1970), especially chap. 7, "It Can Happen Here."

[32] Frederick F. Clark, "Is it Economically Feasible to be Concerned with Educating the Young Humanely?" in *Financing the Independent School of the Future*, p. 30. Mr. Clark is the head of Cate School, California.

entails the use of a great variety of teaching materials and frequent use of short tests which the aides administer, thus freeing the teacher to assess the students' progress and advise and assist them. It is not uncommon for parent-owned schools of the NACS to have parent volunteers working in the school, doing a variety of tasks from clerical and record-keeping to grading papers, even in some cases assisting with the custodial work. The presence of more adults of different kinds in the school appears to be a generally beneficial influence, and judging by the New York evaluation, warmly appreciated by the students.[33] A careful analysis of teacher utilization is almost certain to disclose wasteful practices in all but the most grossly understaffed schools, and even these stand to benefit greatly by volunteer or paid assistance of a kind which releases the full-fledged teachers for the responsibilities which, presumably, only they can perform.

Another potential source of economies lies in closer cooperation with nearby schools for the purpose of sharing library resources, film collections, special speakers, and the purchase of many basic necessities ranging from fuel and food to insurance and computer services. The Taft, Westover, and St. Margaret's schools in Connecticut find that sharing teachers in certain special subjects such as Russian helps make the curriculum more attractive at relatively low cost.[34] The Boston Independent School Computer Center is a good example of cooperation among nine schools. The Chicago Consortium of Schools has an ambitious program of cooperation on many fronts. SPHERE, the consortium of schools in the Hartford, Connecticut, area, designed to promote fruitful interaction of the schools with the community, is another illustration.

There is no good reason why such consortia should not embrace church-related and public schools as well as independents. Such a development would help dispel the myth that these different types of schools have nothing to learn from each other. One of the problems of many small elementary schools is the lack of a good business manager and a development officer because each operation is too small to support full-time salaries for such work. Conceivably, one good manager or a single development man could serve two or three small schools without entailing an excessive cost to any one institution, and all might gain something from the mutual relation. The main deterrent to improved cooperation is the feeling of each school that its situation is very special—in fact, unique. This feeling is to some extent inherent in the concept of the independent school, and has too long prevented such schools from joining with others, not only to reduce costs, but to enjoy the benefits and learn the techniques of mutual aid. Now that a new spirit of cooperation is abroad, it seems incredible

---

[33] As reported in the *New York Times*, May 18, 1971.

[34] See the comments of independent school business managers in *Financing the Independent School of the Future*, pp. 41–42.

that in the past schools which were separated by only a few blocks could be almost totally oblivious of each other's presence. It is a luxury they can no longer afford.

An example of a consortium which embraces public, independent, and Catholic schools is the Secondary School Research Program, a cooperative with over seventy members. Research is an important tool in planning and evaluating school reform, but it is expensive and no single school has sufficient resources to develop a significant program on its own. The first project undertaken by the SSRP is to help member schools gain a better insight into the school's total environment as it is perceived by various constituencies, the students in particular, and what they take to be the reality of the school. The SSRP is based at Andover, with F. A. Peterson, director of research and evaluation at the academy, serving as secretary of the consortium.[35] While cost-cutting or greater immediate efficiency is not the primary aim of this group, its program is an excellent illustration of how schools can by means of joint action accomplish things which none of them alone would be capable of doing.

Given the rising cost of all nonacademic labor and service, the time is ripe for more schools to consider student work programs, not only for savings that might result, which would probably be small, but for their educational value, especially to a generation that is concerned about relating work and study. Examples abound among boarding schools, but some day schools manage to involve not only students but parents in the upkeep of the school and its grounds. The Reverend Frederick H. Sill, founder of the Kent School in Connecticut, developed a plan of self-help which involves all students in the school's maintenance. At the Putney School in Vermont, students work on the construction as well as the maintenance of the school's buildings and grounds. "The self-help policy mixes rich and poor alike," a teacher at the Wooster School in Connecticut told visitors. In the spring the athletic teams devote part of an afternoon each week to campus maintenance. We noted earlier the extensive, well-organized work programs in a number of Seventh-Day Adventist boarding schools such as Auburn Academy near the Cascades and the Blue Mountain Academy in the Poconos, which include, in addition to all sorts of paid office and campus service jobs, a furniture factory which employs students in every operation of furniture making from cutting and joining to crating the finished product. As the hourly and overtime rates of unionized school service employees climb, schools with well-established traditions of student self-help are in a better position than those that rely entirely on outside employees.

---

[35]See "A New Look at Reality in the High Schools or Why the Secondary School Research Program?" *Independent School Bulletin*, October 1970, pp. 25–30. The Institute for Educational Research in Downers Grove, Illinois, located in the Avery Coonley School, is another consortium of private and public schools devoted to research.

Day schools have less opportunity and also somewhat less need to develop a student-help program, but even here student participation can be a beneficial adjunct to the educational program. Students of the John Carroll High School in Alabama, a Catholic institution, schedule "work-play days" during the summer, which bring young people out to wash walls, clean floors and other maintenance jobs in the school, followed by a recreational period. The NACS Delaware County Christian School in Pennsylvania brings parents and students together by groups at the school on weekends for painting and cleaning, on a rotating responsibility which helps build a sense of community between young and old and between the school and the patrons it serves.

We turn finally to one aspect of financial management that more than anything else is the key to success or failure, namely, long-range planning. Though it has been stressed for well over a decade in the college world and more recently by the NAIS, the fact that many schools make little or no serious effort to plan ahead and project income and expenditures for five or ten year periods accounts for much of the financial precariousness which afflicts nonpublic schools. Careful planning is still the exception. The rule is to plod along from year to year in a state of financial myopia, concerned only to make ends meet for that year. We suspect this is attributable not so much to a lack of vision, as to the lack of time and business sense among school heads. They pride themselves above all on being educators, and as such they are steeped in a kind of idealism that carries with it no guarantee of expertise in financial management. And since all but the small fraction of well-off schools are chronically understaffed, even if the head has the necessary insight, there is always something else next to the elbow that must be done immediately and no one else is available to plan ahead.

The NAIS staff has developed "Worksheets for the Development of a Ten-Year Financial Plan for Independent Schools" based on the practice which was recommended by Dexter Merriam Keezer in *Financing Higher Education, 1960-70.*[36] These are readily adaptable to the use of church-related schools, which in so many cases are badly in need of a hard look at their business management procedures. The worksheets encourage the user schools to undergo the useful exercise of spelling out, for purposes of ten-year budget projections, the general assumptions about the trend of the national economy as a whole, as well as the school's assumption about its own goals, policies, and priorities regarding facilities, teaching methods, faculty policies, student-teacher ratio, library acquisitions, intra-institutional cooperation, school size, and related basic questions. It then calls for year-by-year projections, over a ten-year period, for each major item of income and expense, as well as a review of the past ten years'

---

[36] (New York: McGraw-Hill, 1959), chap. 7; McGraw-Hill Book Company's 50th anniversary study of the economics of higher education in the United States.

experience in fund raising. Such projections would entail a revaluation of the present jumble of policies regarding tuition charges, scholarships, and fund raising, and expose to the trustees and supporters the need for keeping accurate accounting records.

And speaking of priorities, we raise a question about the tendency which developed during the fat years to spend excessive amounts on the construction of new buildings and facilities without realistically counting the added maintenance cost that each additional building entails. Bright new surroundings doubtless add to the pleasure that most people find in their school—though the students are often less impressed than the adults—but they have little or no bearing on the quality of the education that goes on inside the buildings. One of the reasons why some of the affluent independent schools are presently in financial straits is that they lavished large sums on new buildings just as the fat years were drawing to a close. And now in the lean years the cost of maintaining the new structures adds to the annual deficits. There is an old axiom in fund raising that money for buildings is easier to come by than money for any other educational need, and so the temptation to overbuild is strong. If the present financial stringency results in a reordering of priorities leading to the use of more capital funds directly in support of the educational program and more restraint in undertaking new construction, something useful will have been learned about the economics of private school education.

The American public's seemingly unbounded faith in the power of education appears to be tempered now by the widely advertised failure of education, even while the cost of education at all levels continues to escalate. American universities today have been held up as examples of the most grossly mismanaged, inefficient institutions in the land. Through decades of staggeringly rapid growth, the public lavished ever-increasing sums upon them. But the day of reckoning is here. The private schools, not having been to any significant degree the beneficiaries of public largess, have not developed wasteful habits to anywhere near the same degree. But they will deserve the state aid for which they are now petitioning only to the extent that they put their financial house in order. The state has no business aiding private institutions, whether schools, colleges, or universities, unless the assistance given does in fact demonstrably and economically serve the public interest.

9

Private Schools and the Racial Question

*"If America in actual practice
could show the world
a progressive trend by which the Negro
became finally integrated
into modern democracy,
all mankind would be given faith again—
it would have reason to believe
that peace, progress and order are feasible.
And America would have
a spiritual power many times stronger
than all her financial
and military resources—
the power of the trust and support
of all good people on earth."*

Gunnar Myrdal[1]

The Background

The moral arguments for the racial integration of private schools are precisely the same as those which obtain for the integration of all schools and institutions of the land. As institutions serving the public interest, nonpublic schools are bound by the nation's professed ideals. The creed of equality, conceived from the beginning of our nationhood as a peculiarly American ideal, setting this country apart from class-conscious Europe, was invoked by militant abolitionists who spoke for the frustrated social conscience of American democracy. For though equal status was accorded all men in principle at the very birth of the nation, the procrastination in effectuating it has been centuries long. Even after Lincoln's Emancipation Proclamation freed the black man from the shackles of legal enslavement, the white world, except for the brief interlude of Reconstruction, denied him access to the rights and privileges of free men by imposing the

[1] *An American Dilemma*, rev. ed. (New York: Harper & Row, 1962), pp. 1021–22.

233

rigid etiquette of segregation. It was not until the New Deal of the 1930s that the "forgotten man," in the form of various minorities within modern American society, became politically effective, and racial discrimination began to abate.

The causes that broke—or eroded—the patterns of segregation were complex. Science, in shedding new light on genetics and anthropology, made it difficult for enlightened men to cling to the old racist mythologies. Unforgettable lessons in the tragic consequences of race theories came with the fascist upheaval in Europe and the unspeakable horrors of genocide. Manpower crises during the Second World War lowered many economic barriers that had prevented Negroes from moving beyond the most menial jobs and intensified the migration of Negroes from rural areas of the South to the industrial cities of the North and West. And successive decisions of the Supreme Court opened the way to the full political participation of Negroes and struck down the legal supports of school segregation and of discrimination in housing and jobs. By the sanctions of law and the mandates of the courts, great breaches have been opened in the formerly solid pattern of segregation. Too many Negroes have either tasted or have a new vision of the fruits of the new freedom to make a return to the old rigid system even thinkable, though the struggle is as yet far from being resolved.[2]

It is apparent, however, that although the "old-style" southern segregation is dying rapidly, the "new style" northern segregation is setting up a different and more subtle set of barriers to the advancement of blacks. The new style segregates as much by class as by race, and the two are intertwined in the inner city society where the lower class is increasingly black, to a point where the urban lower class is mistakenly thought to be largely black.[3] The new style segregation permits upwardly mobile blacks to move into the white world with relatively few impediments; in fact, because of the pressure on employers to integrate, there is some evidence of reverse discrimination which favors blacks over comparably educated or skilled whites in hiring and promotion practices, as well as in admission of scholarship applicants in private colleges and in independent schools. But the Negroes who make it into the white world in a professional or managerial capacity are a minority. The majority are stuck in the ghetto, which is so difficult to climb out of because the whole environment is a drag on the development of talents that would enable the young to rise in the economic and

[2]Even as recently as 1944 Gunnar Myrdal found that in the South, apart from a few liberal intellectuals, statements to the effect that there really is no Negro problem were part of the common stock of southern stereotypes that can be encountered in the North also. He saw it as a moral escape—an effort to see the locus of the problem as somewhere other than in oneself or in the South. *Ibid.*, vol. 1, chap. 2.

[3]See the discussion of this point in Christopher Jencks and David Riesman, *The Academic Revolution* (New York: Doubleday and Co., 1968), especially chap. 10, "Negroes and Their Colleges." The authors point out that although the majority of the urban poor is white, the fact remains that Negroes think they constitute the majority of urban poor, and most middle class whites share this misconception.

social scale. The schools, which are supposed to provide the ladder, are as a rule inferior, lacking the kind of peer group and adult models that could provide for the ghetto child examples of the vocational aspirations, self-worth, and confidence in his own powers that he badly needs.

So it is that the racial question remains one of the most deeply frustrating and bitterly controversial issues of the late twentieth century. A decade and a half after the Supreme Court's 1954 *Brown* decision racial isolation in the public schools remains widespread and is growing in some of the nation's cities. What has been gained by court-enforced integration has often been lost again by the increase in de facto segregation as whites vacate the central cities and move to all-white suburbs. The seventeen years since de jure segregation was outlawed by the Court have been a lesson in how persistent and complex the problems of de facto segregation can be. And even where court-enforced integration does prevail, it is sometimes nullified by segregational practices within supposedly integrated schools.

It is against this background that we undertake in this chapter to review the state of integration in nonpublic schools. We propose to examine the extent to which nonpublic schools are integrated, the attitudes of various school constituencies toward the issue, obstacles in the path of the schools' obtaining a better racial mixture, some successful efforts to surmount them, and the legal and constitutional instruments by which the integration of nonpublic schools could be mandated.

How Integrated Are the Private Schools?

Are nonpublic schools, as a group, the friend or foe of racial integration? The answer to this question is a qualified one. The commitment of some of the church-affiliated schools to integration goes back to earlier Christian missionary work among Negroes, efforts which paralleled similar activities on behalf of the American Indians. The Catholic Church as well as both liberal and fundamentalist denominations of Protestantism were engaged in such endeavors in a limited way long before the furor over school integration began. Many long-established independent schools have been racially liberal from their founding—Andover, Exeter, Northfield, Mt. Hermon, Wooster, Windsor Mountain, Collegiate, Georgetown Day, Francis Parker, and a number of Quaker schools come to mind. But, in company with all American schools, indeed all American institutions, the great host of private schools has been painfully slow to recognize and accede to the Negroes' demand for racial justice and equality of opportunity in education.

Extreme reactions to this demand have not been lacking. On the one hand, private schools are currently being used to circumvent integration by means of the makeshift segregationist academies proliferating in the South. Information about this trend is fragmentary, since some state departments do not keep count of private schools. The Southern Regional Council estimated the enrollment of segregationist academies in eleven states to have been from 450,000 to 500,000 in 1970-71, and the number is expected to increase in the fall of 1971. Yet the 1970-71 estimate represents only slightly more than five per cent of the white pupils in the eleven states concerned and includes older private schools which were not founded explicitly to evade segregation. "The question is not that private schools are expanding," an SRC official commented, "but whether they have begun leveling off. They are at different stages in different places. Undoubtedly there will be new ones this fall, and at other places enthusiasm for them will have waned."[4] It should not be overlooked that legal constraints, inadequate facilities, substandard teachers, precarious financing, and substantial tuition costs serve as effective brakes on the spread of segregated academies.

At the other pole of racial response are the new, largely Negro and Puerto Rican private schools, such as Harlem Preparatory School and the street academies in New York City and elsewhere, the schools of the Christian Action Ministry in Chicago, the Black Muslim schools, and free, community minischools. Similar institutions, aiming to rekindle the educational ambitions of school dropouts and founded to provide an alternative to ineffective public schools, are springing up in Washington, D.C., Detroit, San Francisco, Los Angeles, and other major cities.

While these radical developments capture the public attention, the older, more conventional, established private schools are responding in various ways to the challenge to create equal educational opportunities for black children. The result is that many—even a majority—of all types of nonpublic schools have not only acknowledged their responsibility for achieving a racially integrated student body but have devoted considerable energy and resources to the task. The progress which these schools have made toward this goal, if still incomplete and inadequate, appears to be quite comparable to that made by the private colleges and universities of the land, in spite of the latter's access to greater federal funding for the disadvantaged.[5] Likewise, the degree of integration in many

[4] Kathryn Johnson, "A Crucial Year for Southern Schools," Associated Press dispatch in the *Boston Globe*, July 17, 1971.

[5] According to data obtained by the American Council on Education's Office of Research and reported by Alan E. Bayer and Robert F. Boruch, *The Black Student in American Colleges*, ACE Research Reports 4:2 (Washington, D.C.: American Council on Education, 1969) "less than six percent of all students currently enrolled in American colleges are black, whereas almost 12 percent of the college-age population in the United States is black; ... more than two-fifths of the black students attend the predominatly Negro institutions, which represent four percent of the current 2,300 American undergraduate institutions. ... Fully one-half of all the colleges and universities in the United States each enroll less than two percent black students among their freshmen; 88 percent have an enrollment of black students that is ten percent or less of the entering class" (pp. 1, 13-15).

nonpublic schools is greater than that of countless suburban public schools, where, because of residential de facto segregation, no black people reside within the school district's boundaries; indeed, many private boarding schools have achieved racial integration far in excess of that of neighboring public schools in areas sparsely populated by black families.

According to the testimony of the schools themselves concerning their enrollment of Black American, American Indian, Mexican American, Puerto Rican American, and Oriental American students, three-quarters of the secondary schools reported at least one student enrolled from one or more of these groups, while only slightly over a third of the elementary schools enrolled any "minority" children. But in terms of their proportional enrollment, the pattern is reversed: children of the listed ethnic or racial groups occupy seven out of one hundred elementary school seats, compared to only five out of a hundred in the secondary schools (see table 7). Important variations regionally and among the different kinds of schools show that while in the Northeast the Catholic schools lag behind the independents in percentages both of schools reporting any minority students and their proportionate part of the total enrollment, in the South, Catholic schools far exceed the independents on both counts. In the Midwest and Far West the independents lead all groups of schools reporting any minorities enrolled, with almost 90 per cent of the schools so responding; but these children make up only 4.7 per cent of the total enrollment.

Practices and policies vary, of course, from one denomination to another. For example, less than half of the Seventh-Day Adventist schools reported enrolling any children from the "minority" groups, but the children from these racial or ethnic groups are 13 per cent of all the students enrolled. In line with the older dual-system practice of many Protestant denominations, the Seventh-Day Adventists have maintained separate conferences for whites and blacks within overlapping geographical regions since 1944. There is a movement among the Adventists today to integrate, a movement supported in principle by the General Conference; but the decision to integrate rests with each congregation and its associated schools.

In general, the Protestant schools, Quaker and Episcopal excepted, showed as a whole fewer schools "integrated" and fewer "minority" children enrolled than either the Catholic or the independent schools.

In view of the progress of racial integration in American institutions in the immediate past, the percentages of black and other minority group students enrolled in the nation's nonpublic schools has very probably increased significantly since 1969, the year of our survey. There is a strong likelihood, however that the relationships of the integration patterns among the various groups remain relatively unchanged.

It is instructive to compare these figures with those of other studies. The National Association of Independent Schools has twice conducted and published

Table 7

RACIAL OR ETHNIC GROUP REPRESENTATION IN NONPUBLIC SCHOOLS, 1968-69

Type of School	Number of Schools	Schools Enrolling Any Racial or Ethnic Group Students[a]				Enrollment of Racial or Ethnic Group Students[a]				
		Schools reporting Black American enrollment		Schools reporting racial or ethnic group enrollment		Total student enrollment in schools[b]	Black American enrollment		Total ethnic or racial group enrollment	
		No.	%	No.	%		No.	%	No.	%
Elementary	197	67	34.0	92	46.7	46,931	1,701	3.6	3,220	6.9
Secondary	251	152	60.6	184	73.3	97,930	2,660	2.7	4,808	4.9
Catholic (Elem. & Sec.)	188	101	53.7	126	67.0	84,220	2,833	3.4	5,693	6.8
Northeast	57	29	50.9	35	61.4	34,441	869	2.5	1,655	4.8
South	65	42	64.6	46	70.8	21,385	1,420	6.6	1,917	9.0
Midwest & Far West	66	30	45.5	45	66.7	28,394	544	1.9	2,121	7.5
Protestant (Elem. & Sec.)	101	32	31.7	46	45.5	18,660	383	2.1	691	3.7
Lutheran	36	15	41.7	18	50.0	6,622	104	1.6	193	2.9
Seventh-Day Adventist	27	9	33.3	12	44.4	2,786	192	6.9	352	12.6
Christian Reformed	22	2	9.1	6	27.2	6,488	4	0.1	20	0.3
National Association of Christian Schools	16	6	37.5	10	62.5	2,764	83	3.0	126	4.6

Episcopal (Elem. & Sec.)	28	15	53.6	17	60.7	5,261	178	3.4	321	2.7
Independent (Elem. & Sec.)	119	71	59.7	86	72.3	33,579	967	2.9	1,322	3.9
Secondary only										
Northeast	41	32	78.0	34	82.9	11,588	402	3.5	531	4.6
South	26	4	15.4	10	38.5	7,432	26	0.3	108	1.5
Midwest & Far West	37	28	75.7	33	89.2	12,159	455	3.7	574	4.7

Note: The total U.S. population of those between the ages of 5 and 19 in 1968 was 59,227,000. Of this number, 7,836,000, or 13.2 per cent, were Negro. U.S. Bureau of the Census, *Statistical Abstract of the United States, 1969* (Washington, D.C.: Government Printing Office, 1969), table 8. Another category, nonwhite (defined by the *Statistical Abstract* as American Indian and Oriental American) totaled 706,000, which, combined with the Negro group, accounted for 14.4 per cent of the total age group.

[a] Racial and ethnic groups listed on questionnaire were Black American, American Indian, Mexican American, Puerto Rican American, Oriental American.

[b] Excluding those of foreign citizenship.

239

a "Minority Group Survey" of its entire membership of 770 schools. Of the 752 reporting for the school year 1969-70, 730 (93.1 per cent) stated they had an open enrollment policy, although of these, 99 had never enrolled a black student. The 595 member schools with black students admitted altogether 7,617 black students. It is significant, and a hopeful augury for the future, that the number is more than twice the number admitted in 1966-67.[6]

With the advent of the National Catholic Educational Association's data bank, figures on ethnic and racial minority enrollment in Catholic schools across the country are also available for the school year 1969-70. While the *Statistical Report* does not show the percentages of integrated institutions, it does list the numbers of black, Spanish, and Indian children among the nation's Catholic school enrollment. These figures bear out our finding that minority groups make up a higher percentage of the total enrollment in elementary as compared with secondary nonpublic schools.[7] A Report on U.S. Catholic Schools, 1970-71 also shows that a higher percentage of elementary than secondary Catholic schools are exclusively white as well as a higher percentage of elementary schools

[6]Number of NAIS schools with 5 per cent or more black students enrolled:

Per cent black students	Number of schools
Over 40%	1
30–40%	1
20–30%	5
10–20%	26
5–10%	115
Total	148

Source: Minority Group Survey, 1969-70 (Boston: National Association of Independent Schools, February 1970).

[7]Figures for minority students in Catholic schools for 1969-70:

	Elementary		Secondary	
	Students	%	Students	%
Black	163,134	5.1	34,646	3.7
Spanish	180,149	5.7	34,806	3.8
Indian	9,194	0.3	2,591	0.3
All others	2,815,904	88.9	849,234	92.2
Total reported	3,168,904	100.0	921,277	100.0

Source: A Statistical Report on Catholic Elementary and Secondary Schools for the Years 1967-68 to 1969-70 (Washington, D.C.: National Catholic Educational Association, 1970), p. 10. These figures reflect 87.8 per cent of the elementary enrollment in Catholic schools and 87.7 per cent of the secondary enrollment.

which are all or mostly black.[8] It is evident that the Catholic elementary school is primarily a neighborhood phenomenon reflecting the housing patterns and the ethnic and racial compositions of the sponsoring parish. Secondary school students are more mobile, with the result that Catholic secondary schools, like public schools, can draw students from a larger geographic area and hence present a better racial mix.

Attitudes of School Constituencies Regarding Further Integration

The following sections deal with some of the efforts of nonpublic schools, past and present, to improve the racial mixture of their student population, as well as with the obstacles, real or fancied, to such progress. As a backdrop for this discussion, we propose to explore first what we found regarding the attitudes of various school constituencies concerning the admission of students and the employment of teachers from minorities where the color line and deprivation are issues (see table 8).

To put the question about black students enrollment into a broader perspective, members of governing boards and parents were asked also about their attitudes regarding admission of Catholic, Protestant, and Jewish students as well as children from poor families. The interpretation of the tabulated responses poses a problem. The race issue and other forms of discrimination are for many Americans charged with emotional overtones of fear and diffidence. Moreover, the normal human pleasure in being detected in virtue, might have prompted many to respond in a way that is considered the socially acceptable thing. Yet the fact that the attitudinal responses of the different groups roughly parallel the factual record of integration in nonpublic schools, in direction if not in degree, lends at least some credibility to the expressed attitudes; in general, the respondents are most favorably disposed in school groups where the practice of integration is most prevalent, and least favorably disposed in schools where it lags.

[8]The level of integration in Catholic schools (in per cent):

	All or mostly black	*All white*
Elementary schools[a]	2.8	56.0
Secondary schools[b]	0.7	45.9

Source: A Report on U. S. Catholic Schools, 1970-71 (Washington, D.C.: National Catholic Educational Association, 1971), table 4-2, p. 40.

[a]Based on replies from 87.8 per cent of the Catholic schools.
[b]Based on replies from 88.3 per cent of the Catholic schools.

Table 8

PARENT AND GOVERNING BOARD VIEWS REGARDING A MORE HETEROGENEOUS STUDENT BODY

	Elementary and Secondary Respondents Combined														Secondary Respondents Only					
	Catholic						Protestant								Independent					
Per Cent Favoring Enrollment	North-east		South		Midwest & Far West		Lutheran		S. Day Adven.		Chris. Ref.		NACS		North-east		South		Midwest & Far West	
	P	GB	P	GB	P	GB	P	GB	P	GB	P	GB	P	GB	P	GB	P	GB	P	GB
90 or more	Ca+ Po+	Ca+	Ca+	Ca+ Pr- Je- Bl- Po-	Ca+ Po+	Ca+ Po+	Po+ Pr+	Po+ Pr+		Po+ Pr+ Bl+	Pr+ Po+	Pr+ Po- Bl-	Po-	Pr+ Bl-	Pr+ Je+ Cat+ Bl+ Po-	Pr+ Cat+ Jet+ Bl- Po-	Pr+ Ca+ Je+	Pr+ Je+ Ca-	Pr+ Ca+ Je+ Bl+	Pr+ Ca+ Je+ Bl-
80–89	Po+ Bl+ Pr-	Bl+ Je+ Pr- Je- Bl-	Po+	Po+ Pr- Je- Bl-	Bl+ Pr+ Pr+	Bl+ Je+ Pr+		Bl-	Po+ Pr+ Bl+	Je-			Pr+	Je- Bl- Ca-					Po-	Po-

242

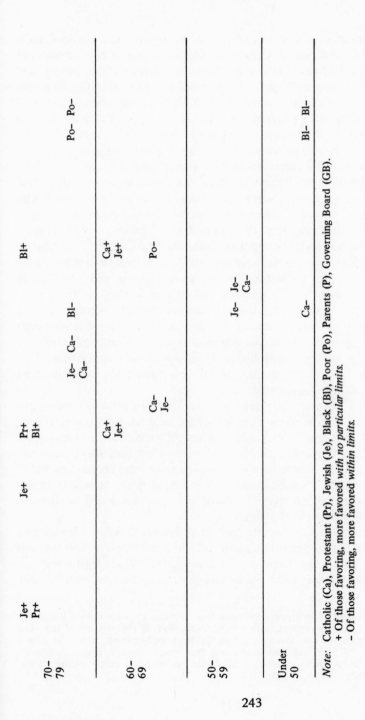

Note: Catholic (Ca), Protestant (Pr), Jewish (Je), Black (Bl), Poor (Po), Parents (P), Governing Board (GB).
\+ Of those favoring, more favored *with no particular limits.*
\- Of those favoring, more favored *within limits.*

The constituencies of Catholic schools in all regions naturally look most favorably on the enrollment of Catholics, with the children of poor families not far behind. Outside of the South, over 80 per cent of the Catholic parents and trustees also favor the enrollment of black students, with most setting no particular limit. Southern Catholic trustees show a high percentage (over 90 per cent) who favor enrolling black children, but, mindful perhaps of the more cautious parental constituents, the trustees would put a limit on black enrollment. Catholic parents in the Northeast are more favorably disposed to the enrollment of black students than to the admission of Protestant children.

As if to reciprocate, the Protestant school constituencies approve the enrollment of black children more highly than the admission of Catholic or Jewish children, while they would welcome the children of the poor, in principle, equally with Protestant children. Protestant parents, however, view the admission of black children with less enthusiasm than do the trustees of their schools.

The independent school constituents are emphatic in their view of the enrollment of black students: parents in the Northeast, Midwest, and Far West are strongly in favor, more so and with less reference to limits than the trustees. Southern independent parents and trustees, however, register a majority opposed to the enrollment of black children.[9] Mindful perhaps of the relatively high tuition charged by their schools, the independent school constituents view with less favor—though still by a majority in all regions of the country—the enrollment of children from poor families. In principle, they make no distinctions about a child's religious background.

Judged by the testimony of parents and trustees, their attitude toward integration is somewhat more liberal than the school head takes it to be (see figure 11). The heads with but a few exceptions see their constituents as more conservative than the responding parents and trustees see themselves, while the heads for the most part believe their own position to be more liberal than that of their constituents. The salient point is that school heads appear to underestimate somewhat the readiness of parents and governing board members to accept a more open admissions policy.

How do the students and faculty feel about this issue? Asked whether they think the number of students from racial and ethnic minorities in their school is sufficient, over half of the total Catholic, student, faculty, and trustee respondents say that not enough or not nearly enough such students are enrolled, with

[9] Evidence accumulates to support the claim that southern attitudes toward integration are changing. For example, according to a 1970 Gallup Poll, in 1963 six out of ten white parents in southern states said that they would object to sending their children to schools enrolling Negroes. In 1970 only one in six said they would object. A similar though less dramatic decline in the number of such objectors was recorded among northern white parents. *The Washington Post*, May 3, 1970.

Figure 11

THE SCHOOL HEAD ON HIS CONSTITUENCIES' VIEWS
REGARDING INTEGRATION OF STUDENT BODY AND FACULTY

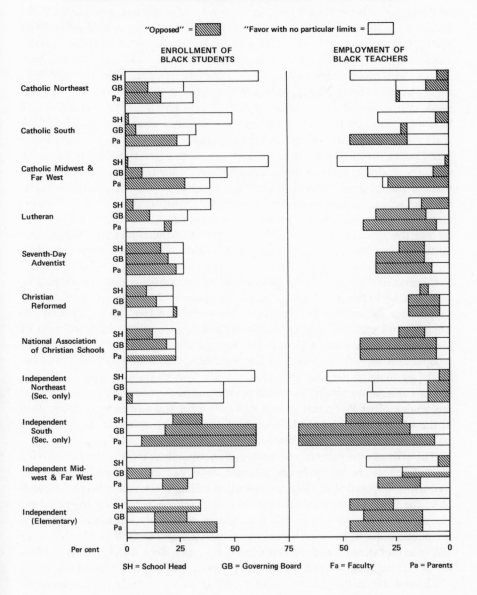

"Opposed" =   "Favor with no particular limits =

ENROLLMENT OF BLACK STUDENTS   EMPLOYMENT OF BLACK TEACHERS

Catholic Northeast

Catholic South

Catholic Midwest & Far West

Lutheran

Seventh-Day Adventist

Christian Reformed

National Association of Christian Schools

Independent Northeast (Sec. only)

Independent South (Sec. only)

Independent Midwest & Far West

Independent (Elementary)

Per cent   0   25   50   75   50   25   0

SH = School Head   GB = Governing Board   Fa = Faculty   Pa = Parents the northeastern constituents giving an emphatic endorsement to the admission of more (see figure 12). In the South the number of those who say there should be more drops below a majority, but again the governing boards are the more approving of a better racial mix. In the Protestant group as a whole only the students muster a majority for such a step, although the Lutherans, viewed apart, show majorities in all three constituencies. In the independent group, students and faculty show clear majorities favoring more students from minority groups, with the faculty endorsement somewhat stronger than the students', while the trustees are less approving. Noteworthy is the solid majority of independent school students and faculty in the South who think their school should have more students from racial and ethnic minorities—perhaps a silent rebellion against the tacit policy of segregation prevailing in some. Also noteworthy is the fact that in the church schools, students are more eager than faculty for more minority students, while in the independent sector the reverse is true. It suggests that for the faculty of church schools the religious or denominational qualification for school admission remains a dominant consideration, but is less important in the eyes of students. Among the independents, where neither the teachers nor the students need be troubled by denominational loyalties, the student attitudes probably reflect upper and upper middle class conservatism respecting the racial question.

General confirmation of the attitudes of private school constituents regarding race is to be found in the school head's estimate of the degree of opposition or support for unqualified enrollment of black children (see figure 11). Catholic heads overall estimate that more parents and trustees favor the enrollment of black children than are opposed. The same is overwhelmingly true among the independent secondary schools of the Northeast, and, with the exception of the heads' estimate of parental opposition, in the western states as well. Lutherans, too, are seen to lean more toward an open enrollment policy with regard to race; but among other Protestant groups, the forces for and against racial integration in the schools seem to be in balance, with the majority opting for an enrollment policy which favors enrolling black children, but "within limits."

The attitudes of parents and trustees of nonpublic schools toward employing black teachers are, in the heads' estimate, more cautiously favorable and more frequently opposed than they are toward enrolling black students. Understandably, the first consideration of those in church schools is for teachers who share the same religious persuasion. It is hard enough to find black teachers to teach in nonpublic schools, let alone to find some who are also Catholic, or Lutheran, or Christian Reformed—religious denominations which do not number many black people among their communicants. Furthermore, the very low admissions rate of black students in the past to prestige colleges—only recently did the ivy gates open to more than a trickle of racial minorities—reduced the numbers of black

Figure 12

WHAT STUDENTS, FACULTY, AND TRUSTEES OF SECONDARY SCHOOLS
THINK OF THE RACIAL DIVERSITY OF THE SCHOOL
("Not nearly enough" and "not enough" responses combined)

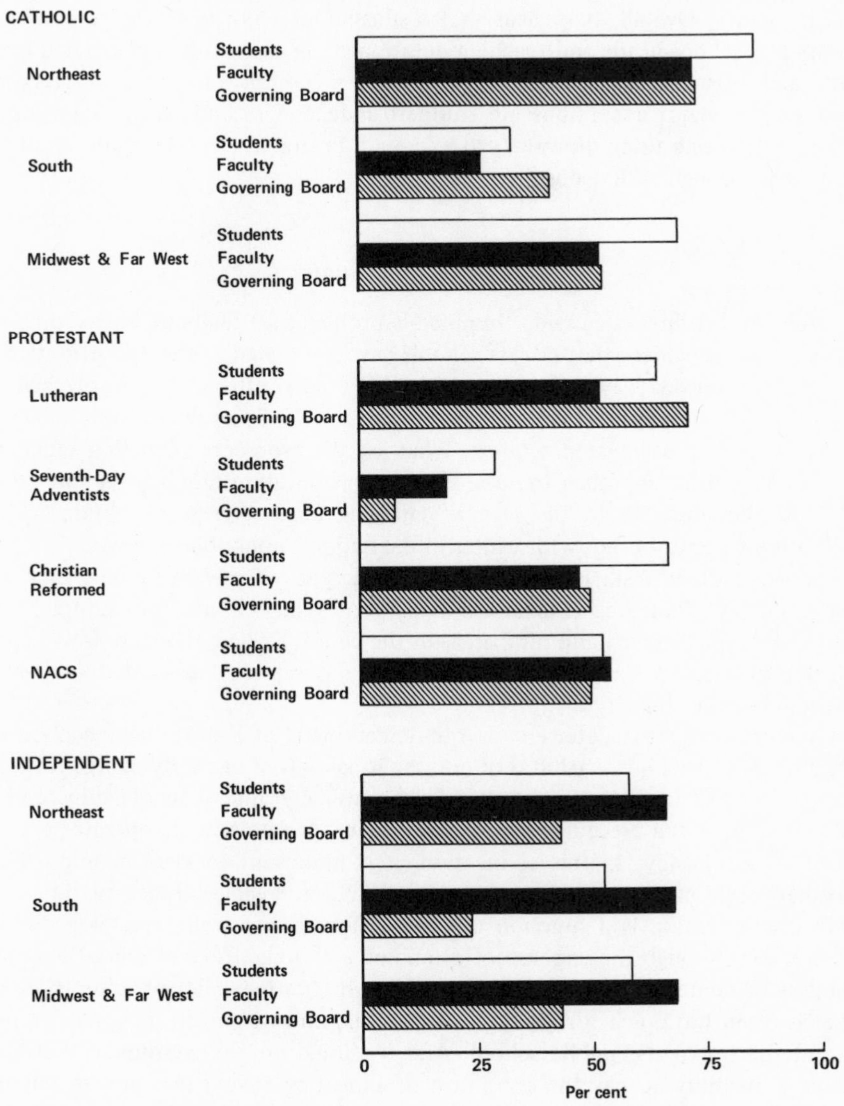

teachers who could meet the teacher qualifications of the strongly college-oriented independent schools.

These, then, are the facts as we found them concerning the extent of racial integration in the nation's nonpublic schools and the attitudes of the various school constituencies regarding the admission of black students and hiring of black faculty. Overall, it is clear that a substantial majority of the responding nonpublic school heads and teachers questioned, as well as their associated parents and trustees, are on record as favoring a basically nonracial admissions policy. The major exceptions are southern independent and certain Protestant schools. It is one thing, however, to express a favorable attitude, quite another to follow through with deeds.

Obstacles and Goals

John W. Gardner once said, "Impossible problems are really unlimited opportunities." It is evident that private schools have responded to the opportunity to integrate in various ways: some have seized it boldly, others have approached it cautiously or timidly, still others have either passed it by or deliberately flouted it by setting up segregated schools. What are the prospects of further tangible gains? A realistic approach to an answer to this question requires that we first look at the obstacles in the way of enabling black youths to obtain equal educational opportunities with whites in the nation's nonpublic schools.

Some of these obstacles are common to all types of private schools. One of these already alluded to is location. Many Protestant schools, for example, are situated in small towns and rural areas of the country where there are few if any blacks, while many Catholic and independent day schools are located in largely white suburbs of big cities.

A more important deterrent to the achievement of a more balanced racial mixture is that all but a handful of nonpublic schools of necessity charge tuition fees, and, with few exceptions, they have extremely limited scholarship funds. We stressed in the preceding chapter that many private schools operate on the brink of insolvency. In this connection, it is important to keep in mind that northern-style race segregation is in part a function of economic segregation and that discrimination is a function of class differences as well as of skin color. Hence, even though the expense of attending a church-affiliated school may be modest in comparison with the cost of certain elite independent schools, even that is often too much for many black parents, however much they may prefer an alternative to the public school. And it should not be overlooked that the parents' inability to pay the extra cost of educating a child in a private school means that private schools have about as few really poor white children as black.

The dimensions of this problem and how they affect the independent schools are illustrated by the NAIS *Minority Group Survey, 1969-70*, which also points up the commitment of many independent schools to a policy of racial integration. The survey shows that almost half of the 8,331 minority group students enrolled in member schools during that year received no financial aid whatever.[10] It is noteworthy, however, that in schools reporting at least five minority group enrollees, the black students receiving aid constituted 20.6 per cent of all scholarship students, and they received a disproportionate amount—one-third—of all the financial aid currently available in the schools. A comparison of scholarship aid in the years 1960-61 and 1970-71, as reported by member schools of the NAIS, is instructive:

SCHOLARSHIP AID AMONG INDEPENDENT SCHOOLS[11]
(Non-Faculty Children Only)

	1960-1961	1970-1971
Total Number Schools Reporting	328	597
Total Amount Granted	$7,569,780	$23,592,698
Total Number Recipients	12,174	21,605
Average Grant per Pupil	$622	$1,092
Per Cent Enrollment Receiving Scholarship Aid	11.3%	12.0%
Per Cent Scholarship Amount	4.9%	5.8%

During the decade the average grant grew by 75 per cent, the percentage of those enrolled who received scholarship aid increased 6 per cent, while the amount of the total operating budget devoted to scholarships rose 18 per cent. On all counts, the scholarship programs of reporting NAIS schools advanced substantially, with the most striking change occurring in the size of the average grant, occasioned in part, no doubt, by rising tuition costs which necessitated comparably larger scholarship grants. This was possible only because of strong, concerted effort to provide educational opportunity to genuinely poor youngsters for whom token grants would be without meaning.

It is clear that the paucity of scholarship funds is a serious limiting factor for schools who wish to enroll more black students. But it must also be said that

[10]*Minority Group Survey, 1969-70*, p. 3.

[11]National Council of Independent Schools, *Report No. 61: Annual Statistics* (Boston, December 1960), p. 4; and National Association of Independent Schools; *Report No. 35: Annual Statistics* (Boston, December 1970), p. 9.

lack of genuine enthusiasm for the admission of more nonpaying black Americans seems a continuing deterrent in some schools. One has only to consider the characteristic ways in which some independent schools use the proceeds of their periodic major fund drives; significant percentages rarely are either planned for or allocated to scholarship funds for minority groups. Indeed if these schools, especially those which already have impressive facilities, chose a different order of priorities in the expenditure of funds, as some now do, appreciable sums could be directed toward the education of an increased number of qualified young black Americans.

The word "qualified" points to a third deterrent to the admission of more black students by nonpublic schools, especially by the independents whose chief reason for being is the maintenance of high academic standards. In their heyday the prestigious schools accepted fewer than one-half, even as few as one-third or one-fourth of those who applied, and rejected others largely on grounds of inability to meet the schools' academic standards, whether through lack of scholastic aptitude, as measured by conventional tests, or inadequate scholastic preparation. Among those rejected were sons and daughters of loyal alumni. In this kind of competition, the average young black American, through no fault of his own, is at a serious disadvantage.

Other deterrents appear more fancied than real. For example, to explain and excuse their failure to admit black students, some private schools continue to say "none ever apply" or "no qualified applicants ever apply," thus implying that they would take suitable black applicants if any showed up. But it is a rare black youth who will on his own initiative attempt to breach the pristine facade of a traditionally all-white school. As Headmaster John D. Verdery of the Wooster School said: "From a practical standpoint the institution that wants Negroes must at first *ask them to come.* If it has none, it is really quite fair to say that it simply does not want them."[12] A related obstacle centers in the interpretation of the word "qualified" and how much reliance the admissions process places on the time-honored but class- and culture-loaded tests and other measures of aptitude and promise. If these are applied unimaginatively to disadvantaged youngsters, few will be chosen in the competition with white, upper-middle class, test-wise young people. Since the admissions process is something of a gamble in any case, alert schools have learned to look for undeveloped potential and do some gambling there.

These, then, are the main deterrents to admitting blacks in large numbers, deterrents shared in varying degrees by many nonpublic schools of whatever kind. They help to explain why many private schools are only minimally integrated. Other deterrents are characteristic of one or another type of nonpublic

[12] David Mallery, *Negro Students in Independent Schools* (Boston: National Association of Independent Schools, 1963), p. 69 (emphasis added).

school. Among the independents, apart from a few that were founded by donors of another era who specified all-white student bodies, there is no legal impediment to their voluntary integration, nor is there for most of these schools an explicit barrier, such as church membership, that might restrict the admission of black applicants.[13] What does restrict, however, is the strong upper middle and upper class orientation of most independent schools, although the meritocratic institutions overcome this constraint by persistent efforts to enroll a cross-section of youth based chiefly on ability. But for most high-tuition private schools the kind of ability that of necessity turns out to be very important, in addition to scholastic ability, is the ability to pay. It was relatively easy for the pioneering independent schools to cross the color line, providing they did not have to cross class lines at the same time.[14] We noted above that about half of the minority students in integrated NAIS schools pay their own way. Since that half fits the social class pattern of white students in these schools, they pose no great problem. Indeed, many independent schools are well equipped to educate the upwardly mobile children of middle and upper class black families, especially those of professional men.

On the other hand, that "other half" who receive substantial financial aid—and the number is increasing—entails not only a financial problem but, as noted, problems of social and educational adjustment as well. Little enough is known by anyone, in school, college, or society at large, let alone by private school teachers used to dealing with advantaged children, about how best to help deprived youth to catch up. Such knowledge is not quickly or easily gained, as many independent school teachers are fully aware. Nor are the whites' stereotypes and ignorance about black Americans easily erased. There is, as a consequence, an understandable hesitation to meet the challenge of dealing effectively with boys and girls from impoverished rural and ghetto backgrounds—children so markedly different from the school's traditional type. Encounters with young people whose emotional and intellectual needs vary strikingly from those of the usual run of white middle and upper class students call for forays into the untried and unknown: new and different remedial work and counseling, special

[13] The legal status of racially restrictive clauses contained in the charters of some educational institutions is reviewed briefly by Norman Dorsen in an essay, "Racial Discrimination in 'Private' Schools." See Donald A. Erickson, ed., *Public Controls for Nonpublic Schools*, (Chicago: University of Chicago Press, 1969), pp. 135–57.

[14] "John F. Gummere, head of the William Penn Charter School in Philadelphia, notes that the school's first Negro student, entering in kindergarten, was the grandson of a president of a distinguished Negro university and the son of educated, professional people. The one or two people who objected to the arrival of a Negro child seemed to be silenced when they heard about his background. . . . Other school heads have found perhaps surprising changes of attitude on the part of a few objecting parents or alumni when a Negro student turns out to have parents of some special kind of professional or social distinction." Mallery, *Negro Students in Independent Schools*, pp. 18–19.

studies, unprecedented social and disciplinary problems, and the unpleasant task of placating loud-talking constituents who if not wholly antagonistic to such experiments are chary of them. Moreover, the outlook of the young blacks who attend these schools is changing under the influence of the militants to a stance of greater belligerency and deliberate separatism; and one cannot be sure that they will find interdependence with whites in largely white schools either appealing or endurable.

In sum, the integration picture for the independent schools remains a mixed one but with many encouraging developments. The pooled experience of schools which have managed integrated student bodies over a period of years provides many insights into how institutions and student communities can restructure themselves in order to have a comfortable relationship between a black minority and a white majority.[15] Furthermore, an increasing number of schools, characteristically the strongest ones, have won the support of a substantial number of alumni who sympathize with the efforts of their alma mater to achieve a just and educationally fruitful racial mixture of students and to extend the school's range to meet new social needs. In some schools, these alumni outnumber the symbolic wearers of the old school tie, and they look upon the school's accomplishments in this respect as conferring a special kind of accreditation or mark of prestige.

A heartening example of a vigorous, concerted effort launched by independent schools is their establishment, in 1963, of the ABC (A Better Chance) Independent School Talent Search, a nonprofit educational organization which enables students from low-income families to prepare for college. In the past six years ABC has obtained scholarships for 1,568 disadvantaged boys and girls who, after intensive remedial work in English and mathematics in summer programs (financed by ABC and located on the campuses of five colleges), attend one of the 110 independent boarding schools (up from 23 in 1964) that are members of the organization. Over 80 per cent of these students are Afro-Americans, the remainder being American Indians, Oriental and Mexican Americans, Puerto Ricans, and poor whites. From 1965–1968 the federal government paid part of the cost of the program, but of the 1969–70 ABC student population over 80 per cent were supported either by full scholarships from the member schools or by partial scholarships matched by grants from ABC, which is in turn supported by corporations, foundations, and private individuals. Since the founding of ABC, its member schools have contributed over six million dollars of scholarship aid to the students of this program, over two million for 1969–70 alone. More

[15] See especially Charles Merrill's article, "Negroes in the Private Schools," *Atlantic Monthly*, July 1967, pp. 37–40; and the December 1970 issue of *The Independent School Bulletin*.

recently the Independence Foundation of Philadelphia awarded grants for scholarships totalling $1.5 million to 29 girl's college preparatory schools.

In addition to this concerted effort, in their admissions procedures for racial minorities certain independent schools are increasingly relying upon evidence of potential ability rather than certified adequacy of preparation and are setting up for these matriculants a variety of new activities to compensate for weakness in previous training: special tutorial and counseling services, special sectioning, special summer session opportunities. These efforts, coupled with recent increases in the number of private schools that actively recruit black Americans, while they provide no ground for complacency, do give promise of an enlarged contribution by the independent schools to the disadvantaged.

When we turn to the problems of integration confronting church schools, we find a quite different set of circumstances. The huge Catholic "system" enrolling about five million youngsters in elementary and secondary schools is in a position to play a major role in the integration of American schools. By comparison, the Lutherans, the Seventh-Day Adventists, the Christian Reformed, the members of the NACS, and other smaller Protestant school groups, can have much less impact nationally, but in the aggregate they too can make a significant contribution. Unlike the independent schools and their allies the Quaker and Episcopal schools, all with a strong appeal to middle and upper class clients, the church schools draw a substantial student contingent from the middle, lower middle, and lower classes, a fact that helps account for certain differences in attitudes about the admission of Negroes in the church-related schools as against the independents.

One would expect the church schools' attitude toward integration to be strongly influenced by the idea of Christian service to the poor and disinherited. The belief in the unique worth and preciousness of each human being is the essence of Christianity, and this doctrine reinforces the American social ideal of democratic equality. It is all too obvious, however, that Christian as well as secular advocates of basic equality before the law have been faithless to that humane idealism over long stretches of our national history. Racially discriminatory attitudes not only proved to be more tenacious and potent than religious scruples; indeed, Christian segregationists have been known to comb the Scriptures for texts to justify the dogma of Negro inferiority.[16] "God meant us to be different." The fact is, up until four decades ago race discrimination was so pervasive and respectable almost everywhere in the United States, the churches could accept it without subterfuge or apology. It has been said that "the most

---

[16]For example, the doctrine of the Latter Day Saints, based on a mythological interpretation of the curse of Ham, still relegates Negroes to an inferior status: while they may become "saints," they may not rise to the priesthood.

segregated hour in the United States is eleven o'clock Sunday morning." With but few notable exceptions the Christian churches until very recently accepted the social status quo, even though that meant the isolation of Negroes, despite the gospel message that in Christ there is neither bond nor free, or Jew or Greek.

Nevertheless, the underlying thrust of Christian teaching, long obscured by custom and unexamined prejudice, helped to keep alive the inner voice of social conscience; there remained a sense of guilt over denying to Negroes the right to develop to their full human stature in keeping with the promise of American life and the Christian virtues which it was expected to exemplify. The old church groups—the Catholics, the Anglicans, the Lutherans, the Quakers, and the Calvinists of various persuasions—draw on memories going back to missionary work in the education among American Indians and later among Negroes. Some of the new evangelical "third force" sects, emerging in the first half of the nineteenth century, were born under the banner of the Abolitionists, although in the South, where the Negro problem was concentrated, the faith of the fathers became quickly embalmed, after the Reconstruction, into a shield for the defense of southern attitudes. But everywhere north of the Potomac and Ohio rivers, piety, while remaining a mighty force, grew "steadily more gentle, more vague, and at the same time more rational."[17] Even in the South, despite the sanctioning of segregation within and by the churches, the ethics of the gospel remained an accusing though barely audible witness to the stubborn persistence of race prejudice imposed by social custom.

But once the repressed black minority began to assert itself and the process of liberalization gained momentum, the dormant seeds of the Christian social ethic became an ally in the battle to lift racial barriers. As H. Richard Niebuhr observed some decades ago, "the ideal of unity and equality has never been recognized in reality until the inferior group, whether women or slaves or a racial group, has asserted that equality and compelled the church to translate its principles into practice."[18] Thus the Catholic Church in particular became a leader in breaching the solid wall of school segregation in the South in the early 1950s, waging a fight against segregation, often in the face of strong lay opposition.[19]

[17]Wilbur J. Cash, *The Mind of the South* (Garden City, N.Y.: Doubleday and Co., 1954), p. 139.

[18]*The Social Sources of Denominationalism* (New York: H. Holt & Co:, 1929), p. 238.

[19]That is not to suggest, however, that this effort was everywhere crowned with success. In Louisiana, for example, a suit is pending against the School Board of the Roman Catholic Diocese of Lafayette, which "seeks to bring about the immediate desegregation of two parochial schools . . . which serve the same area. The all-black Holy Ghost school is separated physically from the Academy of the Immaculate Conception (which has five black children) only by an integrated Roman Catholic cemetery. The public schools of Opelousas were integrated under court order last fall [1969] and the black plaintiffs contend that

Aroused by this example, more churches began to recognize that they could not escape the duty of dealing with the relationships of people as they found them; and their effort to alleviate the lot of Negroes, which until recent times took the form of all-black missionary schools founded in the spirit of carrying the "white Christian's burden," was translated into backing the project of integrating the schools. The work of some Protestant groups, however, notably the Seventh-Day Adventists, and of certain sects sponsoring NACS schools retains much of the flavor of missionary work, though here too the advocates of integration are gaining.[20]

Now that the churches are bestirring themselves about integrating their schools, the question of the extent to which the admission of blacks is restricted by professed religious loyalties or lack of them assumes growing importance. If religious affiliation with the school's denomination is a test of eligibility for admission, there are undoubtedly too few black Catholics or Lutherans to achieve anything more than token integration in parochial or other denominational schools.[21] From our observations, however, we judge that affiliation with the school's denomination is less of a deterrent to the eligibility of such applicants than is commonly supposed.[22] It is true, nevertheless, that certain schools in the South, including some that are broadly denominated "Christian," continue to exclude blacks as a matter of policy based on religious loyalties or other considerations. As we noted earlier, many of these schools are interdenominationally Protestant and under the direct control of a congregational or inter-congregational parent group. The admissions pattern of such schools is accordingly set not so much by denominational policies or doctrines but by the prevailing local social mores; and since each member school of the NACS retains a high degree of independence, the policy respecting the admission of Negroes varies from school to school. The only religious requirement that is exacted of the school and its students is subscription to a doctrinal statement which is broadly evangelical in its tenets, but does not of itself constitute a basis for the exclusion

---

continued operation of the duel Catholic system constitutes a government-supported out for segregationist parents." Center for Law and Education, Harvard University, *Inequality in Education*, no. 6 (n.d.), pp. 17–18.

[20]Ellen White's son began missionary work among the Negroes in the South in 1895; today, it is estimated, one out of every six Seventh-Day Adventists in North America is black. For Mrs. White's teachings on the subject, see *E. G. White and Church Race Relations*, by Ronald D. Graybill (Washington, D.C.: Review and Herald Pub. Assoc., 1970).

[21]According to Brother Joseph Davis, S.M., head of the National Office for Black Catholics, there are 800,000 black Catholics in the United States today. He notes that black converts are rare, as are black religious vocations. *The Catholic Review*, July 10, 1970, p. A4.

[22]A national survey of the nation's Roman Catholic schools, sponsored by the U. S. Office of Education for the school year 1970–71, showed that 38 per cent of black children enrolled in Catholic schools were not of that faith. *New York Times*, April 7, 1971.

of Negroes. Many thousands of Negroes in the South are members of segregated branches of various Protestant church bodies that adhere to the same creed.

The record of Protestant school integration is on the whole spottier and somewhat less consistent than the Catholic, in part because many Protestant schools are located in regions sparsely populated by blacks and in part because the schools are largely controlled by a conservative laity. A Protestant commentator rebukes his colleagues in these words: "The familial quality of Protestant church life rests upon personal congeniality, similarity of taste, equality of social status. We are too often a church family not because of what we share in Christ but because of what we share in the world."[23] Protestant leaders complain that lay control over the application of the church's teachings to the social and political problems has tended to impede rather than increase racial integration. Although our survey found that a majority of Protestant parents support open enrollment, they tend to be, on the whole, conservative when it comes to committing their churches and schools actively to the struggle for racial justice.

Nevertheless, the riptide of change is steadily disrupting old patterns and attitudes. Protestant and Catholic churchmen and laymen who are pressing hard for the elimination of racial discrimination in their schools are gaining new allies in the militant young ministers and laymen who are jabbing at their churches' conscience over the racial question. The radicalization of the younger Catholic clergy portends many changes in outlook, with the battle against racism a prime target. The guidelines suggested by Monsignor James C. Donohue, former director of the Department of Education of the United States Catholic Conference, would assign the highest priority to the ghetto schools, even if needs be at the expense of curtailing the Catholic educational effort at other points.[24] The young people's deepening concern for the plight of humanity in the late twentieth century is a sign to the churches that preoccupation with the church as an institution and its dues-paying communicants no longer commands the respect of the young, unless it embraces a vigorous ministry also to the poor and the dispossessed of the world.

Private School Integration and the Law

After this review of the facts and promise of voluntary racial integration of private schools, it remains to us to explore the legal and constitutional aspects

[23] Kyle Haselden in *What's Ahead for the Churches*, ed. K. Haselden and Martin E. Marty (New York: Sheed & Ward, 1964), p. 213.

[24] "New Priorities in Catholic Education," *America*, April 13, 1968, pp. 476–79.

of private school admissions policies respecting racial discrimination. A ruling of the Internal Revenue Service on July 11, 1970, revoked the tax-exempt status of private schools continuing to practice racial discrimination in admissions; this should provide a strong incentive for schools that have been laggard about integrating. But it is far from the final word on the question. The loss of tax-exempt status would be a severe if not necessarily a fatal financial blow to any private institution, but it falls short of making segregation in private schools illegal. Proprietary schools have survived without tax-exempt status, and presumably some will continue to carry on. The IRS ruling raises some prickly questions, however, regarding the admissions policies of church schools which exist, after all, to serve a religious constituency. Can these schools be coerced into opening the gates to admit racial minorities regardless of their religious persuasions? Furthermore, what percentage of blacks would be deemed necessary to satisfy the new requirement, and how would compliance be determined?

Answers to questions such as these remain in the realm of conjecture. But some light can be shed on them by tracing the development of recent legislative enactments and judicial decisions bearing on racial discrimination in private schools. The process began with recent decisions of the Supreme Court regarding the efforts of certain southern states to maintain schools patently designed to evade integration. The litigation in Virginia, in Prince Edward County in particular, beginning in 1956, came to an end when the court ruled regarding such schools that "grounds of race and opposition to desegregation do not qualify as consitutional."[25] Though that decision shook the segregationists, they were still not through devising schemes to circumvent the mandate to integrate the public schools. Another landmark was the decision in *Poindexter* v. *Louisiana Financial Assistance Commission*, rendered by a federal court in 1966 and upheld by the United States Supreme Court in 1968. In that ruling, pertaining to efforts to establish segregated white private schools with public support by means of tuition grants or vouchers, the court held that a school need not be "predominantly maintained" by the state, but rather that "*any amount* of state support to help found segregated schools or to help maintain such schools is sufficient to give standing to Negro school children" under the Fourteenth Amendment.[26]

Now that state aid to nonpublic schools is in effect in a number of states and in the study or talking stage in many others, while federal aid is also a reality as

---

[25] *Griffin* v. *County School Board of Prince Edward County*, 377 U. S. 231 (1964).

[26] See Norman Dorsen, "Racial Discrimination in 'Private' Schools," in Erickson, ed., *Public Controls for Nonpublic Schools*, p. 142 (emphasis in original). I am indebted in what follows to Dorsen's analysis of the legal and constitutional questions surrounding the issue.

well as on the agenda for further study, the question of the legal standing of segregated private schools, with or without state aid, has become a very real and practical issue. Those that do accept "any amount of state support" are already under the command to maintain a racially nondiscriminatory admissions policy. The church schools pose a special problem in this connection, which is discussed below. But what of the purely secular private schools that receive only marginal state aid? What statutes now in effect cover or can be interpreted to cover these schools?

The Fair Educational Practices Acts existing in six states, with the gist of various provisions incorporated in the Model Anti-Discrimination Act of the Commission of Uniform State Laws, explicitly prohibit racial discrimination in all schools. But though the acts have been in effect for some time, they are without teeth and have exerted at most only a vaguely salutary influence on school admissions policies in peripheral ways. Another statutory alternative— laws prohibiting discrimination in public accommodations—in some states covers private schools. But laws of this type, in the absence of vigorous public support, have also proven to be largely ineffective in combatting racial exclusion.

The Fourteenth Amendment of the constitution offers a better hope. The "equal protection" clause, invoked in the *Poindexter* argument, has been applied to curb racial discrimination in private hospitals receiving even partial public support. Enough state aid is now reaching private schools in the form of property and gift tax exemption, lunch subsidies, health services, transportation, textbook loans, as well as federal aid under the Elementary and Secondary Education Act (ESEA) of 1965 and other special enactments, to make the Fourteenth Amendment applicable. The applicability of this amendment to the problem of racial discrimination in state-aided private schools is clearly demonstrated by the Girard College case. Girard College, located in what is now a predominantly Negro section of North Philadelphia, was established in 1848 by the will of Stephen Girard explicitly to educate poor, male, white orphans. But in 1968 a Federal District Court decision, supported by a United States Court of Appeals, banned further exclusion of students on the basis of race. The court took the position that discrimination against Negro applicants is prohibited by the Fourteenth Amendment because the school's trustees are appointed by the state and the school is tax exempt.

The federal ESEA aid program, covering both public and private schools, is subject to Title VI of the 1964 Civil Rights Act, which bars payment of federal funds for any "program or activity" that discriminates on the basis of race or national origin. Another legal straw in the wind is a ruling by Federal Judge J. Skelly Wright that any school or college which performs a public function that would otherwise be performed by the state should be treated as an agent of the state and is subject, therefore, to the same antidiscriminatory prohibitions as public institutions.[27] In sum, the legal basis under which private schools could be required to eliminate segregation is already there, awaiting only an applicable test. It could happen any time now that Negro parents, aided by civil rights leaders, are more aggressive in seeking admission to private schools.

But if the as yet completely unintegrated private schools were to wait on the legal forum for the signal to eliminate racial discrimination, the time would probably be long deferred. The long-drawn-out and still only partly successful compulsory integration of public schools shows how difficult, complex, and time-consuming that process can be. But in time the compulsory elimination of segregation in private schools of all types appears to be inevitable. The schools which by then have still not taken the step voluntarily will be obliged to do so under terms and conditions not of their own choosing.

If and when all private schools are brought under a clear legal mandate to eliminate segregation, some difficult legal bridges will have to be crossed in connection with the church schools that together compose almost nine-tenths of all nonpublic schools. In the case of parochial schools, for example, where preference is naturally given to members of the school's denomination or faith, could the state validly require the school to cease practicing religious discrimination in order to accommodate a better racial balance? It is an interesting question to which there is no simple or easy answer. To devise a statute that would cope with all the contingencies and conflicting rights involved presents a mare's nest of legal and constitutional difficulties.

This is one of those situations, however, which poses more difficulties in theory than in practice. The religious qualification for admission to church schools is not intended usually to be a racial barrier but to exclude those with contrary or conflicting religious affiliations. Thus, Lutheran or Christian Reformed schools are not at all keen about admitting Catholic students, but an unchurched black applicant is something else again. It is not a question, therefore, of recruiting only black Catholic or black Lutheran youngsters, of whom there are not many. Among the Negroes in the ghettos are hundreds of thousands who are either unchurched or whose church connections are casual and tenuous. It is not uncommon for Catholic and Lutheran parochials, functioning in inner-city situations from which the whites have fled, simply to fill the once-vacated school with a mixture of black, Puerto Rican, and remaining white children of the neighborhood or contiguous neighborhoods, without any particular concern for past religious affiliations or the lack of them. For example, 57 per cent of the students enrolled in the Catholic parochials of Washington, D.C., in 1971–72 were black, and of these 16.4 per cent were non-Catholic.

---

[27]*Guillory* v. *Administrators of Tulane University*, 203 F. Supp. 855, 853–59 (E.D.La. 1962); cited by Norman Dorsen, "Racial Discrimination," pp. 147–48.

The spirit in which many denominations approach the admission of minority group students is illustrated by the guidelines set forth by the Lutheran Church—Missouri Synod for admissions policies in elementary schools:

An application, for a child from a minority group, whether racial, cultural, national, or religious, may be viewed as a problem in some congregations. However, to deny the child admission on such grounds is to deny the all-inclusiveness of the Gospel which the congregation and its school purport to teach. In view of this and to prevent any given child from becoming the focus of controversy, admission policies should clearly indicate that minority status in the community does not constitute valid grounds for denial of admission.[28]

Lutheran parochial schools are encouraged to take care first of the congregation's own children, to minister next to unchurched children, and after these needs have been met to reach out to children belonging to other Christian congregations.

To the extent that the churches are active in inner-city school ventures there is no problem in achieving a high degree of integration as long as the community remains integrated. But these are costly enterprises and a diocese or district can afford to maintain only a limited number without substantial support from the broader religious community or philanthropic assistance from other sources. On the other hand, church schools in largely white suburbs or in small towns—this also pertains to the independents—are confronted with the same conditions of de facto segregation that so seriously impede the integration of public schools. Beyond that, private schools operate within restrictions that tend to generate their own types of religious and class de facto segregation, as we noted above. These restraints indicate that, if and when private schools are required by law or judicial mandate to integrate, many will find it difficult, because of de facto segregation and the paucity of scholarship funds, to achieve a significant racial mixture.

The IRS ruling and future judicial commands to integrate will almost certainly increase the pressure on the state and federal governments to provide financial aid to nonpublic schools in the form of scholarship assistance. A rough gauge of the cost of educating more blacks in private schools is the fact that 34.5 per cent of all nonwhite families in the United States were classed as poor in 1967 (as compared with 8.5 per cent of whites)—in other words, families whose children would need large or full scholarship aid from the private school that accepts them. Many of these are in the cities. And yet it is precisely in the cities that the Negroes' educational need for an alternative to the ghetto public school is greatest. The "purchase of secular services" type of assistance enacted in

---

[28]Frederick Nohl, *Admissions Policies in Lutheran Elementary Schools*, Bulletin 120 (St. Louis: Board of Parish Education, the Lutheran Church—Missouri Synod, n.d.), p. 3.

several states but ruled unconstitutional by the Supreme Court in June 1971, made no provision for scholarship aid to the disadvantaged. Instead, legislation of that type tended to consolidate the status quo among private schools and in subtle ways helped the haves more than the have-nots. True, the easing of the school's teaching salary burden might have released funds for other purposes, including scholarships. But this was entirely at the discretion of the school.

Another predictable consequence of the IRS ruling is the spread of tokenism among schools that reluctantly admit a few blacks in order to maintain their tax-exempt status. The presence in a student body of a very small number of blacks, whether limited by intention (tokenism) or by unavoidable circumstance, is widely condemned as a bad thing, bad for the lonely, conspicuous black youth in a hostile white world, bad for the school in that it receives few institutional benefits from the presence of just one or two minority students. Such a limited number also does not prepare a school for the problems it must be prepared to cope with when it accepts enough black students to become a strongly self-identifying, separatist force on the campus. There is much truth in these contentions. But there is another side. Hitherto segregated institutions are seldom in a position to plunge into integration in a big way, since they are not equipped to deal with a set of radically different problems. And looking at it from the black students' point of view, even the tokens have added up to thousands of black Americans who made it to college and all that that implies for their chances in life. The human cost of tokenism may be high for the tokens, but it has been a lifeline also to a better chance for thousands of black children. Even though the step may be taken for the wrong reasons, there is every likelihood that once taken it will yield unsuspected benefits and insights for all concerned, as the pioneer integrating private schools discovered over the years.

On this issue—the voluntary admission of black and other racial minority youths on the same footing as other students—the concept of the private school's right to choose what it wants to be and whom it wants to admit loses its legitimacy. Freedom of choice exercised by schools with the intention of excluding people just because of their color or race is plainly contrary to the basic principle of justice among men, and it has been so recognized in the law and by the courts of the United States. Private schools as a group, both church-related and secular, have greeted with general satisfaction the antidiscrimination ruling of the Internal Revenue Service. The majority of nonpublic schools accept their responsibility to educate children without regard to race or color. While much remains to be accomplished in respect to numbers of blacks enrolled and the effectiveness of the education given them in predominantly white schools, alert schools have made significant contributions to the integration of American society by voluntarily responding to the right of all to equal educational opportunity.

10

Aspiration and Reality: Notes on the Dynamics of Institutional Change

"Whenever some external sector of society or the schools themselves press for change in the schools, then the schools must in turn make their peace with all other linked sectors of society. Without external pressures or alliances the schools themselves rarely initiate change."

Anthony G. Oettinger [1]

The Urgency of School Reform

Anyone who looks at the development of American education in this century cannot but be struck by the mounting stream of books and articles bearing apocalyptic titles such as *Death at an Early Age, The Blackboard Jungle, Our Children Are Dying, Schools Against Children, The Classroom Disaster, Crisis in the Classroom*, or *Murder in the Classroom*. In the avalanche of criticism, constructive as well as destructive, there is something on the newsstand to suit every taste—weighty sociological and psychological treatises on schools and learning, rhapsodies on kids and angry accusations of betrayal in the classroom, grotesque hopes for education gimmickry, essays on how to put ecstasy and love into the curriculum, and here and there exhortations on the need to return to discipline

[1] *Run, Computer, Run: The Mythology of Educational Innovation* (Cambridge, Mass.: Harvard University Press, 1969), p. 61.

and the no-nonsense school. Education in the United States has never been long without harsh critics of the status quo. What is new in our time is that the criticisms are about fundamentals, about the school as a total environment or ecological system.

Nonpublic schools do not come in for anything like the volume of criticism that is leveled at the public school, for reasons which have been discussed in earlier chapters. Yet there is a considerable ferment of self-criticism within them, a feeling of unease about the future, a gnawing sense that the school is not really reaching the "now" generation and that something must be done. While the private schools have been spared the turmoil that has wracked many urban public schools, the evidence of boredom, grievances, and student impatience with the rigidities of the traditional school is unmistakable. And it worries headmasters and teachers. Boarding, military, and single-sex schools face a struggle for survival. They know they must do something; changes in some schools appear to be virtually dictated by the sharp drop in client interest. But beyond these special cases, all nonpublic schools, except perhaps those of the most separatist, self-isolating religious groups, share a growing awareness that the traditional school is in essential respects obsolete and unsuited to the mission of helping to prepare young people to find themselves and to live in a world of hyperbolic change.

It is not, of course, that public and private schools have remained completely unchanged. They have indeed changed in many respects. The point is, however, that the innovations of schooling in this century, when they made a significant dent at all in the ways of the school, have been superficial. They have missed the wood for the trees. Most of the "experimental" changes of past decades were basically administrative in character, responses not so much to children's as to adults' needs. The new math and the new science which were designed to be fresh and stimulating to the student turned out to be as dull and anxiety-provoking as the old math and the old science; for the new curricula were administered as part of a set school ritual which is designed to turn the student on and off according to schedule. These and other piecemeal innovations, such as tinkering with the English curriculum, adding a bit more work in the arts, rewriting the constitution of the student council, adding advanced placement courses, permitting a few pass-fail options, liberalizing the student dress code a little, and so on, fail to touch the heart of the matter, which is the culture of the school as a whole and its effect on the student.

What are the prospects for such a needed self-renewal among the private schools? We shall explore in this chapter several aspects of the mechanism of decision making as it touches on this question, and what the school people themselves have to say about the need and the direction of change. Thereafter, we shall attempt to identify some of the obstacles to change as well as the levers of school reform.

Decision-Making in Nonpublic Schools

Basic to any valid assessment of the nonpublic school's ability to change is an understanding of "the power structure," as young people like to call it, in the various types of private schools. Who really makes the decisions regarding goals and methods, and who is in a position to influence decisions about basic policies?

The governance of most private schools is on paper relatively simple. The typical independent school operates on the basis of a charter which provides for a self-perpetuating board of trustees. In principle all powers and policy decisions are the board's, though in practice it delegates full administrative authority as well as certain policy-making powers to the school head, to be exercised by him at his discretion but with the advice and consent of the board. The head is thus the pivot of the organization as well as the primary channel of communication between the school and its various constituencies. As previously noted, the headmaster of an independent school occupied in days gone by a position which was unique in the power and authority with which the board invested the office. But although on paper the powers of the headmaster have changed but little, in this age of consensus and democratization, a sensible headmaster knows that his powers are limited in practice not only by the residual power of the board but by what the faculty and, more recently, the students regard as acceptable policy. Thus the head usually shares the exercise of certain of his powers—mainly those concerned with the form and content of the curriculum, admissions policy matters, and student discipline—with the faculty. The faculty's prerogatives, however, do not usually rest on a formal delegation of power but on a working agreement with the head to the effect that certain decisions will be reached in tandem with the faculty. The etiquette of power sharing is by now so deeply implanted that the teaching staff in the sophisticated independent institutions has almost achieved the same standing in the power structure as the faculty in a liberal arts college. Almost, but not quite.

In assessing the part played by nonpublic school parents and students in influencing policy decisions, it is essential to distinguish between "power" and "influence." Except in the Protestant parent-owned schools, parents and students usually have little or no power in the sense of a right to vote on matters of substance affecting the school. Nevertheless, they can and often do materially influence policy decisions by conveying in one way or another their pleasure or displeasure over the way the school conducts its affairs. Moreover, together they hold an ultimate veto power over the school in the sense that if they do not like what is going on they can withdraw. Generally speaking, parents exert a stronger influence in shaping the policies of elementary and day schools than of secondary and boarding schools.

As for the students, in the past the school which took seriously their desire for greater responsibility and trust, as well as their yearning to be heard and understood, was exceptional. In recent years, however, lines of communication between students on the one hand and faculty and administration on the other have been opened in many schools, both church-affiliated and independent. Joint student-faculty committees designed to discuss basic educational goals and ways and means of reaching them have proliferated. In the process, teachers and heads have begun increasingly to see in young people's reactions a source of fresh insight for what is requisite for institutional renewal. It is one of the truly hopeful signs on the horizon of school reform.

The power relationships and the decision-making process within the church schools are difficult to characterize because they vary substantially. Catholic schools, for example, fall into parochial, diocesan and order ("private" or "independent") schools, each defined by reference to the controlling, subsidizing, and owning body. Despite the fact that all are theoretically subject to the ascending levels of the American and international hierarchy, they retain in practice a large measure of local autonomy, and as a result in many localities Catholic schools (and colleges) are in undisguised competition with other Catholic schools. Diocesan school superintendents have limited authority and lack certain prerogatives under canon law which the parish pastor enjoys. The organization of most parochials is usually informal and uncodified, depending more on tacit agreements and established routines than on formal structure and precise definition of responsibilities and duties. In the past, many principals singlehandedly exercised almost total control, subject, however, to general supervision of the superior of the principal's religious order, and the watchful eye of the local pastor, all within the framework of Catholic educational establishment.[2] Recently, however, parish and diocesan school boards, reflecting the constituent community of the

[2] Donald A. Erickson summarizes the complex interrelationships of parochial school governance as follows: "The parochial school has not been *entirely* 'of the parish.' . . . The superior of the order normally appoints the school principal (the position is often rotated among teachers who belong to the order, commonly known as 'religious teachers'). The superior holds ultimate responsibility for supervising the work of the religious teachers. The principal of the school, consequently, has three masters—two major and one minor. She (most parochial school principals are nuns) is responsible to her religious superior and the parish pastor, and (in a more tenuous relationship) she must accommodate to diocesan school officials. The principal obtains money to run the school from the pastor, obtains religious teachers from the religious superior, and obtains educational guidance and advice on numerous questions (such as class size, salaries, teacher bargaining, curriculum, and

school, have been created, and their number as well as influence are growing rapidly, as is the number of laymen who serve on such boards. As this movement gains momentum, and as Catholic schools outgrow their original purely pastoral function and become community schools of a special kind, the authority structure comes to resemble that of the independent schools, with a comparable power and working relationship between the board, school head, and faculty.

The relationship of parents and students to the Catholic school authorities reflects the fact that all together are members of a religious community which the school exists to serve. Catholic parents tend to be more involved in the workings of the school and consulted about a wider range of issues than is true of parents in other schools except in the parent-owned Protestant schools. For example, according to the testimony of school principals, faculties, and governing boards, it is not uncommon for Catholic parents to be consulted not only about disciplinary action and regulations regarding student dress and decorum, they are also listened to on curricular matters and questions pertaining to the admissions policies of the schools, Catholic students, on the other hand, have less voice in curricular and academic matters than do independent school students, though they, like students in all types of private schools, are consulted on those hardy perennials: hair, dress, and personal grooming.

Noteworthy about the Protestant schools in this connection is the prominent role of the governing board in all salient decisions ranging from faculty salary policy through curricular questions, discipline, admissions policy, and down to the omnipresent concern about dress, hair, and decorum. Ideally, Protestant school boards exercise this power on behalf of the parents as well as denomination or sect. Parent-owned and controlled schools are not uncommon—in fact, they are the rule among the "Christian" schools. With "parent power" more than adequately represented on the board, Protestant parents at large exert relatively little direct influence on the school. Since the Protestant churches traditionally never drew as deep a distinction between lay and clergy as have the Catholics, Protestant schools have long been accustomed to having their school boards as well as teaching staffs composed largely of laymen. Protestant school boards typically delegate less of their power to administrators than do boards of other private schools.

By way of summary, one can see a gradual but significant shift toward an increase in sharing power or influence among various constituencies of the nonpublic school. In the nineteenth century, the governing boards of schools, normally containing a generous complement of clergymen, commonly shared the

---

schedules) from the diocesan office." *Crisis in Illinois Nonpublic Schools: Final Research Report to the Elementary and Secondary Nonpublic Schools Study Commission, State of Illinois* (Springfield, 1970), pp. 4-8, 4-9.

decision-making powers in important matters with school heads, who were frequently invested with dictatorial authority. Since then, the growth of academic professionalism has greatly increased the faculty's influence in decision-making, so that the prevailing pattern finds the school head, no longer the benevolent autocrat of old, sharing his powers with the faculty, while the trustees' role is (except among the Protestant schools) restricted to choosing a new head, watching over the institution's financial welfare and real estate, and advising on matters which the school head brings to their attention. In the process of gradual democratization the teachers and, to a still limited extent, the students have acquired a stronger voice, usually at the expense of the authority formerly exercised by the head and the trustees. Parental influence is generally somewhat stronger in the church schools than among the independents, and in the parent-owned Protestant schools there is considerable parent-involvement in school affairs.

What these power and influence interrelationships tell us about the dynamics of institutional change is not immediately apparent. One thing, however, is clear: The school head or principal is in the key position to initiate change. If he is a champion of innovation and possesses the imaginative boldness and charisma to persuade others, the faculty in particular, of the wisdom and excitement of a new approach, he is in a position to move the institution to new and higher ground. However, in some nonpublic schools, boards and parents retain strong veto powers, and in such circumstances much depends upon what these constituencies think about the school's current practice and how it might be improved. As a general rule parents and trustees tend to be far more conservative and content with the status quo than either the head, the faculty, or the students are.

Next to the head, the likeliest source of change is the faculty, for, as we noted earlier, heads consider certain faculty members and the deliberations of certain school committees to be the best source of new thought in education. But before we get too deeply into the levers of change, we must first explore what the various school constituencies have to say about where they now stand in what direction, if any, they desire to move.

The Real versus the Ideal

In exploring the readiness or capacity of the private school to promote change we should distinguish between two basic dimensions of schooling: the moral-religious and the academic or scholastic. Proposals for change take quite different forms, depending upon which aspect is under fire. Reforms of academic practices or goals usually take the form of new teaching methods, improved teacher education, changes in course requirements, new curricula, the addition or subtraction of courses, changing the balance of large and small classes, a changing school mission such as changing from a military to a college preparatory curriculum, and so on. On the other hand, the concern for education in values involves questions about the nature of the religious instruction (if any), the effect that the school's total environment has on the student, questions regarding the content and style of the moral influence the school is expected to exert or not to exert, extracurricular activities including the role of athletics, or questions covering social regulations, discipline, and the kind of person the school desires to produce. The moral dimension of education bulks very large in the eyes of most private school educators. The towering headmasters of the past—men like Endicott Peabody of Groton, Horace Taft of Taft, George C. St. John of Choate, Alfred E. Stearns of Andover, Lewis Perry of Exeter, and Frank Boyden of Deerfield, walking in the footsteps of the great Dr. Thomas Arnold of Rugby—thought of themselves first and foremost as character builders. It is more difficult now to sustain the pose of a father image, of a preeminent moral example, authority and disciplinarian, but that ideal is as yet far from completely eroded in the image of the independent school heads of today. And as for the church schools, their *raison d'être* is clearly to provide an education, by precept and example, in a setting of moral and religious values.

One of the basic issues of moral education is whether the young should be indoctrinated in a traditional moral code, grounded usually in some form of dogmatic religion, or whether young people should be encouraged to formulate their own values. To ascertain the position of various private schools respecting this issue, both as to their current practice and the direction in which they think they should move, various school constituencies were asked for their reactions to the following statement:

Scale A

Some schools take as a primary purpose the transmission and preservation of values and standards that are part of a received tradition, culture or religion, while other schools emphasize a critical examination of established and evolving values and development of a student's capacity to formulate his own values. Circle below the number which best represents the relative emphasis your school places, *in practice*, on the two goals.

Transmit values of culture or religion   1   2   3   4   5   6   Critically examine, develop own values

Using the same scale indicate where you think the relative emphasis *should* be placed.

            1   2   3   4   5   6

For most persons the polar alternatives do not present a satisfactory either/or, since they recognize a degree of validity in both extremes. Hence the scale. In the minds of many educators the transmission of the heritage of the past is a necessary preliminary to the development of personal values. Even elementary education does not begin in a moral vacuum. By the time formal schooling begins, the child has already been habituated in conduct based usually on a pattern of family and community-held values, the basis of which is not yet clear to him. Yet many also believe that the young should not be taught blind acceptance of traditional mores and beliefs but should be helped to compare and weigh the principles that underlie his habitual conduct and to reflect on alternative moral goals. It should be expected, therefore, that most respondents to this question would locate their practice and their ideal somewhere between the two poles, recognizing the tension between the need for a measure of social conformity as against the ideal of personal independence (see figures 13 and 14).

Certain caveats are in order in interpreting responses to a question of this sort. They pertain particularly to the normative part of the question. The descriptions of "what is" appear to be on the whole fairly trustworthy, for they are generally confirmed by other findings. But regarding the reactions to what "should be," it is well to keep in mind that few people willingly admit that their school's present practice is all it should or could be, and so it is to be expected that most respondents probably were inclined to put at least a decent gap between the reality and the ideal. One should therefore allow for an automatic "psychological" shift in one direction or the other. Nevertheless, though it would be misleading to take the "should" responses at their face value, the extent and direction of the shift from the "is" does provide important clues to the nature and nisus of desired changes in schools of different types. It was to be expected that most "should" responses would fall to the right of the "is," for that fits in with the trend of the modern liberal-academic ideal of rational individualism, not to mention the current vogue of contextual ethics and internalized morality. However, it should be noted that a few respondents did stand pat, and a few others moved the other way—hardy counter-cyclical souls who want to reverse the trend or who think things have gone about far enough.

Concentrating first on what teachers and heads of nonpublic schools believe to be the current practice of their schools, we find characteristic differences among the various school types. A majority (or near majority) of both groups believe their school's actual practice is weighted in favor of the transmission of traditional values rather than aiding students to formulate their own. In the frequency and strength of this "conservative"[3] response, the Protestant teachers

---

[3] This use of "liberal" and "conservative" to describe these positions is admittedly open to question, but their meaning in this connection should be apparent. We use the terms

Figure 13

THE "SCALE" QUESTIONS

(Secondary schools only)

The primary purpose of our school is 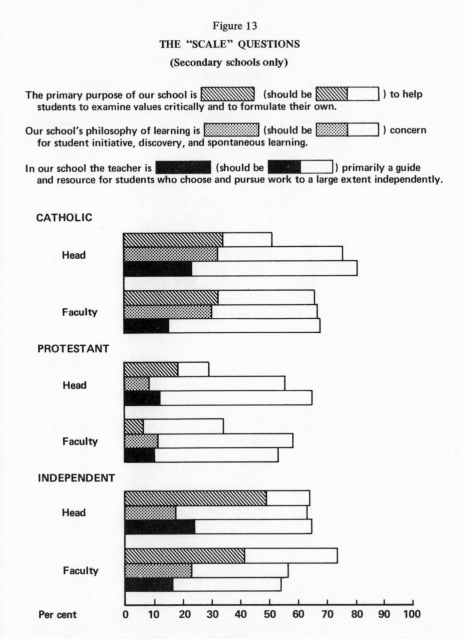 (should be ▨▨▨▨) to help students to examine values critically and to formulate their own.

Our school's philosophy of learning is ▨▨▨▨ (should be ▨▨▨) concern for student initiative, discovery, and spontaneous learning.

In our school the teacher is ▉▉▉ (should be ▉▉) primarily a guide and resource for students who choose and pursue work to a large extent independently.

Note: This chart shows the percentages of school heads and faculty who believe that *present practice*, in greater or lesser degree, is weighted toward agreement with the three statements above, and the percentage of those who think it *should be* so weighted even if current practice differs.

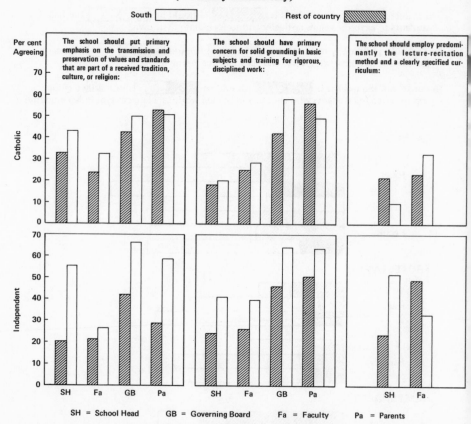

Figure 14

REGIONAL VARIATIONS AMONG SCHOOL CONSTITUENCIES
ON THE "SCALE" QUESTIONS
(Secondary schools only)

South ☐   Rest of country ▨

Note: This chart shows the percentage of school heads, faculty, governing boards, and parents who believe that the school's practice *should be*, in greater or lesser degree, weighted in the direction of agreement with the above three statements.

and heads are far and away in the lead, with approximately 90 per cent so believing. The independents show the smallest number on the "conservative" side of the scale, with majorities only slightly in excess of 50 per cent thus characterizing the present practice of their schools. Catholic schoolmen generally resemble the pattern of the independents, although the Catholic position is in general more centrist.

---

without reference to the political connotations attached to them in other contexts. As the scale is laid out, it happens that the advocates of more freedom land on the right and the stand-patters on the left of center, so that, given the common parlance, it would be even more ambiguous to speak of moving "to the right" or "to the left."

However, these broad composites of attitudes regarding education in values obscure certain differences among the constituencies of various types of schools. For example, in reporting their current practices more heads than teachers say their schools emphasize training in the critical examination of values. One suspects that it may be the desire of the majority of these principals to move in such a direction which prompts a wish-fulfilling judgment that it indeed is taking place. On this score, the word of the teachers, engaged as they are in the day-by-day converse with students and with each other, would seem to be the more trustworthy.

How do these appraisals of the current practice of schools compare with what the constituencies say *should* be the emphasis? Keeping in mind the caveats noted above, we are inclined to discount the "ought" responses except in cases where the discrepancy between the "ought" and "is" is pronounced. Scrutinizing the tables with this in mind, we come upon the following food for thought regarding the dynamics of institutional change.

The most striking outcome is the fact that the shift from the "is" to the "ought" is with but very few exceptions consistently away from the inculcation of traditional values and toward equipping the student to undertake a critical examination of values and formulate his own. Theoretically, it could just as well have gone the other way, except for the plain historical fact that the main thrust of modernism in this century is in the direction of liberating individuals from the shackles of ignorance, superstition, and the religious and moral dogmas of the past, so that they may formulate their own values. "Whirl is King, having driven out Zeus." And yet, considering the strong conservative reaction in some circles to the perils of the present human predicament, one might expect an appreciable resurgence of traditionalism and conservatism in some nonpublic schools—an educational backlash as it were. It is there, but it shows up only in traces among these respondents.

Among those who believe that a school's emphasis should be upon teaching students to examine values critically, independent school faculties lead the way. This response is in keeping with the intellectual-humanistic rather than religious orientation of these schools. Catholic teachers, however, are not far behind in favoring the development of moral independence, though the heads of these schools are somewhat less enthusiastic about moving in this direction. The position of Protestant educators, on the other hand, is a conservative one in the main, with about a third of the heads and faculties following the pattern of their independent and Catholic school counterparts. But in all types of schools, the teachers are more liberal in respect to this issue than are the school heads.

As for the governing boards, those of the Protestant schools reveal themselves as strikingly conservative on this issue. Only one in ten thought that the school should emphasize a critical examination of established values. This compares with four in ten of the board members of independent schools who so believe and over half of those on Catholic boards. In general, the figures reveal a critical difference in the point of view of governing board members compared to that of the faculties and heads of their schools. For example, whereas only one in four of the independent school trustees believe the school should give more emphasis to the critical examination of values, such an emphasis is backed by a solid 64 per cent of the heads and 74 per cent of the faculties of these schools.

What these findings suggest regarding the dynamics of school change in the area of value education can be summed up as follows. The majority of teachers and heads of Catholic and independent schools are disposed to encourage the student's freedom to examine traditional values critically, but the preference of parents and trustees tends to be a restraining influence. In the Protestant schools the teachers, though conservative in the majority, show signs of moving in a liberal direction, particularly those in certain leading schools. However, not only the parents and trustees of these schools but the heads as well favor a traditionalist approach to moral education.

Judging by this survey, many private school educators are prepared—in their minds at least if not institutionally—to place greater trust in the child's capacity to formulate, with the help of adults and in the bosom of the peer group, a philosophy of life's values. Are they equally prepared to accept the academic corollary of that view: the thought, developed most clearly by Piaget, that the child is the principal agent in his own mental development and that each child's needs are unique?

Some private schools, encouraged by the experience of English primary schools as recounted in the Plowden report, have reorganized the classroom to facilitate this approach. Here the teacher is no longer the sole generator of learning but serves as a guide, catalyst, and diagnostician for the activities that the child pursues more or less independently. The learning environment is carefully planned to include a rich array of materials which appeal to various senses in order to open alternative avenues to learning. The informal schoolroom is less of a radical departure than it sounds, for it aims primarily to free the teacher from rigid routines and lesson plans so that he may do better what good teachers have always done, even under the restrictions of the formal classroom: assist the child's learning by capitalizing on his native interest and curiosity, and help him to learn in whatever way he learns best. The new concept rests on trust in and respect for children as persons and a deep concern for the child's affective and cognitive growth. Many elements of this approach were embodied in the progressive school movement which emerged during the 1890s, largely in response to John Dewey's critique of the traditional philosophy of teaching and learning.

Judging by the repeated indictments of public education—Charles E. Silberman's *Crisis in the Classroom* is a recent example—the chief complaint about most public schools is that they are too impersonal and inflexible. Because of the large number of children it must "process," the conventional school selects a common denominator of children's interests, attention span, growth rate, and cultural background and settles on a prescribed program, administered in regular doses under teacher-proof lesson plans. Instead of adapting the curriculum to the child, the child is made to adapt himself to the curriculum and the school culture. The job of the teacher is primarily that of the disciplinarian who maintains order and quiet among students who become restless, evasive, or bored under the enforced routine. And both teacher and child are judged less by what the child learns than by how well the teacher controls the class and how docilely the child fits into the prescribed timetable.

The time-honored concept of schooling is reflected in the shape and furnishings of the traditional schoolroom with its hardwood desks bolted to the floor in neat rows, and the raised dais up front from which the teacher tells authoritatively about this or that subject, makes assignments, hears student recitations and grades the results. The roomful of fidgety, age-graded youngsters is expected to learn largely by rote, drill, and memorization, in a pitiless competition designed to separate the sheep from the goats. By now much of the grimness of yesteryear's schoolroom has been papered over by brightened rooms, improved texts, and a greater concern for the child's personal well-being. It is evident, too, that good teachers somehow get through to many of the students despite the obstacles that the formal classroom poses. Nevertheless, too often the school culture still suppresses curiosity, allows the sensibilities to atrophy, and encourages docility and dependency.

From the evidence at hand it is clear that the nonpublic schools, too, are strongly tethered to the traditional way, though there are important variations by and within the various types. Just how they compare with public schools overall in this respect is hard to say. Most likely the small size and familial atmosphere of most private schools, and the voluntary relationship of clients and school, create a climate which appreciably softens the hard institutional lines of conventional schooling.

How do nonpublic school educators characterize their philosophy of student learning and teaching methods, and are they satisfied with their current practice on these counts? A clue to where they stand on these questions is contained in the ways heads and faculties reacted to the following statements:

Scale B

Classify your school's philosophy of student learning, *as it is currently practiced by the faculty*, on the following scale: at one end primary concern for solid grounding in the basic subjects and training for rigorous, disciplined work; and at the other end, primary concern for student initiative, discovery and spontaneous learning. For many schools both considerations play a part. Circle the point on the scale that represents, in your judgment, the relative weight given the two sets of goals.

| Solid grounding, basic subjects, disciplined work | 1 | 2 | 3 | 4 | 5 | 6 | Student initiative, discovery, spontaneity |

Using the same scale indicate where you think your school's education emphasis *should* be.[4]

1 2 3 4 5 6

Scale C

Identify your school's teaching methods, *in practice*, on the following scale. The left end represents schools that employ predominantly the lecture-recitation method and a clearly specified curriculum. The right end represents schools wherein the teacher is primarily a guide and resource for students who pursue and choose their work to a large extent independently.

| Lecture-recitation, specified curriculum | 1 | 2 | 3 | 4 | 5 | 6 | Teacher as resource and guide for students working independently |

Using the same scale, indicate the teaching methods you think *should* be practiced.

1 2 3 4 5 6

As we noted earlier, while there is no precise way of measuring the general trustworthiness of the responses to questions of this sort, our direct observations and interviews, as well as related survey findings, lead us to accept the responses as reflecting in the main the actual state of affairs. One caution is in order, however. The various school samples were drawn from a national list, compiled by the United States Office of Education covering the year 1965-66, and augmented by new or hitherto unidentified schools that came to our attention in one way or another. Nevertheless, even an augmented list is bound to contain a greater proportion of well-established schools in comparison with new experimental ones, since the latter are often short-lived and difficult to track down. In other words, whatever distortion is reflected in these findings, it is probably in the direction of making the nonpublic schools as a whole appear to be somewhat more conservative than they are in fact. But on the basis of our overview of the whole private school world we judge the distortion, if indeed there is one, to be

[4] Governing board members and parents were asked only to react to the normative part of scale B.

276

slight; and it may be more than compensated for by the human tendency to put the school and its work in the best possible light, which in this case would mean exaggerating the liberal stand of the school, in keeping with the prevailing trend.

Looking first at how private school educators characterize the philosophy of student learning prevailing in their school, we find that most heads and teachers in Catholic, Protestant, and independent schools see it as predominantly conventional, with emphasis on solid grounding in basic subjects and disciplined work. The Protestant educators are much more strongly so inclined than the Catholics and independents. Secondary schools of all types consistently place more emphasis on rigorous, disciplined work than do elementary schools. The college preparatory track with its stress on "hard" academic subject-orientation probably accounts for much of this emphasis.

In the what "should be" scale, however, the heads and teachers of all groups, without exception, in great numbers desire to move toward more reliance on student initiative and discovery. Sixty-seven per cent of Catholic elementary and just over three-quarters of Catholic secondary heads would shift in that direction, joined by a comparable, if somewhat smaller, majority of teachers. While less than half of Protestant elementary heads and teachers would emphasize student initiative, their colleagues in Protestant secondary schools favor such an emphasis by comfortable majorities. It appears then that many schoolmen who were hitherto content with conventional objectives and methods are desirous of moving toward a more "liberal" philosophy of student learning.

As to teaching methods, an overwhelming majority of teachers and heads in all types of elementary and secondary schools characterize theirs as consisting mainly of lectures and recitations within the confines of a well-structured curriculum. Such differences as do come to light between Catholic, Protestant, and independent schools are small. Teaching methods in elementary schools are consistently reported to be freer and more flexible than those in the secondaries. Among the secondary schools there is little to choose—overall the current teaching methods are reported to be almost unrelievedly conventional. There is only a little leavening of the traditional lump here and there reported by schools that experiment with more flexible student-centered alternatives designed to help children learn by and for themselves.

The "should be" part of this question, interpreted with the cautions noted above, yields some general clues regarding the extent of the dissatisfaction with the methods currently employed, and the direction of potential or desired change. Most school heads—81 per cent of the Catholic and 65 per cent of the Protestant and independent secondaries—believe their schools should move toward greater flexibility in teaching and more encouragement to student initiative in learning. The teachers are somewhat less eager for such a change. We noted in an earlier chapter that most teachers believe that they lack the skill and training to teach in this way. Secondary school educators in all groups show a stronger inclination in this direction than do their elementary colleagues, which is not surprising since the former's present practice is much more conventional to begin with. The educators in "Christian" secondary schools are the most contented of all with things as they are. Of particular interest, however, is the desire for a more experimental approach to teaching and learning expressed by large numbers of teachers in Lutheran schools. Since most of the Lutheran schools are Missouri Synod institutions—one of the more conservative branches of Lutheranism in the United States—the progressive attitude of Lutheran teachers in both the leading and representative schools signals a struggle within between the forces of religious conservation and academic progressivism.

A comparison of the teaching methods currently in use at randomly selected schools and certain "leading" schools (the latter identified by chief offices of the various national school associations) brings to light a revealing difference. The practice of leading secondary schools in the NAIS, Episcopal, Catholic, and Lutheran groups (as reported by teachers and heads) is appreciably more progressive than that in the corresponding general school group, while the Seventh-Day Adventist and "Christian" leaders by contrast are more closely tethered to the old ways in comparison with the randomly selected schools. This curious outcome evidently reflects the basic differences between schools having a predominantly academic orientation and those for which religious and moral education is the chief aim. It is to be expected that the leaders among the academically oriented independent schools would employ more advanced teaching methods than do the typical schools of that same group. There is a comparable difference among the church-related Episcopal schools. However, even the Catholic and Lutheran leading schools differ from their representative schools in showing a stronger tendency toward progressivism. It suggests that these leading schools, even though church-related, stress academic goals, while the typical schools of the same denominations are more concerned with their religious mission.

There are others besides the head and the teachers—not to mention the students themselves—who must be listened to and at times consulted when significant changes in a school's education program are at issue. Chief among these are the trustees and parents. We noted above the discrepancy between the "liberal" tendencies of heads and teachers, on the one hand, and the "conservative" posture of governing boards and parents on the other hand in regard to the proper mission of a school in respect to moral and religious education (scale A). A similar discrepancy comes to light in the reactions to the scale questions concerning a school's preferred philosophy of learning and teaching techniques (scales B and C). The evidence at hand seems to support the generalization that, other things being equal, those closest to the students in the daily round of teaching and learning are more likely to be stronger advocates of encouraging student initiative in developing personal values and in academic learning. As the distance from the daily workings of education increases, the view of the school's goal and techniques becomes more conservative.

Finally, certain geographical differences in the reactions to the scales should not be overlooked. Our data provided for a regional breakdown of only the constituents of Catholic and independent schools. Few striking regional differences were disclosed among the Catholic schools. There were sharp differences, however, between constituents of the southern independent secondary school group and those of corresponding schools in all other sections of the country. For example, in regard to whether a school's primary mission is to transmit traditional values or help students to formulate their own (scale A), the southern schools reveal a "conservative" cast: only about a fifth of the independent school heads in the North and West, compared with well over half the southern school heads, opted for the traditionalist position. There is a similar difference in the attitudes of governing boards. On this issue only the faculty attitudes reveal negligible regional differences.

Comparable variations are revealed regarding whether the school should emphasize solid grounding in basic subjects or student "discovery" and initiative (scale B). The percentage of those who say they favor a philosophy of rigorous, disciplined work is appreciably stronger among all southern constituencies than among those of the other regions. The sectional pattern in favor of employing predominantly the lecture recitation method runs true to form for independent school heads, with those in the South more conservative than those in other sections. However, a majority of southern teachers approve the use of teachers primarily as a guide and resource for students working independently.

Obstacles to Change

From the foregoing it is evident that many private schoolmen appear to be dissatisfied with the prevailing philosophy and practice of their institutions. In substantial majorities they incline to the view that learning, in both the academic and value dimensions, should build on the learner's interests rather than on the teacher's, and that the teacher's role should not be so much that of a teller or instructor as a guide, catalyst, and stimulator. This should come as no surprise. The major trend of proposed reforms is persistently away from the subject-centered, teacher-dominated program designed as a common denominator among children of varying talents, emotional differences, and growth-rates, and toward a plan that adapts the materials and pace of learning to the interests and needs of children. It is one thing, however, to define the direction of the desired change, quite another to redirect and augment the resources of established schools to carry out any such mandate, if indeed it be a clear one. What is holding them back—the private school educators with their vaunted freedom to move with the times? It is time to consider briefly the most important obstacles to effecting far-reaching educational change—obstacles that are common to private schools in particular.

First and most obvious, perhaps, is the problem of cost. Certain types of individualized instruction, which may seem in some respects educationally made to order for private schools, entail costs that appear to place them out of the reach of many private schools. Individualized instruction, as it is conceived in well-endowed independent schools, requires an expensively low pupil-teacher ratio. Other more precise experiments in Individually Prescribed Instruction (IPI), such as the special program developed by the University of Pittsburgh's Learning Research and Development Center and tried out in the Pittsburgh Oakleaf and McAnnulty elementary schools where normal public school pupil-teacher ratios prevail, is estimated to add from $35 to $115 a year more per pupil than conventional teaching methods.[5] And those figures do not take into account the added administrative duties, special teacher training, new materials and general retooling and restructuring that are entailed by installing the system. Similarly, the high cost of other overtouted, not yet perfected devices of educational technology should spare most private schools the agony of being caught up prematurely in a frenzy of innovation along those lines. But in time, once some of the devices emerge as tested, reliable aids to teaching, private schools may be faced with a serious cost problem.

Or will they? Perhaps the lack of financial resources, the small size and familial character of many private schools will naturally channel their innovative efforts into a deeper exploration of how an open, warm, school climate, characterized by cordial relationships between students and adults, can serve the educational needs of young people best. Perhaps the most directly human methods will prove to be most effective. It seems unlikely that the needed humane qualities will be developed by commodity-oriented innovative programs which invite into the classroom technological devices that, however clever they may be in teaching marketable skills, abstract logic, or factual knowledge, kill the spirit in the process. It takes activity and communion in the "adventurous presence of other real persons," in the words of Peter Marin, to nourish the qualities that young people need for psychic survival in a world of all-encompassing technology.[6] So it may be the special destiny of private schools to perfect counter-cyclical "models" of the humanizing school dedicated to reawakening in the

[5] See Oettinger and Marks, *Run, Computer, Run*, especially pp. 140–50.

[6] "Children of the Apocalypse," *Saturday Review*, September 19, 1970, p. 73.

young the sense of community between old and young and the continuity of past, present, and future of the human adventure.

A second potent deterrent to change is inherent in the very concept of "school" as an institutionalized process which comes to have an identity and life of its own with traditions, precedents, and routines hardened into an inert, change-resistant armor. Doing things repeatedly in the same way endows them with a sacrosanct quality: it is our way, the right way, the only way. The private school, in particular, tends to build up a staff and clientele of likeminded people who harbor certain expectations regarding the character of the school. To the extent that it becomes the prisoner of its constituencies, it can change only as they do.

Thus it is that even the new ideas that do get tried out have tough sledding, despite optimistic predictions that they herald a major breakthrough in education. The radio, team teaching, television, the ungraded school, the curriculum reforms of the 1950s and '60s, programmed and computer-assisted instruction, individually prescribed instruction after the IPI pattern—each in turn was hailed as marking a historic turning-point in teaching and learning. But they have rolled over the durable, unchanging schools like transient waves to recede again, leaving behind little that is either new or a solid improvement. John I. Goodlad, after visiting one hundred schools in thirteen states, summed it up: "We are forced to conclude that much of the so-called educational reform movement has been blunted on the classroom door."[7] Goodlad was speaking of public schools, but visits to private schools convinced the writer and his colleagues that the burden of proof is equally on the private school.

Beyond the school walls, a strong obstacle to innovation is of course the economic, religious, or intellectual conservatism of many of the parents who constitute the clientele of the private schools in all their variety. The "market" of the avant-garde school is limited and precarious. Most parents do not wish their children to be the subjects of any "far-out" experimentation which would imperil their acquisition of the three R's and the virtues and values of the middle-class establishment. And so the instinctive resistance by society at large to far-reaching social change makes it difficult for private school leaders to shape education as they wish and for bold new ideas to gain a sufficiently secure beachhead on which to build a financially viable school.[8] There are reasons to believe, however, that more parents are now alert to the need for school reform

---

[7]"The Schools vs. Education," *Saturday Review*, April 19, 1969, p. 60.

[8]As a teacher in a Catholic girls' school reported to a study visitor: "We want to create the whole woman and parents want us to create the college-prepared child. I think a lot of times parents completely miss the point of what we are trying to do with the whole woman."

than was the case even a decade ago. In fact, in some private school communities it is the parents and alumni(ae) who are pushing for new approaches.

Finally, we come to the human factor, the quality of the men and women who direct the schools and teach in them. Although some of them admit that they feel the constraints of trustees, parents, or alumni to be serious obstacles, many appear to lack the intensity of conviction needed to bring about changes they themselves say they desire. The overall impression is that teachers and heads are hesitant to change the status quo, because of the uncertainties and risks that charting a new course entails. Educators, whether in private or public schools, tend to be cautious, prosaic, respectable people who are not eager to risk the opprobrium of working for untried and conceivably unpopular reforms. Moreoever, most school heads well appreciate the hazards of getting caught between the upper and nether millstones of conservative parent-trustee pressures and the demands of disaffected students and young faculty insurgents. In such a game, where you are damned if you do and damned if you don't, the temptation is strong to indulge in tactics of evasion and compromise or to quietly defuse the factions that rock the boat, in order "to avoid trouble." In the face of widespread belief that today's schools are not as good as they could be or should be, observers are often discouraged by the seemingly limited numbers of private school leaders of established schools who are not only imbued, in Whitehead's words, with "a noble discontent" with things as they are, but bold enough to do something about it.

We recognize, then, powerful forces that oppose fresh attacks on old and new problems of the schools, forces that are compounded of the human factor—a too-limited supply of vigorous, imaginative, courageous leadership—and the built-in resistance of deep-going change that characterizes formal, institutionalized education the world over. Yet not all private schools by any means are merely the obedient servants of their clients. Headmasters and principals worthy of their salt, and the same should be said of teachers, have their own ideas of what the proper ends and means of education are, ideas that are not always fully in tune with their clients'. A vigorous head and faculty have to educate their patrons as well as their students. And today's questioning students are spurring their teachers and the head as well as their parents to a reexamination of many aspects of school life hitherto taken for granted.

The Levers of Change

"To move from schools wherein expectations for pupils, content, grouping, and so on are determined by grades," says Dean John I. Goodlad, "to schools where chronological age, grade level, and group norms are unimportant in determining what children are to learn and how they shall be classified for instruction is to make a mighty leap."[9] It is time now to examine what persons or groups in the private school are in the best position to exert the leverage necessary to produce such a leap.

Doubtless the school head, in virtue of his power and authority, is in a stronger position than anyone else to introduce and diffuse innovative ideas or to champion and encourage innovative members of his staff to experiment. If he is bent on introducing ideas of his own, he must first win allies among the faculty, and perhaps among his trustees, to create a reasonably secure beachhead from which to win further cooperation and support; or if he aims to further the plans of innovative members of his staff he can use his power to clear the way for them and devise ways of enlarging the circle of those who are involved in the new approach, while remaining closely involved himself. Goodlad reports that the key characteristic of six forward-looking and genuinely innovative public schools in California was that "the person identified with having authority for curriculum and instruction in the school system was involved in or very close to the changes taking place in the schools. In brief, the physical and psychological distance between the actuality of change and the responsibility for effecting change was very short. No complex hierarchy existed between the classroom teachers and the top authority of the school system or his immediate associate to whom responsibility for curriculum and instruction had been delegated."[10]

The Goodlad quotation underlines the difficulties of trying to improve a system of schools from the top down, or by remote control at the end of a long bureaucratic line. This is to some extent a problem of those church schools that are under relatively firm hierarchical control, causing the heads and teachers in the schools to feel hamstrung and deprived of initiative. The remedy that Goodlad suggests is basically two-fold. First, allow the local school greater leeway and responsibility in educational decision-making so that spontaneity and creativity may flourish within it. Second, provide the local school with experimental models so that the heads and teachers, who often have little time for study or reflection, can encounter concrete new ideas and see how old habitual school patterns can be successfully restructured.

It is in this connection that the leverage of the national associations of non-public schools takes on added importance. It is not the function of these associations to set guidelines for member schools; this is usually done, in the case of the church schools, directly through the ecclesiastical hierarchy, if any. Rather these groups, such as the National Catholic Educational Association, the Lutheran Education Association, and the National Association of Independent Schools,

[9]"The Structure of Catholic Schooling," in *Catholic Education Today and Tomorrow*, ed. Michael J. Sheridan and Russell Shaw (Washington, D.C.: National Catholic Educational Association, 1968), p. 70.
[10]*Ibid.*, p. 71.

are the servants of their constituents. In practice, one of their important functions is to serve as a channel of communication between members about what is going on in the world of education. The NCEA and the NAIS, for example, devote much of their energies to keeping their memberships informed about new departures in education, at home and abroad, so that the busy head and teacher whose schedule is too crowded to enable him to dig this information out of professional journals has ready access to news about new developments, in a form that is tailored to his own special situation and interests. Similarly, through the conferences and workshops that the association makes available to administrators and teachers, the word about new thought and new ways spreads. Whether this dissemination of new ideas has any effect on a local school depends in part upon the degree of freedom and initiative which it is able or willing to exercise.

The independent schools come nearest to being in an ideal situation in this respect. As unitary, autonomous institutions, independent schools are not subject to a hierarchy that is empowered to issue authoritative guidelines or directives. Yet autonomy alone carries no guarantee that the school is indeed quite free to foster educational experimentation. Self-governing schools are not always as free as they appear to be or say they are. An experimentally inclined headmaster who presides over a school in which faculty control is deeply entrenched, or one in which the voice of the patrons is strongly on the side of maintaining traditional values and solid respectability, may find himself stymied in his efforts to move the school into new channels. Alumni too have been known to raise querulous voices about what is transpiring at the old school.

So under these circumstances it is often necessary to involve all the key constituencies in the process of change—teachers, students, trustees, administrators, alumni, and possibly parents working on joint committees. The composition of such committees needs to be planned with great care, lest the outcome be merely a series of watered-down compromises resulting from a balanced representation of conflicting interests. For example, a faculty committee made up of department heads has little chance of producing a fresh approach, since each head has a vested interest to protect and is bound to be to a large extent the prisoner of the special interests and colleagues of the department. One of the difficulties of bringing about change is that every school has people in various constituencies who are satisfied with things as they are and drag their feet when others introduce alternatives.

Next to the make-up of the committees, it is vitally important to provide optimum conditions for the major planning sessions, preferably in an environment free of the pressures and distractions of day-to-day burdens—a place such as a quiet live-together retreat where the planning group gets to know and understand each other, and has ample time to air ideas. Schools that have used this technique find that such sessions are most productive when proper preparatory steps have been taken. These may consist variously of sending teams of two or three faculty, who are to be keys to the process of change, to visit schools that have been selected because they illustrate certain specific innovative practices; faculty sabbaticals for the particular purpose of working on the improvement of the curriculum and teaching methods; the participation of teachers in summer workshops and conferences; the use of knowledgeable, imaginative consultants who can bring first-hand information of new practices and serve as stimuli and catalysts.

The school of the future, recognizing that the constant acceleration of change imposes a new task on schooling, will do well to reorganize itself so that time for thinking and planning is built into the schedule. As matters now stand, beginning teachers often do not begin at the forefront of current school practice, while experienced teachers have little opportunity to study, let alone change, the teaching habits which they acquired over the years. As the need for in-service teacher education increases, and as the need to keep schools abreast of the changing world expands, more time must be set aside for study and planning, More and more schools are wisely setting up long-range planning committees on a permanent basis, with rotating membership, and are allocating a percentage of the budget to continuing education research. The school which has the foresight to provide for its own continual self-renewal is in the best position to produce the responsive human environment that young people desire and need.

Despite the wave of optimism over school reform that has been generated by the acknowledged success of the informal classroom in England and here and there in the United States, it would be foolish to underestimate the weight and severity of the encumbrances to change. Critics of education tend to forget that the schools reflect society and that many of the school's problems lie outside the school and are beyond the power of the school to eradicate. Furthermore, nonpublic schools are parts of a complex set of interrelated institutions, and as such what they can accomplish, or what they could accomplish by a change in their form and character, depends in the last analysis on what the public expects of them. And there is reason to believe that the public's expectations of the nation's schools are already unreasonably high in certain respects. Only occasionally does a sensible voice suggest that perhaps we expect much too much of formal schooling, much more than even the most ideally functioning institution could deliver. People tend to forget that so many of the formative influences lie, for better or worse, beyond the school—in the peer group, the home, the news media, and the community with its complex of interrelated social, political, economic, cultural, and religious institutions. As a people we harbor extravagant expectations of what the schools are capable of doing or could be capable of doing to save individuals and society from various forms of personal or collective perdition.

And yet, after taking these caveats into account, we persist in believing that the schools can and should do a much better job of helping young people to cope with a world wherein the only constant is change itself. It is the very unprecedented nature of the tumultuous times in which we live that raises fresh hope. The schools can be better because they must be better. The social turmoil of the sixties spelled out with painful clarity how ill prepared we are to control the technological world of our devising. And yet the fresh start the schools are making, in building on the needs and interests of the young in an atmosphere of trust and humane concern instead of fitting them for ready-made slots in the military-industrial complex, raises the hope that a new spirit is emerging, and the schools can be more effective in helping to raise the quality of human life.

III

Private Schools and the Public Interest

11

State Aid: Salvation or Trojan Horse?

*"What is right and proper
or what is going 'too far'
depends largely on how
public opinion sees the case
in the context of time,
place and circumstance;
it cannot be gauged
by any general formulas."*

Will Herberg[1]

Where Matters Stand

The issue of state aid to nonpublic schools is commonly put as a choice between whether private schools should or should not be assisted by public funds. But to put it thus is an archaism. Aside from the exemption which these schools enjoy from both state and federal taxes—an indirect but nonetheless appreciable bene-fit—at least 23 of the 50 states provide pupil transportation, either statewide or within some local school districts; nine "loan" textbooks, and more have legisla-tion to this effect pending; and at least eight provide health services either statewide or in some local jurisdictions. State or county contracts with private schools covering the provision of special kinds of education or under special circumstances, though not widespread, are significant in that they continue an

---

[1] *Religion in America—Original Essays on Religion in a Free Society*, ed. John Cogley, (New York: Meridian Books, 1958), p. 134.

289

old New England tradition of reimbursing available private schools for public services rendered instead of building competing schools under public control. For example, Alaska contracts with certain parochial schools to provide "educational opportunities" for students in rural areas; in Massachusetts the State Development Commission is authorized to fund selected privately-run experimental schools; in Maryland the state pays certain specialized private schools the full cost of educating physically handicapped children, a practice which is duplicated by a number of other states. Hawaii provides a tax credit on a fixed schedule for student dependents. A few states have encouraged shared time or dual enrollment so that private school students can take advantage of programs in public schools.[2] The issue of state aid has never been, in the United States, a question of whether the state shall or shall not aid nonpublic schools: it is in most states a question of how and how much.

These efforts taken together define a new national concept of "public education" embracing all schools that serve a broadly useful social purpose. It is a natural development out of the "new pluralism" which conceives American society and its institutions as an outgrowth of a succession of religious, ethnic, and racial conflicts. The price of peace is the gradual accommodations that are negotiated as new groups rise to challenge the dominant ethnic group—in our national history the white Protestant establishment which long dominated the public school system. As E. Digby Baltzell concludes, "Prejudices are only overcome . . . *after and not before* the members of different ethnic and racial groups have lived and worked together over long periods of time, perhaps for several generations."[3] Although opponents tend to view the current pressure for state aid as a devious, underhanded, and largely Catholic process, it is inherent in the normal mechanism by which a democratic society adjusts to changing demands.

It is politically significant that the current agitation for state aid is just as vociferous in states with explicit constitutional prohibitions regarding state aid to church-related schools as in states that have no such impediment. These prohibitions owe their origin to times past when anti-immigrant or anti-Catholic sentiments were rampant. A majority of the states have such restrictive clauses. New York State's so-called "Blaine amendment," for example, pointedly proscribes the use of the state's "property or credit or any public money, directly or indirectly, in aid or maintenance . . . of any school or institution of learning wholly or in part under the control of or direction of any religious denomination, or in which any denominational tenet or doctrine is taught."[4] The amendment was passed by the Protestant majority in the convention of 1894 during a

[2] See the summary of "State Programs for Support to Nonpublic Schools" in *Compact*, published by the Education Commission of the States, February 1970, pp. 14–17.

[3] *The Protestant Establishment: Aristocracy and Caste in America* (New York: Random House, 1964), p. 304 (emphasis in the original).

[4] Article XI, section 3.

ground swell of anti-Catholicism. An attempt in 1967 to substitute for Blaine the more moderate and general language of the first amendment to the United States Constitution failed, along with the proposed new state constitution in which it was incorporated. Efforts to repeal Blaine continue unabated. In the meantime the Blaine amendment has the force of law. Nevertheless, on Governor Nelson Rockefeller's initiative a variety of aid programs to private schools and to higher education have been enacted, including the issuance of loans by an "independent authority" for educational facilities, a "scholar incentive program," the so-called Bundy program which reimburses qualifying colleges for each degree granted, and most recently a program under which schools are reimbursed for certain administrative and "mandated services." Each of these programs in one way or another circumvents the Blaine amendment (or simply ignores it), to the consternation of embattled church-state separationists. New York is not alone in this respect; other states are pursuing the same course.

Despite the stout resistance of First Amendment fundamentalists who test proposed innovations in welfare and education by whether they maintain the mythical "wall of separation" between church and state "high and impregnable," in Mr. Justice Black's rhetorical flourish, the dominant trend recently in the politics of state aid appears to be an accommodating pragmatism, rather than a polarization into absolute either/ors.

This is well illustrated by the brief but controversial history of titles I, II, and III of the Federal Elementary and Secondary School Education Act (ESEA) signed into law by President Lyndon Johnson in April 1965. Federal aid to public schools (as distinct from colleges) had been effectively blocked during the Kennedy administration by the conflict over aid to church-related private schools. The deadlock was broken early in 1965 by a formula which limited federal assistance to compensatory programs for poor and educationally deprived children, whether in public or private schools. The formula satisfied neither the public school–oriented separationists, who opposed any sort of aid to nonpublic schools, nor the private school accommodationists who felt it did not go far enough. But by means of some arm-twisting persuasion the rival National Education Association, championing the public schools, and the National Catholic Welfare Conference (now the United States Catholic Conference), battling for the nonpublic schools, gave their grudging consent and drew the diffident National Council of Churches into the agreement along with several other moderate separationist groups. But hard-core separationists such as the American Jewish Congress, the ACLU, and the Americans United for the Separation of Church and State remained unconvinced.

The passage of the bill, far from ending the process of negotiating an acceptable course among conflicting demands, raised all sorts of prickly administrative problems. It is too long a story to be detailed here. Suffice it to say that the guidelines issued by the Office of Education for the administration of the

ESEA by the states precipitated another controversy about exactly what it was that Congress had legislated. The issue has not yet been fully resolved. But on balance, the enactment of the ESEA marked an important breakthrough in public support, though the provisions of the act fall far short of supplying the massive assistance which the advocates of parity (equal support for private as for public schools) claim as their due.[5]

The case for federal aid to nonpublic schools was reopened by President Richard M. Nixon's executive order of March 1970, establishing a President's Commission on School Finances which was charged with the task of helping "states and communities to analyze the fiscal plight of their public and non-public schools." In the words of the president, "New methods of organization and finance must be found, and public and nonpublic schools should together begin to chart the fiscal course of their educational planning for the seventies."[6] The special interests and concerns of private schools are represented on the commission by a Panel on Nonpublic Schools.

Since the efforts to secure public assistance for private institutions—not only schools but hospitals, day-care centers and welfare agencies—have revived the dormant issue of church and state, it may be useful at this point to identify the major adversaries as they are presently aligned over the school aid issue. A major clue to the way people think about this problem is the theologically grounded concepts—the ideology—that members of various religious groups have about the nature and role of the state. But it has a more personal dimension also. "The fact of our discrepant histories creates the second experience of the pluralist society," said the late John Courtney Murray. "We are aware that we not only hold different views but have become different kinds of men as we have lived our several histories."[7]

The Catholic church in America takes the position that there is no necessary or inherent conflict between church and state, and it favors cooperation between the institutions of the state and church within the limits prescribed by due regard for the principles which each incorporates. Thus Catholics find it difficult to accept the interpretation of the First Amendment which holds religion to be a purely private concern, since Catholics see both the state and the church as subject to a higher, divine law. The "wall of separation" interpretation is the result of "the seemingly inveterate Protestant tendency to theologize the First Amendment, to read into it certain tenets of Protestant theological dogma."[8]

---

[5] For a lively capsule history of the political sparring that the enactment and subsequent definition of guide lines entailed, see Richard E. Morgan, *The Politics of Religious Conflict: Church and State in America* (New York: Pegasus, 1968), pp. 84–94.

[6] *New York Times*, March 4, 1970. The full text of the president's message to Congress is to be found in H. Doc. no. 91–267, 91st Cong., 2nd sess. (1970), p. 9.

[7] In John Cogley, ed., *Religion in America*, pp. 29–30.

[8] *Ibid.*, p. 36.

Catholics believe the government should be impartially friendly to religion, not simply neutral. Most Catholics, therefore, are numbered among the strong supporters of state aid to nonpublic schools, though the church also harbors a dissident group known as the National Association of Catholic Laymen, as well as others who vociferously oppose state aid. In addition to church agencies, in particular the United States Catholic Conference, the Catholic case is vigorously promoted by the all-lay, largely Catholic, Citizens for Educational Freedom and a miscellany of other organizations.[9]

Just as there is no such thing as Protestantism in the strict sense of a single coherent theology, so there is no such thing as a Protestant theory of the political state. Episcopalians generally hold quite different views about the state than do the constituents of evangelical denominations, while the Lutherans and Calvinists are somewhere between. Nevertheless one can identify some common themes that serve to explain the Protestant outlook regarding the proper relation of church and state, themes that owe as much to the circumstances of the origin of different Protestant denominations as to their theologies.

Protestantism was a revolt against established authority and the organizations, laws, rituals and traditions over which the reigning authority presided. The Protestant case stressed the vocabulary of resistance, the appeal to the individual, his rights, and his liberty of conscience. Unlike the Catholic church, which has long maintained an international organization having some of the attributes of state power, Protestantism had to make terms as best it could with various territorial powers, because it was itself usually without any pretense of sovereignty or political authority. Opportunity permitting, however, Protestants were not averse to identifying with the state, as they did in Henry VIII's England, or in Geneva, or Boston; and when this happened early Protestantism turned out to be neither tolerant nor democratic. For in the tension of its birth Protestantism was a ferocious, heaven-storming enterprise, striving for an unearthly perfection in this life—a project made the more difficult by Protestantism's pessimistic appraisal of man's ability to lead the good life in this world. At bottom, the final authority before which the Protestant must bow is not that of an ecclesiastical hierarchy nor of princes or potentates. It is nothing more or less than the real, incontrovertible authority of the Bible: God's word, not man's.

This broad Protestant inheritance was deeply influenced by the development of Protestantism in America. Religious toleration was not among the original goals of the major Protestant churches, but grew because of the enormous proliferation of sects who became weary, in this expansive land, of trying to put each other down as heresies. As the sects multiplied, the chief concern of each was to be protected in the right to be itself and to propagate its own faith. And they

[9]For a thumbnail description and *modus operandi* of these and other accommodationist and separationist agencies see Richard E. Morgan, *The Politics of Religious Conflict*, chap. 2.

asked of the state nothing more than to be protected in the private freedom to worship as they pleased. In contrast to the Catholic view that the state should be in a friendly partnership with religion, the Protestant conception requires that the state be kept at arm's length from religion and that it be entirely neutral as between the various competing church groups. To the Protestant consciousness it seems hazardous, therefore, to call on the state's power to further religious and social objectives. But just as the state's power should be limited, so too should the churches'. The inherent individualism and congregationalism of the Reformation tradition led the fragmenting church bodies to cherish the freedom of the church—freedom from state interference and freedom for independent-minded individuals and groups to strike out on their own and establish new sects. In the course of time Protestantism gloried in the posture of Christian unity amidst denominational and sectarian diversity.

It is probably safe to say that a majority of Protestant laymen was opposed to public aid for nonpublic schools. Certainly this was the case several decades ago, but one cannot be sure now. The extent to which Lutheran, Christian Reformed, and some of the Evangelical, Episcopal, and Protestant-oriented independent school people are shifting from opposition to support is discussed in the following section. Yet the largely Protestant, moderately separationist National Council of Churches and the militant Protestants and Other Americans United for the Separation of Church and State, along with agencies representing the Baptists and Seventh-Day Adventists, are among the leading spokesmen for strict construction of the First Amendment.

The Jewish position is influenced less by doctrinal convictions than by the brutal lessons of Jewish history. As a small minority in a predominantly Christian state it sees its best hope in living under a government that pursues a "hands off" policy respecting religion. In consequence, Jewish intellectuals and liberals identify strongly with secularizing forces which, they believe, will afford a security they have never known. Jewish intellectuals in America are reinforced in this stance by the generally anti-religious posture of non-Jewish liberals and academicians with whom they consort. The result is that lay Jews make common cause with Protestant and secular separationists, much to the dismay of Orthodox rabbis who teach in and manage the budgets of Jewish schools. In the absence of an overall organization of the Jewish community in the United States, the American Jewish Congress, uncompromising in its First Amendment fundamentalism, along with the somewhat more moderate American Jewish Committee and Anti-Defamation League, are the chief spokesmen for Jewish interests. But they do not speak for the entire Jewish community. The people who staff and patronize Jewish schools are often in vigorous dissent from the separationist position of the Jewish community at large.

As for the secularists, their chief concern is to protect the public order from involvement with religion. Although it is often said that the United States is a religious nation, the secular tradition has long been an influential strain in American political thought with antecedents in the Enlightenment and the Jeffersonian tradition. Secularists are by no means all irreligionists or antireligionists; their point is to insist that religion—or lack of it—is a private matter which is none of the state's business, that the price of the state's "integrity" is total uninvolvement with religion. It is ironic that Protestant separationists, many of whom are religious fundamentalists, find among their bed fellows in the church-state issue secularists who include agnostics and atheists whom the fundamentalists abhor. They reach the same conclusion from opposite directions. Protestant separationists are concerned above all to keep the churches free from state interference, while the concern of the secular separationists is to avoid the contamination of the state by religion. The outstanding spokesman for the secularist position is the American Civil Liberties Union. Other agencies include the public school groups such as the National Education Association, the American Association of School Administrators, the Horace Mann League, and state and county school offices which are usually more or less active in behalf of separationism, though here and there public school administrators are sympathetic to public aid for private schools.

Where the School People Stand

Where do school people themselves stand on the issue of state aid? A decade ago only the Catholic educators were strongly for it. Protestant and independent school people took the position that acceptance of state aid might lead to state control and the compromising of the school's distinctive aims, traditional freedom, and autonomy. Where do they stand today?

We found in our survey that now only the heads and trustees of Seventh-Day Adventist schools continue to say they are strongly opposed in principle to any form of state aid; here as in other groups, the trustees are characteristically in stronger opposition than the schoolmasters. Only a negligible per cent of Catholic school heads and trustees are opposed in principle. The independent school people are somewhat more cautious—the trustees noticeably more so than the headmasters—but with a substantial majority of both unopposed. The schools of the Protestant groups, however, show the greatest variation. The range is from zero opposition among the Christian Reformed people to a large majority of the Adventists who are opposed, while the heads and trustees of NACS schools are mixed but leaning toward acceptance of state aid. Substantial majorities of the Episcopal and Lutheran school people favor it. While our data on Jewish schools are inadequate to justify a firm conclusion, it is generally known—and confirmed by our school visits—that the rabbis who conduct the schools strongly favor state aid, though their governing boards, if they reflect the dominant attitudes of Jewish constituents at large, are generally opposed. In

January 1971, the New York Board of Rabbis, representing more than one thousand Reform, Conservative and Orthodox rabbis, was reported as having abandoned its long-standing opposition to state aid.[10]

The attitude of the Seventh-Day Adventists is an interesting one. The heads, and even more emphatically the governing boards, declare their stubborn opposition to state aid in principle. Nevertheless, the church sees no inconsistency in accepting from the state "certain limited favors, such as tax exemption, police and fire protection," and it recognizes, moreover, "the right of its individual members to accept assistance from the state under such programs as the public health service, school lunches and similar programs of direct student aid designed for the benefit of both parent and child." But it specifically enjoins the schools from accepting "gifts of land, buildings, or equipment from the government, or public tax money for capital improvements, the salaries of teachers, or the maintenance, operation, or support of the services which the schools supply." Acquisition of government surplus is permitted, however, as are research grants or government contracts, as long as they do not interfere with "the stated policies, objectives, and programs of the school."[11] One is tempted to reprove the Adventists for wanting to eat their cake and have it too; for the policy statement says in effect that they see no harm in accepting forms of state aid that demonstrably do not compromise the autonomy or stated purposes of their schools—a position taken by virtually all nonpublic school groups. It appears, then, that the degree of caution with which the various school groups approach state aid depends on the degree of separatism that a given school group desires to maintain. The Amish, for example, wish only to go their own way without harassment or interference. Church schools with a strong fundamentalist orientation can usually be counted on to be lukewarm to state aid, even though the need for financial assistance is acute.

In this connection the shift of Lutheran educators is revealing. Only a decade ago they were chary of all save very marginal state aid, but the swing is now vigorously in favor, to a point where the Lutheran school heads and governing board members of the Missouri Synod are encouraged to "actively promote and, where possible, help to shape legislation which is acceptable in terms of the Detroit resolution." That resolution deemed federal aid acceptable "so long as it does not interfere with the distinctive purposes for which such schools are maintained."[12] Most Lutheran educators have come around to the view that

---

[10] *New York Times*, January 28, 1971.

[11] From a statement on "Church-State Relationships in the United States," issued by the North American Division Committee on Administration, General Conference of Seventh-Day Adventists, February 12, 1969.

[12] From William A. Kramer, *Public Aid to Church-Related Nonpublic Schools* (St. Louis: Board of Parish Education, The Lutheran Church—Missouri Synod, April 1970).

state aid can be administered under terms and conditions that leave the autonomy of the school and the integrity of their Lutheranism unimpaired, though they stress the need for vigilance. They believe, moreover, that state aid may require of the church a more vigorous effort to maintain a proper level of voluntary support to guard against any contingencies that may arise, such as the sudden withdrawal or scaling down of aid once it has been made available.

The aggressive approach of Catholic educators in pursuit of state aid is conditioned to some extent by past conflicts which led some Catholic leaders to demand as a *right* full public support of church schools on a parity with public schools. This objective is presently openly advocated by the Citizens for Educational Freedom on the grounds that it is essential to the "free exercise" of religion as guaranteed under the First Amendment to the federal constitution. When one takes into account the fact that Catholics have been for over a half century footing the bill for the operation of the huge Catholic school system while also bearing their share as taxpayers in the financing of public schools, one can begin to understand why more people are listening to their case. But the attitude of the Catholic majority is even more strongly conditioned today by the bleak financial outlook of many of their schools. Since they see the alternatives as surviving with government aid or perishing without it, they are prepared to accept greater risks, even to the point of becoming in effect public schools with Catholic overtones. Nuns, priests, brothers, lay teachers, and parents are in hot pursuit of aid, often with seemingly little thought of the possible effects of certain forms of aid on the distinctive qualities of Catholic education. But the large Catholic community is not without its spokesmen who point to the need for a statesmanlike approach to the aid question. Among them is William B. Ball, a prominent Catholic layman who believes that limited state aid is both constitutionally permissible and wise, but who warns that "Catholics must not approach the aid question with anything less than the most discriminating evaluation of what their schools will need in order to survive and the nature of the controls which will follow public dollars."[13]

These differences in the degree of caution with which different schools approach the issue of state aid are reflected in the opinions of heads and trustees regarding the merits or demerits of various specific forms of aid which are available or under discussion in various states. These opinions give only a rough indication of the school people's attitudes, since questions about what specific forms of aid they prefer or oppose are general and hypothetical; yet much depends upon the definite terms and conditions under which this or that form of categorical aid would be made available. One of the major points of difference is

[13]"A Roman Catholic Viewpoint," in *Public Controls for Nonpublic Schools*, ed. Donald A. Erickson (Chicago: University of Chicago Press, 1969), p. 195.

the attitude of various school groups toward salary supplements or "purchase of secular services," a form of aid which the Supreme Court found unconstitutional in the opinions handed down in late June 1971. Protestant and independent school leaders were wary of this form of assistance, while most Catholic school leaders strongly favored it, chiefly because it proffered assistance where the pinch has become hardest, namely, in meeting faculty salaries. There is a comparable split among nonpublic school educators regarding "shared time and dual enrollment" programs, though the extremes of opposition and approval are not nearly as great as in the case of the purchase of secular services, except in the case of the leaders of the Christian Reformed schools, whose unanimous opposition to shared time and strong inclination toward purchase of services resembled the Catholic position. We found that the leaders of all types of schools are on the whole most favorably inclined to various pupil-family benefits such as scholarships, tuition vouchers, textbook loans, transportation, or tax credits for tuition costs, while they look with much less favor on various programs of direct institutional aid. All in all, the cautious approach of Protestant and independent schools to state aid and the more indiscriminate willingness of Catholic school leaders to embrace state aid in almost any form is clearly apparent.

The Urgency of the State Aid Issue

It is unmistakably clear from the survey of school finances in chapter 8 that the nonpublic schools, along with all educational institutions in the United States, higher and lower, public and private, face a severe financial crisis. It is by now a familiar story to every newspaper reader. Inflation, the present recession, rising teacher salaries, the soaring costs of all goods and services, have contributed to a deepening financial plight which threatens the survival of large segments of nonpublic schools. As the inflation reduces the disposable income of many families, private school charges, even in the low tuition schools, are beyond the reach of more and more families. Even in the tiny minority of well-endowed schools deficit financing has become the rule rather than the exception. If one were to sort nonpublic schools into the three categories employed by Dr. Earl F. Cheit's December, 1970, report on behalf of the Carnegie Commission on Higher Education, we would place them, on the basis of an informed guess, as follows: 10 per cent "not in trouble," 40 per cent "headed for trouble," 50 per cent "in financial difficulty." It is not only Catholic schools that are in trouble. Many schools of other church groups are engaged in a grim struggle for survival. As for the independent school realm, though it contains a substantial number of well-established schools that are by dint of long-range planning, good management, and realized fund-raising potential in better shape than many improvident nonpublic schools, the predictions of experienced head-masters is that "many schools won't make it."[14] Moreover, the life expectancy of new experimental schools, which should be serving as a leaven in the lump of traditional private schooling, is usually all too brief, chiefly because of the inability of most new schools to establish a sound financial footing.

The weight of evidence shows beyond reasonable doubt that the cost of nonpublic education now exceeds the combined resources of individual and organized private support. Unless state and federal aid are forthcoming in signifi-cant amounts, the private school sector will be seriously weakened either by accelerated school closings or by progressive deterioration in the quality of education the surviving schools are capable of offering.

Such a development would be viewed by single-minded advocates of public education as a consummation devoutly to be desired. Following the lead of Horace Mann's messianic vision of public schools' mission, they maintain that the very existence of private schools is divisive, that the public schools alone are the great engine of Americanization. Until quite recently the public school was idealized by many Americans as a sacred institution, a bulwark of American society, of whose benevolent ministrations no child should be deprived. A care-ful reading of school history in the United States does not bear out such a complacent interpretation. For one thing, the public schools enjoyed only a partial success in assimilating the poor and the immigrants; too often these minorities were treated with a degree of contempt that drove them to build their own schools. And while it is true, on the other hand, that in their early history the religious schools were as much concerned with perpetuating a separate ethnic culture as with providing education in citizenship, times have changed, and religious and ethnic cleavages are not nearly as deep as before. Nor is American-ization the problem it once was. Indeed, the religious schools are turning out "Americans" just as efficiently as the public schools. In the most comprehensive study of the influence of Catholic schools, Andrew M. Greeley and Peter H. Rossi concluded, *"No confirmation was found for the notion that Catholic schools are 'divisive.'* Community involvement, interaction with non-Catholics, concern about 'worldly problems,' attitudes toward other groups were not af-fected by attendance at Catholic schools."[15]

---

[14] See the addresses of Carl W. Andrews, then headmaster of the Collegiate School, and of Howard L. Jones, president of Northfield and Mt. Hermon Schools, in *Financing the Independent School of the Future* (Boston: National Association of Independant Schools, 1968), pp. 10–18 and 48–57.

[15] *The Education of Catholic Americans* (Chicago: Aldine Publishing Co., 1966), p. 224 (emphasis in the original). This study was financed by grants from the Carnegie Corporation and the U.S. Office of Education.

The unity of American life has never been monolithic; it has always been essentially pluralistic. The people of varied ethnic, religious, and national backgrounds who settled here found that America recognized no permanent national or cultural minorities of the European type. Within two generations the assimilative process had usually done its work. In the process religion was the primary context of self-identification and the medium through which ethnic concerns were represented and refined—the "triple melting pot" of Protestant, Catholic, and Jewish religious communities.[16] Public education, on the other hand, is now not nearly as "public" as it was thought to be a half-century ago, because of the self-sorting of neighborhoods by income, race, and social background. Under the circumstances the fear of private school divisiveness is not only of doubtful validity, it looms as a demand for an oppressive conformity to the "mainstream" of American life—a term that is abhorrent in its implications of overriding all differences in order to create a common type. The outcry over divisiveness is peculiarly out of place in the context of the present, marked as it is by a renewed search for roots and ethnic identity, brought about in part by the disappointment with public schools and the critical need to try to adapt education to the differing needs of young people of diverse backgrounds.

The allegation that nonpublic schools, Catholic schools in particular, are divisive is often a mask for prejudices which cloud the discussion of the merits and demerits of public and private schools. "Educators have taught us," writes Christopher Jencks, "to use 'public' as a synonym for 'democratic' or just plain 'good', and to associate 'private' with 'elitist' and 'inequality'."[17] Attributions of this sort obscure more than they reveal. Posh country-club boarding schools make up only a tiny fraction of nonpublic schools, and most of them are straining at great cost to diversify their student body. The church schools, on their part, enroll many thousands of children from poor and lower class families who must sacrifice to send their children to them. As Jencks notes, "if we are to judge schools by their willingness to subsidize the poor, we would have to say that private schools have shown *more* interest in the poor than public ones. Has any suburban board of education used its own money to provide scholarships for slum children? Most refuse to admit such children even if their way is paid. Many private boards of trustees, on the other hand, have made such efforts, albeit on a small scale."[18] And, as we have shown above, many nonpublic schools would willingly do much more in this respect if financial assistance were made available.

[16] See Will Herberg, *Protestant, Catholic, Jew: an Essay in American Religious Sociology*, rev. ed. (Garden City, N.Y.: Doubleday and Co., Anchor Books, 1960), pp. 36–41.

[17] *The Public Interest* 2 (Winter 1966): 24.

[18] *Ibid.*, pp. 24–25.

The demise of large numbers of private schools, which seems likely unless means are found to assist them, would create a virtual state monopoly in public schooling, a cheerless prospect which is inimical to American democracy. Pluralism has contributed greatly to making American society a diverse, free, and self-renewing organism. The forces that would compulsively level individual and group differences under state-dominated programs are always at work. They should be impeded rather than encouraged. Moreover, the public school needs the private school as a salutary point of reference. It is not only a matter of competition in innovation and fresh approaches. The very presence of nonpublic schools, the fact that parents choose them because they believe these schools offer a better or a different kind of education and do more for their students, is a standing challenge to the public schools. The prudent course for American education is not to put all the eggs in one basket, but to encourage schools with a diversity of goals, methods, and types of management so that parents will have options and alternatives. The problem is to make such options available to the poor as well as to the rich.

Not the least of the reasons that causes many a taxpayer to lend a sympathetic ear to the advocates of state aid is the prospective cost of shifting millions of youngsters from parochial to public school rolls. President Nixon stated that if all nonpublic schools were forced to close the United States would be obliged to spend $4 billion per year more on public school operations and at least $5 billion for new facilities. It is safe to predict that no such wholesale closing of nonpublic schools will take place. But enough Catholic schools have closed or are on the verge of closing to alarm the beleaguered taxpayer, who is in many localities already in revolt over present public school costs. The operation of private schools has saved the states many billions of dollars that would otherwise have been spent on the public education of children who attended private schools at virtually no cost to the taxpayer. It makes good sense economically to support in part the education of children in nonpublic schools so that the state need not support them fully in public schools.

Support for the Status Quo or for School Reform?

The main drawback of the argument that limited aid to nonpublic schools is a bargain for the state is that it fails to confront important questions of educational policy that hinge or could be made to hinge on state aid. Different forms of state aid can have quite different educational consequences, depending upon the purpose, how, to whom, and under that terms and conditions aid is given. Is the intention simply to keep the nonpublic schools open to do what they have always done, or should state aid be used as a lever of improvement among private and public schools? If the intention is merely to keep the schools going, any form of support will do as long as it is (a) limited but adequate, (b) does not seriously jeopardize the school's autonomy, and (c) does not run afoul of the First Amendment. But some critics of public schooling in the United States see in the concern over state aid an opportunity to effect substantial school reforms, looking to the equalization of opportunity, wholesome competition among schools, stimulation of experimentation and new approaches, and encouragement for the development of diverse new schools.

The now prohibited "Pennsylvania Law," the prototype for similar enactments in Connecticut, Rhode Island, Michigan, and Ohio, is a prime illustration of a state aid statute designed merely to maintain the status quo among the nonpublic schools of the state. That law provided for the purchase by the state of "secular educational services" in private schools. Specifically, the state was empowered to pay the "reasonable cost" of the salaries of teachers teaching in certain nonreligious subjects as well as the cost of instructional materials, although the amount paid in fact was limited by the necessity of prorating in the event that the valid requests exceeded the available funds in any given year.[19] The law did nothing to improve the educational bargaining position of poor or lower middle class parents but left them with the same lack of options as before. In fact, the first effect of the operation of the law was to widen the gap between prosperous and impecunious schools.[20]

The Connecticut law differed in offering financial incentives to schools that enroll substantial numbers of educationally deprived children. But in other respects the Connecticut act incorporated several provisions that had the effect of restricting the growth of diversity. For example, to qualify for salary reimbursement teachers had to have the same certification as public school teachers, and the act ruled out reimbursement for any teacher who conducted any kind of religious exercise at any time during the regular school day. A priest or nun who taught mathematics or English but conducted a religious meditation some time during the day did not qualify. The act also required what amounted to a three-year waiting period for any newly founded school before it became eligible to be considered for aid—an effective way of assuring that the status quo would not be disturbed by some lively newcomers. All of the enacted secular service plans contained provisions that tended to discourage the founding of new schools and, with the exception of the Connecticut act just noted, they did little to increase the options of the poor.

---

[19]The moneys paid into the Nonpublic Elementary and Secondary Education Fund came from the proceeds of horse racing, which fell far short of covering the legitimate requests in full.

[20]In the first distribution, the elitist Baldwin School at Bryn Mawr received $102.68 per student, while the average of parish and diocesan schools, some of which serve substantial numbers of poor and lower middle class students, received only $8 per pupil. See *Time*, December 19, 1969, p. 54.

At the same time, these acts seriously restricted the freedom of private schools by requiring that, as the price of limited support, the core of the academic curriculum be modeled on that of the public schools. The Ohio law is most explicit in this respect. In order to qualify for state aid, the law not only requires that nonpublic teachers must hold state certificates, it prescribes that "such services, instructional materials, or programs provided for pupils attending nonpublic schools shall not exceed in cost or quality such services . . . as provided for pupils in the public schools of the district," and prohibits the use of services, materials, or programs not available in public schools. And as if to make sure that private schools would not conjure up some interesting deviations from standardized public school practice, the state superintendent is empowered to review courses, teacher and student evaluations, and test scores.[21] It would be difficult to design a better way of crushing whatever spontaneity and variety exists in the private school domain. The Ohio act condemned the private schools of the state to replicating the failures and uniformities of the public schools, the very traits which in their founding the private schools hoped to avoid.

But by far the most disturbing feature of these laws was the evident fact that they did little to prevent the perpetuation of unlawful or improper discrimination beyond requiring "compliance" with title VI of the Civil Rights Act of 1964. In the absence of specific standards and enforcement procedures, the probable effect of state aid *in this form* would be to increase the difficulties of integrating the public schools.

The fate of the purchase of secular services concept of state aid was sealed when the Supreme Court, in reviewing two lower court decisions—*Lemon* v. *Kurtzman* in Pennsylvania and *DiCenso* v. *Robinson* in Rhode Island—ruled that both these state laws are unconstitutional. In a decision distinguished far more by its pragmatic reasoning than by any enunciation of a new principle, the court, while admitting it could "only dimly perceive the lines of demarcation in this extraordinarily sensitive area of constitutional law," held that financial aid of this type involves "excessive entanglement between Government and religion."[22] At the same time the court upheld, by a five to four margin, the Federal Higher Education Facilities Act of 1963 under which the federal government provides grants for the construction of academic buildings on the campuses of private colleges, including church-related ones. The court seems to imply that there is one criterion of constitutionality for federal aid and another for state aid, and one for aid to colleges and another for aid to schools.

The Pennsylvania state legislature responded to the Supreme Court's invalidation of the purchase of services concept by enacting in its place the Parental

[21] For a good discussion of the restrictions of the Ohio law see Stephan Arons, "The Joker in Private School Aid," *Saturday Review*, January 16, 1971, pp. 45ff.

[22] "Excerpts from High Court Opinions on Financial Aid to Church-Related Schools," *New York Times*, June 28, 1971.

Reimbursement Act for Nonpublic Education, which provides flat payments of $75 and $150 to parents of each elementary and secondary private school student respectively, regardless of means. This provision, signed into law in August 1971, is funded by a state cigarette tax. While the law is doubtless of significant assistance to low-tuition church-related private schools in particular, as it stands it quite ignores the need for school reform and equalization of education opportunity as between rich and poor.

The Logic of Various Voucher Plans

There are other forms of aid that do not involve the risk of exposing nonpublic schools to arbitrary treatment by state officials to the extent the purchase of secular services laws did. Various plans are under discussion for either partial or full support of the cost of educating children in private schools, or in both public and private schools, by giving parents tuition grants, scholarships, or vouchers redeemable for a specified sum in the school of their choice. Contrary to current impressions, the voucher idea is not a recent invention; it has been around in one form or another for over 200 years, advanced by advocates as ideologically diversified as Adam Smith, Tom Paine, John Stuart Mill, and in recent times, Milton Friedman, the conservative economist and adviser to President Nixon.[23]

Although various voucher proposals differ substantially in their intentions and regulatory constraints, they all propose to give more control to the ultimate consumers of education—the parent and child—by affording them a choice among alternatives. With the schools beholden to the parents instead of the other way round, parents would be in a position to react to the school directly, rather than through the cumbersome political process, by simply taking their children out of a school they did not like and sending them elsewhere. The result would be the creation of an educational market in which schools would have to compete for customers.

Friedman's original plan proposes that the government finance a minimum level of schooling by means of vouchers given to parents and redeemable for a specified sum per child annually. The voucher would be usable only for ap-

---

[23] See Friedman's essay, "The Role of Government in Education," first published in *Economics and the Public Interest*, ed. Robert A. Solo (New Brunswick, N.J.: Rutgers University Press, 1955), and later expanded in Milton Friedman, *Capitalism and Freedom* (Chicago: University of Chicago Press, 1962). Voucher plans have been advanced by English economists associated with the Institute of Economic Affairs. See E. G. West, *Education and the State* (London: Institute of Economic Affairs, 1965), and *Education: A Framework for Choice* (London: Institute of Economic Affairs, 1967). A brief history of voucher plans is given in Phillip Whitten, "Antecedents of the Poor Children's Bill of Rights" (qualifying paper, Harvard Graduate School of Education, 1970).

proved educational services rendered either by nonprofit institutions or enterprises operated for profit which meet certain minimum requirements. "Here as in other fields," Friedman argues, "competitive enterprise is likely to be far more efficient in meeting consumer demand than either nationalized enterprises or enterprises run to serve other purposes."[24] He sees this plan as preferable also because it would foster diversity, which the present nationalized public school monolith is largely incapable of doing.

One of the common objections to the Friedman plan is its total reliance on a free, uncontrolled market mechanism. While it might in the large provide greater educational benefits than the present bureaucratic public school system, it would almost certainly aggravate the existing inequality of educational opportunity as between rich and poor, since the wealthy would be free to buy a superior education by adding to the voucher, but the poor would not. Moreover, the uncontrolled market would in all likelihood lead to an even greater racial and social imbalance in the schools than now exists.[25] Just a few years back "vouchers" were in bad odor precisely because they were used in the abortive schemes of certain southern states to circumvent the mandate to integrate the public schools. Though the courts have repeatedly thrown out such transparent evasions, vouchers in a totally free market would entail going over once again the whole tedious process of integrating the public schools that began in 1954, in order this time to integrate the school population as reshuffled by vouchers.

Friedman's voucher model is but one of several which are the subject of a flurry of discussion and controversy just now. A more specialized plan, sketched out by Dean Theodore Sizer of the Harvard Graduate School of Education and Phillip Whitten, entitled "A Proposal for a Poor Children's Bill of Rights," would provide vouchers for poor children only, as a corrective to the gross imbalance of educational opportunities available to children from poor and from rich families. *"We must discriminate in favor of the poor,"* say the authors. The proposed plan would "give money in the form of a coupon to a poor child who would carry the coupon to the school of his choice, where he would be enrolled. The school chosen could use the sum as it saw fit. And the supplementary grant which the child would give to his school must be large enough to motivate the school to compete for it. Our judgment is that a grant of $1,500 per child per year (about three times the current per-pupil national expenditure) is a necessary figure."[26]

---

[24] *Capitalism and Freedom*, p. 91. The "other purposes" the author has in mind are schools run primarily for their religious effect. He thinks such schools might decline rather than grow under a voucher system.

[25] See the critique of Friedman's plan by Henry Levin in "The Failure of the Public Schools and the Free Market Remedy," *Reports Digest* (Washington, D.C.: U.S. Office of Education, September 1968), pp. 1–6.

[26] *Psychology Today* 2 (August 1968): 60–61 (emphasis in the original).

The $1,500 subsidy would decrease on a sliding scale as family income rose, with the cut-off point reached at family incomes of six to seven thousand dollars. The subsidy is estimated to cost nationally from $11 to $17 billion per year, depending on the subsidy formula used and various regional adjustments in the light of variable per-pupil cost of education. It is argued that this substantial investment in compensatory education would repay itself in time by raising taxable income and cutting the costs of welfare, unemployment, crime, and poverty programs.

This plan, like Friedman's, is designed to encourage free enterprise in education by encouraging the founding of new schools, thus increasing the range of choice and the degree of control exercised by parents. But it differs from Friedman's plan in that the Poor Children's Bill of Rights would set up competition between public and private schools, whereas Friedman's plan would in effect convert all schools into private venture institutions. While the proposed Sizer-Whitten subsidies would enable some poor children to buy their way into private schools which they could not otherwise afford, it would not extend a comparable opportunity to middle class children. American politics being what it is, most legislators would most likely find it inexpedient to support such a scheme.

The voucher plan that attempts to maximize the impact of vouchers as a lever of educational reform is the so-called Jencks plan, named after Christopher Jencks, the director for the Center for the Study of Public Policy, in Cambridge, Massachusetts. The preliminary research and planning for this plan and feasibility studies of experimental demonstration projects using education vouchers are funded by the Office of Economic Opportunity. If and when the feasibility studies uncover one or several locales wherein substantial community support is forthcoming, it will be up to the OEO to determine under what conditions a voucher demonstration project might take place, for a recommended period of from five to eight years.

The Jencks plan proposes to pay the full operating costs of all participating public and private schools by means of vouchers given to parents, who in turn give them to the school they select for their children. This shift in the source of public school funding away from legislators, school boards, and educators, where it is now vested, into the hands of parents is expected to make the schools accountable to the parents who select them rather than to the bureaucracies and political agencies, which are often unresponsive to the complaints of citizens. Competition and diversity are the magic words in the latest push for school reform, which aims to decentralize the monolith of public education. The increase in parent power is expected to open up new alternative choices for every parent, regardless of family income, by creating a competitive but controlled education market, regulated so as to curb the tendency of schools to segregate by race, income, or ability.

How would private schools be affected by this plan if it were implemented in a demonstration project?[27] The question is best answered by spelling out the eligibility requirements (as presently conceived) which any nonpublic school would have to meet in order to become an "approved voucher school":

a. accept a voucher as full payment of tuition;
b. accept any applicant so long as it had vacant places;
c. if it had more applicants than places, fill at least half these places by picking applicants randomly and fill the other half in such a way as not to disciminate against ethnic minorities;
d. accept uniform standards established by the Educational Voucher Agency (EVA) regarding suspension and expulsion of students;
e. agree to make a wide variety of information abouts its facilities, teachers, program, and students available to the EVA and to the public;
f. maintain accounts of money received and disbursed in a form that would allow both parents and the EVA to determine whether a school operated by a board of education was getting the resources to which it was entitled on the basis of its vouchers, whether a school operated by a church was being used to subsidize other church activities, and whether a school operated by a profit-making corporation was siphoning off excessive amounts to the parent corporation;
g. meet existing state requirements for private schools regarding curriculum, staffing, and the like.[28]

Private schools that accept these terms and conditions in return for voucher support would become for all practical purposes "public" in function, even though they would continue to be privately owned and managed and retain control over all the policies and practices other than those that would be surrendered to the Educational Voucher Agency established to administer the voucher system. Offhand one can predict that private schools would see both advantages and disadvantages in the scheme and would perhaps be hard put to decide whether or not to join in.

The signal advantage of becoming a voucher school would be the assurance of economic stability. The staff of the school so aided could devote its full time to the education of children and plan intelligently for the future without the gnawing uncertainties over red ink budgets and threatened insolvency. On this basis alone it should be highly attractive to all nonpublic schools except those that are opposed to full state aid in principle. Moreover, most private schools would not

---

[27]In the original proposal an initial project would include only kindergarten through sixth grade pupils.

[28]*Education Vouchers–A Preliminary Report on Financing Education by Payments to Parents* (Cambridge, Mass.: Center for Study of Public Policy, March 1970), p. 15.

find it difficult to comply with the agreement to provide ample information about the school and to maintain accurate accounts of receipts and disbursements open to public inspection. The latter requirement would exert a salutary influence on the Catholic parochials, whose accounting practices are often highly informal—carried around in the pastor's head. Nor would compliance with existing state requirements for private schools pose a problem, since they already satisfy these. Conceivably some schools might balk at EVA-established uniform standards regarding suspension and expulsion of students, but much would depend upon precisely how these were spelled out. In general, these conditions do not loom as stumbling blocks for private school participation in the Jencks voucher plan.

But certain eligibility requirements and regulations would probably prove to be strong deterrents. Chief among them is the requirement that voucher schools fill at least half their places by lottery among applicants. Well-placed private schools that regard selective admissions as an essential ingredient of the school's purpose would be loath to comply. The problem is not so much making available places for selected poor and disadvantaged children. Many schools are already doing that to some extent on their own initiative and at considerable cost. They probably would balk, however, at being obliged to abandon selective admissions for as much as half the student body. Whether or not selective admission is all that vital or important is another question. Recent research raises some fundamental questions regarding the wisdom of the policy of picking only those young people who are easy to educate, "the winners."[29] But the point is, many independent and some church school educators and their clients see it as the hallmark of their schools; to forgo it would mean becoming a different kind of institution. Conceivably the pressures of change may force the elitist schools to undergo a transformation into somewhat more egalitarian institutions in order to survive—vouchers or no vouchers. Elitism as an educational objective no longer commands the automatic deference and respect it once did. So if a voucher plan were in being, these schools might be drawn into it gradually.

The reception of the Jencks plan by educators has not been a good omen for its eventual acceptance. Most public school people, along with the NEA, see it as a threat to the established school order, which indeed it is, for reasons clearly stated in the prospectus. Opposition from that quarter was expected as a matter of course. But people who are favorably disposed to "giving the money to the parents," parental choice, alternatives, school improvement through competition, and free enterprise in education are taken aback by the labyrinth of regulations that the controlled market calls for, and they fear that the EVA, if instituted, would loom as another mindless bureaucracy shunting children here and

[29] See, for example, the reports of Alexander W. Astin, "Undergraduate Achievement and Institutional 'Excellence'," *Science*, August 16, 1968, pp. 661–68; and "The Folklore of Selectivity," *Saturday Review*, December 20, 1969, pp. 57ff.

there. Even though the plan is devised chiefly to equalize educational opportunity for poor and environmentally deprived children, it has drawn the fire of the NAACP for which "voucher" is still a dirty word. Catholic spokesmen generally expressed a preference for the purchase of secular services, before that form of aid was voided by the court. That concept, though loaded with the educational flaws noted above, had the virtue of simplicity. The First Amendment fundamentalists on their part generally condemn vouchers as they do every form of aid to nonpublic schools.

Despite these caveats and reservations we believe the voucher experiment deserves to be tried. Much of the opposition stems from the human reluctance to change, which is so prevalent among schoolmen. "The devil you live with is better than the devil you don't know." In some cities the public school system is at the brink of collapse, and many suburban schools foster a bland conformity at a time when our problem is to foster more diversity. The old refrain that more money poured into the same channels will somehow turn the ailing schools around is losing credibility. Even compensatory education under the same management procedures has been disappointing. A drastic restructuring in the form of an experiment in a new form of control, or in achieving a better balance of the power and influence exerted by parents, teachers, and government could teach us much about what might be accomplished by the restructuring of schooling. We hope the experiment will take place and under conditions that enable those who operate the voucher agency to ascertain, on the basis of experience, how much regulation is necessary to achieve the stated objectives. Fortunately, the Jencks plan has a built-in evaluation concept designed to test the success of the demonstration projects.

The voucher plans surveyed above by no means exhaust the possibilities of public aid given to parents and children for tuition support. Another proposal provides for educational allowances graduated inversely to family income, using tax returns to determine the variable value of individual allowances.[30] For students choosing a public school, the allowance would cover the full cost per student, regardless of family income, but allowances for students from poor families would be enriched in order to encourage schools to recruit such children and to enable the school to cover the cost of needed compensatory programs. Students choosing a private school would receive allowances inversely proportional to income on a curve which would provide a high-value allowance for poor children, with the value of allowances decreasing as family incomes rise until the allowance value declines to zero. Each student would be assured admission to the public school of his district, but would be free to apply to other schools, public or private. It would be essential to have effective controls to prevent

[30] A draft entitled "A Proposal for Educational Allowances" was prepared by A. D. Ayrault, Jr., assistant director of this study (1967–69) and now headmaster of Lakeside School, Seattle, Washington. It was circulated privately for discussion and comment.

deliberate racial segregation, and a procedure for admissions to over-applied schools affording the poor at least a chance of entrance.

The basic assumptions of this plan are threefold: (1) increasing the bargaining power of poor parents would enable them to exercise greater choice among alternatives and greater control over their children's education; (2) enriched allowances for the poor would provide for the schools an incentive to enroll more poor and environmentally disadvantaged children as well as an incentive to establish new schools to take advantage of public bounty; (3) by making public as well as private schools subject to choices, competition between schools would ensue, thereby creating a climate conducive to school reform.

This scheme could be linked with the tax mechanism at either the state or federal level, and it could be readily integrated with a guaranteed annual wage, if that were to be adopted, as a coordinated welfare concept.

Voucher plans have thus far remained in the dream or proposal stage, apart from special and limited exceptions such as direct state subsidies for handicapped children, for children of families living in remote areas, and the traditional practice, surviving in some New England localities, of subsidizing the education of children in private schools in lieu of building public schools. Several state legislatures have been considering bills embodying state aid in the form of scholarships, mini-vouchers, or tuition grants for pupils of private schools only. These aim at some of the objectives which the more ambitious voucher plans embody more fully. Early in 1971 the Maryland Commission to Study State Aid to Nonpublic Education recommended to Governor Marvin Mandel and the General Assembly a scholarship program guided by the following principles:

a. The aid should be effective in providing selective and meaningful assistance to lower income families, who, of all groups, have the least practical option in terms of where and how their children are to be educated;
b. The aid should, at the same time, be of material assistance to middle income families who, with increased general expenses and often more than one child in school, are also feeling the economic "pinch" of higher tuition costs;
c. The aid concept should encourage more open enrollment in nonpublic schools;
d. The aid program should be easy and inexpensive to administer, and involve the state as little as possible in the operation of nonpublic schools;
e. The program should be as free as possible from legal and constitutional uncertainties, and be within the bounds of financial and political realities;
f. For the sake of safeguarding the independence of nonpublic schools and for the sake of the public purse the aid should be limited so as not to dry up the sources of private and philanthropic support.[31]

[31] A Report to the Governor and General Assembly of Maryland, by the Commission to Study State Aid to Nonpublic Education, January 1971, p. 3.

A bill incorporating the commission's recommendations was enacted by the state assembly in the spring of 1971. It authorizes scholarships of $200 per child for children of families with incomes under $6,000, with the amount decreasing in steps up to incomes of $12,000, which is the cut-off point. This plan goes at least part way in providing improved options for children of lower and middle income families and thereby indirectly benefits private schools, particularly those that serve substantial numbers of inner-city and other poor children. But the amount of the aid proferred would be insufficient to produce a strong leverage for school reform in other respects, since it in no direct way affects the status quo of the public schools.[32]

One other form of state aid designed to provide financial assistance to families whose children attend nonpublic schools is a tax credit (as distinct from a tax deduction) for all or part of the tuition paid. Hawaii and Minnesota have laws to this effect on the books. The major advantage of such a plan is that it averts any transfer of monies from the state directly to the schools, so that the entanglement of the state with religion is minimal as is the temptation of the state to exercise undue regulatory authority over the schools. A decade ago there was a strong national movement to interest the Congress in enacting this form of aid as a federal benefit for private colleges, but the various bills introduced in the Senate and House failed of passage. The tax credit method of indirectly aiding schools and colleges runs into two major objections. First, a tax credit inevitably favors the affluent over the poor, since the poor have no tax on which to earn a credit. Second, public officials and the revenue people in particular are leery of using revenue laws to support social or educational goals, however worthy they may be. Moreover, it is feared that once the gate is opened a little to help private education, private hospitals and welfare and other agencies will demand that they too participate. Conceivably the first objection can be met in part by legislation that would help only the lower income families and not grant assistance to those who do not need it. But even so, it would be manifestly unfair to those Americans (almost one in five) who are too poor to incur a tax but whose need for an educational alternative is often desperate. All things considered, we believe a scholarship or voucher plan to be a better solution. Under it, the taxpayer can readily ascertain how much is being appropriated out of public funds to assist private institutions, and the legislation can be drafted, as in the case of the Maryland law, to help enhance the educational opportunities of the poor.

In this overview of state aid we have barely touched on the constitutional and other legal questions that voucher proposals and other forms of aid precipitate. It would serve no useful purpose to attempt to review here all the various

[32] This legislation was petitioned to referendum and will be voted on in the November 1972 elections.

decisions of the courts bearing upon the question, since opinions differ as to their meaning, and the courts will in any event have to decide the open questions. It is generally held that public aid to parent and child is constitutionally less vulnerable than direct aid to the schools or any segment thereof. But since various legal theories have come to the fore in constitutional decisions covering different situations, only time can tell.

The future of vouchers as a device for equalizing educational opportunity is bound to be affected by the trend toward greater state participation in the financing of public schools and the growing awareness of the need for an equitable distribution of educational resources. Discussions of how the cost of public education should be divided between the local districts and the state generally do not take into account the resources of the nonpublic schools and the contribution they make to the overall educational accomplishments of the state. Now that all educational institutions confront a deepening financial crisis, the role of the state vis-à-vis the private school needs to be reexamined with an eye to making the most effective use of this resource. A voucher plan that would make nonpublic as well as public schools accessible to a wider range of children in an open educational market is a logical alternative to the present system.[33] No truly statesmanlike solutions of the problem of equality of opportunity in schooling can be found short of having legislators take into account, state by state, not only the equitable financing of public schools, but also the financial health of the alternative private schools.

[33] For an insightful analysis of equalizing educational opportunity among public schools by financial and legal means see John E. Coons, William H. Clune, III, and Stephen D. Sugarman, *Private Wealth and Public Education* (Cambridge, Mass.: Harvard University Press, Belknap Press, 1970).

12

Public Policy for Nonpublic Schools: State Regulation and the Improvement of Teaching

*"It is cardinal with us
that the custody, care, and nurture
of the child reside first
in the parents, whose primary function
and freedom include preparation
for obligations the state
can neither supply nor hinder."*

U.S. Supreme Court[1]

*"The alternative to furnishing
ready-made subject matter
and listening to the accuracy
with which it is reproduced
is not quiescence, but participation,
sharing, in an activity.
In such shared activity, the teacher
is the learner, and the learner is,
without knowing it, a teacher—
and upon the whole
the less consciousness there is,
on either side, of either giving
or receiving instruction, the better."*

John Dewey[2]

Pluralism and the Rationale of State Regulation

The presence of private venture schools in many communities raises a number of prickly questions about how much state regulation they should be subjected to so that the citizen at large may be assured that the operation of such schools truly serves the public interest. One of the major functions of government is the regulation of activities initiated by persons, groups, or corporations in order to protect the consumer against fraud, malpractice, nuisances, and danger to life and limb. And so everything from hospitals to barbershops is licensed, as are the professionals and practitioners who provide the services. No sensible person questions the general need or the benefits of all this regulation, licensing, and

---

[1] *Prince* v. *Massachusetts*, 64 S. Ct. 438 (1944). The Supreme Court's decision in this case denied the power of the state to prohibit Jehovah's Witnesses parents from having their children below a certain age sell religious tracts. The child in question was nine years old.

[2] *Democracy and Education* (New York: The Macmillan Co., 1916), p. 188.

313

inspecting. Yet many people have occasion to question the extent, degree, or purport of such regulation. Regulatory agencies, like other instrumentalities of government, can become empires with a life and rationale of their own; and when that happens they are often tempted to use their power to stifle initiative or to discourage change and variety.

The potential for "lawful" interference in the affairs of private institutions is considerable in the world of nonpublic schools. Most government regulatory activities concern goods and services in which the government is involved only as a regulator, not as a producer of goods or supplier of services. But in the matter of education, the states centrally and through their subdivisions own and operate the elementary and secondary schools in which 88 per cent of American children receive their schooling. The remaining 12 per cent receive their pre-college education in nonpublic schools which most states undertake to regulate, at least to some extent, via agencies made up largely of state department of education officials aided by professors of education and public school administrators. There are, fortunately, among these officials those who recognize the value of alternatives to the public school and work in a spirit of partnership with private school educators. Yet there are also many, including the leadership of the National Education Association, whose attitude ranges from skepticism of the need or value of nonpublic schools to downright hostility—as though the 12 per cent somehow pose a dire threat to the welfare of the 88 per cent.

Actually, the states rarely impose undue or unreasonable regulations on the nonpublic schools, and most of the statutes or criteria employed in this connection are beneficial to all concerned. But even seemingly beneficent regulations (such as teacher certification and health and safety codes) can be used as tools by an intolerant officialdom bent on suppressing pluralism or experimentation. The troubles that the Amish have encountered recently in various states, reviewed briefly in our first chapter, show what can happen. Fortunately the piety and moral uprightness of the Amish raised for them a host of defenders. But what would happen if Black Muslims or other types of black schools, or schools for the poor, or radical experimental schools came under attack by officials wielding state sanctions? The rationale behind current state enactments providing for regulation of nonpublic schools is as yet both too fragmentary and too incoherent to enable one to predict whether or not the schools' freedom of dissent would stand a chance of being sustained.

The fact that numbers of states are considering various forms of increased state aid to nonpublic schools will undoubtedly precipitate some second thoughts regarding state regulations. As long as private schools wanted most to be let alone to do their special work, state legislatures paid them little heed. But the debate over state aid has given these schools much greater visibility, and that of itself may elicit a regulatory response. It is to be expected that state aid made

314

available in substantial amounts would entail a measure of public accountability of which nonpublic schools have been largely free in the past. For example, in Ohio, as we noted earlier, recent state aid laws include terms and conditions which exact strict equivalency with certain public school programs. It is imperative that much thought be given to the form and limits of state regulation of private schools, lest the schools suddenly find themselves shackled by hastily conceived regulations which would deprive them of the freedom and diversity which are their *raison d'être*. The potential for severe and crippling regulation continues to create an element of uncertainty and apprehension in the minds of many private school educators. Up to now the regulatory problems have been solved pragmatically rather than theoretically. So the complex issue remains.

The issue has been put forthrightly by Donald Erickson in these words: "How can nonpublic education be both responsible and *free*? Responsible to serve the public interest; free to experiment and disagree. *Without* regulation, some schools may victimize patrons and endanger the general welfare. *With* regulation, dissent is in jeopardy. Where should the balance be struck?"[3]

In the attempt to discover guidelines which might point to an answer to this question, we turn first to an examination of the rationale and scope of state regulations of nonpublic schools as well as to its limits.

The same decision of the Supreme Court that affirmed the right of the parent to educate his children as he saw fit ("the child is not the chattel of the State") and denied the state the power to compel all children to attend public schools also reaffirmed the power of the state to regulate all schools, private as well as public. The court's concept of the scope of the states' regulatory power was expressed as follows:

No question is raised [by this decision] concerning the power of the state to regulate all schools, to inspect, supervise and examine them, their teachers and pupils; to require that all children of proper age attend some school, that teachers shall be of good moral character and patriotic disposition, that certain studies plainly essential to good citizenship must be taught, and that nothing be taught which is mainifestly inimical to the public welfare.[4]

The case for the legitimacy of governmental regulations of nonpublic schooling rests on the basic proposition that a state must, in order to promote the public welfare, require that schools be so conducted as to give each child an

[3] Donald A. Erickson, ed., *Public Controls for Nonpublic Schools*, (Chicago: University of Chicago Press, 1969), p. 2. Emphasis in the original. Our own treatment of the problem is indebted to this pioneering book which grew out of a conference on "State Regulation of Nonpublic Schools," held at the University of Chicago's Center for Continuing Education, March 28–29, 1967.

[4] *Pierce v. Society of Sisters*, 268 U.S. 510 (1925).

opportunity to grow and prosper and to contribute as a citizen to the common good. The question of state regulation of private schools came under scrutiny with the passage of compulsory school attendance laws for all children. If the state could force every child to go to school, the state, it was argued, had an equal obligation to require all schools, private as well as public, to meet minimum educational standards. This requirement, it should be noted, embraced not simply the laws governing building codes, health and sanitation codes, and safety—laws that apply generally to all organizations and institutions as well as to schools—but regulations that apply specifically to schools as educational institutions, such as those mandating subjects of study, textbooks, educational standards, length of the school year, requirements for graduation, and so on.

In keeping with this principle, most state legislatures have enacted some type of compulsory standard for nonpublic school instruction. Yet no common patterns of regulation exist among the separate states. Only a few states require official approval or recognition of private schools, or subject them to state inspection and evaluation specifically as educational institutions. Most state laws affecting nonpublic schools reflect the "equivalency" principle, that is, that nonpublic school instruction shall be equivalent to that provided in the public schools and that the subjects taught shall be comparable to those taught in public schools. The intent of regulatory legislation in most states is merely to require nonpublic schools to meet the minimal standards deemed necessary for public school children, so that the students enrolled satisfy quantitatively the compulsory attendance laws of the state.

The case for maximum feasible freedom for nonpublic schools from state controls is also compelling. A private school cannot achieve its distinctive and varied objectives unless it is free to follow its own educational philosophy, to select teachers whom it considers most competent to carry out the school's objectives, to select an appropriate curriculum, and if it is so inclined, to experiment and innovate out of the desire to open other than the conventionally approved or state-sanctioned paths. Indeed, the very right of existence of responsible schools, along with the special benefits which the schools confer—for example, schooling of high quality to millions of children at virtually no cost to the taxpayer—could be wholly nullified if state requirements forced nonpublic schools to replicate the public schools.

Closely related to the freedom of the nonpublic schools is the question: Who is to make the judgment of what is best for the child? For the public school child it is the district or municipal school board acting with the advice of a hierarchy of professional educators and under the sanction of the collective will of society. But for the private school child, as we have argued repeatedly, the mutual voluntariness of choice on the part of the family and the school means that the school and the teachers are primarily an extension of parental responsibility. Nonpublic schools carry out a state responsibility only secondarily, inso-

316

far as they enable the pupil to fulfill the compulsory education requirement. In the private school it is the parent, not the state, that sits in direct judgment upon the school, for he will not long accept inferior services, and his patronage or withdrawal of it exerts an immediate, direct influence on the school's operation. The power of the patrons' purse is a potent force, a force which in the long run is probably less of a threat to quality in education than are standardizing state regulations and bureaucratic control.

Considering the legitimacy of the state's regulatory power on the one side, and on the other side the need of private schools to be safeguarded in their constitutionally grounded freedom to be different, what principle can provide a philosophic framework within which to reconcile and adjudicate the conflicting demands of control and freedom? Basically, this issue is but one facet of the broad problem of state power versus personal and institutional freedom.

The one principle that should be uppermost in judging the justification and limits of the state's intervention in education is the importance of pluralism in a democratic society—the recognition that variety, alternatives, choices, and multiple centers of initiative are essential for continuous social renewal. Applied to the schools, this means that the state should encourage both the pursuit of pluralistic goals and diverse approaches to the achievement of these goals. The aim is not to reduce the multiplicity of schools to the same kind, but to encourage many kinds and encourage each school to be *good of its kind.* "I think it a priceless principle," says Donald Erickson, "that radically different educational purposes are not only tolerable but desirable in our democracy," and he points out that different educational goals presuppose different programs, personnel, and facilities.[5] "Standardization and regimentation in the field of learning," affirmed the Supreme Court of North Carolina in *The State* v. *Williams,* "is contrary to the American concept of liberty. It would be difficult to overemphasize the contribution of private institutions of learning to the initiative, progress and individualism of our people. Regulation should never be resorted to unless the need is compellingly apparent."[6]

In short, if there were no nonpublic schools, people would have to invent them—which in fact they are doing every day, as new free schools mushroom. Particularly in these times, when revolutionary thoughts are burgeoning in all departments of human life, it is inconceivable that schools should be under one management, or that the state should have a monopoly in the education of children.

What would be the characteristics of a good working relationship between nonpublic schools and those who are charged with administering the regulatory power of the state? In the first place, the private schools must accept the

[5] *Public Controls for Nonpublic Schools*, p. 162.
[6] Quoted in *ibid.*, p. 119.

principle of reasonable controls, if for no other reason than to help in identifying and coping with charlatans that seek to infiltrate their ranks, the "fly-by-night schools," which bilk the gullible public and cast discredit on private venture schooling. However, the line between a quack and a far-out but basically legitimate experimental school is not always easy to draw. To help citizens make sound judgment, it is advisable to establish good communication between the state's nonpublic schools and the state officers charged with administering state school regulations. Various steps can be taken to facilitate better communication. Occasional conferences could be held between private school heads and chief state officers concerned for the purpose of discussing common problems. The Association of Independent Maryland Schools has done this with constructive results. Public school educators could be invited to a place on the boards of private schools. Private and public educators have much to learn from each other, and in the process of discussing both their common and their peculiar problems they usually come to have a broader appreciation of the importance of diversity in education.

Next, it is incumbent upon the state officers to reach decisions affecting nonpublic schools only after becoming thoroughly familiar with the objectives and methods of all nonpublic schools under their jurisdiction. It is of first importance that the chief officer responsible be basically sympathetic to educational pluralism, and that he be given sensible latitude in the application of regulations. For example, many states spell out in uniform school laws precisely how many hours per day and how many days per year schools must be open. Doubtless, some sort of quantitative standard is needed, but as any informed person knows, one hundred days in a truly stimulating school may be worth more than two hundred in a boring, listless one. And now that "schools without walls" are multiplying and students are outward bound in all sorts of community projects, "days in school" becomes not only an impossible but a meaningless criterion of student educational attainments. The judgment that a school is substandard should not rest on its failure to comply with conventional criteria, which may be irrelevant to the school's basic goals and methods. As John Elson rightly says, "The constant intellectual ferment in educational thought precludes the possibility that anyone can make rules to meet all school situations solely on the basis of his own belief in certain enduring principles of sound education."[7]

Above all, it is vital that public and private school leaders should seek partnership in evolving a regulating and accrediting procedure that is sensitive to the philosophy and aims of each individual school—a partnership that would foster a mutually enriching relationship between the public and private educators while it furthers the diversity that makes private education such a valuable and needed option in a pluralistic society.

[7]*Ibid,,* p. 130.

The Accreditation Jungle

States that undertake any significant surveillance of nonpublic schools usually keep a list of schools which meet the minimum legal requirements and are therefore "approved" or "recognized," meaning that the state accepts both the right of such institutions to exist and permits students to fulfill the compulsory school attendance requirement in them. But many private schools, desirous of demonstrating their true competence and attainments, seek a higher kind of approval, or "accreditation" as it is called. So there have come into being, in addition to state agencies, a variety of extralegal or nongovernmental voluntary accrediting associations whose membership consists of accredited schools and colleges. Chief among these agencies are the six regional associations spanning the country (New England, Middle Atlantic, Southern, North Central, North-west, and Western), each with separate commissions to evaluate secondary schools and colleges. The Southern association is unique in having a separate commission for elementary schools, and the New England association is distinctive in having a separate one devoted to independent schools. Although the regional associations are in fact and in principle extralegal, nevertheless being a member of the club—or, above all, being denied membership—is fraught with many consequences; much depends on the educational lights of those who sit on the commissions.

The states covered by the various regional associations are usually glad to accept the appropriate agency's verdict on the schools because it saves the state officers time, and besides, considerable prestige attaches to such accreditation, much more so within than outside of academia. Besides these big boys there is also a proliferation of more or less freelance state and regional independent school associations which undertake to evaluate independent elementary and secondary schools only. Some of these associations live uneasily under a nego-tiated peace or in a state of more or less open hostility with one or another of the six regionals. To complete the picture, mention should be made of special-ized accrediting agencies in chemistry, music, teacher education, and so on; but these pay little or no attention to the schools. Finally, the National Accrediting Association attempts to bring some order out of this chaos—the jungle of ac-creditation agencies.

Although much of the accrediting machinery was sponsored originally by private institutions—the Middle States Association of Colleges and Secondary Schools, for example, was founded over a half century ago by a group of private colleges and universities interested in regularizing college entrance require-ments—in some regions it has been dominated for a long time by public school educators who could see no reason why the same "standards" should not be applied to private as to public schools. Generally speaking, however, where nonpublic school leadership has been accepted in a cooperative working relation-

319

ship with the states and with regional associations, nonpublic education has served well its role of providing alternatives and diversity within the area concerned. There are signs recently that some of the more hidebound associations are showing an interest in a more flexible approach, acknowledging that schools can be different in kind and yet provide a good, and even an excellent, useful education. The North Central Association, for example, long bypassed by leading nonpublic schools in its nineteen-state jurisdictional area because of the rigidity of its requirements and their irrelevance to nonpublic school goals and objectives, has relented, and recently developed evaluation criteria and procedures primarily directed toward college preparatory nonpublic schools.

The successful functioning of the regional accrediting associations that have developed flexible techniques, suggests that the best way to ensure and to enhance the quality and variety of nonpublic education is to encourage the schools in ever increasing numbers to regulate themselves in concert with others of their kind, under the aegis of the appropriate regional association. The process of the school's self-evaluation in preparation for a visit from representatives of its regional association usually entails months of self-analysis of the school's goals and practices. In the last analysis, a school's achievements are not revealed by a check list of quantitative school inputs; the true test is the actual performance of a school and its teachers, their proven ability to encourage and promote in their students a genuine concern for learning.[8] To this end we strongly recommend a modification of the structure of existing regional accrediting associations to include in each a separate commission for nonpublic schools (secondary or elementary and secondary), using separate criteria and procedures applicable to such schools, such as those long in use by the New England association.

Whatever the failings of the regional associations, which have in the past generally been characterized by excessive rigidity and the belief that there is only one kind of academic excellence, matters of accreditation are far better left in their hands than in the states'. Therefore, in our view it is wise to create a partnership of public and nonpublic school educators charged with setting flexible criteria for the evaluation of public and nonpublic schools, so that each kind of school can show its special virtues and the particular contribution which it makes to the education of American youth.

The Defects of the Teacher Certification Process

No problem involving the nation's diverse schools, both public and private, has resisted satisfactory solution more stubbornly and persistently than that of

[8] Donald Erickson suggests that, in the interest of public knowledge, the state might itself publish a handbook on nonpublic schools summarizing the main findings of these periodic evaluations. He writes, "If parents are given systematic findings concerning the

determining who are competent to teach in these schools and how their competences can best be developed. What knowledge and skills should prospective teachers be expected to acquire? Is there, as many believe, a common "professional expertness" which teachers should be required to possess, an expertness "derived from a body of knowledge which is unique to the profession and without which expertness would be absent"?[9] What agency or agencies should be empowered to certify that a prospective teacher has acquired such expertness? Should teachers of private schools be required to undergo the same training and acquire the same knowledge and skills as teachers in public schools? These and similar critical questions have agitated concerned laymen and educators for decades.

Contrary to the licensing process in most professional fields such as law or medicine, where state governments have granted licensing authority to professtional organizations of practitioners, state legislatures have vested authority for certification of public school teachers in state departments or boards of education which lay down specific requirements for the properly ordained teacher. These requirements, which vary widely from state to state, are usually formulated with the advice of university professors of education, state associations of public school teachers, and such national organizations as the National Education Association's National Commission on Teacher Education and Professional Standards and the National Council for Accreditation of Teacher Education. Such alliances have been the main instruments in bringing pressure on the states to mandate the courses in education deemed essential for the professional training of public school teachers. To date, only a handful of states require certification of nonpublic school teachers.

In addition to these agencies there are, as previously noted, the six extralegal regional accrediting associations, whose task is to develop and apply standards in the evaluation of schools and colleges, both public and private, which seek membership on a voluntary basis. Certain of these associations have strict quantitative semester-hour credit requirements in professional education courses for teachers of schools which they accredit.

Historically, the study of education, on which the certificaton requirement is based, has been hard pressed to establish respectable intellectual credentials. From their earliest beginnings, courses in pedagogy and "education" have been quarantined in schools and departments of their own, greatly to the detriment both of "education" and of the liberal arts subjects with which they are intertwined. The divorce was occasioned by the staggering growth of the public

---

effectiveness of the schools they patronize, in most cases they will be far more vigorous than any state in demanding excellence." *Ibid.*, p. 173.

[9] Margaret Lindsey, ed., *New Horizons for the Teaching Professions* (Washington, D.C.: National Education Association, 1961), p. 24.

schools in the late nineteenth century, creating a need for the preparation of vast numbers of teachers, a burden which the faculties of arts and sciences in most universities and colleges refused to shoulder. It fell, therefore, to the lot of the old normal schools. But as the level of education across the nation rose steadily, the normal schools evolved into the state teachers colleges of recent memory, while many universities created departments and schools of education on the theory that education was not only a profession but a distinct discipline and a science as well. Most academicians, however, rejected this claim and haughtily relegated the educationists to second-class citizenship or worse in the academy. They also turned their backs on the problems of mass education. It is only within the last two decades that concerted efforts have been made to reconcile these hostile factions. In the meantime, however, the educational "establishment" became deeply entrenched not only in the control of schools by states and nationally, but especially by virtue of its stranglehold on teacher certification.

At the present time, an observer of the nation's nonpublic schools is immediately struck by differences between the attitudes taken by independent and by church-related schools toward the professional preparation of private school teachers and the requirements for their certification or licensing. We found that an overwhelming majority of teachers in all major private school groups have taken at least some courses in teacher education, such as the history and principles of education, as well as various courses in teaching methods and so on. However, almost a fifth of all independent school teachers say they have taken no courses whatever in education. Quite a few independent school people are still skeptical or openly scornful of "education" courses, a traditional attitude which is being debated now within the fraternity. In the process of teacher recruitment and selection, the independents give more weight to the candidate's education in appropriate subject fields and to personal qualities. The church schools, on the other hand, show a greater willingness to accommodate themselves to the prevailing state requirements for professional teacher preparation. This difference is borne out by comparison of the number of teachers in the major private school groups who hold state teacher certificates. About 71 per cent of Catholic teachers say they are certified, compared to 58 per cent of the Protestant and only about 47 per cent of the independent school teachers.

Since most states do not require certification of nonpublic school teachers, the Catholic effort to match the standards set down for public school teachers, compared to the relative indifference of the independent schools in this regard, provides an oblique insight into the kind of image each of the schools wishes to project. Catholic educators desire to provide an education in secular academic subjects at least comparable to that provided by the public schools. This is true generally of most church schools. To what an extent this is a defensive reaction

322

to the public's skepticism over the quality of academic offerings in church schools is hard to say. The public sees them as different, but the schools do not want to be regarded as too different, above all in the academic dimension. Understandably, if the secular education offered on church schools is indeed as good as that in the public schools, the whole project of religious schooling is more secure. And now that state aid for nonpublic schools is under debate, church schools that are reaching for aid have an added incentive to improve academically. The outlook of independent schools, however, rests on quite different premises. As a group they believe themselves to be qualitatively comparable to the public schools; many regard themselves as distinctly superior. Accordingly, they are less inclined than the church schools to toe the mark drawn by the state. And they are not above making a virtue out of the noncertification of their teachers, since it differentiates them from the public schools and their concept of mass education. Yet this attitude has changed steadily during the past twenty years, and independent schools are now debating vigorously the benefits and disadvantages of teacher certification.

Whatever the percentages of nonpublic school teachers who hold degrees in education or are certified, certification requirements have been vigorously attacked by teachers and administrators of public as well as private schools, and indeed by many representatives of state departments of education who administer them. Charles E. Silberman sums up their common dissatisfactions in these words: "That the preparation of teachers should be substantially different from what they now receive seems hardly open to debate; there is probably no aspect of contemporary education on which there is greater unanimity of opinion than that teacher education needs a vast overhaul."[10] Although some of the dissatisfaction stems from the mediocrity of many college courses in professional education, the main target of the critics—and the the major obstacle to change, although state attitudes toward teacher preparation are broadening—has been the rigidity of the state certification and licensing requirements, which have too often consisted of a quantitative measurement of a candidate's readiness to teach, a largely automatic accumulation of credit hours in professional education with minimum regard to a teacher's classroom performance or personal qualities. The difficulty, as Koerner states, is that "no way has yet been discovered of measuring the connection, if any, between Education courses and the actual performance of teachers in the classroom."[11] James Bryant Conant puts it even more sharply. "The assumption that prescribed programs of teacher education,

---

[10]*Crisis in the Classroom: The Remaking of American Education* (New York: Random House, 1970), p. 413.

[11]James D. Koerner, *The Miseducation of Teachers* (Boston: Houghton Mifflin Co., 1963), p. 51.

323

or certification procedures," he says, "can insure public protection from individual incompetence is largely illusory"; and, again, "The policy of certification based on the completion of state-specified course requirements is bankrupt; of this I am convinced."[12]

Toward Improved Teacher Education

So much has been said about the ineffectiveness of teacher certification on the basis of a prescribed number of credits, there is no point in belaboring the subject further. Rather, we state simply our conviction—increasingly shared by countless public as well as private school educators and officials of state departments of education—that nonpublic schools should collectively resist being locked into rigid state-mandated certification requirements based on prescribed courses in education. The constructive report on teacher preparation which best supports this conviction is *New Horizons for the Teaching Profession*, prepared in 1961 by a task force of the National Education Association under the direction of its National Commission on Teacher Education and Professional Standards. Many of the recommendations of this task force can form the potential basis of agreement among leaders of both public and private education. They were largely foreshadowed in an earlier report entitled *Preparation of Secondary School Teachers*, which was prepared in 1958 by the Committee on Teacher Training of the National Association of Independent Schools.

New Horizons envisages "the imperatives" of teacher education as four-fold:

a. A first-rate general or liberal education which encourages the development of human understanding and commitment to high ethical values;
b. Specialized knowledge of one's teaching field;
c. Professional knowledge of teaching and of education, i.e., the specific knowledge which is unique to the teaching profession and hence necessary for professional expertness;
d. Student teaching, or internship, which results in demonstrated classroom competence.

The responsibility for the education of teachers, according to this report, must be vested in a whole institution, not simply in its department of education, and the path to a teacher's acquisition of the necessary personal qualities, knowledge, and skills is not that of the lockstep of uniform credits in courses of education. The report states that "much more is required than the all too common hit-or-miss collection of courses, credits and degrees," and it calls for flexibility, for close adaptation of program to the particular needs and capabilities of

[12] *The Education of American Teachers* (New York: McGraw-Hill, 1963), pp. 54, 56.

the individual candidate, for an evaluation process based on qualitative rather than quantitative standards and for the provision of a variety of ways for a student to achieve the desired goal.

In this connection the report states:

No longer can it be assumed that a course meeting regularly through an academic year for three or more hours a week is the only channel for teaching and learning. Nor can it be assumed that all duly credited scholarly pursuits must take place at college. This shrinking world will, in the years ahead, make study round the world an integral part of some students' programs. . . . Some will gain the needed understandings through discussion of basic intellectual concepts; others, lacking an experience background, will need first-hand contact against which to reflect ideas. . . . Provision should be made for some individuals to carry out [a] delayed decision [to teach], meeting the requirements of the professional competent educator through work which recognizes their variants.[13]

The "imperatives" laid down by the *New Horizons* report today find a large measure of support among private school leaders. They have long required of their new teachers a sound liberal education in addition to solid grounding in their teaching field. Increasingly, too, heads of private schools are recognizing that the process and philosophy of education are legitimate objects of intellectual inquiry and that, while their study will not alone transform a poor teacher into a superior one, there is truth in the statement made in 1930 by the Massachusetts Board of Education before it established the first normal school:

No one can entertain a doubt that there is a mastery of teaching as in every other art—nor is it less obvious that within reasonable limits this skill and this mastery may themselves be made the subject of instruction and communication to others.[14]

More specifically, the ends of the study of education for the teacher appear to be seven-fold:

a. the aims of education, viewed historically or philosophically, including the consideration of what knowledge is most worthwhile and what ways of thinking, feeling, and acting schools should help their students develop;
b. how young people learn and fail to learn, how they grow and develop, individual differences and the dynamics of group behavior;
c. knowledge of self, particularly of personal strengths and weaknesses as they bear on teaching;

[13] Lindsey, ed., *New Horizons*, pp. 32, 79.
[14] Conant, *Education of American Teachers*, p. 113.

d. the most effective methods of dealing with specific subject matter in the light of the process of learning and growth in young people;

e. knowledge of and practice with the most common technological aids to education, i.e., sufficient familiarity with these aids to eliminate the fear which inhibits their use;

f. for teachers who will teach in schools enrolling children from minority groups, knowledge of their social and economic background, their intellectual and psychic handicaps, and their potential for significant educational gain;

g. for many, if not all teachers, an experience with the "free day" or informal approach to elementary education being developed in England and recently introduced experimentally into the United States.[15]

About the only aspect of teacher education that all critics agree is indispensable is practice (or student) teaching ("the best way to learn anything is to teach it"). It is by far the most valuable part of a beginning teacher's education, whether it is done in preparation for one's first job or as part of an internship program or on-the-job training. As the NAIS committee report on teacher training says: "Nothing is more valuable, we believe, than work as an apprentice to a great teacher in a dynamic school; and a strong case can be made for the contention that it is a lamentable waste of talents of our best teachers if they are not used, in part, to teach new teachers."[16] To James Bryant Conant, well supervised practice teaching so far exceeds in value any other component of teacher training that he makes it central in his program of reforming teacher education. He proposes to eliminate all state-mandated course requirements in professional education, arguing that a candidate for teacher certification need present only the following evidence:

a. that he has a baccalaureate degree from an accredited college;

b. that he has successfully performed as an intern under the direction of a state-approved supervisor;

c. that his college or university attest that the institution as a whole considers him fit to teach. In this way, the state would rely on the judgment of the college to determine what instruction was necessary in addition to practice teaching.

The heart of Dr. Conant's proposal for teacher certification is evidence of successful performance as a teacher, that is, successful internship under the

[15] The objectives and methods of the "free" or "integrated day" in the informal classroom are discussed with many illustrations in Silberman's *Crisis in the Classroom* part 3, pp. 207–369.

[16] *Preparation of Teachers for Secondary Schools* (Boston: National Council of Independent Schools, 1958), p. 27.

scrutiny of an accomplished practicing teacher in the intern's field and the counsel of a college professor on theory and method. This intensive experience would become the basis for certification. To base certification largely on demonstrated teaching competence via a carefully supervised internship was the heart of a proposal made to the Massachusetts legislature in 1968 by the Massachusetts Advisory Council on Education;[17] more recently, the New York State Education Commissioner, Ewald B. Nyquist, made a similar proposal, in part to permit a weeding out of candidates whose temperament and quality of mind give no promise of successful teaching.[18]

It should be stressed in this connection that practice teaching is most effective when educational theory is presented *concurrently* with practice. Ideally, so important is it to tie theory closely with practice that student teaching is best overseen by the same person as the one who presents the theory. Furthermore, this person should himself be an active teacher, not divorced from the realities of the classroom.[19] Making the improvement of clinical practice a priority offers perhaps the greatest promise of maximum gain in quality of teachers produced.

But even the beneficial effects of practice teaching are nullified if (1) there is a lack of correlation between theory presented in formal courses and the actual teaching experience, so that theory has nothing to tie to or is forgotten; or (2) the practice is done in a detached school in which the supervisor is a poor model or is ignorant of the theory taught the trainee, or suspicious of it, and distrustful of experimentation and all the newfangled ideas put forth by the professors of education; or (3) the student teacher perforce is obliged to accept the supervisor's class plans and make no attempt to influence the spirit or atmosphere of the class. Indeed, practice teaching may even be self-defeating where an intelligent, sensitive student teacher, well versed in the most recent knowledge of how children learn and develop, is sent for her practice teaching into a classroom that controverts all she has learned.

Discussion of teacher education usually assumes that the study of theory should precede actual teaching. A strong case can be made that the formal study of education should not be undertaken before two or more years of actual teaching, which have laid bare the basic problems of the classroom and revealed

---

[17] *Teacher Certification and Preparation in Massachusetts: Status, Problems and Proposed Solutions, Report Number 1* (Boston, 1968).

[18] *New York Times* editorial, January 20, 1971.

[19] "Much of the work in methods and psychology," says Conant, "is almost meaningless when given to undergraduates. The same material has meaning when it is presented to a teacher after he has struggled with the problems of the classroom. Hence, the amount of professional education in the undergraduate program should be cut to the bone, and opportunities should be provided in graduate summer sessions for continuing such work." Conant, *Education of American Teachers*, p. 203.

to the young or intern teacher his own strengths, weakness, and special needs. As a result of this experience, graduate work in education can come into focus and take on real meaning. Many experienced teachers agree with this thesis.

The extent to which private school leaders agree with the new thought regarding the ingredients of effective teacher education is revealed by the following statement which the NAIS Board of Directors approved in June 1963:

The National Commission on Teacher Education and Professional Standards is making an important contribution toward such progress by focusing national attention on the need for better teacher education. With many of the TEPS' objectives and recommendations, the National Association of Independent Schools is warmly in sympathy. Better identification and selection of those preparing to teach are clearly desirable. It is equally clear that the preparation of teachers of quality must be a continuing process which assures each teacher a sound liberal education, advanced study in the subject matter of the field to be taught, systematic study of education and its problems, adequate apprenticeship as a beginning teacher, and suitable provision for further growth as an experienced teacher. Nor can there be any doubt that a sound national program for the accreditation of teacher education be useful. We endorse these broad objectives of the National TEPS Commission and are anxious to contribute in whatever ways we can toward their attainment.

At the same time, the NAIS group of schools expressed concern over the rigidity of the TEPS approach to policing the teaching profession in the following words:

Most of our disagreement arises from what appears to us to be a tendency on the part of TEPS to favor the imposition of a uniform structure on the teaching profession and on the procedures for entering it. We seriously question these TEPS proposals: there should be only one recognized accrediting agency to approve programs of teacher education; there should be a governmental licensing system for teachers which would approve only graduates of those programs endorsed by this single accrediting agency; and membership in professional associations should be limited to graduates from these approved programs. These proposals seem unnecessarily and unwisely restrictive and monolithic. Furthermore, they assume a high degree of certainty as to what constitutes proper teacher training and who is a competent teacher, as well as an ability to define related standards in universally applicable terms. These assumptions appear unwarranted in the light of our present knowledge of the educational process. . . . We are deeply concerned about any program which would attempt to cope with so sensitive a field as teacher education through uniform procedures backed by statutory authority.[20]

[20]"NAIS Statement on Teacher Education," in National Association of Independent Schools, *Report No. 5* (Boston, June 1963), pp. 5-6.

Unexpressed in this statement, but remaining always at issue between the private and public school (or state board of education) view of the essential qualities of a good teacher, is the relatively greater emphasis placed by the private school world on the *personal* traits of the prospective teacher. While freely acknowledging the difficulty of isolating the component parts of good teaching and of determining what characteristics good teachers have in common, private school heads, of both nonsectarian and church-affiliated schools, place great store in the attitudes, values, and moral and emotional qualities possessed by the men and women whom they choose as teachers of the young. To these heads, human qualities such as integrity, warmth, emotional stability, humor, respect for the young and genuine interest in helping children develop to their full potential are more essential to successful teaching than any professional knowledge or skills whatsoever. Yet they cannot be acquired or readily cultivated by formal training. The NAIS statement on teacher training notes: "The quality of the individual human being is the most important factor in the educational process. . . . Effective teaching will depend less on the teacher's preparation than on his qualities as a person."[21] What the Plowden committee report said of the teachers in the schools of Great Britain has long been a cardinal tenet of the teachers in American Schools, held by public as well as private school teachers— if perhaps given less weight in governmental or public school formulations of the responsibilities of a teacher; namely, the expectation that he will "carry the burden of teaching by example as well as by precept," that he will be a "good man and . . . influence children more by what he is than by what he knows or by his methods."[22]

A possible way to dispose of the embattled issue of teacher certification while still maintaining and even raising standards has been suggested by Ralph O. West, director of evaluation of the Commission for Independent Secondary Schools, a subdivision of the New England Association of Colleges and Secondary Schools. In place of state certification of individual teachers on the basis of an approved course of training, he proposes a system of evaluation of a school's total program by an approved agency—an evaluation which would include every phase of staff competence: how the school recruits and selects its staff, how it initially orients the teacher to the life of the school, what it does for his on-going professional development, and what the school does by way of evaluating its teachers. If by this method the school with its total program and its implementation were to be evaluated and approved, rather than individual teachers, the whole question of individual teacher licensing would become academic, and the school would have a new incentive to plan carefully for the in-service training of teachers.[23]

[21] *Ibid.*, p. 6.

[22] Silberman, *Crisis in the Classroom*, p. 227.

[23] See Ralph O. West, "The Teacher in his School," *The New England Association Review* 18 (Summer 1970): 13–14.

While it is true that teaching has so far defied the development of a wholly adequate evaluation procedure, it is clear that certification as presently managed is a poor substitute. And legislation enabling private schools to receive public tax monies will almost certainly stimulate new interest in valid measurements of teaching competency.

Such periodic evaluations of the performance of a school's faculty would also have the supreme advantage of facilitating an aspect of teacher education even more important than that of training a novice; namely, his continuing professional development, now largely ignored by the schools and almost wholly neglected by the states except insofar as they provide salary increments for graduate study, or require a master's degree for permanent licensure, on the same tired old unproved assumption that more courses make better teachers. Over and over again, school heads admitted to the school visitors the general neglect of in-service training of teachers. Teachers in all types of schools said there should be more in-service training in the form of supervision of new teachers, more voluntary inter-class visiting, a reduction of the teaching load for beginners and so on. Some teachers thought it would be a good idea to use videotapes of teaching performances for self-analysis. The Cranbrook School in Michigan uses this technique with the cooperation of the education staff of Wayne University. Though in principle independent school teachers say they are for in-service teacher training, yet they place a high value on the sanctity of their classrooms and strongly resist having them invaded by either a camera or a colleague. Many methods of enlivening teaching require little or no special equipment. But despite the best of intentions they are not often practiced; or once tried they quickly lose momentum and peter out. One of the main problems, of course, is time. Teachers in many of the church schools in particular are often overburdened with multitudinous, time-consuming tasks that spare the teacher neither the time nor the energy to work systematically at improving his teaching competence.

One of the measures that does work and that faculties are eager to have more of are the conferences, institutes, and fellowship meetings convened by national school organizations and by district or regional school offices of various denominations. These are devoted variously to curriculum planning, the discussion of new teaching methods, teacher recruitment, financial and management problems, the exploration of goals and objectives, and to inspiration and good fellowship. The number of summer workshops and institutes, both here and abroad, devoted to early childhood education and training teachers and heads for the informal classroom is growing. Many of these are conducted by associations of private schools for the benefit of member schools. The NAIS sponsors a steadily expanding number of such summer workshops in localities all over the

United States, designed to acquaint teachers with the philosophy and practice of English schools.[24] These have benefited both public and private teachers. The "Five-Year Cooperative School Assessment and Improvement Project for Lutheran Elementary Schools: 1968–1973," conducted by the Board of Parish Education of the Lutheran Church–Missouri Synod, while it is concerned primarily with "up-grading" the conventional school rather than reforming it, provides a vigorous forum for the discussion of goals and means and sets precise targets for the in-service training of teachers. Several university centers offer new experiences in fresh educational approaches; the work of Lillian Weber at the City College of New York, Vincent R. Rogers at the University of Connecticut, and Vito Perrone's statewide project under the auspices of the University of North Dakota's New School of Behavioral Studies in Education stand out.[25]

In summary, the time has come for public and private school educators to work together with full and sympathetic understanding toward the establishment of criteria for genuinely effective teacher education. It is recognized on the one hand that the state is obligated to see that children are taught only by teachers who are competent according to the best professional judgments obtainable. On the other hand, there is much truth, as we have seen, in the contention of many independent school educators that past and present requirements for obtaining a license to teach fail to signify true competence, fail to permit a sufficient variety of ways to meet individual differences, and often deter able young people from entering a profession for which the mandated training is so often not only irrelevant but inexcusably dull. Private school leaders have much to contribute to the important task of making explicit the content of teaching expertness—and effective ways of obtaining it—and we urge that, for the good of all, they will share in the national responsibility for the quality of teaching in the great variety of American schools. Only through such cooperation can the vital interests of educational diversity and public welfare be maintained.

The type of agency which regulates teaching, whether state or private, seems far less important than the principles which guide it. We urge the following three principles as a platform to a new approach to teacher certification. First, mindful that countless outstanding teachers have never taken a course in professional

[24] Edward Yeomans, *Education for Initiative and Responsibility—A Visit to the Schools of Leicestershire County, England* (Boston: National Association of Independent Schools, 1967); and Yeomans, *The Wellsprings of Teaching—a Discursive Report of a Teachers' Workshop in the Philosophy and Techniques of the Integrated Day* (Boston: National Association of Independent Schools, 1969). See also by the same author, *Preparing Teachers for the Integrated Day* (Boston: National Association of Independent Schools, 1972).

[25] For a helpful analysis of the whole problem of the continuing professional development of teachers and suggestions for an in-service training program of high quality the reader is referred to David Mallery's *The Nurture of a First Class Faculty* (Boston: National

education, we urge that alternative paths into the teaching profession be permitted and encouraged, and that suitable equivalencies for formal course work be recognized which will enable schools to welcome to their teaching staff any person of distinction—artist, musician, writer, social worker, government official—whether his expertise was acquired in formal academic courses, his own study, or his own life experience. Second, we urge that the overriding consideration in the education of teachers by colleges and universities be not the number of semester hours of credit obtained but the quality of the total program successfully undertaken. Third, we suggest that the vital test of the candidate's readiness to teach—or receive regular rather than internship appointment—be his classroom performance, judged by experienced and competent observers.

Effective preparation for teaching in the ever-changing world of the future must focus with sharpened intensity on the ends of education. Much of the controversy that pits advocates of the traditional liberal arts education against supporters of a more narrow pedagogical training for teachers is academic. Neither method has enjoyed great success in preparing teachers. If the conventional teacher certification process too often represents a kind of technical training from which the candidate emerges with a more or less useful bag of pedagogical tricks, many "liberally educated" college graduates freely acknowledge that their college work failed to arouse interest in any sustained effort to think about or insight into the ends and means of education. The reason may well be that even today liberal education consists essentially of "covering" a certain number of slabs of subject matter, often without regard to how a given subject relates to others, to knowlege as a whole, or to life generally. Without a group of underlying philosophical principles and an insight into the interrelationships of parts and wholes, the implications of any subject for a theory of learning and its bearing upon current moral, social, and political problems are lost. And the educator who holds to a theory of education which he has accepted without comprehending the philosophical and psychological ideas on which it is based is certain to be bewildered when confronted with the obsolescence of that theory in the face of a major transformation of the environment and fundamental change in the human condition such as we are witnessing today. Moreover, many liberal arts graduates achieve their B.A. without having to think deeply about the process of human growth and development or how the process may be furthered under diverse conditions. Yet an insight into that process and the capacity to diagnose clinically what is needed to further it are as essential to the educator as the pharmacopoeia is to the physician.

Association of Independent Schools, 1966), and the report of a workshop held July 21–23, 1970, at the Taft School, sponsored by the New England Association of Colleges and Secondary Schools, Inc.

For these reasons, it seems clear that significant improvement in teacher education entails a general reorientation of higher education. It is also evident that the time is overripe for larger numbers of the nation's most distinguished intellects to devote themselves to what Alfred North Whitehead called "the art and science of education" which "require a genius and study of their own."[26]

[26] Alfred North Whitehead, *The Aims of Education* (New York: Macmillan, 1929), p. 6.

13

The School of the Future?

*"When one considers in its length
and breadth the importance
of this question of the education
of a nation's young, the broken lives,
the defeated hopes, the national failures,
which result from the frivolous inertia
with which it is treated,
it is difficult to restrain
within oneself a savage rage."*

Alfred North Whitehead[1]

*"We must rethink our ideas
of childhood and schooling.
We must dismantle them and start again
from scratch. Nothing else will do.
Our visions of adolescence and education
confine us to habit, rule perception out.
We make do at the moment with a set of ideas
inherited from the nineteenth century,
from an industrial, relatively puritanical,
repressive and "localized" culture. . . .
Everything has changed. . . .
What emerges through these children
is post-industrial, relatively unrepressed . . .
a new combination of elements,
almost a new strain."*

Peter Marin[2]

The Lesson of the 1960s

If the turmoil of the 1960s taught us anything about education, it is that the traditional, formal, authoritarian "school" is no longer suited to the needs of young people who will live most of their lifespan in the twenty-first century. Ever since colonial times more and more functions have been piled on the school—functions formerly performed by the home, the community, apprenticeship arrangements, and various social, commercial, political, and religious agen-

---

[1] *The Aims of Education* (New York: The Macmillan Co., 1929), p. 26.
[2] The Open Truth and Fiery Vehemence of Youth: A Sort of Soliloquy," *The Center Magazine*, January 1969, pp. 61–62.

335

cies. In the process, young people became shunted off into a contrived school environment which not only retrogressively excluded them from the responsibilities of adulthood, but also prolonged the period of dependency. In a way, the pent-up human explosion in the schools and colleges during the 1960s was finally triggered by the post-Sputnik emphasis on the single-minded pursuit of academic excellence. It was the straw that broke the camel's back. When the reaction came, people were dismayed at its suddenness and ferocity. But it had been long in the making. And in the aftermath it became clear that a whole new agenda for education had been precipitated. No longer could it be assumed that learning is something that is imposed by adults on obedient, passive children. The conclusion is by now inescapable: the traditional school, whether it be public or private, is simply not good enough.

Why, one may ask, should the sense of crisis in education be so pervasive just now when American children are demonstrably learning more in school than their older brothers and sisters did a decade ago and far more than their fathers and grandfathers did? The chief reason seems to lie in the "revolution of rising expectations," the social discontent which is spurred by the fact that the old "scarcity culture" is vanishing, and under the new dispensation many hitherto impossible things have become possible. Once people are persuaded that the resources and knowhow for making a better world are there, they become impatient and restless with their lot. "This retroactive impatience over things previously accepted," says Charles Silberman, "in turn leads men to misconstrue improvement in their condition as deterioration, for the improvement rarely keeps pace with their expectations."[3] Hence, the sentimental fallacy of "the good old days." But at the same time, the technology which is the source of so many improvements poses severe new threats which arouse deep anxieties and a growing concern over what is happening to the environment and to the quality of life. Moreover, the very fact that men have gained a growing measure of control over the environment has produced a bewildering range of options for the individual to choose among—a curse as well as a blessing, since the burden of choice is not easy to bear. All of these developments have a direct bearing on how we conceive the mission of education.

It is times such as these that prove the mettle of private schools. Though people differ over the rationale of the private school in a public-school oriented society, almost everyone agrees that the most valuable service private venturing in education can render is to demonstrate new and better ways. Most private schools are small and flexible enough for a quick turn-about. "The fact is that the public schools need—and need desperately," says Fred Hechinger, "the freewheeling presence of the independent schools." And though some public educa-

[3] *Crisis in the Classroom: The Remaking of American Education* (New York: Random House, 1970), pp. 19–20.

tors are inclined to shrug them off, they forget that many improvements incorporated in public schools would not have occurred "had not the independent schools—boldly risking the errors that may follow from each trial—pioneered, experimented, risked public scorn."[4]

The School of the Future

Four crucial considerations, all outgrowths of recent human experience, mark out a new pathway for education in the future. One important upshot of today's strange new world of miracles and anxieties, with its confusing signposts to utopia and oblivion, is the heightened awareness of the acceleration of change and the rapid obsolescence of knowledge, an awareness accompanied by a pervasive feeling that education is failing to prepare young people to cope with the speed of change, however successful schools may be in preparing them for college, for the professions, or for one or another vocation. The schools tend to look upon learning as a commodity rather than an activity and students are expected to acquire quantities of "knowledge stock," in Ivan Illich's phrase.[5] Yet "knowledge," said Whitehead, "does not keep any better than fish." Since, as Margaret Mead observed, we must teach children things that we ourselves don't know, the chief concern of education should not be so much the acquisition of knowledge as the training of the mind to utilize effectively the tremendous resources of information, research, analysis, and criticism which are available in modern communities, and to bring them to bear on the unprecedented problems that confront individuals and society.

The second point is the compelling need, in secondary education particularly, to shift the emphasis from narrow, intellectual-academic preparation for college toward a concern for full human excellence, including the development of the aesthetic, emotional, and ethical life of the young. Most schools still concentrate largely on verbal-intellectual learning—reading books and listening to lectures—despite the fact that a succession of philosophers of education going back to Rousseau, Pestalozzi, Dewey and Piaget, not to mention Plato, advocated a more comprehensive approach utilizing a variety of modes and developing all the senses in the learning process.

---

[4] *Teaching and Learning* [Journal of the Ethnical Culture Schools], 1959, p. 6.

[5] "The Alternative to Schooling," *Saturday Review*, June 19, 1971, p. 44. Illich argues that the "hidden curriculum" in schools all over the world, regardless of whether the prescribed curriculum is designed to teach fascism, liberalism, Catholicism, or socialism, is the same in that it conveys the message that only what is learned in school is worth knowing and only through schooling can the individual prepare himself for adult society. To Illich, the solution is a truly radical step: disestablish the schools. Although Illich's writings contain many fresh insights, his suggested program for the future of education is, in our view, sheer anarchy.

The third need is to integrate the work of the schools and the colleges more effectively with the ongoing life of the larger community in its cultural, occupational, civic, and recreational dimensions. Education involves much more than formal schooling. The school is one among many educational influences in the community, and to the extent that it functions in isolation as a contrived limbo in which children are confined from nine to three-thirty, Monday through Friday, for the purpose of preparing them for college (and incidentally for life) it will continue to be the target for charges of irrelevance and organized boredom and frustration. Much of the criticism of the schools by the youth counterculture stems from their blandness and lack of excitement, for to a generation which is maturing earlier and yet is expecting to live in prolonged dependency, the school is more than ever in competition with an exciting world where real things are happening.[6]

Fourth is the growing concern for the school's total environment, for the emotional as well as the intellectual climate in which learning and growth take place. In the 1950s and 1960s the zeal to "raise standards" and to improve instruction in the "hard" academic subjects forming the core of the college preparatory program seemed to the critics necessary and laudable steps in the pursuit of excellence, as it was then conceived. But as so often happens in piecemeal school reforms, a step forward in one area entails a step backward in another. In the process of toughening the curriculum and making learning speedier and more efficient, too little attention was paid to the human equation, to the young people themselves who were being goaded to step up the pace in a race which many of the entrants were unenthusiastic to run at all. Too often, instead of experiencing an atmosphere of openness in human relations, and the warmth and trust which they crave, students experienced education as an impersonal academic rigmarole of grading, competition, tracking, certification, and status-conferring classifications by which the sheep are separated from the goats—occupationally, economically, and socially.

The conventional academic exercises of yesterday were intended primarily to fit children for a place in society, using either the stick or the carrot to bring them safely into the orbit of established values. But the old verities and the old life styles are disintegrating in an avalanche of change. The present and future no

---

[6]It is easy to exaggerate the volume of discontent of today's students and thus draw some extravagant conclusions. A 1969 survey of 100,000 college students by the Carnegie Commission on Higher Education found seven of ten satisfied with their education. The Scranton Commission on Campus Unrest reached a similar conclusion. Nevertheless, the student protest has caused college officials to undertake a searching review of the ends and means of college education. The situation of the schools is quite comparable. Here too the radicals and critics are a minority, but they expose defects which cannot be ignored any longer.

longer replicate the past. Out of the torrent of criticism over the shortcomings of schools and the voluminous literature about how they can be improved, though they point in many directions, there emerges a main theme which should serve as a guide to the school of the future: You start with living children and build a teaching staff, a curriculum, and a school from there. Instead of trying any longer to fit the student to the school, the new school turns around 180 degrees and fits itself to the needs of the students, now and in the future.

Enough has already begun to happen so that one can discern the new role that the school is called on to play and chart the direction of change—the direction in which private schools should move in order to be relevant and effective. It involves a new role not only for the school as a whole, but for the teacher, the curriculum, and the student.

The changing role of the teacher is amply illustrated by what is happening in innovative public and private schools. The old order has the teacher up front as an authoritarian figure who, having presumably attained "mastery" of his subject, not only knows all the answers, but asks the questions also. As the source of learning he spends much of the class time lecturing or telling the age-graded students about the subject, listening to recitations, drilling the students, and setting the assignments for the next task. He devotes much time to keeping order and enforcing the rule of silence so that each student can carry out his appointed task with a minimum of distraction according to a set schedule. Another part of his time is spent grading the students' exercises in numerical or letter grades and recording these as inexpungible accretions of the students' permanent record.

In the new role, by contrast, the teacher is the facilitator rather than the source of learning, with the child himself being the source and principal agent of his own development. The teacher helps the child to become self-motivated for learning by building on his natural curiosity and interests and encouraging him to dig up his own answers. The elementary classroom is transformed from the silent, rigid, authoritarian, largely verbal-formal exercise room into an inviting, informal learning center abounding with concrete materials that children can manipulate, measure, compare, join, separate, and move. The secondary classroom is similarly diversified, as is the teacher's relation to students, in that the student has ready access to a central learning center stocked with books, records, tapes, pictures, and projectors, so that learning may go on in various modes, depending on what is best suited to the learner. The schedule is flexible, allowing for individual teacher-student conferences or for groups of various sizes to meet for discussion, for lectures, to view films, to watch or to present a demonstration, or to participate, alone or in groups, in off-campus community projects or apprenticeships. The teachers in such a situation are not so much specialized instructors in set subjects; they are stimulators, advisors, coordinators, and partners in the learning process. The point is to help the child help himself.

339

The old method of "telling" by the teacher and by the textbooks does not disappear in the school of the future; rather, it fans out into many alternative ways of learning. The alternative in the Montessori and Leicestershire schools has rekindled interest in manipulative instructional materials, a special form of "learning by doing," advocated long ago by John Dewey. Audio-visual approaches, teaching machines, and programmed learning, the latter two still in the experimental stage, present other alternatives. Some new curriculum projects make use of programmed techniques, breaking down the learning process into series of sequential steps or sets as in the Pittsburgh Individually Prescribed Instruction program. Another alternative—computer-based instruction—is still in its infancy, but it seems unlikely to find a large place in private school instruction because of the cost.

Teaching in the new schools increasingly subordinates the goal of the acquisition of knowledge for its own sake and "coverage" of subjects to helping the student gain the power to grasp key concepts and controlling principles, in order to develop his capacity for solving problems. The idea, in short, is knowledge for use, instead of for dead storage or nostalgic remembrance. The change in emphasis means a diminishing role for specialization within rigid departments and greater stress on inter- or cross-disciplinary approaches which help the student to integrate his knowledge and increase its relevancy to the problems he is called on to solve. A corollary of this approach is a diminished emphasis on college admissions requirements and a greater stress on the student's growth.

Another aspect of the new teaching and curriculum is the stress on the directly human purposes of education—values, feeling, appreciations—the concern for the student's individual fulfillment and personal development as well as his interpersonal relationships. Good teachers manage, even under the most conventional system, to touch the individual student as a person, and for that more than anything else they are fondly remembered and respected. Much has been learned in this century about the way the feelings, the emotions, and psychological sets can inhibit learning, and how fear, lack of confidence, or low self-esteem can ruin the child's life at an early age. Just how the school can be most helpful in engendering in children a positive, constructive self-concept is as yet far from clear. Much more thorough research is needed in this complex area. To what an extent sensitivity groups, games techniques, role playing, and improvisation can help the student to a fuller and more satisfying emotional life remains to be seen. It is safe to say that reliable answers will be slow in coming. Many schools are understandably wary of experimenting with direct "psychological" education.

But short of conducting experiments in this subjective area, schools are not without tested options. One way is to create more outlets for students to work intensively in nonverbal dimensions. Many private schools—this is true of certain church schools most particularly but not limited to them—sadly neglect the arts. Children who grow sullen or hostile under the unyielding demands of verbal-intellectual learning may "find" themselves in painting, sculpture, music, drama, dance, or film-making. The long arm of college-entrance requirements reaching into the schools is nowhere more evident than in the short shrift that many schools give to the arts. For example, a well-known independent girls' boarding school in Connecticut until very recently allowed the student no more than one-half credit in the arts (though students were welcome to take more extra-curricularly, and many did), while there was no ceiling on the number of earnable credits in classics, which few students elected.

Another tested pathway to the psychological education of young people is by means of student participation in school governance. We do not have in mind the well-known charade of "student government," which in too many schools is designed as a tool for co-opting the students rather than to accord them a truly serious voice in school government. The role of students in decision-making is one aspect of the total environment of many private schools which needs a drastic overhaul. Just how this is to be accomplished and what form of student participation in school governance evolves depends upon the style and character of the school's "self," and the degree of mutual trust and sense of partnership which is present to start with. The aim is to facilitate the student's growth in independence, responsibility and maturity. How are students to gain an insight into the democratic process if they are not permitted to experience it personally in a significant way? What they are taught about American democracy in the school books is not how it actually works, but only theoretically how it ought to work. And the sham experience of democracy to which they are so often exposed in school makes cynics rather than believers of them. "Our schools are now educating millions of students," said Alan Westin, director of the Center for Research and Education in American Liberties, "who are not forming an allegiance to the democratic political system because they do not experience such a democratic system in their daily lives at school."[7]

The new goals of the school of the future are achievable only if schools are willing to change the total learning environment from the conventional, routinized, cut-and-dried curriculum to an open invitation to learning by means of discovery and problem-solving, much of it, at the secondary level, taking place beyond the walls of the school. In the process the school is transformed from a dispenser of learning into a home base from which students set forth and to

---

[7]From the "Westin Report" as reported in the *New York Times*, September 22, 1970, p. 25. In the same article Dr. John F. DeCecco, professor of psychology and education at San Francisco State, declares, "Of all American institutions it is particularly ironic that the one institution charged with the mission of teaching democracy is usually perceived by the student as one that leaves him powerless."

which they repair for guidance and help as they use the outside community as their learning laboratory. We have maintained repeatedly that the central problem of "school" as such is the cultivation of the child's mind in a limbo of dependency, separated from the adult environment and removed from life's real responsibilities. Students talk about the real world as "out there" and about the school as "in here"—the unreal, protected hot-house world. One of the ways in which alert schools are meeting this problem is to build bridges connecting the two worlds in order to present students with opportunities for total involvement in learning. Such experiments presented as accredited parts of the school program (not merely as extracurricular opportunities) hold promise of satisfying the students' appetite for real life involvement in a working relationship with adults—in other words, for a relevant education.

Illustrations abound. At St. Paul's School seniors may undertake nonacademic projects as part of the independent study program (ISP), which necessitates living off campus for one or two terms. Under this arrangement students are able to design most or all of their senior year curriculum. The ISP work may be either academic, or artistic, or wholly experimental or job-oriented. In 1970–71 most of the students chose some form of social service. Among the jobs chosen were Black Business Development in New York City; the Center for the Study of Responsive Law in Washington, D.C.; environmental conservation on Long Island; teaching ghetto children in Miami, Florida, and in a street academy in Springfield, Massachusetts; a theater internship in New York City; the Boston Redevelopment Authority; the Smithsonian Institution; South End House, Boston; Dartmouth College's Outward Bound program; a film apprenticeship. The school keeps a file of various agencies interested in taking boys, usually on a volunteer basis, and is considering among its long-range planning objectives the possibility of creating in the nation's capital a "learning center" functioning as a satellite operations base. The ISP at St. Paul's simultaneously satisfies the student's desire for an outreach into the community and for individual study.

Dana Hall, a boarding school for girls in Wellesley, Massachusetts, has another conception of how the boarding student can profitably intermingle book learning and community experience. The school initiated this year a program for a limited group of seniors who will devote two-thirds of their time during the day to such work as laboratory assistants, assistant teachers in public schools, and apprenticeships in government offices. The group, which will live in a separate house with their own house parents, will participate in informal seminars and a broad humanities course in the evenings. In the following year the program will be available to a much larger group of seniors as well as some graduates who will substitute this program for a freshman year at college.

At Andover, a course in Man and Society, an elective for seniors, consists of a term of classroom study of the problems of the city. It includes two weeks of a

342

physical-challenge group-relations program on Outward Bound lines, nine weeks of residence in Boston's South End, where students work in a variety of apprenticeship jobs, and a final term in which they pursue individual study projects derived from their practical experiences in Boston. The last term is seen as vital to the goal of using practical experience as an incentive to further study and informal involvement in community action.

Programs of this sort are not limited, of course, to boarding schools. Dynamy is a school without walls located in Worcester, Massachusetts. Instead of attending a formal school or college as a high school senior or college freshman, a Dynamy student or intern spends five six-week periods during the regular school year on a variety of civic, business, and sociological projects. Programs of this sort which allow for a "creative break"—the thirteenth year or perhaps the twelfth—while they appeal now to small but growing numbers of students, encounter some fairly stiff parental resistance from those who fear that an interruption of the traditional school-college sequence means the end of the child's education. Hence, programs that do not rupture the school-college sequence but still manage to involve the student in the community are more common. Maumee Valley Country Day School, in Toledo, Ohio, began in 1965 to send "all its seniors 'out' for the last four to six weeks of the school year, into newspaper offices, city planning centers, settlement houses, businesses, labor unions, investment houses, hospitals, museums, rehabilitation centers. Students are expected to serve as well as to watch, to act as well as to learn."[8]

Though the church schools appear to be doing less experimenting with special horizon-expanding programs for seniors than the independent schools, the Catholic schools in particular have been active in various kinds of innovation. The hard times that have befallen Catholic education have spurred some schools to try new approaches in the classroom. The Pittsburgh, Pennsylvania, diocese was one of the first in the country to introduce in parochial schools the nongraded system for English and mathematics, with the children placed according to ability rather than age. At the same time, the three diocesan high schools added more opportunities for students to engage in unstructured independent study.[9] Some of the new thought enlivening the academic aspect of Catholic schools is attributable to the influence of Lloyd Trump of the National Association of Secondary School Principals, Dean Dwight Allen of the School of Education,

---

[8] David Mallery, *A New Look at the Senior Year* (Boston: National Association of Independent Schools, 1967), p. 17. This booklet contains a lively account of what was astir in this respect among independent schools up to 1967. Since then the pace of experimenting with programs designed to add experiential depth by community involvement has been stepped up. See also by the same author, *Independence and Community in Our Schools* (Boston: National Association of Independent Schools, 1971).

[9] George Vessey, "Catholic Schools Today: Challenged and Changing," *New York Times*, March 1, 1971.

University of Massachusetts, and the Education Research Council of America in Cleveland, Ohio. Another impetus to reform is the National Catholic Education Association's Practicum in Educational Programs which is developing pilot programs in flexible scheduling, individual study, nongraded schools, team teaching, and school-community involvement. The pattern developing at the diocesan Camden Catholic High School (2000 students) in Cherry Hill, New Jersey, under the principalship of the Reverend Charles J. Giglio, consists of a substantial offering of electives including courses in fine arts and practical (vocational) arts, as well as in foreign languages; a limited commitment to team-teaching; flexible scheduling to provide for both large and small group meetings in courses;[10] individualized instruction and counseling; generous use of volunteer teacher aids throughout the program; and extensive use of visual aids. As the principal said to school visitors, "There is no point in having teachers do anything that machines can do equally well." He reasons that a judicious use of machines releases the teacher for more personal attention to students. The in-service teacher training program takes the form chiefly of discussions of teachers with the department head or principal, and two- or three-day visits by consultants to advise teachers about teaching materials and methods of instruction. Elements of the Camden design are incorporated in Fontbonne Academy in Milton, Massachusetts, a school enrolling 555 girls, which is conducted by the Sisters of St. Joseph of Boston.

Contrary to the prevailing impression of many intellectuals who in the past consistently underestimated the quality of the educational output of Catholic schools, there is among these institutions a rising potential for innovation and reform. The ecumenicism of Pope John and the theological radicalism of the younger clerics are having all sorts of repercussions in the schools. Because Catholic schools are affiliated with parishes, dioceses, and a great variety of religious orders, they have many windows on the world which are not open to most other nonpublic or to public schools. The strong desire of various dioceses and orders to minister to the human and educational needs of children in the ghetto is gaining momentum. It is one outgrowth of the concept of the church's mission in the world which Vatican II did so much to further. Of the numerous illustrations of this trend we select a few as indicative of one special type of Catholic school of the future which is filling a critical social need.

The Ralph Young School, located in Baltimore's Model Cities Area B, is an outgrowth of earlier summer programs for black inner-city boys. Using an old unremodeled school building, this tuition-free school opened in 1969 under

[10] A typical course meets weekly for one large motivational period, three small group discussion periods and one period in the resource center. Homerooms have been dispensed with because they are not needed.

Father Leo Gafney's principalship with 60 seventh grade boys, about a third of whom come from families living on welfare with the mother the sole parent. More grades are to be added later. Student ability levels are very mixed—some entering students were reading at the first grade level or below—so the instruction, which stresses five basic areas including special emphasis on skills in English and math, is individualized. Hour-long daily periods in each subject planned by a teaching team are designed to meet the needs of each student, which means that the teachers can divide the class into smaller groups at their discretion. The program as a whole aims to develop the basic skills and assist the student to think clearly, make good judgments, and to listen with comprehension. Cooperation is emphasized rather than competition, for competition and failure so readily discourage these students.[11]

Serving a comparable but more specialized purpose is the Monsignor Kelley Junior High School for Boys located on West 83rd Street in New York City, on the third floor of the Holy Trinity Parochial School. It is conducted and largely staffed by the Brothers of the Christian Order with Brother Jude O'Brien serving as principal. Since its founding in 1965 the school has been committed to the goal of rescuing the gifted child from the boredom, frustration, and apathy of ghetto life. The enrollment, consisting of 150 tuition-free students in grades six through eight who have survived a vigorous screening process, has been "fudged" so as to include about a third Negro, a third Puerto Rican and a third white students. The school is unique in that here bright black students are not in the minority. The daily schedule is extraordinarily fluid and adapted to the needs of the individual student; small groups, spun off of the large classes in basic subjects, are sent to work on their own in hallways, on the stairs or in separate rooms with individual students assigned as group leaders. Proficient students are put to work helping the slower ones. In all meetings large or small, the focus is on teaching verbal and communication skills as well as on developing self-confidence; for one of the aims of the school is to develop leadership for the ghetto. The visitors noted that discipline was not a problem; the school is noisy, except in the library where the rule of quiet is firmly enforced, yet there prevails throughout a definite order and purpose. Respect for the individual is the cardinal rule. Students as well as teachers are given a voice in the selection of new teachers, who are chosen only after visiting the school for a full day to meet with and to be observed by all.

The main thrust of reform in the Protestant schools, apart from the Episcopal and Quaker schools which closely resemble and indeed affiliate with the independent schools, is largely in the direction of curricular improvement—better teaching materials and more effective teaching largely within the framework of

[11] Gerard Pereghin, "Black Belt," in *Momentum*, April 1970, pp. 8–12.

the conventional, carefully structured school. Excepting only the Seventh-Day Adventist boarding schools and their well-conceived campus work programs and curricular stress on the applied arts, there is little evidence of innovation among the schools of the conservative Protestant denominations. Some Lutheran schools make a fairly extensive use of visual aids as well as volunteer teacher aides, a few have experimented with team teaching, modular scheduling, individual instruction, learning centers, and the like, but few of the teachers and principals appear to be either comfortable with or enthusiastic about the new ways in education.

The reason is not far to seek. Many of the schools in question belong to congregations affiliated with denominations which have strong fundamentalist leanings. Paternalism and the acceptance of authority come naturally to them, because all genuine authority proceeds directly from God. They take their religion quite seriously, and quite literally from the Bible. Fear of "modernism" is usually part of the same syndrome. While they appreciate the reasons behind the religionless curriculum of the public schools and would not have it otherwise, and while they readily conform to public school teacher education standards wherever they are required, they deplore the public school peer group pressure in dating, drinking, smoking pot, sexual permissiveness, flamboyance in matters of hair, dress, and so on; and in some cases (the Christian Scientist schools, for example) they deplore above all what is taught in the classroom of public schools. And so they strongly believe it is their mission to inculcate the true faith and apply gentle but firm discipline.

What we have described as the school of the future involves an assessment of human nature that is at odds with certain strains in Protestant theology which fundamentalists are prone to emphasize, among them the inherent sinfulness of man. The integrated day, independent study, the school without walls, student voice in school governance—these and related features of the new school assume that a more open, trustful attitude toward the child will lead to a better outcome than the effort to fit the child into a preconceived social role by means of external discipline. It is not that the discipline in the Protestant schools in question is harsh or severe. We observed during our visits to these schools that the relationship of students with teachers and principals was usually warm and caring. Nevertheless, there is a clear understanding all around about what is and what is not permissible in the student's conduct. The lines can be drawn quite tightly without risk of student rebellion because the school, the home, and the adult church community are all highly supportive of each other in matters of conduct, morality, and religion. The conventional classroom with its emphasis on order and quiet is tailor-made for the purpose of indoctrinating the young in the accepted ways.

We believe that, given the human dilemmas of our time and the need for helping young people cope with an increasingly complex, interdependent social world, the Protestant schools of the future will find that they must deal in a new way with social and emotional problems of the young. The materials of instruction are of secondary importance compared to the conditions and setting of learning. Unless the atmosphere of the school is conducive to the opening of the child's mind, even the "best" curriculum will not provide a useful education. The problems of learning—intellectual, emotional, moral—go far deeper than the formal pattern of schooling which engages teachers, curriculum, and students in the setting of the conventional classroom.

After years of intense criticism, searching, and piecemeal reform of education in the sixties, there begins to emerge now a new positive sense of direction and threads of unity. Behind the more flexible curriculum, the growing concern over effective education, individualized instruction, more involvement in the community, the de-emphasis of grades and competition as well as of the surfeit of petty student regulations, and the granting to students of a greater voice in school affairs—though these projects seemed at first helter-skelter and ofttimes incoherent attacks on the rigid school inherited from the nineteenth century— behind them all lies the unifying idea of a more humane, person-fulfilling, civilizing education of the heart as well as the head. Many of the changes, it has to be said, were forced upon reluctant educators by idealistic young people who took literally the rhetoric about the American dream that fell from the lips of parents and teachers who had, however, by imperceptible degrees accommodated themselves in practice to the idea that the main purpose of education is to provide manpower for industry, war, government, and the professions. Some private schools, as we noted above, are already well along the road toward a new destination. But in others there remains much understandable uncertainty and confusion, and not a little yearning for the good old days seen through rose-colored glasses. An enormous opportunity awaits the private school, an opportunity to move forward, to assume again its historic mission, to demonstrate its potential to respond to a new challenge, to exert leadership, to utilize its flexibility and innovative capacity to redefine the goal of the American elementary and secondary school, and to redesign its own structure to enable the school to fulfill its new role effectively.

Breaking the Academic Lockstep

One thing wrong with the curricular reforms of the fifties and sixties was that they proceeded largely from the top down. Few educators questioned the sacrosanct process of "academic forwarding,"[12] in which each step on the educational ladder is made subservient to the one above it by the mechanisms and minutiae of admissions procedures, with the process as a whole ultimately controlled by

[12] The phrase is Betty Hall's, president of Simon's Rock.

the highly specialized professors of the graduate schools. Thus, the college program is expected to qualify students for the graduate school, the secondary school for the college, and the elementary school for the secondary. For the student, the next barrier casts its anxiety-provoking shadow over his present stage. Moreover, the high school, the college, and the graduate school each function as gate-keepers in the certification and status-awarding process which largely determines where, when and with what prospects the graduate enters the occupational, social, and economic worlds. Once in this academic lockstep, the private secondary schools, and to some extent the elementary ones too, lost much of their freedom and initiative. The independent schools in particular committed themselves fully to college prepping and meshed their programs with college admissions requirements.

The time is ripe now to proceed with educational reform from the bottom up, to begin with the needs of the child rather than with the imperatives of the academic lockstep. Alert elementary and secondary schools are experimenting with ways to break this regimentation by using a flexible ungraded approach in which advancement is based on achievement rather than time-serving. Elementary schools are pointing the way by providing for continuous pupil progress uninhibited by grade barriers, by providing for alternative group placement for students based on differences in individual rates of growth, and by organizing subject matter around fundamental concepts and principles instead of presenting it in isolated fragments. The secondary schools are somewhat more timid, chiefly because they are tied firmly to the mechanism of college admissions and have staked their reputation with parents on guarantees of college acceptance. Many preparatory schools, scarred by the highly competitive college admissions race of the recent past, are afraid of the colleges, But there is good reason to think that if schools and colleges got together they could largely eliminate the present system of entrance requirements based on credits and grades. In selecting their students, more and more colleges give weight to the applicants' personal qualities, special talents, and recognized potential, instead of selecting on the basis of accumulated credits and College Board scores. Perhaps an investigation comparable to the Eight-Year Study of Schools and Colleges (1933–1941) would be useful at this stage. However, judging by the rate colleges and universities are retreating from their old stance of strict enforcement of regulations governing admissions and academic studies, we believe the schools can gain the needed freedom without becoming involved in another long and costly study of that kind.

One of the major objectives of the more flexible program is to seek ways and means of reducing the total length of schooling and the prolonged, uninterrupted dependency under which today's young people chafe. It may be that three years of high school suffice (in place of the nine through twelve sequence), particularly in schools that cater to well-motivated middle or uppper class students where the educational influence of the home and peer group is strong. Thousands of students went to college early during the 1950s and '60s by way of the Early Admissions Program or shortened their college program by matriculating with Advanced Placement.[13] Yet despite these demonstrations showing that many young people can progress more rapidly, the system as a whole remains firmly rooted in the standardized four high school—four college years time-serving sequence. The reasoning of the Carnegie Commission in recommending a three-year college and the proposals of the Frank Newman task force contain food for thought also for secondary schooling.[14] The arguments have been touched on at many points in this book. Earlier intellectual maturation of young people, the speeding up of learning both within and outside school, and the growing desire of young college people to interrupt the long road of kindergarten through graduate school by getting involved in action programs outside the academic world—these and related considerations require a loosening up of the time-worn organizational patterns depending upon age-grading and grouping at fixed levels—elementary, junior high, high school, college, graduate school, and postdoctoral training. All sorts of new combinations and permutations are possible. Moreover, various other paths to education and self-fulfillment besides formal attendance at school are being tried, such as combinations of work and study, or alternatives of work or study, open at various stages in life.

A three-year high school diploma opens up a variety of possible options regarding the student's fourth year:

a. to go directly to college;
b. to re-enroll at the school to take advanced courses, independent work, or to pursue special projects under faculty direction;
c. to enroll in a school-connected satellite campus, such as a year abroad or in a Washington, D.C. apprenticeship;
d. to go on his own, traveling, getting a job, or studying, or combining a job with evening study.

Evidently the number of secondary school graduates who prefer to exercise one of these options, while not large, is increasing.

The fact that the once sharp line between school and college is becoming blurred, while the hitherto automatic forwarding from school directly to college is being questioned by young people, opens new possibilities for schools that are

[13] See *They Went to College Early* (New York: Fund for the Advancement of Education 1957).

[14] The Newman task force was commissioned by the Department of Health, Education and Welfare in 1969 and issued its final report in October 1971. See *New York Times*, August 8, 1971, p. E-7.

casting about for a new or enlarged mission. Some independent boarding schools equipped with a good faculty, excellent facilities, and a sturdy reputation are operating with some dormitories half filled or closed. The situation cries for imaginative thought about how these educational resources can be used more effectively. To go down bravely with flags at full mast because the leadership cannot conceive of any other mission than the kind of college prepping that worked for the last one hundred years is pathetically pointless. Education is in exceptional ferment. A period of hyperbolic change renders old goals obsolete or insufficient, but is also creates new opportunities. Combining the last two years of school with the first two of college, as Mrs. Livingston Hall has done successfully at Simon's Rock, is one possibility. Converting a tired boarding school into a lively community college is another. Enlivening the boarding school by making it an operating base for a multitude of on-campus and off-campus projects—a learning center of a special kind—is still another. There would be problems galore in taking any of these steps. But they would be problems eminently worth working at because they are creative undertakings, rather than the dispirited endeavor to shore up an institution whose once shining mission is declining.

The history of private schools shows that there is nothing sacred or immutable about the particular form a school takes at a given period of time. In earlier chapters we traced the history of the church and independent schools, noting the many mutations and permutations which they underwent. The oldest independent schools began as academies rivaling the colleges, then became boarding schools, and in the same transition turned gradually into the prep schools we know today. Mary Lyon's Mt. Holyoke Female Seminary evolved into a college, as did many other nineteenth century academies, once schools of their kind were no longer viable institutions; others were transformed into the normal schools which emerged subsequently as teachers' colleges and more recently as state liberal arts colleges. On the other hand, the history of private schools is liberally strewn with schools that perished for want of a new idea and, of course, for want of money—the two are often associated in failures.

The Future of the Church Schools

The future of the church schools is tied closely to the fate of the denominations they serve. Dramatic and bewildering changes have come over institutionalized religion so rapidly during the last two decades it is impossible to assess confidently either the substance or direction of what is in the making for the established churches. Of critics of the churches there is certainly no dearth at this point in time. Are the thought patterns of the present so radically new in human history that Christianity, with its roots in another age, has become simply irrelevant? Kyle Haselden, bemoaning the failure of the churches generally to become involved in the acute social problems facing this generation, wrote in 1963, "It may well be . . . that the healthiest sound in the white churches today is the angry rumbling of dissatisfaction which sweeps through the churches among young ministers and laymen. . . . In loud, sometimes uncouth voices young Christians remind us that Christians are not custodians of a shrine, not imprisoned caretakers of a sacred institution, but were created, gathered, sent as God's priests to serve Him in that great church which is the world."[15] The impact of those angry voices is now apparent in the new breed of clergymen who take the social gospel seriously and sharply challenge the mission of churches that would be content with a comfortable ministry to the middle class. To some observers, including apocalyptic young revolutionaries, pessimistic theologians, and many academicians, the present dilemmas of the churches represent the death rattle of institutionalized religion, a development which many of the intelligentsia believe to be long overdue, though there are plenty of others who now feel no sense of triumph in secularity.

Those who argue that institutionalized religion is declining usually point to the spread of scientific rationalism, beginning with the scientific revolution in the seventeenth century and the accompanying rapid secularization of western institutions; and they maintain that this trend has now reached the point where religion, at least the institutional variety, is rapidly withering away. The well-known view of Auguste Comte, shared by other nineteenth-century philosophers and sociologists, that religion belongs to the mythological stage of human evolution and has no place in the scientific stage, is still very much alive in intellectual circles. The epitaph of religion has been written over and over by scientists for more than one hundred years. And since many of the scientifically minded believe that religion is an anachronism, they tend to conclude that it is in fact disappearing.

Part of the plausibility of that conclusion rests on the assumption that people were much more religious in the past than they are today. Yet there is no solid evidence to support such a view. The religious history of the United States during the century and a half since the disestablishment of the church-states is one of upswings and downswings of religious concern, for reasons which are not readily apparent. Moreover, such empirical evidence as is available does not lend support to the notion that religion is in a sudden steep decline. Andrew M. Greeley, program director for higher education at the National Opinion Research Center at the University of Chicago, a man who is both a Catholic priest and a professional sociologist, after reviewing the limited empirical evidence bearing on the hypothesis of massive secularization, concludes that "the data . . . do not

[15] Kyle Haselden and Martin E. Marty, eds., *What's Ahead for the Churches?* (New York: Sheed & Ward, 1964), p. 213.

prove that religion is 'healthy' today, nor do they prove that there is no crisis nor hypocrisy nor unbelief nor doubt nor anxiety. They don't prove much of anything, I suppose, but what they don't prove in a great spectacular way is the secularization hypothesis."[16] The available data provide only the "most tenuous and marginal support" for the secularization hypotheses, but they fall far short of documenting either a rapid or serious decline of religion, whether measured by church attendance or manifestations of a persistent search for the meaning of life in spiritual terms.

Indeed, to many student revolutionaries today as well as to theologians and even to a spate of sociologists, religion remains the expression of a fundamental, enduring spiritual need of man, his "ultimate concern," the "dimension of depth," in Paul Tillich's words, which changes its mode with the times but persists in new forms. Many thoughtful observers believe that the troubled times through which the world is passing, with the heavy awareness of the shattered dreams of inevitable progress toward utopia, can only intensify the search for sprirtual insight and the yearning to explore the mystery beyond the garishly illuminated present.

In fact, much evidence of a growing religious awareness is to be found in contemporary society. Among the young the psychedelic culture is in open rebellion against the hyperrationalist world and its assumption that the capacity for abstract reasoning is the chief measure of human worth and the key to human happiness. At universities across the country students are enrolling in courses on religion in record numbers. Professor Huston Smith of MIT describes his experience as advisor to a student-directed independent study project in these words: "I cannot recall the exact progression of topics, but it went some-thing like this: Beginning with Asian philosophy it moved on to meditation, then yoga, then Zen, then Tibet, then successively to the *Bardo Thodol*, tantra, the kundalini, the chakras, the *I Ching*, karati and aikido, the yang-yin macro-biotic (brown rice) diet, Gurdjieff, Maher Baba, astrology, astral bodies, auras, UFO's, Tarot cards, parapsychology, witchcraft and magic. And underlying everything, of course, the psychedelic drugs. . . . What *they* (the students)

---

[16]Greeley, *Religion in the Year Two Thousand* (New York: Sheed & Ward, 1969), p. 53. The data in question are from Gallup polls and various opinion surveys, reported chiefly in the following (as cited by Greeley): Guy A. Swanson, "Modern Secularity," in Donald R. Cutler, *The Religious Situation: Nineteen Sixty-Eight* (Boston: Beacon Press, 1968), pp. 811–13; "The Religious Behavior of Graduate Students," *Journal for the Scientific Study of Religions*, 1 (1965): 34–40; Martin Marty, Andrew M. Greeley, and Stuart Rosenberg, *What Do We Believe: The Stance of Religion in America* (New York: Hawthorn Books, 1968), pp. 101–2; David Martin, "Toward Eliminating the Concept of Secularization," in Julius Gould, ed., *Penguin Survey of the Social Sciences* (Baltimore: Penguin Books, 1965). The articles by Professors Swanson and Martin include data on people in certain countries of western Europe.

learned in the course of the semester I don't know. What I learned was that the human mind stands ready to believe anything—absolutely anything—as long as it provides an alternative to the totally desacralized mechanomorphic outlook of objective science."[17] The absorption of some of the best young minds in psychedelia and the occult—a search in which religion and the new politics mix in strange ways—is a commentary on the sterility of scientific rationalism when taken as a way of life as well as on the irrelevance of much of the formal, conventionalized religion which the established churches stand for.[18] The young critics are not opposed to religion as such but to what they conceive to be sham religion. That the Catholic and Protestant churches have been visibly shaken by these developments is clear from the emergence of the underground churches, from the appearance of men such as the Berrigan brothers, Ivan Illich, and William Sloane Coffin, Jr., and from the relentless questioning of everything from liturgy to hierarchical authority—a questioning which is itself inherently religious in nature.

The true gauge, however, of the depth of America's religiosity is not to be found in the strange transitory phenomena of the last decade or two, but in the perspective of history. Despite the great stir caused a decade ago by the radical theses of Dietrich Bonhoeffer and the "God is dead" theologians, western civilization remains deeply rooted in the Judeo-Christian values. And even though the price of religious renewal may be, as some believe, the disengagement of Christianity from the Judeo-Christian world view,[19] much of the institutional structure of the older Christianity is bound to survive by gradual adaptation to change; it will survive because it is intertwined in the democratic culture of the West. As Herbert Butterfield shows in his chapter on "Christianity and Western Civilization," the ideals of democracy, liberty, individualism, and equality, as we know them today, represent social implications that were drawn out of Christianity.[20] And it was no accident that even modern science grew out of the bosom of a Christian civilization. Whitehead makes the same point in *Science and the Modern World*: "My explanation is that the faith in the possibility of science, generated antecedently to the development of modern scientific theory,

---

[17]"Secularization and the Sacred: The Contemporary Scene," in Cutler, ed., *The Religious Situation*, pp. 594–95. Quoted in Greeley, *Religion in the Year Two Thousand*, pp. 58–59.

[18]Professor Marcia Cavell of New York University presents an illuminating account of the search by today's young people for a new and private heaven, or "paradise now," in "Visions of a New Religion," *Saturday Review*, December 19, 1970, pp. 12ff.

[19]See for example the essay by Michael Novak, "Christianity: Renewed or Slowly Abandoned?" in *Religion in America*, ed. Wm. G. McLoughlin and Robert N. Bellah (Boston: Houghton Mifflin, 1968), pp. 384–413.

[20]In *Christianity in European History* (London: Collins, 1952), pp. 24–44.

is an unconscious derivative from medieval theology."[21] Max Weber's famous essay, "The Protestant Ethic and the Spirit of Capitalism," delineates the influence of certain Protestant doctrines on the developing economic system in the West. Likewise, Talcott Parsons, pointing out how the Protestant Reformation "individuated" religion, shows how strongly the moral judgment of individuals as well as the goals of western institutions are influenced by Judeo-Christian values; even the rationale of individual and social criticism of malfunctioning institutions is inherently Christian and characteristically Protestant.[22]

Present-day criticism of the institutions and ideas shaped under the influence of Judeo-Christian values yields but questionable support for the "massive secularization" hypothesis. Christian principles are appealed to in support of civil rights, the peace movement, and the war against poverty; and clergymen are in the van in many communities in advocating a radically humane reappraisal of our institutional and societal goals. "By being here," Butterfield says, "the Church stands as a perpetual centre from which the whole process can be for ever starting over again."[23] The church in a sense creates its own underground, its heretics, and its rebels, as it has done throughout its history. And so the religious dialogue in the United States is a rich and varied one, replete with manifestations of superstition, magic, and folk-religion, with the sophisticated, modern discourse in the divinity schools and seminaries, with the religious fundamentalism and evangelism of grass-roots sects, and with religious radicalism in urban areas where social conflicts and tension abound.

Our purpose in surveying these thoughts on the future of religion was to gain some perspective regarding the prospects of the church schools. The weight of the evidence, in our view, does not support the contention that religion is withering away and that the church schools are becoming or are due to become irrelevant. But what does seem clear is that the church schools will be swept away in the tide of change, unless they, like their supporting denominations and all other institutions, respond effectively to the need for renewal in both their educational and religious dimensions.

But our probe needs to be carried a step farther. The church schools are expressions not only of religion but more particularly of denominational and sectarian religion. The historical growth and fluctuations of denominational schools are essentially expressions of religious pluralism and denominational zeal that provided the major incentives for establishing and maintaining church schools. Now that ecumenicism is in the air and interdenominational clusters are

---

[21] *Science and the Modern World* (New York: Macmillan, 1925), p. 19.

[22] Talcott Parsons, "Christianity in Modern Industrial Society," in *Sociological Theories, Values, and Socio-cultural Change*, ed. Edward A. Tiryakin (Glencoe, Ill.: Free Press, 1962).

[23] *Christianity in European History*, p. 55.

forming in the Protestant world, how are the denominational schools likely to be affected?

Professor Martin E. Marty of the University of Chicago Divinity School and associate editor of *The Christian Century* speculates about what might be a creative future for denominations in the ecumenical era. He states: "There is no reason to believe that the denomination will fade because it becomes increasingly implausible. It continues to serve as an efficient organizing center for personal and social integration of religion. The denominations . . . do serve potentially as incarnations of much that is good in the traditions of the church and of much that is vital in the confessions of the church."[24] Reasoning of another sort lends support to Marty's assessment. In the pluralistic society of the United States, religious denominations have long served as a primary means of individual self-definition and community identification, as well as an outward expression of common and cherished ethnic backgrounds. This deeply set pattern is likely to affect the outlook of people for a long time to come. "It is in the religiously pluralistic countries," says Andrew Greeley, "that one can expect religion to have its greatest intellectual and social vitality. . . . Something of a multiplier effect is at work; it is precisely in those countries where religion is most vigorous that the organizations and mechanisms appear which tend to reinforce the vigor."[25] Religious groups that produce an elaborate institutional structure, including not only schools and hospitals but also publishing firms, universities, magazines, newspapers, and a denominational bureaucracy, have a stronger motivation to adjust to the changing social realities than do those that have little or no institutional commitments.

In view of denominationalism's deep roots in our national history, in theology, in the social structure, and in the culture of the United States, there is good reason to believe that, whatever transformation religion may undergo in the foreseeable future, it will not totally erode the denominational capacity or the felt need to maintain and adapt its own institutional structure to changing times. or to generate new institutional forms. Rather, the fact that a denomination has a strong institutional structure is usually one indication of a high degree of denominational vigor and identity. The fact that the long season of denominational mergers in this century has had little negative effect on the number of parochial schools offers empirical confirmation of this general hypothesis. In fact, the rapid growth of Protestant parochial schools in the period from the end of the Second World War up to 1965 coincided with a period of intense ecumenical activity and many mergers. It is as if the schools were built to insure a firm denominational identity within the context of hyperbolic religious change.

[24] "The Forms of the Future," in *What's Ahead for the Churches?* pp. 24–25.
[25] *Religion in the Year Two Thousand*, pp. 97–98.

What has been said about denominationalism applies chiefly to the Protestant schools and to some extent to Jewish schools, though the distinction among Jewish religious groups is not strictly speaking denominational. If our conclusion is correct, however threatened the Protestant schools may be for other reasons, they are not in jeopardy for the reason that the supporting denominations are about to disappear or lose their vitality, or because religion in general is going to the dogs. This appears to be equally true of the schools of highly separatist denominations and sects such as the Amish, Mennonite and Seventh-Day Adventists, as of the middle-ground Christian Reformed and Lutheran Schools, and the Episcopal and Friends schools.

The Catholic schools present a special case. The conditions under which that vast system was founded, as we noted earlier—a time of militant anti-Catholic prejudice when even the Protestant-oriented public schools were pressed into the first line of attack against Catholicism—no longer prevail.[26] Though the mandates "a Catholic school for every parish," and "every Catholic child in a Catholic school," were never achieved, the immense Catholic educational system that grew up alongside the public one, with a phenomenal rate of growth in this century, eventually reached a point, in the middle 1960s, when accelerating costs caused the schools to absorb a growing and disproportionate share of the church's available religious personnel and funds; in other words, the Catholic educational effort was overextended.[27] The crisis that now rocks the Catholic educational world forces the church to make choices. One diocese after another is engaged in or has completed a thorough self-study, usually followed by consolidation, some school closings, and the implementation of plans to strengthen and improve the remaining schools. Though it would be foolish to underestimate the financial factor, the crisis in Catholic education is by no means attributable merely to the lack of money. Not all Catholics by any means regard the schools as the essential or sole means of providing a suitable religious education for their children. Some Catholic families question the value of parochial education compared with various alternatives which are being explored, such as released time or dual enrollment; separate religious instruction offered under the Confraternity of Christine Doctrine; ecumenical cooperation between teachers of different religious faiths; public school courses in biblical literature, comparative religions, and social science with a religious emphasis; and church-related social groups (such as the Newman clubs and DeMolay) enabling young people to meet with

[26] A good account of the excesses committed in the battle over "the school question" is to be found in Lloyd P. Jorgenson, "The Birth of a Tradition," *Phi Delta Kappan*, June 1963, pp. 407–14.

[27] According to Neil G. McCluskey, at the peak about half of elementary school–age Catholic children and about a third of the secondary school–age group attended Catholic schools. *Catholic Education Faces Its Future* (New York: Doubleday & Co., 1969), p. 263.

clergy and chaplains for religious discussions. For many Catholic families, however, the all-day Catholic school is still the best choice and will probably remain so for some time to come.

That the future of all types of church schools—Catholic, Protestant, and Jewish—depends on other factors besides the continuing vitality of religion and denominationalism is readily apparent. The parochialism and conservatism that often stalk religious education, heightened in many cases by financial stringency, cause the faithful to settle too often for barren traditional schoolrooms staffed by underpaid and overburdened teachers, who offer an unimaginative program which is too readily justified by saying, "We are Christians doing what God wants us to do with his children." There is a point in William Sloane Coffin, Jr.'s remark that "little Christian schools make little Christians."

That God does, however, tolerate other ways is evident from the small but growing number of church schools which are experimenting with the informal classroom, and from the interest displayed by many church schools in new curricula, methods, and the transformation of the teacher from a classroom authority to the stimulator, catalyst, and guide of student learning. How much these ideas, promoted by means of workshops and institutes, actually affect the day-to-day teaching it is hard to say. The fact that many well-intended reforms are greeted with initial enthusiasm only to be "blunted on the classroom door," is by now well documented, not only for church schools but for other private and public schools as well. Yet the informal classroom, with its design for good rapport between the teacher and each individual student, seems particularly well suited to the classrooms of the many small, familial church schools.

The special problem of the church school is that it sets out to reach two distinct goals: to provide an academic education as well as a religious education of a special kind. Few church schools are satisfied with their program of religious education and indeed with some reason, since there is no conclusive evidence that school instruction of itself makes better adherents to the faith. Yet in most church schools a peculiar fealty to the values held by the group comes through clearly, not so much as a consequence of direct teaching as from the whole complex of a school's total environment, the personal examples of teachers, and the shared ethnic and religious and, to some extent, class background of teachers and students. On the other hand, the number of church schools that have reason to take pride in their purely academic accomplishments is limited. And it is in this area that the church schools will be judged more closely in the future, especially in the event that more public aid is forthcoming.

We believe the church schools are going to survive for an indefinite future. Enrollments may decrease in some, and increase in others, and almost all are likely to face a continuing crisis in finance and personnel, though in this respect they do not differ from public or independent schools. They will continue to exist because they perform a needed public service which the public schools, by their very nature, are incapable of rendering, and as such the church schools contribute significantly to the diversity of American education.

The Need for Entangling Alliances

"If any group has held fast to Washington's admonition against entangling alliances," said Harold Howe, II, in 1967 while he was United States Commissioner of Education, "it is the independent schools." He might just as well have included the church-related schools, for they too have been, until recently, even more wary of working in concert with schools not of their own kind. "The balance of effort," he continued, "has turned inward rather than outward" toward the public schools and the community with its urgent social and economic problems.[28] The traditional policy of noninvolvement offered the advantages of freedom to shape an educational experience peculiarly fitted to the needs of those whom the schools elected to serve. But the price of that inwardness was the segregation of advantaged young people in an environment largely unsullied by the most pressing social and political problems of the time, and the minimizing of the influence of private schools as a state and national educational resource. Howe pointed to the Independent School Talent Search, to independent summer teacher preparation programs for public school teachers, and to a variety of other horizon-expanding projects as hopeful signs of a more positive attitude by private schools toward the community and the public schools. But he urged private schools to make their voice heard in the debate over the future course of education and to become more fully engaged in state and national educational concerns.

Much water has gone over the dam since 1967. Many private schools in 1971 are much less preoccupied with nursing their privateness, and instead are devising projects to utilize their resources effectively, for their own students' and the community's benefit, in a wider collaboration with public and other private schools as well as with community agencies combatting poverty, ignorance, and delinquency.[29] Moreover, as the issue of state aid for nonpublic schools is raised in one state after another, legislators and the public are becoming steadily better informed about the nature and resources of private schooling. Also, the various associations of nonpublic schools are doing a more effective job of alerting member schools to the social and political issues—state and federal—affecting

[28] "The Need for Entangling Alliances" (an address delivered before the Annual Conference of the NAIS, New York, March 4, 1967), printed in *The Independent School Bulletin*, May 1967.

[29] For brief descriptions of some of the projects in which NAIS member schools are involved, see David Mallery, *Independence and Community in Our Schools*.

school policies. And finally a move is afoot to form a national federation or council of all types of academic nonpublic schools to serve as a deliberative body and spokesman in furthering the interests of nonpublic schools. With the formation of the Council for American Private Education (CAPE), the day of the insular, self-sufficient, withdrawn private school appears to be fast drawing to a close.

The founding and definition of CAPE—a movement gathering momentum just now because important public policy decisions are pending respecting nonpublic schools—poses special difficulties. The various school groups represent a variety of purposes, philosophies, styles, and beliefs which preclude general agreement on many questions. They seek the comfort of mutual reinforcement not in order to overcome these differences—that would destroy their *raison d'être*—but to form a united front on the basis of what they have in common. The common denominator is the concept of independence, the right to be different, the mutual acceptance and mutual protection of diversity in education. It is a position on which church-related and independent schools can stand comfortably together, realizing that the principle which unites them is indivisible: all are in jeopardy if the survival of diverse groups of schools is imperiled. Catholic, Protestant, Jewish, and independent schools can work together profitably on issues pertaining to their relationship to the state in the basic dimensions of support, control, and in seeking the mutual reinforcement of public and nonpublic schools in the interest of the welfare of all schooling in the United States. A national federation of nonpublic schools should function also as a primary channel of communication and cooperation among the various kinds of private and public school agencies, and as the spokesman for nonpublic schools at hearings before federal legislative bodies, the United States Office of Education, and other government bureaus and officials concerned with education. Hitherto the nonpublic schools have had no more than a barely audible voice in the nation's educational councils, and in consequence have usually been ignored, except as Catholic educational leaders generated sufficient muscle to influence the legislative process, as they did in the passage of the federal Elementary and Secondary Education Act in 1965.

But education is above all a concern of the states. The same logic that draws the leaders of nonpublic school associations together to act in concert nationally applies to the need for state-wide federations. The internal organizations of different types of church schools as they stand is by dioceses, districts, or conferences, often drawn with little regard for state lines, while the independent schools form either state or regional associations of their own kind. If nonpublic schools desire to become politically effective in state legislative councils and before state departments of public education, they are well advised to consider federating state-by-state, while retaining their own existing denominational or associational organizations. The organization and purposes of statewide federations will vary from state to state, depending upon local historical developments of nonpublic schools, the number of schools of different types, the potentialities for cooperation, the nature of the relationship with public school officers, and other factors. No two states are alike in this respect, nor can any one be regarded as typical.

Much can be learned, however, from the experience of the pioneer Washington (State) Federation of Independent Schools, which, it should be noted, employs the word "independent" as a synonym for nonpublic.[30] The articles of incorporation of the WFIS declare the purposes of the organization as follows:

1. To provide a framework for communication and cooperation between the different types and groups of independent schools, between independent schools and their public school counterparts, and between independent schools and the State Department of Public Instruction.
2. To promote a vigorous diversity in education to match our country's heritage of pluralism, taking care that the welfare and spirit of the whole society are enhanced in the process.
3. To insure that all families have a realistic choice among schools for their children.
4. To encourage a broad public commitment to excellence in education.
5. To foster a close sharing by independent schools in the state's educational task.
6. To insure that the public interest is well served by the state's independent schools through the maintenance of standards appropriate to the purpose of each institution.
7. To assist in a sound management of the educational dollar, whether from public or private sources, and to promote the full utilization of all existing and potential resources of the state.[31]

Noteworthy in this statement is the emphasis given to the positive responsibility of nonpublic schools in furthering the public interest by promoting diversity, alternatives, excellence, a concern for the state's total educational task, and cooperation with public schools.

One problem likely to prove troublesome in organizing state federations is the representation of Catholic schools, which in most states greatly outnumber all other kinds. The WFIS solved it by providing for Catholic representation on the twelve-member executive committee as follows: The superintendent of schools

[30] Similar state-wide federations of nonpublic schools are being organized in Michigan and Florida.

[31] Dexter K. Strong and A. D. Ayrault, Jr., "The Washington Federation of Independent Schools" (undated 15-page statement prepared early in 1971 and privately circulated).

of each of three dioceses that together span the state, and a representative of the Catholic private (order) academies. The plan of representation for all types of member schools relies on the various associations already in existence and utilizes these also for purposes of communication. In other words, the WFIS, far from trying to replace or substitute for the member associations, simply provides an agency through which they can work in concert.

Besides the state and national federations of nonpublic schools, two other steps are essential to bring the schools more effectively into national and state educational councils. First is the need for appropriate representation of the interests and contribution of nonpublic schools in the United States Office of Education. There are over five million children in the United States who receive their elementary or secondary education in nonpublic schools, yet the Office of Education is almost wholly concerned with the problems of public education. Even the periodic survey of enrollment and other statistical information about nonpublic schools gathered by the USOE is underbudgeted and understaffed, so that the published results leave much to be desired. The neglect of private schooling led the President's Panel on Nonpublic Education to include in its "Interim Report" the following recommendation:

Plans for a reorganized Office of Education should include provision for creation of a structure to deal directly with nonpublic schools and to make effective recommendations to top officials in the Department of Health, Education and Welfare.[32]

The second step is the inclusion of adequate nonpublic school representation on the state delegations to the Education Commission of the States.[33] This body is likely to play an increasingly influential part in the development of state policies vis-à-vis the role and support of public and private schools. On the whole, the ECS has brought a fresh, inquiring approach to the mounting problems of education, and has been assessing with vigor and objectivity the need for more comprehensive planning with reference to public and private education.

It would be misleading to leave the impression that these steps—national and state federations of nonpublic schools, the inclusion within the USOE of officers specifically charged with looking after the interests and contributions of nonpublic schools, and appropriate representation on the Education Commission of the States—will solve the complex problems of the role and future of nonpublic schools as partners with the public schools in the education of the nation's

[32] "Interim Report" to President Nixon forwarded by the President's Commission on School Finance, dated February 12, 1971.

[33] The state and territorial members have as their goal to further a working relationship among governors, legislators, and educators for the improvement of education.

children. These steps would, however, provide a basis for the progressive solution of those problems and the furtherance of constructive relationships and improved communication. As matters stand, the public schools move in one direction, largely disregarding what is happening in the private sector. Private schools, in similar fashion, tend to go their own way, largely oblivious of the public schools, except insofar as public school officials are in a position to exercise a measure of control over the private sector. The result of this communications vacuum is a lack of appreciation of what each can contribute to the common good, and how they can cooperate in the public interest. The goal, then, is the policy of the middle ground, which acknowledges the validity of public and private schools, recognizing that the dual system adds alternatives, richness, and diversity to the opportunities open to the young, while it strives to bring the two spheres into a harmonious working relationship.

Appendix

Outline of the Research Plan for the
Questionnaire Survey and School Visits

The goals of this study, originally conceived as "A Study of the American Independent School," but expanded to take in all academic nonpublic schools in the United States, were set forth as follows:

The primary aim of this Study is to map the profuse variety of nonpublic schools in order to characterize the dominant types in respect to (1) what they take to be their educational goals and philosophy; (2) how their various constituencies see the school and their place in it; (3) the prevailing climate of learning in the schools; (4) their financial condition; (5) their attitude towards various minority groups; (6) their readiness and capacity for change; (7) issues of public policy pertaining to nonpublic schools; (8) their prospects in the future. The project is not conceived as a precise in-put out-put study of the kind that attempts to measure the variable effectiveness of given institutions in achieving a predetermined end, such as academic effectiveness measured by achievement tests, and so on. We proceed on the general assumption that there is no single goal of education, such as vigorous intellectual training, for example, which is clearly superior to all others. Rather, we assume that, given the infinite variety of human talents, abilities, aptitudes, and the changing conception of educational goals, schooling serves the ends of individuals and society best if it provides a variety of goals and methods among which persons may choose. The Study does not aim, therefore, to identify a single type of institution which could serve as a model for private or for public schools; it aims instead to trace the effects of voluntary choice in schooling and its implications for educational practice and theory.

Population Definition

The first step in the pursuit of these goals was to define the school population which was to be characterized and analyzed. Since no adequate list of nonpublic schools in the United States was available, it was necessary to compile our own, using as a base the information on magnetic tape compiled by the United States

363

Office of Education in 1965–66. We attempted to bring this up to date by using other sources such as the Porter Sargent *Handbook of Private Schools*, lists provided by state education offices (which vary widely in the attention given to nonpublic schools), regional accrediting associations, various national private school associations such as the NAIS, and the denominational school offices. The latter were particularly important because the sampling plan, described below, called for stratification by religious affiliation or lack of it.

By comparing these sources we compiled as complete a list of nonpublic schools in the United States as the available time permitted, state by state. The list included elementary and secondary schools which offer either a general or college preparatory academic program, but excluded private schools which exist primarily to offer vocational programs, such as secretarial training, cosmetology or electronics. We arbitrarily limited the population to schools which include grade 6 or higher, thus eliminating many schools which offer *only* nursery, kindergarten, or the first five grades. The list included boarding and day schools, single sex and coeducational, large and small, schools from all regions of the United States and, within the limitations described above, represented all grade levels from kindergarten through grade 12.

The Survey Instruments

Six survey instruments were prepared and pretested, one questionnaire each for general information about the school, for the school head, the faculty, the students, the parents, and the members of the governing boards. Three carry-in question formats were prepared also for use in interviews with the head, the faculty, and the students during school visits. Because of limitations of space these instruments are not reproduced here in full. But the major dimensions of each of the six questionnaires are listed below. Some dimensions are general, that is, they appear in three or four instruments, making possible comparisons between the views of different constituencies of the same school. Other dimensions are limited to one or two questionnaires. The major dimensions or aspects of nonpublic schools to which the six questionnaires were directed are the following:

1. General Questionnaire
(37 questions, 311 variables)

School Type, Setting and Characteristics
The Structure of School Governance
Curricula Offered
Affiliations and Accreditation
Composition of Faculty

Income, Expenditures, Assets and Debts
Tuition and Scholarship Policy
Composition of Student Body
Destination of Graduates

2. *School Head Questionnaire*
(57 questions, 265 variables)

Personal Characteristics, Background and Education
Civic and Professional Activities
Assessment of the School's Philosophy of Education
Teachers, Teaching Competence and How to Improve It
The Extent and Influence of Religion in the School
Discipline and Student Participation in Shaping Policies
Attitude Toward Enrollment of Minority Group Students
Ways of Economizing and Attitude Toward State Aid
Problems Facing the School
Sources of New Ideas and Inspiration

3. *Faculty Questionnaire*
(47 questions, 273 variables)

Personal Characteristics, Background and Education
Duties and Compensation
Appraisal of the School Head
Motivations for Independent School Teaching
Self-Assessment of Teaching Competencies
Assessment of School's Philosophy of Education
Relationships to Students and Assessment of the Students' Role
Student Grievances—are they Justified?
The Learning Environment in the School
The School's Strengths and Weaknesses
Relationships to Administration and Faculty Role in Governance
Academic Freedom and Tenure
Current Sources of Educational Ideas
Attitude toward Educational Innovation

4. *Student Questionnaire*
(32 questions, 142 variables)

Personal Characteristics, Background and Previous Schooling
Reasons for Selecting a Private School
Assessment of School's Educational Program

365

Reactions to Formal Moral-Character Training Environment
Desired Changes in Above
Reactions to Grades, Work-Load, School Regulations
Discipline in the School
Student Unrest
Reactions to Informal Environment of Peers and Adults
Desired Changes in Own Ingroup Peer Culture
Expected Adult Role—College Plans, Life and Career Goals
Desired Outcomes of School Experience
The Learning Environment in the School

5. *Parent Questionnaire*
(30 questions, 168 variables)

Personal Characteristics, Background and Education
Reasons for Selecting a Private School
Degree of Satisfaction or Dissatisfaction With the School
Reactions to Student Grievances
Reactions to School's Admission Policies Respecting Minority Group Students
Assessment of the Moral Influence of the School
The Learning Environment in the School

6. *Governing Board Questionnaire*
(27 questions, 165 variables)

Personal Characteristics, Background and Education
Estimate of Time Spent on School's Affairs
Assessment of the School's Philosophy of Teaching and Learning
Ways of Economizing and Attitude Toward State Aid
Appraisal of Best Way to Meet Financial Problems
Appraisal of the School Head
Reactions to School's Admission Policies Respecting
    Minority Group Students
Assessment of the School's Religious Emphasis
Discipline and the Role of Students in Governance

The three carry-in question formats designed to lend structure, objectivity, and comparability to interviews with heads, faculty, and students included the same dimensions respectively as the questionnaires devised for each of these constituencies.

The Sampling Plan

It was assumed that the median or average school encountered in the non-public school population would have about 300 students and 25 faculty members.

In order to collect representative data from among the over 18,000 nonpublic schools, two samples were selected: a 750-school general sample, and a 250-school in-depth sample. The primary stratification criterion employed in the sampling process was denominational affiliation or lack of it. Preliminary study of the differentiating characteristics of the schools made it plain that church-relationship or its absence was the major dimension of difference within the whole school population. Most denominations tend to exert a unifying influence upon their schools, thus reducing the impact of other differentiating characteristics (such as boarding or day schools, single sex or co-ed schools, regional factors, and so on). This approach was fortunate with respect to our problem of population definition since some of the most useful statistical information about segments of the school population came from denominational offices. The 750-school general sample was drawn with the help of random numbers, while the 250-school depth sample was selected as a stratified subsample within the randomly selected 750.

Each school in the general sample received a general and a school head questionnaire, and each school in the depth sample received multiple questionnaires also for faculty, students, parents, and governing board members as shown in table A below:

Table A

Questionnaire Type	Sample	No. per School	Totals per Type Q's
School Head – Personal	750	1	750
– General	750	1	750
Faculty	250	8	2,000
Students (Sec. schools only)	135	10	1,350
Parent (Sec. schools)	135	10	1,350
Parent (Elem. schools)	115	8	920
Governing Board	250	5	1,250
Grand Total Questionnaires			8,370

Table B, below, shows the total number of schools operated by the larger denominational systems, as well as the number of schools to be selected from each denomination for the sample of 750 and the subsample of 250. In general, we deliberately overrepresented secondary schools, with the result that the study emphasizes secondary, or secondary and elementary schools combined, more than schools which offer elementary grades only. While we consider the work of nonpublic elementary schools of great importance, and suspect that more innovation is taking place at the elementary than the secondary level, the questionnaires were better suited to secondary than to elementary schools, particularly the student questionnaire. We believe, however, that our samples include a significant number of elementary schools, though not proportional to their actual numbers.

Roman Catholic schools constitute over 75 per cent of all nonpublic schools. Our stratification approach deliberately underrepresented Catholic schools in order to avoid having the study become essentially an investigation of those schools. This procedure enabled us the better to disclose the full diversity of nonpublic schools overall. It also took cognizance of the fact that two recent national studies of Roman Catholic schools, *The Education of Catholic Americans* by Andrew M. Greeley and Peter H. Rossi, and *Catholic Schools in Action* by Reginald A. Neuwien, had provided data concerning them. In our survey, Catholic schools were sampled regionally in each of three geographic areas.

The 2,369 religiously unaffiliated schools were deliberately oversampled because they presumably lack the unifying influence of denominational membership, and we reasoned that there might be more diversity and less uniformity in this group. Here, too, as is indicated in table B, below, we sampled regionally.

Finally, a third sample of 50 "leading schools" was chosen with the advice and assistance of the officers of the various national church and independent school associations. Occasional comparisons of data regarding this group of schools with the randomly sampled schools are enlightening. Each of the selected leading schools received a full battery of the six questionnaires.

School Visits

About 60 schools were visited by members of the study staff, augmented for this purpose by a special group of visitors who are identified in the preface. The list of schools visited included several public schools widely known for their innovative programs. Our aim in the visits was to maximize diversity rather than to obtain a proportional or representative sample. The list included new black schools, such as the Harlem Preparatory School and a street academy. Most but not all of the schools visited were in either the general, the depth, or the leading school sample.

Table B summarizes the distribution of schools in each of the samples:

Table B

Kind of School [a]	750-School Sample	250-School Sample	50 Leading Schools
Roman Catholic (13,150)	240[b]	60[b]	10
Lutheran (1,700)	45 (30E,15S)	15 (10E,5S)	5
Adventist (1,150)	45 (30E,15S)	15 (10E,5S)	5
Jewish (270)	30	10 (5E,5S)	5
Episcopal (350)	30	10 (5E,5S)	5
Christian Reformed (210)	30	10 (5E,5S)	5
Other church related (680) (e.g., Presbyterian, Methodist, Christian Science)	110	50	5
Not religiously af- filiated (2,375)	220	80	10
Secondary	180[c]	60[c]	
Elementary	40	20	
Totals	750	250	50

[a]Figures in parentheses in this column are the approximate number of elementary and secondary schools in each category.

[b]Regional stratification as follows (number in 750–school and 250–school samples respectively):

	Northeast	South	Other
Elementary	40; 10	40; 10	40; 10
Secondary	40; 10	40; 10	40; 10

[c]Regional stratification for secondary schools only (number in 750–school and 250–school samples respectively):

Northeast	60; 20
South	60; 20
Other	60; 20

The Response

The response to the questionnaire survey was somewhere between our fondest hopes and our darkest fears. All in all, considering the diversity of the population and the lack of an accurate up-to-date listing—one which clearly discriminated between schools which combine elementary and secondary levels and those which are either one or the other—the response was good, though as one would expect, variable. It was particularly good in view of the fact that the study must have appeared to many of the church schools as an "outside" agency. Each batch of questionnaires was accompanied by a letter from the appropriate national school association officer urging cooperation with the study. These proved to be exceedingly helpful. The response of schools in the general and the depth sample is tabulated in tables C and D. The response of the 50 "leading schools" was highest of all.

Table C

RESPONSES—GENERAL SAMPLE SCHOOLS

| Type of School | Number of Schools | | | Number of Questionnaires Received and Cross-tabbed | |
	In sample	Meeting study criteria	Non-respondents	General	School head
Catholic					
Northeast elementary	40	39	10	28	29
South elementary	40	42	6	36	36
Midwest & Far West elementary	40	38	3	33	35
Northeast secondary	40	39	9	29	30
South secondary	40	35	5	29	30
Midwest & Far West secondary	40	39	5	33	34
Lutheran					
Elementary	30	31	4	27	27
Secondary	15	12	1	9	11
Seventh-Day Adventist					
Elementary	30	21	7	13	13
Secondary	15	16	1	14	13
Christian Reformed					
Elementary	30	19	2	17	17
Secondary		7	2	5	5
Other Church					
Elementary	110	56	33	21	23
Secondary		41	18	22	22
Episcopal					
Elementary	30	14	2	12	12
Secondary		16	–	16	16
Jewish					
Elementary	30	12	5	5	7
Secondary		17	8	7	9
Independent					
Elementary	40	33	16	15	15
Northeast Secondary	60	58	16	41	42
South Secondary	60	49	22	26	27
Midwest & Far West secondary	60	55	17	37	36
Total	750	689	192	475	489

Comments on Table C

1. A word of explanation is in order regarding the column designated "Number of schools meeting study criteria." When the returns began to come in, we soon learned that some schools drawn randomly from the USOE list as "elementary" were in fact, by our definition, secondary schools, and vice versa. That explains the apparent oversampling of Catholic south elementary schools. The undersampling of Lutheran secondary schools is attributable to the very small number of such schools on our list and in the country. In many cases schools listed in the 1965 USOE Directory had closed by 1969; in such cases we filled in new randomly selected schools from the same cell, but eventually ran out of time. Closings, mergers, and changes in grade level of selected schools necessitated some deviations from the proposed sampling plan.
2. The column "nonrespondents" consists of schools which were still in operation, according to all available information, but which did not respond to our mailings or which declined to take part in the survey. If we had no proof that a school no longer existed, it was listed as a nonresponding school.
3. The apparent discrepancy between nonresponding schools, the total number of schools which met the study criteria, and the number of general and school head questionnaires received is explained by the fact that a few schools returned one but not the other of the two questionnaires addressed to the school.

Comments on Table D (pages 372-73)

1. The depth questionnaires (faculty, student, parent, and governing board) were distributed by the school according to explicit instructions intending to insure random selection of faculty and student respondents. Parents (usually mothers) were matched with student respondents. Instructions covering distribution of questionnaires to governing board members were intended to ensure having the chairmen among the respondents.
2. The questionnaires numbered in the "general" and "school head" columns are *not* in addition to those received in the general sample. Consequently, the total number of questionnaires from general and depth samples is 4,308.
3. The columns entitled "distributed" mean that we had reasons to believe each type of questionnaire had been distributed by the school. The fact that so few faculty questionnaires were distributed, e.g., in the Seventh-Day Adventist elementary cell, suggests that the schools were much smaller—which we now know to be true—than our original supposition about school size in the sampling plan. The 9 Adventist elementaries should have distributed 72 faculty questionnaires; in fact they distributed only 28.

Table D

RESPONSES–DEPTH SAMPLE SCHOOLS

Type of School	Number of Schools				Number of Questionnaires Returned								
	In sample	Taking part	General	School head	Faculty			Parents		Students		Governing board	
					Distributed	Ineligible	Used	Distributed	Used	Distributed	Used	Distributed	Used
Catholic													
Northeast elementary	10	10	9	10	79	7	56	80	55	–	–	15	13
South elementary	10	10	10	10	65	12	46	80	58	–	–	34	24
Midwest & Far West elementary	10	7	7	7	51	12	31	56	38	–	–	14	10
Northeast secondary	10	9	9	9	72	9	58	90	64	90	75	18	15
South secondary	10	10	9	10	77	3	49	98	71	98	80	24	12
Midwest & Far West secondary	10	10	10	10	80	7	54	100	64	100	71	35	25
Lutheran													
Elementary	10	10	10	10	54	10	30	79	55	–	–	45	34
Secondary	5	5	4	5	39	4	21	50	33	50	39	25	21
Seventh-Day Adventist													
Elementary	10	9	8	8	28	3	12	63	35	–	–	35	16
Secondary	5	6	5	6	37	3	11	53	21	53	17	25	14
Christian Reformed													
Elementary	5	6	6	6	20	2	17	42	28	–	–	24	12
Secondary	5	3	2	2	24	0	17	30	25	30	24	15	12

Other Church													
Elementary	50	15	15	15	98	29	41	105	59	—	—	68	39
Secondary		15	14	14	105	14	60	148	106	148	120	66	40
Episcopal													
Elementary	5	6	6	6	39	9	15	48	31	—	—	20	13
Secondary	5	6	6	6	46	1	37	60	50	60	54	30	25
Jewish													
Elementary	5	3	2	3	18	1	7	24	8	—	—	—	—
Secondary	5	3	3	3	24	10	7	30	15	30	16	—	—
Independent													
Elementary	20	14	12	12	98	9	46	111	63	—	—	54	33
Northeast secondary	20	19	19	19	152	15	89	190	124	190	145	76	49
South secondary	20	15	14	15	111	7	67	147	89	147	104	63	39
Midwest & Far West secondary	20	14	13	14	111	9	73	140	86	140	90	54	41
Total	250	205	193	200	1,428	176	844	1,824	1,178	1,136	835	740	487

373

4. The "used" columns mean "received and cross-tabbed."
5. The number of questionnaires actually distributed to governing board members is small among the Catholics because many of the schools replied they did not have such boards.
6. Faculty respondents were considered "ineligible" if the questionnaire revealed that they did not meet our definition of "faculty," that is, full-time teachers who teach at least grade four or higher. In coding the returned questionnaires it became apparent that many of the teachers did not meet our criteria; for example, they devoted more than 25 per cent of their time to library work, coaching, and so forth.

Index

Index

Index

Index

Index

Index

Index

Index

THE JOHNS HOPKINS UNIVERSITY PRESS

This book was composed in Press Roman text by the Jones Composition Company
from a design by Laurie Jewell. It was printed by Universal Lithographers, Inc.
on 55-lb. Sebago Regular and bound in Columbia Llamique by L. H. Jenkins, Inc.